Everyday Family Suppers 2008

More than 450 Recipes and Tips
Make Beating the Kitchen Clock Easier than Ever

Between bustling careers, keeping up with household chores and driving the kids to soccer practice, family cooks need meals that come together in a pinch. That's why moms from coast to coast turn to *Everyday Family Suppers* from Pillsbury!

With hundreds of dishes to choose from, this collection of no-fuss favorites makes it a snap to set hearty, home-cooked dinners on the table—even on the busiest of nights. Best of all, every recipe is sure to turn out right because they're all from Pillsbury…America's most-trusted Test Kitchen. Featuring common kitchen staples, step-by-step directions, preparation timelines and gorgeous color photos, *Everyday Family Suppers 2008* ladles out homemade comfort with ease.

You can't go wrong with the dishes in the chapter "All-Time Favorites." Here you'll find classics bound to receive thumbs-up approval. Beef Stroganoff with Parsley Noodles (p. 8), Easy Chicken Parmigiana (p. 20) and Black Bean Enchiladas (p. 28) are only a sample of what this chapter has to offer.

The "Soups & Sandwiches" section makes menu planning as simple as can be. Just consider Hot Sourdough Chicken Sandwiches (p. 42) paired with Easy Corn Chowder (p. 44). Or, turn to "Salads & Breads" and toss together Curry Wild Rice Salad (p. 68) served alongside Cheddar and Canadian Bacon Muffins (p. 69).

Looking for a swift yet satisfying main course? See the mouthwatering specialties in the chapters "Beef & Ground Beef" or "Chicken & Turkey." There you'll find Mexican Beef 'n Bean Pizza (p. 109) or Quick Chicken Divan (p. 158). And when it's time to switch your supper routine, turn to the chapters "Fish & Seafood" and "Pork, Ham & Lamb." They also offer dozens of options for hurried weeknights.

TIME-SAVING STRATEGIES

Looking to get out of the kitchen even quicker? To prepare comforting meals on your very most harried nights, look for recipes labeled with the following categories:

✻ super fast: These tasty choices are ideal for swarming schedules because they're ready in less than 30 minutes. Add them to your weekly meal plan, and you'll see just how simple a homemade dinner can be.

✻ meal-in-one: When it comes to suppertime lifesavers, nothing beats one-dish specialties. Colorful stir-fries, refreshing entree salads and hearty chowders offer today's cooks the fix-it and forget-it flair they crave. Just set these items on the table and dinner is served!

✻ plan ahead: Slow-cooked favorites and bubbling casseroles sometimes require additional cooking time. With a little planning, you'll come out ahead by assembling these no-fuss dishes early in the day or the night before.

Bake-Off® Contest Winners: Sometimes deciding what to serve can take just as long as preparing it. Turn to these reliable recipes when you're looking for a surefire taste sensation. They're bound to please because they're considered the best of the best from a Pillsbury Bake-Off® Contest.

You'll also find helpful cooking secrets, ingredient substitutions and minute-saving tips scattered throughout so you can feed your gang in a snap. In addition, "Prep" and "Ready to Serve" timelines let you know which dish best fits your schedule.

So when your calendar is full with dance lessons, softball practice, after-work meetings and other weeknight activities, grab *Everyday Family Suppers 2008*. You'll be amazed at just how easy it is to please your hungry bunch while skimming minutes from the kitchen timer.

Everyday Family Suppers 2008

All recipes have been tested in the Pillsbury Kitchens and meet Pillsbury's standards of easy preparation, reliability and great taste.

PUBLISHED BY
Taste of Home Books
Reiman Media Group, Inc.
5400 S. 60th St., Greendale WI 53129
www.reimanpub.com

This edition published by arrangement with Wiley Publishing, Inc.

Printed in U.S.A.

International Standard Book Number (10): 0-89821-602-8
International Standard Book Number (13): 978-0-89821-602-8
International Standard Serial Number: 1935-5157

CREDITS
General Mills, Inc.
PUBLISHER, COOKBOOKS: Maggie Gilbert/Lynn Vettel
EDITOR: Lois Tlusty
RECIPE DEVELOPMENT AND TESTING: Pillsbury Test Kitchens
PHOTOGRAPHY: General Mills Photo Studios

Reiman Media Group, Inc.
VICE PRESIDENT, EXECUTIVE EDITOR/BOOKS: Heidi Reuter Lloyd
SENIOR EDITOR/BOOKS: Mark Hagen
ART DIRECTOR: Gretchen Trautman
LAYOUT DESIGNERS: Nancy Novak, Catherine Fletcher
CONTENT PRODUCTION SUPERVISOR: Julie Wagner
PROOFREADER: Linne Bruskewitz
PROJECT EDITOR: Kathy Pohl
PROJECT INDEXER: Jean Duerst
EDITOR-IN-CHIEF: Catherine Cassidy
CHIEF MARKETING OFFICER: Lisa Karpinski
VICE PRESIDENT/BOOK MARKETING: Robert Graham Botta
CREATIVE DIRECTOR: Ardyth Cope
CREATIVE DIRECTOR/CREATIVE MARKETING: James Palmen

Reader's Digest Association
PRESIDENT AND CHIEF EXECUTIVE OFFICER: Mary G. Berner
PRESIDENT, FOOD & ENTERTAINING: Suzanne M. Grimes

For more great recipes, visit Pillsbury.com.

FRONT COVER PHOTOGRAPH:
Beef and Spinach Deep-Dish Pizza, p. 112

BACK COVER PHOTOGRAPHS:
Beef Pepper Steak Casserole, p. 117
Grands!® Strawberry Shortcakes, p. 257
Chicken Pot Pie with Flaky Crust, p. 138

contents

roasted chicken and vegetables provençal * p. 13

vegetable-split pea soup * p. 34

beef stew casserole * p. 131

picadillo wraps * p. 129

all-time favorites

chicken taco stew in bread bowls ✳ p. 18

grilled fresh vegetable pizza ✳ p. 12

swiss steak ✳ p. 8

braised pork chops with cream gravy ✳ p. 7

roasted chicken and vegetables provençal * p. 13

chicken taco grande

PREP TIME: 25 MINUTES
READY TO SERVE: 50 MINUTES
SERVINGS: 8

✳ meal-in-one

taco ring
- 1 tablespoon oil
- 1¼ lb. boneless skinless chicken breast halves, cut into ¼ to ½ -inch pieces
- 2 cups frozen whole kernel corn
- ½ cup chopped green bell pepper
- ⅓ cup water
- 1 (1.25-oz.) pkg. taco seasoning mix
- 4 oz. shredded Cheddar cheese (1 cup)
- 2 (8-oz.) cans Pillsbury® Refrigerated Crescent Dinner Rolls

topping
- 1 cup shredded lettuce
- ½ cup chopped tomato
- ¼ cup sliced ripe olives

garnish
- ½ cup sour cream
- ½ cup chunky-style salsa

1. Heat oven to 375°F. Spray large cookie sheet with cooking spray. Heat oil in medium skillet over medium heat until hot. Add chicken; cook 5 minutes or until no longer pink in center, stirring frequently.

2. Add corn, bell pepper, water and taco seasoning mix; mix well. Heat until bubbly. Reduce heat to medium; cook 10 to 15 minutes or until liquid evaporates, stirring occasionally. Remove from heat. Stir in cheese. Set aside.

3. Separate both cans of dough into 16 triangles. Arrange triangles on sprayed cookie sheet with short sides of triangles toward center, overlapping into wreath shape and leaving 5-inch round opening in the center. Lightly press the short sides of dough to flatten slightly.

4. Spoon chicken filling onto widest part of dough. Pull end points of triangles over filling and tuck under dough to form ring. (Filling will be visible.)

5. Bake at 375°F for 20 to 25 minutes or until golden brown. Meanwhile, in small bowl, combine lettuce, tomato and olives; toss gently to mix.

6. Loosen baked ring with spatula; slide onto serving platter. Spoon lettuce mixture into center of ring. Serve with sour cream and salsa.

Nutrition Information Per Serving: Calories 450 • Total Fat 24g • Saturated Fat 8g • Cholesterol 65mg • Sodium 1130mg • Total Carbohydrate 34g • Dietary Fiber 2g • Sugars 7g • Protein 24g. Dietary Exchanges: 2½ Starch • 2½ Very Lean Meat • 4 Fat OR 2½ Carbohydrate • 2½ Very Lean Meat • 4 Fat.

hearty meatball stew

PREP TIME: 30 MINUTES
READY TO SERVE: 1 HOUR
SERVINGS: 5

1 lb. ground turkey

1 egg

¼ cup chopped onion

½ teaspoon garlic salt

¼ teaspoon pepper

1 tablespoon oil

1 beef-flavor bouillon cube or 1 teaspoon beef-flavor instant bouillon

1½ cups boiling water

1 (10-oz.) can condensed golden mushroom soup

4 carrots, cut into ½-inch pieces

3 stalks celery, cut into ½-inch pieces

1 medium onion, sliced

1 (11-oz.) can vacuum-packed whole kernel corn

1. In medium bowl, combine ground turkey, egg, onion, garlic salt and pepper; mix well. Shape into 1½-inch meatballs.

2. Heat oil in Dutch oven over medium-high heat until hot. Add the meatballs; cook until browned.

3. In small bowl, dissolve bouillon in boiling water. Add bouillon mixture and all remaining ingredients to meatballs; stir gently. Cover; bring to a boil. Reduce heat to low; simmer 25 to 30 minutes or until vegetables are tender.

Nutrition Information Per Serving: Calories 350 • Total Fat 18g • Saturated Fat 4g • Cholesterol 110mg • Sodium 1040mg • Total Carbohydrate 26g • Dietary Fiber 4g • Sugars 8g • Protein 23g. Dietary Exchanges: 1½ Starch • 2½ Lean Meat • 2 Fat OR 1½ Carbohydrate • 2½ Lean Meat • 2 Fat.

braised pork chops with cream gravy

PREP TIME: 15 MINUTES
READY TO SERVE: 55 MINUTES
SERVINGS: 4

4 pork loin chops (½ inch thick)

½ cup water

2 teaspoons dried parsley flakes

¼ teaspoon salt

¼ teaspoon onion powder

¼ teaspoon dried thyme leaves

¼ teaspoon Worcestershire sauce

⅓ cup milk

2 tablespoons all-purpose flour

1. In large skillet over medium-high heat, brown pork chops on both sides. Add water, parsley flakes, salt, onion powder, thyme and Worcestershire sauce. Cover; simmer 20 to 30 minutes or until pork chops are tender.

2. Remove pork chops from skillet; keep warm. In small bowl, combine milk and flour; blend until smooth. Gradually stir into hot mixture in skillet. Cook until mixture boils and thickens, stirring constantly. Serve gravy with pork chops.

Nutrition Information Per Serving: Calories 180 • Total Fat 8g • Saturated Fat 3g • Cholesterol 65mg • Sodium 190mg • Total Carbohydrate 4g • Dietary Fiber 0g • Sugars 1g • Protein: 24g. Dietary Exchange: 3½ Lean Meat.

beef stroganoff with parsley noodles

READY TO SERVE: 40 MINUTES
SERVINGS: 6

* meal-in-one

8 oz. uncooked medium egg noodles (4 cups)

1 teaspoon dried parsley flakes

3 tablespoons margarine or butter

1 (8-oz.) pkg. fresh whole mushrooms, sliced

½ cup chopped onion

1 garlic clove, minced

1 lb. boneless beef sirloin steak, cut into 1-inch strips

1 (10½-oz.) can condensed beef consommé

2 tablespoons ketchup

½ teaspoon salt, if desired

3 tablespoons all-purpose flour

1 cup sour cream

1. Cook noodles to desired doneness as directed on package. Drain. Add parsley and 1 tablespoon of the margarine; toss to combine. Cover to keep warm.

2. Meanwhile, in large nonstick skillet over medium heat, melt 1 tablespoon of the remaining margarine. Add mushrooms, onion and garlic; cook 2 to 3 minutes or until tender. Remove mushroom mixture; set aside.

3. In same skillet, melt remaining 1 tablespoon margarine. Add beef; cook and stir until browned. Reserve ⅓ cup of the beef consommé. Add remaining consommé, ketchup, salt and mushroom mixture to skillet; mix well.

4. In small jar with tight-fitting lid, combine reserved consommé and flour; shake well to blend. Gradually add to beef mixture, stirring constantly. Cook and stir until thickened. Stir in sour cream; cook until thoroughly heated. Do not boil. Serve over parsley noodles.

Nutrition Information Per Serving: Calories 420 • Total Fat 19g • Saturated Fat 8g • Cholesterol 95mg • Sodium 630mg • Total Carbohydrate 37g • Dietary Fiber 2g • Sugars 5g • Protein 24g. Dietary Exchanges: 2½ Starch • 2½ Lean Meat • 2 Fat OR 2½ Carbohydrate • 2½ Lean Meat • 2 Fat.

swiss steak

PREP TIME: 15 MINUTES
READY TO SERVE: 1 HOUR 45 MINUTES
SERVINGS: 6

* plan ahead

¼ cup all-purpose flour

1 teaspoon salt

¼ teaspoon pepper

2 to 2½ lb. beef round steak (½ to ¾ inch thick), cut into serving-sized pieces

1 to 2 tablespoons oil

1 large onion, sliced

1 (8-oz.) can whole tomatoes, undrained, cut up

1 (8-oz.) can tomato sauce

1. In small bowl, combine flour, salt and pepper; mix well. Coat beef with flour mixture, using all of mixture.

2. Heat the oil in large skillet over medium-high heat until hot. Add the beef; cook until browned.

3. Add all remaining ingredients. Bring to a boil. Reduce heat to low; cover and simmer 1¼ to 1½ hours or until beef is tender. If desired, serve with hot cooked potatoes or noodles.

MAKING IT EASY

When preparing the Swiss Steak, you can always combine a 10¾-oz. can of condensed tomato soup with ½ cup of water as a substitution for the canned tomatoes and the tomato sauce. To add a little more color to the main course, simply add some sliced mushrooms, peas and green beans to the recipe. Add the mushrooms along with the onion, but don't add the peas and green beans until the last 10 to 15 minutes of cooking time.

beef stroganoff with parsley noodles

swiss steak

classic chicken pot pie

PREP TIME: 25 MINUTES
READY TO SERVE: 1 HOUR 5 MINUTES
SERVINGS: 6

✳ meal-in-one

1. Heat oven to 425°F. Prepare pie crust as directed on package for two-crust pie using 9-inch glass pie pan.

2. Melt margarine in medium saucepan over medium heat. Add onion; cook and stir 2 minutes or until tender. Add flour, salt and pepper; stir until well blended. Gradually stir in broth and milk, cooking and stirring until bubbly and thickened.

3. Add chicken and mixed vegetables; mix well. Remove from heat. Spoon chicken mixture into crust-lined pan. Top with second crust; seal edges and flute. Cut slits in several places in top crust.

4. Bake at 425°F for 30 to 40 minutes or until crust is golden brown. If necessary, cover edge of crust with strips of foil during last 15 to 20 minutes of baking to prevent excessive browning. Let stand 5 minutes before serving.

Nutrition Information Per Serving: Calories 590 • Total Fat 34g • Saturated Fat 11g • Cholesterol 70mg • Sodium 860mg • Total Carbohydrate 47g • Dietary Fiber 2g • Sugars 4g • Protein 23g. Dietary Exchanges: 3 Starch • 2 Lean Meat • 5½ Fat OR 3 Carbohydrate • 2 Lean Meat • 5½ Fat.

crust

1 (15-oz.) pkg. Pillsbury® Refrigerated Pie Crusts, softened as directed on package

filling

⅓ cup margarine or butter

⅓ cup chopped onion

⅓ cup all-purpose flour

½ teaspoon salt

¼ teaspoon pepper

1 (14-oz.) can chicken broth

½ cup milk

2½ cups shredded cooked chicken or turkey

2 cups frozen mixed vegetables, thawed

DRESSED FOR SUCCESS

Instead of cutting basic steam vents into the top crust of Classic Chicken Pot Pie, why not jazz things up a bit? Cut out tiny shapes using small cookie cutters or the tip of a knife. Be creative and cut out a tiny chicken, or use a small chicken-shaped cookie cutter to make the cutouts and dress up the pie.

---

chili dog pizza

PREP TIME: 30 MINUTES
SERVINGS: 6

✳ meal-in-one

1 (10-oz.) can Pillsbury® Refrigerated Pizza Crust

1 (7.5-oz.) can chili with beans

½ lb. hot dogs, cut into ½-inch slices

¼ cup drained sweet pickle relish

1 cup (2 to 4 medium) chopped Italian plum tomatoes

4 oz. finely shredded mozzarella cheese (1 cup)

1. Heat oven to 425°F. Grease 12-inch pizza pan. Unroll dough; place in greased pan. Starting at center, press out dough to edge of pan, forming ½-inch rim. Bake at 425°F for 7 to 9 minutes or until light golden brown.

2. Remove partially baked crust from oven. Spoon and spread chili over crust. Sprinkle with hot dogs, relish, tomatoes and cheese.

3. Return to oven; bake an additional 15 to 18 minutes or until the crust is a deep golden brown.

Nutrition Information Per Serving: Calories 350 • Total Fat 18g • Saturated Fat 7g • Cholesterol 35mg • Sodium 1090mg • Total Carbohydrate 32g • Dietary Fiber 2g • Sugars 8g • Protein 15g. Dietary Exchanges: 2 Starch • 1½ High-Fat Meat • 1 Fat OR 2 Carbohydrate • 1½ High-Fat Meat • 1 Fat.

chicken-broccoli au gratin

PREP TIME: 20 MINUTES
START TO FINISH: 45 MINUTES
SERVINGS: 2

KIBBY JACKSON ✲ GRAY, CALIFORNIA
BAKE-OFF® CONTEST 42, 2006

1 tablespoon olive oil

1 cup sliced fresh mushrooms

1 small onion, sliced (½ cup)

1 (10-oz.) box frozen broccoli in a zesty cheese sauce

⅔ cup ricotta cheese

1 cup chopped cooked chicken

1 (4-oz.) can refrigerated crescent dinner rolls (4 rolls)

1. Heat oven to 375°F. In 10-inch skillet, heat oil over medium-high heat. Add mushrooms and onion; cook 5 to 7 minutes, stirring frequently, until tender. Meanwhile, microwave broccoli with cheese sauce as directed on box.

2. Spread ⅓ cup ricotta cheese in bottom of each of 2 ungreased 2-cup au gratin dishes or individual casseroles. Top each evenly with chicken, mushroom mixture and broccoli with cheese sauce.

3. Unroll dough; separate into 2 rectangles. Place 1 rectangle over top of each dish, tucking corners into dish as needed.

4. Place dishes on cookie sheet; bake 20 to 25 minutes or until tops are golden brown and edges are bubbly.

Nutrition Information Per Serving: Calories 560 • Total Fat 27g • Saturated Fat 7g • Trans Fat 3g • Cholesterol 70mg • Sodium 1170mg • Total Carbohydrate 43g • Dietary Fiber 3g • Sugars 16g • Protein 38g. **Dietary Exchanges:** 1 Starch • 1 Other Carbohydrate • 2 Vegetable • 4½ Lean Meat • 2½ Fat.

easy cheesy pizzas

PREP TIME: 15 MINUTES
READY TO SERVE: 35 MINUTES
SERVINGS: 8

✲ **meal-in-one**

1 (16.3-oz.) can Pillsbury® Grands!® Refrigerated Buttermilk Biscuits

1 (14 or 15-oz.) jar pizza sauce

6 oz. shredded mozzarella cheese (1½ cups)

1. Heat oven to 375°F. Spray 2 cookie sheets with cooking spray. Separate dough into 8 biscuits; place 2 inches apart on sprayed cookie sheets. Press or roll each to form 6-inch round.

2. Spread 3 tablespoons pizza sauce evenly over each round. Sprinkle each with cheese. If desired, add favorite pizza toppings.

3. Bake at 375°F for 12 to 17 minutes or until biscuits are golden brown and the cheese is bubbly.

Nutrition Information Per Serving: Calories 280 • Total Fat 14g • Saturated Fat 5g • Cholesterol 15mg • Sodium 1040mg • Total Carbohydrate 28g • Dietary Fiber 1g • Sugars 7g • Protein 10g. **Dietary Exchanges:** 1 Starch • 1 Fruit • 1 Medium-Fat Meat • 1½ Fat OR 2 Carbohydrate • 1 Medium-Fat Meat • 1½ Fat.

grilled fresh vegetable pizza

PREP TIME: 30 MINUTES
SERVINGS: 4

✳ meal-in-one

1 cup fresh small broccoli
florets

1 (10-oz.) can Pillsbury®
Refrigerated Pizza Crust

2 teaspoons olive oil

1 small yellow summer
squash, sliced lengthwise

¹⁄₂ cup pizza sauce

2 Italian plum tomatoes,
sliced

6 oz. shredded mozzarella
cheese (1¹⁄₂ cups)

1. Heat grill. In small microwave-safe bowl, combine broccoli and 3 tablespoons water; cover with microwave-safe plastic wrap. Microwave on high for 2 to 3 minutes or until broccoli is bright green. Drain; set aside.

2. Cut 18x12-inch sheet of heavy-duty foil; spray with cooking spray. Unroll dough; place on sprayed foil. Starting at center, press out dough to form 13x9-inch rectangle. Brush dough with 1 teaspoon of the oil. Brush squash with remaining teaspoon oil.

3. When ready to grill, place squash on grill. Invert dough onto grill rack and peel off foil. Cook on gas grill over medium-low heat or on charcoal grill 4 to 6 inches from medium-low coals for 3 to 5 minutes or until bottom of dough is golden brown and squash is crisp-tender and grill-marked, turning squash occasionally.

4. Remove squash from grill; place on cutting board. Cut squash into bite-sized pieces. Turn dough; grill 1 to 2 minutes or until bottom is set. Carefully remove from grill. Top crust with pizza sauce, tomatoes, squash and broccoli. Sprinkle with cheese.

5. Return pizza to grill. Cook an additional 3 to 5 minutes or until crust is browned and thoroughly cooked, and cheese is melted.

Nutrition Information Per Serving: Calories 370 • Total Fat 13g • Saturated Fat 6g • Cholesterol 25mg • Sodium 750mg • Total Carbohydrate 42g • Dietary Fiber 4g • Sugars 7g • Protein 20g. Dietary Exchanges: 2¹⁄₂ Starch • 1 Vegetable • 1¹⁄₂ Medium-Fat Meat • 1 Fat OR 2¹⁄₂ Carbohydrate • 1 Vegetable • 1¹⁄₂ Medium-Fat Meat • 1 Fat.

slow-cooked chicken and sausage stew

PREP TIME: 15 MINUTES
READY TO SERVE: 8 HOURS 15 MINUTES
SERVINGS: 4

✳ plan ahead

¹⁄₂ cup thinly sliced carrot

2 tablespoons brown sugar

1 teaspoon dry mustard

¹⁄₂ cup ketchup

1 tablespoon vinegar

¹⁄₂ lb. kielbasa sausage, cut into
¹⁄₄-inch slices

2 boneless skinless chicken
breast halves, cut into thin
bite-sized strips

1 medium onion, thinly sliced,
separated into rings

1 (16-oz.) can baked beans,
undrained

1 (8-oz.) pkg. frozen cut
green beans in a pouch,
thawed

1. In 3¹⁄₂ or 4-quart slow cooker, combine all ingredients except green beans; mix well. Cover; cook on low setting at least 8 hours or until chicken is no longer pink and carrot slices are tender.

2. Ten minutes before serving, stir in green beans. Increase heat to high setting; cover and cook 10 minutes or until green beans are crisp-tender.

Nutrition Information Per Serving: Calories 460 • Total Fat 18g • Saturated 6g • Cholesterol 75mg • Sodium 1520mg • Total Carbohydrate 47g • Dietary Fiber 8g • Sugars 20g • Protein 28g. Dietary Exchanges: 1 Starch • 1¹⁄₂ Fruit • 2 Vegetable • 3 Medium-Fat Meat • ¹⁄₂ Fat OR 2¹⁄₂ Carbohydrate • 2 Vegetable • 3 Medium-Fat Meat • ¹⁄₂ Fat.

roasted chicken and vegetables provençal

PREP TIME: 30 MINUTES
READY TO SERVE: 1 HOUR 35 MINUTES
SERVINGS: 4

✳ **meal-in-one**

8 small new red potatoes, quartered

1 small yellow squash, cut into 1-inch pieces

1 small zucchini, cut into 1-inch pieces

1 red bell pepper, cut into 1-inch pieces

1 medium red onion, cut into eighths

1 (8-oz.) pkg. fresh mushrooms

¼ cup olive oil

2 teaspoons dried basil leaves

2 teaspoons dried thyme leaves

½ teaspoon salt

½ teaspoon coarse ground black pepper

3 garlic cloves, minced

3 to 3½ lb. cut-up frying chicken, skin removed

1. Heat oven to 375°F. In ungreased 13x9-inch (3-quart) baking dish, combine potatoes, squash, zucchini, bell pepper, onion and mushrooms.

2. In small bowl, combine oil, basil, thyme, salt, pepper and garlic; mix well. Brush half of oil mixture on vegetables. Place chicken pieces, meaty side up, over vegetables. Brush chicken with remaining oil mixture.

3. Bake at 375°F for 45 minutes. Baste with pan juices; bake an additional 15 to 20 minutes or until chicken is fork tender and juices run clear, and vegetables are tender. Baste with pan juices before serving.

Nutrition Information Per Serving: Calories 550 • Total Fat 24g • Saturated 5g • Cholesterol 115mg • Sodium 390mg • Total Carbohydrate 41g • Dietary Fiber 6g • Sugars 7g • Protein 43g. **Dietary Exchanges:** 2 Starch • 2 Vegetable • 4½ Lean Meat • 2 Fat OR 2 Carbohydrate • 2 Vegetable • 4½ Lean Meat • 2 Fat.

mexican beef pie

mexican beef pie

PREP TIME: 15 MINUTES
READY TO SERVE: 40 MINUTES
SERVINGS: 6

* meal-in-one

1 lb. lean ground beef

1 (1.25-oz.) pkg. taco seasoning mix

½ cup water

⅓ cup sliced olives

1 (8-oz.) can Pillsbury® Refrigerated Crescent Dinner Rolls

1 cup crushed corn chips

1 (8-oz.) container sour cream

4 oz. shredded Cheddar cheese (1 cup)

1 cup corn chips

Shredded lettuce, if desired

Salsa, if desired

1. Heat oven to 375°F. Brown ground beef in large skillet over medium-high heat for 5 to 7 minutes or until thoroughly cooked, stirring frequently. Drain. Stir in taco seasoning mix, water and olives. Reduce heat to low; simmer 5 minutes.

2. Meanwhile, separate dough into 8 triangles. Place triangles in ungreased 9-inch pie pan; press in bottom and up sides to form crust. Sprinkle 1 cup crushed corn chips evenly in bottom of crust.

3. Spoon hot beef mixture over corn chips. Spread sour cream over beef mixture. Sprinkle with cheese and remaining 1 cup corn chips.

4. Bake at 375°F for 20 to 25 minutes or until crust is golden brown. Cut into wedges. Top with lettuce and salsa.

Nutrition Information Per Serving: Calories 640 • Total Fat 43g • Saturated Fat 16g • Cholesterol 85mg • Sodium 1050mg • Total Carbohydrate 38g • Dietary Fiber 3g • Sugars 6g • Protein 24g. **Dietary Exchanges:** 2½ Starch • 2½ Medium-Fat Meat • 5½ Fat OR 2½ Carbohydrate • 2½ Medium-Fat Meat • 5½ Fat.

MAKE-AHEAD EASE

To make the Mexican Beef Pie ahead of time, prepare it through the end of Step 3, but don't sprinkle with the corn chips. Cover the pie with foil and refrigerate it for up to 2 hours before topping it with the corn chips and baking it as directed. To reheat, cover the baked pie with foil and bake at 375°F for 25 to 30 minutes or until thoroughly heated.

grandma's potato salad

PREP TIME: 30 MINUTES
READY TO SERVE: 1 HOUR 30 MINUTES
SERVINGS: 6

* plan ahead

salad

3 eggs

2 cups cubed peeled cooked potatoes

¾ cup sliced celery

¼ cup chopped onion

dressing

½ cup salad dressing or mayonnaise

1½ teaspoons cider vinegar

1 teaspoon prepared mustard

½ teaspoon sugar

¼ teaspoon salt

⅛ teaspoon pepper

Paprika

1. Place eggs in medium saucepan; cover with cold water. Bring to a boil. Reduce heat; simmer about 15 minutes. Immediately drain; run cold water over eggs to stop cooking.

2. Peel eggs. Chop 2 of the eggs; reserve 1 egg for garnish. In large bowl, combine chopped eggs, potatoes, celery and onion.

3. In small bowl, combine all dressing ingredients except paprika; blend well. Spoon dressing over salad; mix well. Cover; refrigerate at least 1 hour or until chilled.

4. Just before serving, slice reserved egg. Garnish potato salad with sliced egg; sprinkle with paprika.

Nutrition Information Per Serving: Calories 170 • Total Fat 9g • Saturated Fat 2g • Cholesterol 110mg • Sodium 280mg • Total Carbohydrate 17g • Dietary Fiber 1g • Sugars 4g • Protein 4g. **Dietary Exchanges:** 1 Starch • 2 Fat OR 1 Carbohydrate • 2 Fat.

pork stew

PREP TIME: 20 MINUTES
READY TO SERVE: 1 HOUR
SERVINGS: 6

1 tablespoon oil

1½ lb. boneless pork loin, cut into ¾-inch cubes

1 (14-oz.) can ready-to-serve chicken broth

1 cup water

1 medium onion, cut into 8 wedges

½ teaspoon salt

½ teaspoon dried marjoram leaves

⅛ teaspoon pepper

10 to 12 small red potatoes, quartered

1½ cups sliced carrots

1 cup frozen sweet peas

½ cup half-and-half

¼ cup all-purpose flour

1. Heat oil in 4-quart saucepan or Dutch oven over medium-high heat until hot. Add pork cubes; cook 3 to 5 minutes or until browned, stirring occasionally. Add broth, water, onion, salt, marjoram and pepper. Bring to a boil. Reduce heat to low; cover and simmer 20 minutes.

2. Add potatoes, carrots and peas. Return to a boil. Reduce heat to low; cover and simmer an additional 15 to 20 minutes or until vegetables are tender.

3. In small bowl, combine half-and-half and flour; blend until smooth. Gradually stir into pork mixture. Cook and stir over medium-high heat until the mixture is bubbly and thickened.

Nutrition Information Per Serving: Calories 350 • Total Fat 13g • Saturated Fat 5g • Cholesterol 70mg • Sodium 500mg • Total Carbohydrate 31g • Dietary Fiber 4g • Sugars 5g • Protein 28g. **Dietary Exchanges:** 2 Starch • 3 Lean Meat • ½ Fat OR 2 Carbohydrate • 3 Lean Meat • ½ Fat.

chicken provençal

READY TO SERVE: 20 MINUTES
SERVINGS: 4

* super fast

1 tablespoon olive oil or vegetable oil

4 boneless skinless chicken breast halves

1 large onion, sliced

1 cup cherry tomatoes, halved

1 (14-oz.) can artichoke hearts, drained, quartered

12 pitted extra-large ripe olives, halved

2 garlic cloves, minced

½ teaspoon dried rosemary leaves, crushed

¼ teaspoon fennel seed, crushed

½ cup ready-to-serve fat-free chicken broth with ⅓ less sodium

1. Heat oil in large nonstick skillet over medium heat until hot. Add chicken; cook 4 minutes. Turn chicken; add onion. Cover; cook 3 minutes, stirring occasionally.

2. Add remaining ingredients. Cover; cook over medium-low heat for an additional 5 minutes or until onion is crisp-tender, vegetables are hot, chicken is fork tender and juices run clear. If desired, season to taste with salt and pepper.

Nutrition Information Per Serving: Calories 260 • Total Fat 9g • Saturated 1.5g • Cholesterol 75mg • Sodium 460mg • Total Carbohydrate 15g • Dietary Fiber 5g • Sugars 4g • Protein 30g. **Dietary Exchanges:** 3 Vegetable • 3 Lean Meat.

lazy-day overnight lasagna

PREP TIME: 20 MINUTES
READY TO SERVE: 13 HOURS 35 MINUTES
SERVINGS: 12

* plan ahead

1 lb. ground beef or mild Italian sausage

1 (28-oz.) jar spaghetti sauce

1 cup water

1 (15-oz.) container ricotta cheese

2 tablespoons chopped fresh chives

½ teaspoon dried oregano leaves

1 egg

8 oz. uncooked lasagna noodles

1 (16-oz.) pkg. sliced mozzarella cheese

2 tablespoons grated Parmesan cheese

1. In large skillet, cook ground beef over medium heat for 8 to 10 minutes or until thoroughly cooked, stirring frequently. Drain well. Add spaghetti sauce and water; blend well.

2. In medium bowl, combine ricotta cheese, chives, oregano and egg; mix well.

3. In ungreased 13x9-inch (3-quart) baking dish or lasagna pan, spread 1½ cups of the meat sauce. Top with half each of noodles, ricotta cheese mixture and mozzarella cheese. Repeat with 1½ cups meat sauce and remaining noodles, ricotta cheese mixture and mozzarella cheese. Top with remaining meat sauce. Sprinkle with Parmesan cheese. Cover; refrigerate 12 hours or overnight.

4. Heat oven to 350°F. Uncover baking dish; bake 50 to 60 minutes or until noodles are tender and casserole is bubbly. Cover; let stand 15 minutes before serving.

Nutrition Information Per Serving: Calories 350 • Total Fat 17g • Saturated Fat 9g • Cholesterol 75mg • Sodium 580mg • Total Carbohydrate 23g • Dietary Fiber 2g • Sugars 1g • Protein 25g. **Dietary Exchanges:** 1½ Starch • 3 Medium-Fat Meat OR 1½ Carbohydrate • 3 Medium-Fat Meat.

chicken taco stew in bread bowls

PREP TIME: 10 MINUTES
READY TO SERVE: 35 MINUTES
SERVINGS: 3

✳ meal-in-one

1 (11-oz.) can Pillsbury® Refrigerated Crusty French Loaf

1 (6-oz.) pkg. refrigerated southwestern flavor chicken strips, coarsely chopped

1 (15 or 15.5-oz.) can kidney beans, drained, rinsed

1 (10-oz.) can diced tomatoes and green chiles, undrained

1 cup frozen whole kernel corn

1 cup chicken broth

1 tablespoon cornstarch

2 oz. shredded Cheddar cheese (½ cup)

1. Heat oven to 350°F. Spray cookie sheet with cooking spray. Cut dough into 3 equal pieces. Shape each into ball, placing seam at bottom so dough is smooth on top. Place dough balls seam side down on sprayed cookie sheet.

2. Bake at 350°F for 18 to 22 minutes or until golden brown. Cool 5 minutes.

3. Meanwhile, in medium saucepan, combine all remaining ingredients except cheese; mix well. Cook over medium heat until mixture boils and thickens, stirring occasionally.

4. Cut top off each bread loaf. Lightly press center of bread down to form bowls. Place each bread bowl in individual shallow soup plate. Spoon about 1 cup stew into each bread bowl. Sprinkle with cheese. Place top of each bread bowl next to filled bowl.

Nutrition Information Per Serving: Calories 655 • Total Fat 14g • Saturated Fat 6g • Cholesterol 70mg • Sodium 1920mg • Total Carbohydrate 98g • Dietary Fiber 13g • Sugars 12g • Protein 47g. Dietary Exchanges: 5 Starch • 1 Fruit • 1 Vegetable • 4 Very Lean Meat • 1½ Fat OR 6 Carbohydrate • 1 Vegetable • 4 Very Lean Meat • 1½ Fat.

sage and rosemary roast chicken

PREP TIME: 15 MINUTES
READY TO SERVE: 1 HOUR 45 MINUTES
SERVINGS: 4

* plan ahead

- 3 to 3½ lb. cut-up or quartered frying chicken
- 4 medium baking potatoes, unpeeled, quartered
- 1 bunch (about 8) green onions, trimmed, cut into 2-inch pieces
- ½ teaspoon dried sage leaves
- ½ teaspoon dried rosemary leaves, crushed
- ¼ teaspoon salt
- ¼ teaspoon coarse ground black pepper

1. Heat oven to 375°F. Arrange chicken, potatoes and onions in ungreased 13x9-inch (3-quart) baking dish. Sprinkle with sage, rosemary, salt and pepper.

2. Bake at 375°F for 1¼ to 1½ hours or until chicken is fork tender and juices run clear, and potatoes are tender.

Nutrition Information Per Serving: Calories 590 • Total Fat 21g • Saturated 6g • Cholesterol 135mg • Sodium 280mg • Total Carbohydrate 53g • Dietary Fiber 6g • Sugars 3g • Protein 48g. **Dietary Exchanges:** 3½ Starch • 5½ Lean Meat • 1 Fat OR 3½ Carbohydrate • 5½ Lean Meat • 1 Fat.

cheeseburger skillet hash

PREP TIME: 15 MINUTES
READY TO SERVE: 40 MINUTES
SERVINGS: 5

* meal-in-one

- 4 slices bacon
- 1 lb. lean ground beef
- 3 tablespoons chopped onion
- 3 tablespoons oil
- 2½ cups frozen hash-brown potatoes, thawed
- 1 (11-oz.) can vacuum-packed whole kernel corn with red and green peppers, drained
- 1 (4.5-oz.) can chopped green chiles, drained
- ½ cup barbecue sauce
- 8 oz. shredded Cheddar cheese (2 cups)
- ¼ teaspoon salt, if desired
- ¼ teaspoon pepper, if desired
- 1 (16.3-oz.) can Pillsbury® Grands!® Refrigerated Buttermilk or Reduced Fat Buttermilk Biscuits

1. Heat oven to 400°F. Cook the bacon until crisp. Drain on paper towel; crumble. Set aside.

2. In 12-inch cast iron or ovenproof skillet, brown ground beef and onion over medium heat until beef is thoroughly cooked, stirring frequently. Drain. Place beef mixture in medium bowl; cover to keep warm.

3. Add oil to same skillet. Heat over medium-high heat until hot. Add potatoes; cook 3 to 5 minutes or until browned, stirring constantly. Add cooked ground beef, corn, chiles, barbecue sauce, cheese, salt and pepper; mix well. Cook until thoroughly heated, stirring occasionally. Sprinkle with bacon.

4. Separate dough into 8 biscuits. Arrange biscuits over hot mixture.

5. Bake at 400°F for 16 to 24 minutes or until biscuits are deep golden brown and bottoms are no longer doughy.

Nutrition Information Per Serving: Calories 880 • Total Fat 53g • Saturated Fat 20g • Cholesterol 110mg • Sodium 1950mg • Total Carbohydrate 62g • Dietary Fiber 4g • Sugars 12g • Protein 38g. **Dietary Exchanges:** 3 Starch • 1 Fruit • 4 Medium-Fat Meat • 6 Fat OR 4 Carbohydrate • 4 Medium-Fat Meat • 6 Fat.

EARLY-MORNING ALTERATION

If you're charged with satisfying hearty appetites or you need to whip up a no-fuss breakfast fast, simply convert this skillet specialty into "Hash Ranchero."

All you need to do is prepare the recipe as instructed, but offer it alongside poached eggs. Include sour cream, salsa and guacamole with each serving.

fettuccine alfredo

READY TO SERVE: 25 MINUTES
SERVINGS: 6

✳ super fast

12 oz. uncooked fettuccine
¾ cup butter
1 cup whipping cream
¼ teaspoon white pepper
1¼ cups grated Parmesan cheese
2 teaspoons chopped fresh parsley, if desired
¼ teaspoon nutmeg, if desired

1. Cook fettuccine to desired doneness as directed on package. Drain; cover to keep warm.

2. Meanwhile, melt butter in 6-quart Dutch oven over low heat. Stir in cream and pepper. Cook about 5 minutes or until mixture thickens slightly, stirring frequently.

3. Stir in Parmesan cheese; cook over low heat just until cheese is melted, stirring constantly. Immediately stir in cooked fettuccine; toss to coat with sauce. Stir in parsley and nutmeg. If sauce begins to separate, stir in a little more cream and cook over low heat until smooth.

Nutrition Information Per Serving: Calories 650 • Total Fat 46g • Saturated Fat 28g • Cholesterol 185mg • Sodium 650mg • Total Carbohydrate 42g • Dietary Fiber 2g • Sugars 3g • Protein 18g. Dietary Exchanges: 3 Starch • 1 High-Fat Meat • 7 Fat OR 3 Carbohydrate • 1 High-Fat Meat • 7 Fat.

easy chicken parmigiana

READY TO SERVE: 30 MINUTES
SERVINGS: 4

6 oz. uncooked penne (2 cups)
¼ cup grated Parmesan cheese
¼ cup plain bread crumbs
4 boneless skinless chicken breast halves
1 tablespoon oil
1 (14.5-oz.) can Italian-style tomatoes with olive oil, garlic and spices, undrained
1 small zucchini, cut into 1½-inch-long thin strips
2 tablespoons chopped ripe olives

1. Cook pasta to desired doneness as directed on package. Drain; cover to keep warm.

2. Meanwhile, in shallow bowl combine cheese and bread crumbs; mix well. Coat chicken breast halves with cheese mixture. Heat oil in large skillet over medium-high heat until hot. Add chicken; cook 3 to 5 minutes on each side or until browned.

3. Stir in tomatoes and zucchini. Bring to a boil. Reduce heat to low; cover and simmer 12 to 15 minutes or until chicken is fork tender and juices run clear, stirring and turning chicken occasionally. Serve chicken mixture with pasta. Sprinkle with olives.

Nutrition Information Per Serving: Calories 430 • Total Fat 12g • Saturated 3g • Cholesterol 80mg • Sodium 800mg • Total Carbohydrate 43g • Dietary Fiber 3g • Sugars 7g • Protein 37g. Dietary Exchanges: 2 Starch • 2 Vegetable • 4 Lean Meat OR 2 Carbohydrate • 2 Vegetable • 4 Lean Meat.

slow-cooked beans

PREP TIME: 15 MINUTES
READY TO SERVE: 8 HOURS 15 MINUTES
SERVINGS: 18

✳ plan ahead

½ lb. bacon, diced
½ cup firmly packed brown sugar
¼ cup cornstarch
1 teaspoon dry mustard
½ cup molasses
1 tablespoon vinegar
4 (16-oz.) cans baked beans
1 medium onion, chopped
1 green bell pepper, chopped

1. In large skillet, cook bacon over medium heat until crisp. Drain, reserving 2 tablespoons drippings.

2. In 3½ to 4-quart slow cooker, combine cooked bacon, reserved 2 tablespoons drippings and all remaining ingredients; mix well.

3. Cover; cook on high setting for 1 hour.

4. Reduce heat to low setting; cook an additional 5 to 7 hours.

Nutrition Information Per Serving: Calories 200 • Total Fat 4g • Saturated Fat 1g • Cholesterol 4mg • Sodium 460mg • Total Carbohydrate 35g • Dietary Fiber 5g • Sugars 17g • Protein 6g. Dietary Exchanges: 2 Starch • ½ Fruit • ½ Fat OR 2½ Carbohydrate • ½ Fat.

chicken breasts with wild rice

PREP TIME: 15 MINUTES
READY TO SERVE: 2 HOURS 30 MINUTES
SERVINGS: 6

✳ meal-in-one

1 cup uncooked wild rice

½ cup chopped onion

3 cups water

½ cup sour cream

1 (10¾-oz.) can condensed cream of chicken soup

½ teaspoon dried thyme leaves

½ teaspoon dried marjoram leaves

½ teaspoon salt

¼ teaspoon pepper

1 (9-oz.) pkg. frozen asparagus cuts in a pouch, thawed, drained

6 bone-in chicken breast halves, skin removed

½ teaspoon seasoned salt

1. Heat oven to 350°F. In medium saucepan, combine wild rice, onion and water. Bring to a boil. Reduce heat to low; cover and simmer 45 to 55 minutes or until rice is tender and water is absorbed. Do not drain.

2. Add sour cream, soup, thyme, marjoram, salt and pepper to rice mixture in saucepan; blend well. Spread mixture evenly in ungreased 13x9-inch (3-quart) baking dish. Top with asparagus. Place chicken breast halves over asparagus, meaty side up; sprinkle with seasoned salt.

3. Bake at 350°F for 1 to 1¼ hours or until chicken is fork tender and juices run clear.

Nutrition Information Per Serving: Calories 350 • Total Fat 11g • Saturated 4g • Cholesterol 85mg • Sodium 820mg • Total Carbohydrate 28g • Dietary Fiber 3g • Sugars 3g • Protein 34g. **Dietary Exchanges:** 1½ Starch • 1 Vegetable • 4 Lean Meat OR 1½ Carbohydrate • 1 Vegetable • 4 Lean Meat.

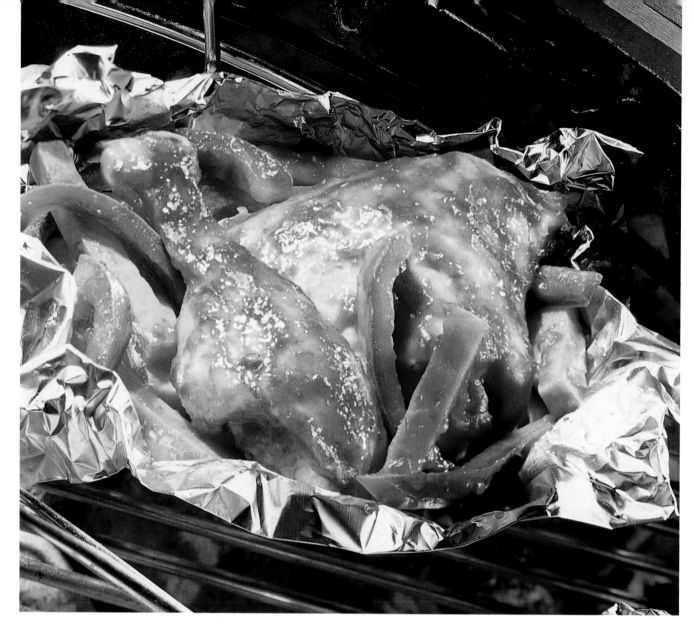

sweet and spicy chicken dinner packets

READY TO SERVE: 1 HOUR 10 MINUTES
SERVINGS: 4

* meal-in-one

½ cup chili sauce

3 tablespoons brown sugar

2 tablespoons fresh lime juice

½ teaspoon ginger

¼ teaspoon ground red pepper (cayenne)

2 medium sweet potatoes, peeled, cut into thin strips

1 green bell pepper, cut into thin strips

4 chicken drumsticks, skin removed if desired

4 chicken thighs, skin removed if desired

1. Heat grill. In small bowl, combine chili sauce, brown sugar, lime juice, ginger and ground red pepper; blend well.

2. Cut four 18x12-inch pieces of heavy-duty foil. Place ¼ of the sweet potatoes and bell pepper in center of each piece of foil; top each with drumstick and thigh. Spoon chili sauce mixture evenly over the vegetables and the chicken. Wrap securely using double-fold seals.

3. When ready to grill, place packets, seam side down, on gas grill over medium-high heat or on charcoal grill 4 to 6 inches from medium-high coals. Cook 40 to 50 minutes or until chicken is fork tender and juices run clear, turning packets once during cooking. Open packets carefully to allow hot steam to escape.

Nutrition Information Per Serving: Calories 420 • Total Fat 16g • Saturated 4g • Cholesterol 105mg • Sodium 570mg • Total Carbohydrate 36g • Dietary Fiber 3g • Sugars 20g • Protein 32g. **Dietary Exchanges:** 2 Starch • ½ Fruit • 3½ Lean Meat • 1 Fat OR 2½ Carbohydrate • 3½ Lean Meat • 1 Fat.

easy chicken tetrazzini

READY TO SERVE: 20 MINUTES
SERVINGS: 4

* super fast

1 (7-oz.) pkg. uncooked spaghetti, broken into thirds

1 tablespoon margarine or butter

½ cup sliced green onions

1 (8-oz.) pkg. fresh mushrooms, sliced

3 tablespoons all-purpose flour

¼ teaspoon garlic powder

⅛ teaspoon pepper

1 cup chicken broth

½ cup skim milk

2 cups cubed cooked chicken

1 (2-oz.) jar sliced pimiento, drained

2 tablespoons dry sherry

¼ cup grated Parmesan cheese

1. In large saucepan, cook spaghetti to desired doneness as directed on package; drain and set aside in colander.

2. In same saucepan, melt margarine over medium-high heat. Add onions and mushrooms; cook and stir until tender. In small bowl, combine flour, garlic powder, pepper, broth and milk; blend well. Add to onion mixture in saucepan. Cook until mixture boils and thickens, stirring constantly.

3. Add chicken, pimiento and sherry; cook until thoroughly heated, stirring occasionally. Stir in cheese. Add cooked spaghetti; toss gently. If desired, serve with additional grated Parmesan cheese and chopped fresh parsley.

Nutrition Information Per Serving: Calories 430 • Total Fat 11g • Saturated 3g • Cholesterol 70mg • Sodium 470mg • Total Carbohydrate 48g • Dietary Fiber 3g • Sugars 5g • Protein 34g. **Dietary Exchanges:** 3 Starch • 1 Vegetable • 3 Lean Meat OR 3 Carbohydrate • 1 Vegetable • 3 Lean Meat.

beef 'n beans with cheesy biscuits

PREP TIME: 15 MINUTES
READY TO SERVE: 40 MINUTES
SERVINGS: 5

* meal-in-one

1 lb. lean ground beef

½ cup chopped onion

1 (16-oz.) can barbecue beans or pork and beans with molasses

1 (10¾-oz.) can condensed tomato soup

1 teaspoon chili powder

¼ teaspoon garlic powder

1 (12-oz.) can Pillsbury® Golden Layers™ Refrigerated Flaky Biscuits

4 oz. shredded Cheddar or American cheese (1 cup)

1. Heat oven to 375°F. In large skillet, cook ground beef and onion over medium-high heat until beef is thoroughly cooked, stirring frequently. Drain.

2. Stir in beans, soup, chili powder and garlic powder; mix well. Bring to a boil. Reduce heat; simmer 5 minutes.

3. Separate dough into 10 biscuits. Spoon hot beef mixture into ungreased 8-inch square (2-quart) glass baking dish or 2-quart casserole. Arrange biscuits over hot mixture. Sprinkle with cheese.

4. Bake at 375°F for 20 to 25 minutes or until mixture is bubbly, and biscuits are golden brown and no longer doughy.

Nutrition Information Per Serving: Calories 640 • Total Fat 30g • Saturated Fat 12g • Cholesterol 80mg • Sodium 1570mg • Total Carbohydrate 61g • Dietary Fiber 6g • Sugars 16g • Protein 32g. **Dietary Exchanges:** 4 Starch • 3 Medium-Fat Meat • 2½ Fat OR 4 Carbohydrate • 3 Medium-Fat Meat • 2½ Fat.

CUSTOM-MADE CUISINE

After the beef and bean mixture has been warmed through, go ahead and taste it. Then you can adjust the seasonings to best suit your family's preferences. Try adding a pinch of your favorite herb!

chicken à la grands!®

1. Bake biscuits as directed on can.

2. Meanwhile, place chicken on microwave-safe plate. Microwave on high for 1½ to 2½ minutes or until thawed. Melt margarine in large saucepan over medium-low heat. Add flour; stir until well blended. Gradually stir in broth and milk, cooking and stirring until bubbly and thickened.

3. Add chicken and all remaining ingredients; mix well. Simmer 5 minutes or until thoroughly heated.

4. Split warm biscuits; place bottom halves on individual serving plates. Spoon hot chicken mixture over each biscuit half. Place top halves of biscuits over chicken mixture.

Nutrition Information Per Serving: Calories 490 • Total Fat 24g • Saturated Fat 6g • Cholesterol 55mg • Sodium 1480mg • Total Carbohydrate 40g • Dietary Fiber 3g • Sugars 10g • Protein 28g. **Dietary Exchanges:** 2½ Starch • 3 Lean Meat • 3 Fat OR 2½ Carbohydrate • 3 Lean Meat • 3 Fat.

- 1 (10.2-oz.) can Pillsbury® Grands!® Refrigerated Buttermilk Biscuits (5 biscuits)
- 1 (9-oz.) pkg. frozen diced cooked chicken breast
- ¼ cup margarine or butter
- ⅓ cup all-purpose flour
- 1 (10½-oz.) can condensed chicken broth
- 1¼ cups milk
- 1 cup frozen sweet peas
- 1 (4-oz.) can mushroom pieces and stems, drained
- 1 (2-oz.) jar diced pimientos, drained
- ¼ teaspoon salt
- ¼ teaspoon pepper

IMPRESSIVE USE OF EXTRAS

If you don't have frozen peas on hand, use a cup of frozen cut green beans, chopped broccoli or whole kernel corn. And if you have some leftover cooked chicken or even turkey, you can try it in this easy recipe. Use 1⅓ cups of the poultry as a substitution for the frozen cooked chicken breast.

tomato-basil-cheese pizza

- 1 (10-oz.) can Pillsbury® Refrigerated Pizza Crust
- 8 oz. shredded mozzarella cheese (2 cups)
- 2 Italian plum tomatoes, sliced
- ¼ teaspoon salt
- ⅛ teaspoon pepper
- ¼ cup chopped fresh basil
- 1 tablespoon olive or vegetable oil

1. Heat oven to 425°F. Lightly grease a cookie sheet. Unroll dough; place on greased cookie sheet. Starting at center, press out dough to form 12-inch round with ½-inch rim.

2. Sprinkle 1 cup of the cheese over dough to within ½ inch of edge. Arrange tomato slices over cheese. Sprinkle with salt, pepper and 2 tablespoons of the basil. Sprinkle with remaining 1 cup cheese. Drizzle with oil.

3. Bake at 425°F for 18 to 20 minutes or until crust is golden brown and cheese is melted. Sprinkle with remaining 2 tablespoons basil before serving.

Nutrition Information Per Serving: Calories 380 • Total Fat 16g • Saturated Fat 7g • Cholesterol 30mg • Sodium 960mg • Total Carbohydrate 37g • Dietary Fiber 1g • Sugars 6g • Protein 22g. **Dietary Exchanges:** 2½ Starch • 4 Medium-Fat Meat • 2½ Carbohydrate • 4 Medium-Fat Meat.

baked chicken and spinach stuffing

PREP TIME: 35 MINUTES
READY TO SERVE: 1 HOUR
SERVINGS: 2

ANNA GINSBERG ✳ AUSTIN, TEXAS
GRAND PRIZE WINNER ✳ BAKE-OFF® CONTEST 42, 2006

- 3 tablespoons maple-flavored syrup
- 2 tablespoons peach preserves
- ½ teaspoon Worcestershire sauce
- 2 bone-in skin-on chicken breasts (1 lb.)
- ¼ teaspoon salt
- ¼ teaspoon pepper
- 4 squares frozen homestyle or buttermilk waffles
- 1 tablespoon butter or margarine
- ½ cup chopped onion (1 medium)
- ¼ cup chicken broth
- ½ teaspoon poultry seasoning
- ½ teaspoon chopped fresh sage
- 1 tablespoon beaten egg white
- 1 (9-oz.) box frozen spinach, thawed, drained
- 1 tablespoon chopped pecans

1. Heat oven to 350°F. Spray 9-inch glass pie plate or 8-inch square pan with cooking spray. In small bowl, mix syrup, preserves and Worcestershire sauce. Place chicken, skin side up, in pie plate; sprinkle with salt and pepper. Spoon syrup mixture over chicken.

2. Bake uncovered 40 to 45 minutes. Meanwhile, toast waffles until golden brown. Cool slightly, about 2 minutes. Cut waffles into ¾-inch cubes; set aside. Spray 1-quart casserole with cooking spray (or use 9x5-inch nonstick loaf pan; do not spray). In 10-inch nonstick skillet, melt butter over medium heat. Add onion; cook and stir 2 minutes or until tender. Stir in waffle pieces and broth, breaking up waffle pieces slightly to moisten. Sprinkle with poultry seasoning and sage. Remove from heat; cool about 5 minutes. Stir in egg white and spinach. Spoon stuffing into casserole. Sprinkle pecans over top.

3. Twenty minutes before chicken is done, place casserole in oven next to chicken in pie plate. Spoon syrup mixture in pie plate over chicken. Bake chicken and stuffing uncovered 20 to 25 minutes longer or until juice of chicken is clear when thickest part is cut to bone (170°F) and stuffing is thoroughly heated. Spoon remaining syrup mixture in pie plate over chicken. Serve chicken with stuffing.

Nutrition Information Per Serving: Calories 640 • Total Fat 22g • Saturated Fat 8g • Trans Fat 1.5g • Cholesterol 105mg • Sodium 1140mg • Total Carbohydrate 68g • Dietary Fiber 5g • Sugars 28g • Protein 42g. **Dietary Exchanges:** 2 Starch • 2 Other Carbohydrate • 1 Vegetable • 5 Lean Meat • 1 Fat.

biscuit-topped lasagna

PREP TIME: 30 MINUTES
READY TO SERVE: 1 HOUR
SERVINGS: 6

✳ meal-in-one

- 1 lb. lean ground beef
- 1 (14-oz.) jar tomato pasta sauce
- 1 (4-oz.) can mushroom pieces and stems, drained
- 1 cup ricotta cheese
- 1 cup chopped fresh spinach
- 8 oz. shredded mozzarella cheese (2 cups)
- 1 (12-oz.) can Pillsbury® Golden Layers™ Refrigerated Flaky Biscuits
- 1 tablespoon chopped fresh parsley

1. Heat oven to 375°F. Spray 12x8-inch (2-quart) glass baking dish with cooking spray. Brown ground beef in large skillet over medium-high heat until thoroughly cooked, stirring frequently. Drain. Stir in pasta sauce and mushrooms. Cook until thoroughly heated, stirring frequently.

2. In small bowl, combine ricotta cheese and spinach; mix well. In sprayed baking dish, layer half each of beef mixture, ricotta cheese mixture and mozzarella cheese. Repeat the layers.

3. Separate dough into 10 biscuits; separate each into 3 layers. Arrange biscuits over cheese layer, overlapping slightly. Sprinkle with parsley.

4. Bake at 375°F for 25 to 30 minutes or until golden brown. Let stand 5 minutes before serving.

Nutrition Information Per Serving: Calories 530 • Total Fat 29g • Saturated Fat 12g • Cholesterol 80mg • Sodium 1230mg • Total Carbohydrate 33g • Dietary Fiber 3g • Sugars 4g • Protein 34g. **Dietary Exchanges:** 2 Starch • 1 Vegetable • 4 Medium-Fat Meat • 1½ Fat OR 2 Carbohydrate • 1 Vegetable • 4 Medium-Fat Meat • 1½ Fat.

easy baked chicken and potato dinner

PREP TIME: 15 MINUTES
READY TO SERVE: 50 MINUTES
SERVINGS: 4

* meal-in-one

- 4 bone-in chicken breast halves, skin removed
- 4 medium russet or Idaho baking potatoes, unpeeled, cut into 1-inch cubes
- 1 red or green bell pepper, cut into 1x½-inch pieces
- 1 medium onion, cut into 8 wedges
- 2 tablespoons margarine or butter, melted
- ¼ cup grated Parmesan cheese
- 1 teaspoon garlic powder
- 1 teaspoon paprika

1. Heat oven to 400°F. Spray 15x10x1-inch baking pan with cooking spray. Place 1 chicken breast half in each corner of sprayed pan. Place potatoes, bell pepper and onion in center of pan. Pour melted margarine over chicken and vegetables; sprinkle evenly with cheese, garlic powder and paprika.

2. Bake at 400°F. for 30 to 35 minutes or until chicken is fork tender and juices run clear, stirring vegetables once halfway through cooking.

Nutrition Information Per Serving: Calories 370 • Total Fat 11g • Saturated 3g • Cholesterol 80mg • Sodium 260mg • Total Carbohydrate 35g • Dietary Fiber 4g • Sugars 4g • Protein 33g. Dietary Exchanges: 2 Starch • 1 Vegetable • 3 Lean Meat • ½ Fat OR 2 Carbohydrate • 1 Vegetable • 3 Lean Meat • ½ Fat.

slow-cooker chicken and dumplings

PREP TIME: 20 MINUTES
READY TO SERVE: 9 HOURS 50 MINUTES
SERVINGS: 5

* plan ahead

- 1 teaspoon oil
- 1 lb. boneless skinless chicken thighs, cut into 1-inch pieces
- 1½ cups sliced celery
- 1½ cups fresh baby carrots
- 1 cup sliced fresh mushrooms
- 1 (1.8-oz.) pkg. dry leek soup mix
- 4 cups water
- 1 (10.8-oz.) can Pillsbury® Grands!® Refrigerated Flaky Biscuits (5 biscuits)
- 1 tablespoon cornmeal
- 1½ cups frozen sweet peas
- ¼ teaspoon pepper

1. Heat oil in medium skillet over medium-high heat until hot. Add chicken; cook and stir until browned.

2. In 4 to 6-quart slow cooker, combine chicken, celery, carrots, mushrooms, soup mix and water; mix well.

3. Cover; cook on low setting for 7 to 9 hours.

4. About 35 minutes before serving, separate dough into 5 biscuits; cut each into 8 wedges. Sprinkle wedges with cornmeal. Stir coated biscuits pieces into the hot chicken mixture.

5. Increase heat setting to high; cover and cook an additional 25 to 30 minutes or until biscuits are no longer doughy in center.

6. About 10 minutes before serving, microwave peas in covered microwave-safe dish on high for 3 to 4 minutes or until hot. Just before serving, stir peas and pepper into chicken mixture.

Nutrition Information Per Serving: Calories 440 • Total Fat 19g • Saturated Fat 5g • Cholesterol 60mg • Sodium 1220mg • Total Carbohydrate 43g • Dietary Fiber 4g • Sugars 8g • Protein 24g. Dietary Exchanges: 2½ Starch • 1 Vegetable • 2 Lean Meat • 2 Fat OR 2½ Carbohydrate • 1 Vegetable • 2 Lean Meat • 2 Fat.

NO PEEKING!

Lifting the slow-cooker lid lets the heat escape and can often prolong the cooking time. Wait until the minimum amount of cooking time has passed before uncovering the pot. If you are purchasing a new slow cooker, consider one with a removable lining for the easiest cleanup.

black bean enchiladas

PREP TIME: 20 MINUTES
READY TO SERVE: 40 MINUTES
SERVINGS: 8

- 2 (10-oz.) cans enchilada sauce
- 1 tablespoon olive or vegetable oil
- 1 onion, sliced, separated into rings
- 1 small red bell pepper, sliced
- 3 garlic cloves, minced
- 1 (15-oz.) can black beans, drained, rinsed
- 8 (6-inch) soft corn tortillas, heated
- 8 oz. shredded colby-Monterey Jack cheese blend (2 cups)

1. Heat oven to 425°F. Spoon ⅔ cup of the enchilada sauce in bottom of ungreased 12x8-inch (2-quart) baking dish.

2. Heat oil in medium skillet over medium-high heat until hot. Add onion, bell pepper and garlic; cook and stir 2 to 3 minutes or until onion is tender.

3. In medium bowl, combine onion mixture and beans; mix well. Spoon about 2 tablespoons bean mixture down center of each tortilla. Top each with 2 tablespoons cheese; roll up. Place, seam side down, over enchilada sauce in baking dish.

4. Spoon remaining enchilada sauce over filled enchiladas. Sprinkle with remaining 1 cup cheese.

5. Bake at 425°F for 15 to 20 minutes or until thoroughly heated.

Nutrition Information Per Serving: Calories 270 • Total Fat 13g • Saturated Fat 6g • Cholesterol 25mg • Sodium 570mg • Total Carbohydrate 25g • Dietary Fiber 4g • Sugars 3g • Protein 12g. Dietary Exchanges: 1½ Starch • 1 Vegetable • 1 Very Lean Meat • 2 Fat OR 1½ Carbohydrate • 1 Vegetable • 1 Very Lean Meat • 2 Fat.

grown-up mac and cheese

PREP TIME: 30 MINUTES
SERVINGS: 4

- 8 oz. uncooked mostaccioli or penne (2½ cups)
- 2 tablespoons margarine or butter
- 2 tablespoons all-purpose flour
- ¼ teaspoon salt
- ⅛ teaspoon white pepper
- Dash nutmeg
- 1¼ cups half-and-half
- 2 oz. shredded fontina cheese (½ cup)
- 2 oz. shredded Swiss cheese (½ cup)
- 2 oz. shredded fresh Parmesan cheese (½ cup)
- 2 tablespoons dry white wine
- 2 Italian plum tomatoes, thinly sliced
- 1 teaspoon olive or vegetable oil
- 2 tablespoons sliced green onions

1. Heat oven to 350°F. Spray 1½-quart casserole with cooking spray. Cook mostaccioli to desired doneness as directed on package. Drain.

2. Meanwhile, melt margarine in large saucepan over medium heat. Stir in flour, salt, pepper and nutmeg; cook and stir until bubbly. Gradually add half-and-half, stirring constantly. Cook until mixture boils and thickens, stirring frequently. Remove from heat. Stir in fontina, Swiss and Parmesan cheeses until melted. (Cheeses will be stringy.) Stir in wine.

3. Add mostaccioli to cheese sauce; stir gently to coat. Pour into sprayed dish. Arrange sliced tomatoes around outside edge of dish. Brush the tomatoes with the oil; sprinkle with onions.

4. Bake at 350°F for 20 to 25 minutes or until edges are bubbly and mixture is thoroughly heated.

Nutrition Information Per Serving: Calories 570 • Total Fat 29g • Saturated Fat 15g • Cholesterol 70mg • Sodium 650mg • Total Carbohydrate 51g • Dietary Fiber 2g • Sugars 6g • Protein 24g. Dietary Exchanges: 3½ Starch • 2 High-Fat Meat • 2 Fat OR 3½ Carbohydrate • 2 High-Fat Meat • 2 Fat.

black bean enchiladas

soups & sandwiches

vegetable-split pea soup ✳ p. 34

chicken and apricot bagel sandwiches ✳ p. 60

vegetarian navy bean soup ✳ p. 32

sweet 'n smoky chicken wraps ✳ p. 36

chicken quesadillas ✳ p. 41

vegetarian navy bean soup

PREP TIME: 30 MINUTES
READY TO SERVE: 10 HOURS 30 MINUTES
SERVINGS: 8

* plan ahead

1 (16-oz.) pkg. dried navy beans, sorted, rinsed

2 quarts water (8 cups)

1 cup finely chopped carrots

1 cup finely chopped celery, including leaves

½ cup finely chopped onion

1 cup vegetable juice cocktail

1 tablespoon chicken-flavor instant bouillon

⅛ teaspoon crushed red pepper flakes

1. In large saucepan or Dutch oven, combine beans and water. Bring to a boil. Boil 30 minutes. Remove from heat; let stand 1½ hours or until beans are tender.

2. In 3½ to 4-quart slow cooker, combine beans with water and all remaining ingredients; mix well. Cover and cook on low setting for 6 to 8 hours or until beans and vegetables are very tender.

3. If desired, in blender container or food processor bowl with metal blade, puree part or all of soup until smooth.

Nutrition Information Per Serving: Calories 210 • Total Fat 1g • Saturated Fat 0g • Cholesterol 0mg • Sodium 470mg • Total Carbohydrate 39g • Dietary Fiber 9g • Sugars 6g • Protein 12g. **Dietary Exchanges:** 2½ Starch • ½ Very Lean Meat OR 2½ Carbohydrate • ½ Very Lean Meat.

hearty grain burgers

READY TO SERVE: 20 MINUTES
SERVINGS: 6

* super fast

½ cup cornmeal

¼ cup uncooked instant rice

¼ cup quick-cooking rolled oats

¼ cup uncooked bulgur

¼ cup uncooked couscous

1 cup boiling water

½ cup low-fat cottage cheese

¼ teaspoon garlic powder

¼ teaspoon pepper

2 tablespoons soy sauce

6 burger buns, split

1. Heat grill. In medium bowl, combine cornmeal, rice, oats, bulgur and couscous. Stir in boiling water. Cover; let stand 5 minutes.

2. Add cottage cheese, garlic powder, pepper and soy sauce; mix well. Shape into 6 patties, ½ inch thick. Spray both sides of each patty with cooking spray.

3. When ready to grill, place patties on gas grill over medium heat or on charcoal grill 4 to 6 inches from medium coals. Cook 6 to 10 minutes or until thoroughly heated, turning once. Serve in buns.

Nutrition Information Per Serving: Calories 260 • Total Fat 3g • Saturated Fat 1g • Cholesterol 0mg • Sodium 670mg • Total Carbohydrate 47g • Dietary Fiber 4g • Sugars 6g • Protein 10g. **Dietary Exchange:** 3 Starch OR 3 Carbohydrate.

smoky hot beef chili

PREP TIME: 20 MINUTES
READY TO SERVE: 1 HOUR 15 MINUTES
SERVINGS: 6

chili

1 tablespoon oil

¾ lb. beef sirloin, cut into 1-inch pieces

1 cup chopped onions

1 medium green bell pepper, seeded, chopped

2 garlic cloves, crushed

2 (28-oz.) cans Italian plum tomatoes, undrained, cut up

2 to 3 chipotle chiles, cut up

1 teaspoon salt

1 teaspoon Liquid Smoke

½ teaspoon pepper

topping

1 avocado, peeled, pitted and chopped

1 teaspoon lime juice

½ cup sour cream

1. Heat oil in large saucepan or Dutch oven over medium-high heat until hot. Add beef; cook 8 to 10 minutes or until beef is well browned. Stir in onions, bell pepper and garlic. Cook 4 to 5 minutes or until vegetables are crisp-tender.

2. Stir in all remaining chili ingredients. Bring mixture just to a boil. Reduce heat to low; simmer 45 to 55 minutes or until slightly thickened, stirring occasionally.

3. In small bowl, combine avocado and lime juice. To serve chili, ladle chili into bowls; top with sour cream and chopped avocado.

Nutrition Information Per Serving: Calories 260 • Total Fat 14g • Saturated Fat 5g • Cholesterol 40mg • Sodium 780mg • Total Carbohydrate 19g • Dietary Fiber 5g • Sugars 9g • Protein 15g. **Dietary Exchanges:** ½ Starch • 2 Vegetable • 1½ Lean Meat • 2 Fat OR ½ Carbohydrate • 2 Vegetable • 1½ Lean Meat • 2 Fat.

"SHEAR" MAGIC

Looking for another way to shave a few moments off of the kitchen clock? Consider the benefits of kitchen shears. A sharp pair of culinary scissors allows you to cut up a large assortment of ingredients without having to dirty (and wash) a cutting board. They're great for snipping chives, parsley and green onions directly onto a dish. In the recipe for Smoky Hot Beef Chili, you can use kitchen scissors to cut the Italian plum tomatoes right in the can.

vegetable-split pea soup

PREP TIME: 15 MINUTES
READY TO SERVE: 3 HOURS
SERVINGS: 7

✳ plan ahead

2 cups dried green split peas, sorted, rinsed

5 cups water

2 (11.5-oz.) cans tomato juice (3 cups)

3 garlic cloves, minced

1 teaspoon salt

1/2 teaspoon pepper

2 cups coarsely chopped cabbage

1 cup chopped carrots

1 cup chopped peeled turnip or potato

1/3 cup grated or shredded Parmesan cheese, if desired

1. In Dutch oven or stockpot, combine split peas and 12 cups (3 quarts) water. Bring to a boil. Boil 2 minutes. Remove from heat; cover and let stand 1 hour.

2. Drain and discard liquid from peas; return peas to Dutch oven. Add 5 cups water, tomato juice, garlic, salt and pepper. Bring to a boil. Reduce heat; cover and simmer 1 hour or until peas are tender.

3. Add cabbage, carrots and turnip; simmer 20 to 30 minutes or until vegetables are tender.

4. To serve, ladle soup into bowls; top with cheese.

Nutrition Information Per Serving: Calories 250 • Total Fat 2g • Saturated Fat 1g • Cholesterol 4mg • Sodium 760mg • Total Carbohydrate 42g • Dietary Fiber 16g • Sugars 7g • Protein 17g. Dietary Exchanges: 2 1/2 Starch • 1 Vegetable • 1 Very Lean Meat OR 2 1/2 Carbohydrate • 1 Vegetable • 1 Very Lean Meat.

italian sausage crescent sandwiches

PREP TIME: 25 MINUTES
READY TO SERVE: 45 MINUTES
SERVINGS: 8

1 lb. bulk Italian sausage, crumbled

1/2 cup chopped green bell pepper

1/3 cup chopped onion

1 (16-oz.) can pizza sauce

2 (8-oz.) cans Pillsbury® Refrigerated Crescent Dinner Rolls

1 (6-oz.) pkg. mozzarella cheese slices, halved, folded

1. Heat oven to 375°F. In large skillet, cook sausage, bell pepper and onion over medium-high heat until sausage is no longer pink and vegetables are tender, stirring frequently. Drain. Add 3 tablespoons of the pizza sauce; mix well.

2. Separate dough into 8 rectangles. Firmly press perforations to seal. Place about 1/4 cup sausage mixture and 1/2 slice of cheese, folded, on one end of each rectangle. Fold dough in half over filling; press edges with fork to seal. Place on ungreased cookie sheet.

3. Bake at 375°F for 15 to 18 minutes or until golden brown. Meanwhile, in small saucepan, heat remaining pizza sauce over low heat until hot. Serve sandwiches with warm pizza sauce.

Nutrition Information Per Serving: Calories 430 • Total Fat 27g • Saturated Fat 9g • Cholesterol 45mg • Sodium 1280mg • Total Carbohydrate 29g • Dietary Fiber 1g • Sugars 9g • Protein 18g. Dietary Exchanges: 2 Starch • 1 1/2 High-Fat Meat • 3 Fat OR 2 Carbohydrate • 1 1/2 High-Fat Meat • 3 Fat.

vegetable-split pea soup

sweet 'n smoky chicken wraps

READY TO SERVE: 30 MINUTES
SERVINGS: 8 WRAPS

PATRICE HURD ✳ BEMIDJI, MINNESOTA
BAKE-OFF® CONTEST 42, 2006

½ cup mayonnaise or salad dressing

¼ cup finely chopped English (seedless) cucumber

1½ to 3½ teaspoons Spanish smoked sweet paprika

½ teaspoon freshly cracked black pepper

2 tablespoons honey

2 teaspoons olive oil

1½ lb. chicken breast strips for stir-fry or 1½ lb. boneless skinless chicken breasts, cut into thin bite-size strips

1 cup chunky-style salsa

1 (11.5-oz.) pkg. flour tortillas for burritos, 8 inch (8 tortillas)

8 leaves Bibb lettuce

1. In small bowl, mix mayonnaise, cucumber, ½ teaspoon of the paprika, the pepper and 1 tablespoon of the honey; cover and refrigerate.

2. Heat 10-inch skillet over medium-high heat; add oil and heat until hot. Add chicken; cook 5 to 8 minutes, stirring frequently, until no longer pink in center. Stir in salsa, 1 teaspoon of the paprika and remaining tablespoon honey. Reduce heat to medium-low; simmer uncovered 5 minutes, stirring occasionally. For more paprika flavor, stir in up to 2 additional teaspoons paprika.

3. Heat tortillas as directed on package. Spread about 1 tablespoon mayonnaise mixture on each warm tortilla. Top each with 1 lettuce leaf and scant ½ cup chicken mixture. Fold bottom of each tortilla up over chicken mixture; roll sides in toward center. If necessary, secure with toothpicks; remove toothpicks before eating.

Nutrition Information Per Serving: Calories 380 • Total Fat 19g • Saturated Fat 3.5g • Trans Fat 0g • Cholesterol 55mg • Sodium 670mg • Total Carbohydrate 30g • Dietary Fiber 0g • Sugars 6g • Protein 22g. **Dietary Exchanges:** 1½ Starch • ½ Other Carbohydrate • 2½ Very Lean Meat • 3½ Fat.

cheddar cheese soup

READY TO SERVE: 35 MINUTES
SERVINGS: 6

½ cup finely chopped onion

¼ cup finely chopped carrot

¼ cup finely chopped celery

3 cups vegetable or chicken broth

1 tablespoon cornstarch

2 tablespoons water

4 oz. diced sharp Cheddar cheese (1 cup)

1 (10¾-oz.) can condensed cream of potato soup

1 (8-oz.) jar pasteurized process cheese spread

1. In large saucepan, combine onion, carrot, celery and broth. Bring to a boil. Reduce heat to low; cover and simmer 10 minutes or until vegetables are tender.

2. In small bowl, combine cornstarch and water; mix well. Stir into broth mixture. Bring to a boil. Reduce heat to low. Add Cheddar cheese, potato soup and cheese spread. With wire whisk, stir until cheese is melted and mixture is well combined. Do not boil.

Nutrition Information Per Serving: Calories 240 • Total Fat 16g • Saturated Fat 10g • Cholesterol 45mg • Sodium 1580mg • Total Carbohydrate 13g • Dietary Fiber 1g • Sugars 7g • Protein 12g. **Dietary Exchanges:** 1 Starch • 1½ High-Fat Meat • ½ Fat OR 1 Carbohydrate • 1½ High-Fat Meat • ½ Fat.

hot chicken hoagie

READY TO SERVE: 15 MINUTES
SERVINGS: 6

* super fast

1 (10 or 10.5-oz.) pkg. frozen breaded chicken breast patties

1 (1-lb.) loaf French bread, cut in half lengthwise

½ cup purchased ranch salad dressing

6 leaves lettuce

8 slices bacon, cooked until crisp

1 avocado, thinly sliced

1 medium tomato, thinly sliced

1. Prepare chicken breast patties as directed on package.

2. Meanwhile, spread cut sides of bread halves with salad dressing. Layer bottom half of bread with lettuce, bacon, chicken patties, avocado and tomato. Cover with top half of bread. If desired, secure sandwich with skewers or picks. To serve, cut into slices.

Nutrition Information Per Serving: Calories 580 • Total Fat 33g • Saturated Fat 8g • Cholesterol 40mg • Sodium 1060mg • Total Carbohydrate 52g • Dietary Fiber 5g • Sugars 5g • Protein 18g. **Dietary Exchanges:** 3½ Starch • 1 Lean Meat • 6 Fat OR 3½ Carbohydrate • 1 Lean Meat • 6 Fat.

mom's chicken noodle soup

PREP TIME: 15 MINUTES
READY TO SERVE: 50 MINUTES
SERVINGS: 5

* meal-in-one

1½ cups cubed cooked chicken

1 cup sliced carrots

½ cup chopped celery

½ cup chopped onion

1 parsnip, peeled, cubed (¾ cup)

2 teaspoons chopped fresh parsley

1 teaspoon chopped fresh dill

4 (14½-oz.) cans ready-to-serve chicken broth

3½ oz. uncooked wide egg noodles (2 cups)

1. In Dutch oven or large saucepan, combine all ingredients except noodles; mix well. Cook over medium heat 20 minutes or until vegetables are tender, stirring occasionally.

2. Add egg noodles; cook 15 minutes or until of desired doneness.

Nutrition Information Per Serving: Calories 230 • Total Fat 6g • Saturated Fat 2g • Cholesterol 55mg • Sodium 1110mg • Total Carbohydrate 23g • Dietary Fiber 3g • Sugars 4g • Protein 22g. **Dietary Exchanges:** 1½ Starch • 2½ Very Lean Meat • ½ Fat OR 1½ Carbohydrate • 2½ Very Lean Meat • ½ Fat.

chicken muffuletta

READY TO SERVE: 10 MINUTES
SERVINGS: 6

* super fast

1 round loaf Italian or sourdough bread, cut in half lengthwise

¼ cup soft cream cheese with olives and pimiento

3 leaves lettuce

4 oz. thinly sliced cooked chicken

1 cup drained pickled mixed vegetables, coarsely chopped

4 oz. thinly sliced provolone cheese

1. Spread cut sides of bread halves with cream cheese. Layer bottom half of bread with lettuce, chicken, vegetables and cheese. Cover with top half of bread.

2. To serve, cut into wedges. If desired, secure each wedge with skewer or pick.

Nutrition Information Per Serving: Calories 330 • Total Fat 11g • Saturated Fat 6g • Cholesterol 30mg • Sodium 1090mg • Total Carbohydrate 42g • Dietary Fiber 3g • Sugars 3g • Protein 16g. **Dietary Exchanges:** 2½ Starch • 1 Vegetable • 1 Medium-Fat Meat • 1 Fat OR 2½ Carbohydrate • 1 Vegetable • 1 Medium-Fat Meat • 1 Fat.

hearty chicken and cheese calzones

READY TO SERVE: 30 MINUTES
SERVINGS: 4

2 oz. shredded Cheddar cheese (½ cup)

2 oz. shredded Swiss cheese (½ cup)

1 cup chopped cooked chicken

½ cup chopped green or red bell pepper

¼ teaspoon dried basil leaves

1 (10-oz.) can refrigerated pizza crust

1. Heat oven to 425°F. Grease cookie sheet. In medium bowl, combine all ingredients except pizza crust; mix well. Press pizza crust into 14x8-inch rectangle on greased cookie sheet. Cut into four 7x4-inch rectangles; separate slightly.

2. Spoon about ½ cup chicken and cheese mixture onto one half of each rectangle; fold crust over filling. Press edges with fork to seal; prick tops with fork.

3. Bake at 425°F for 11 to 16 minutes or until golden brown.

Nutrition Information Per Serving: Calories 350 • Total Fat 13g • Saturated Fat 7g • Cholesterol 60 mg • Sodium 500mg • Total Carbohydrate 34g • Dietary Fiber 1g • Sugars 4g • Protein 24g. **Dietary Exchanges:** 2 Starch • 2½ Medium-Fat Meat OR 2 Carbohydrate • 2½ Medium-Fat Meat.

mom's chicken noodle soup

chicken quesadillas

chicken quesadillas

* super fast

2 cups cubed cooked chicken

4 oz. shredded taco-flavored Cheddar cheese (1 cup)

2 cups purchase thick and chunky salsa

2 tablespoons margarine or butter, softened

8 (8 to 10-inch) flour tortillas

1/2 cup sour cream

1. Heat griddle or large skillet to 375°F. In large bowl, combine chicken, cheese and 1 cup of the salsa. Spread margarine on 1 side of each tortilla.

2. Place 1 tortilla, margarine side down, on hot griddle. Top with 3/4 cup chicken mixture. Place second tortilla, margarine side up, on chicken mixture. Cook until bottom is lightly browned. Turn quesadilla over; cook on second side until quesadilla is lightly browned and chicken mixture is thoroughly heated. Repeat with remaining tortillas and chicken mixture.

3. To serve, cut each quesadilla into 4 wedges; top the wedges with remaining 1 cup salsa and sour cream.

Nutrition Information Per Serving: Calories 630 • Total Fat 31g • Saturated Fat 14g • Cholesterol 105mg • Sodium 860mg • Total Carbohydrate 51g • Dietary Fiber 4g • Sugars 7g • Protein 36g. **Dietary Exchanges:** 3 Starch • 1 Vegetable • 3 1/2 Lean Meat • 4 Fat OR 3 Carbohydrate • 1 Vegetable • 3 1/2 Lean Meat • 4 Fat.

biscuit bowls with chili

* meal-in-one

1 (16.3-oz.) can Pillsbury® Grands!® Refrigerated Buttermilk Biscuits

2 (15-oz.) cans chili with beans or chili without beans

Sliced green onions, if desired

Sour cream, if desired

Shredded Cheddar cheese, if desired

1. Heat oven to 350°F. Cut 8 (25x12-inch) pieces of aluminum foil. Shape each into 3 1/2-inch ball by slightly crushing foil; flatten balls slightly. Place foil balls on large cookie sheets.

2. Separate dough into 8 biscuits. Press or roll each to form 5 1/2-inch round. Place 1 biscuit round over each foil ball, shaping biscuit gently to fit. (Dough should not touch cookie sheets.)

3. Bake at 350°F for 15 to 18 minutes or until golden brown. Meanwhile, in large saucepan, heat chili until thoroughly heated.

4. Carefully remove biscuit bowls from foil balls; place in individual shallow soup bowls or on plates. Spoon 1/2 cup chili into each bowl. Top each with onions, sour cream and cheese.

Nutrition Information Per Serving: Calories 275 • Total Fat 9g • Saturated Fat 2g • Cholesterol 0mg • Sodium 1040mg • Total Carbohydrate 40g • Dietary Fiber 4g • Sugars 11g • Protein 8g. **Dietary Exchanges:** 2 1/2 Starch • 2 Fat OR 2 1/2 Carbohydrate • 2 Fat.

powerful peanut butter sandwiches

* super fast

1/2 cup peanut butter

1/4 cup shredded carrot

2 tablespoons shelled sunflower seeds

2 tablespoons raisins

2 tablespoons honey or sugar

4 bagels, split, or 8 slices whole wheat bread

1. In small container, combine all ingredients except bagels; mix well.

2. Spread mixture on 4 bagel halves or bread slices; top with remaining bagel halves or bread slices.

Nutrition Information Per Serving: Calories 480 • Total Fat 20g • Saturated Fat 4g • Cholesterol 0mg • Sodium 560mg • Total Carbohydrate 58g • Dietary Fiber 4g • Sugars 15g • Protein 17g. **Dietary Exchanges:** 4 Starch • 1 High-Fat Meat • 1 1/2 Fat OR 4 Carbohydrate • 1 High-Fat Meat • 1 1/2 Fat.

garden vegetable quesadillas

READY TO SERVE: 40 MINUTES
SERVINGS: 4

1 tablespoon olive or vegetable oil

1 cup thinly sliced fresh mushrooms

1 medium onion, cut into thin wedges

1 red bell pepper, cut into thin strips

2 garlic cloves, minced

1/4 teaspoon salt

1/4 teaspoon pepper

4 cups fresh spinach leaves, cut into strips

1 tablespoon chopped fresh cilantro

4 (10-inch) flour tortillas

4 oz. shredded mozzarella cheese (1 cup)

1/2 cup chunky-style salsa

1. Heat oil in 12-inch skillet over medium-high heat until hot. Add mushrooms, onion, bell pepper, garlic, salt and pepper; cook and stir 3 minutes. Reduce heat to low; add spinach leaves. Cook an additional 1 to 2 minutes or until spinach is wilted. Remove from heat; stir in cilantro.

2. Place 1/4 of vegetable mixture on half of each tortilla; sprinkle each with 1/4 cup cheese. Fold remaining halves of tortillas over filling. Place the tortillas on ungreased cookie sheet.

3. Broil 6 to 8 inches from heat for 2 minutes. Turn quesadillas over; broil an additional 1 to 2 minutes or until the quesadillas are golden brown and cheese is melted. Serve with salsa.

Nutrition Information Per Serving: Calories 280 • Total Fat 11g • Saturated Fat 4g • Cholesterol 15mg • Sodium 660mg • Total Carbohydrate 31g • Dietary Fiber 4g • Sugars 4g • Protein 14g. **Dietary Exchanges:** 1 1/2 Starch • 1 1/2 Vegetable • 1 Medium-Fat Meat • 1 Fat OR 1 1/2 Carbohydrate • 1 1/2 Vegetable • 1 Medium-Fat Meat • 1 Fat.

hot sourdough chicken sandwiches

READY TO SERVE: 15 MINUTES
SERVINGS: 4

* super fast

1/3 cup reduced-calorie mayonnaise or salad dressing

2 tablespoons finely chopped green onions

4 (1/2-inch-thick) slices sourdough bread, toasted

1 (6-oz.) pkg. thinly sliced oven-roasted chicken breast

1 pear, thinly sliced

1 oz. shredded reduced-fat sharp Cheddar cheese (1/4 cup)

1/8 teaspoon paprika, if desired

1. In small bowl, combine mayonnaise and onions. Spread evenly on toasted bread slices. Layer chicken and pear slices evenly over bread. Place on broiler pan.

2. Broil 4 to 6 inches from heat for 5 minutes. Sprinkle evenly with cheese; broil an additional 1 to 2 minutes or until cheese is melted. Sprinkle with paprika.

Nutrition Information Per Serving: Calories 250 • Total Fat 10g • Saturated Fat 3g • Cholesterol 45mg • Sodium 380mg • Total Carbohydrate 21g • Dietary Fiber 2g • Sugars 5g • Protein 18g. **Dietary Exchanges:** 1 1/2 Starch • 2 Lean Meat • 1/2 Fat OR 1 1/2 Carbohydrate • 2 Lean Meat • 1/2 Fat.

TIME-SAVING STRATEGY

Save a few moments by preparing these satisfying, open-faced sandwiches in your microwave. Begin by simply assembling the sandwiches as directed above, sprinkling with the Cheddar cheese. Place one sandwich on a microwave-safe paper towel. Next, microwave the sandwich on high for 1 to 2 minutes or until the cheese has melted to your satisfaction. Repeat with the remaining three sandwiches. Sprinkle all with paprika and serve.

italian meatball hoagie braids

PREP TIME: 15 MINUTES
READY TO SERVE: 35 MINUTES
SERVINGS: 8

2 (8-oz.) cans Pillsbury® Refrigerated Crescent Dinner Rolls

16 (1½-inch) frozen fully cooked Italian meatballs (about 1 lb.), thawed, halved

1 cup tomato-basil pasta sauce

4 oz. shredded mozzarella cheese (1 cup)

1 egg, slightly beaten

¼ cup grated Parmesan cheese

1. Heat oven to 375°F. Spray 2 cookie sheets with cooking spray. Separate dough into 8 rectangles. Place rectangles on sprayed cookie sheets. Firmly press perforations to seal.

2. Place 4 meatball halves lengthwise down center of each rectangle. Top each with 2 tablespoons sauce and 2 tablespoons mozzarella cheese. With scissors or sharp knife, make cuts 1 inch apart on each side of filling. Alternately cross strips over filling. Brush dough with beaten egg. Sprinkle with Parmesan cheese.

3. Bake at 375°F for 15 to 20 minutes or until golden brown.

Nutrition Information Per Serving: Calories 450 • Total Fat 29g • Saturated Fat 11g • Cholesterol 75mg • Sodium 1110mg • Total Carbohydrate 28g • Dietary Fiber 3g • Sugars 4g • Protein 19g.
Dietary Exchanges: 2 Starch • 2 High-Fat Meat • 2 Fat OR 2 Carbohydrate • 2 High-Fat Meat • 2 Fat.

easy corn chowder

READY TO SERVE: 30 MINUTES
SERVINGS: 3

1 (11-oz.) can vacuum-packed whole kernel corn, undrained

$\frac{1}{2}$ cup chopped onion

$\frac{1}{2}$ cup cubed peeled potatoes

$\frac{1}{3}$ cup water

2 teaspoons chicken-flavor instant bouillon

$1\frac{3}{4}$ cups milk

1 tablespoon margarine or butter

2 tablespoons all-purpose flour

1. In large saucepan, combine corn, onion, potatoes, water and bouillon. Bring to a boil. Reduce heat to low; cover and simmer 10 minutes or until potatoes are tender, stirring occasionally.

2. Stir in $1\frac{1}{2}$ cups of the milk and margarine. In small bowl, combine remaining $\frac{1}{4}$ cup milk and flour; beat with wire whisk until smooth. Add flour mixture to chowder; cook and stir until bubbly and thickened.

Nutrition Information Per Serving: Calories 260 • Total Fat 8g • Saturated Fat 3g • Cholesterol 10mg • Sodium 1080mg • Total Carbohydrate 39g • Dietary Fiber 3g • Sugars 15g • Protein 17g. **Dietary Exchanges:** $\frac{1}{2}$ Starch • $\frac{1}{2}$ High-Fat Meat • $1\frac{1}{2}$ Fat OR $2\frac{1}{2}$ Carbohydrate • $\frac{1}{2}$ High-Fat Meat • $1\frac{1}{2}$ Fat.

LIVELY LEFTOVERS

Easy Corn Chowder is the perfect dish to toss together when you're looking to clear the refrigerator of leftovers. The next time you prepare the hearty chowder, consider stirring in last night's chicken or even pork. Cut the meat into bite-sized pieces so it heats through quickly. In addition, you can feel free to add extra peas, cooked carrots or any other veggies you may still have on hand from side dishes you served earlier in the week.

baked potato soup

* meal-in-one

4 large baking potatoes

4 slices bacon

6 cups milk

½ cup all-purpose flour

4 green onions, sliced

5 oz. shredded sharp Cheddar cheese (1¼ cups)

¾ teaspoon salt

¼ teaspoon pepper

1 (8-oz.) container sour cream

1. Pierce potatoes with fork; place on microwave-safe paper towel or roasting rack in microwave. Microwave on high for 15 to 20 minutes or until tender, turning once halfway through cooking. Cool slightly.

2. Meanwhile, cook bacon in Dutch oven over medium heat until crisp. Remove from skillet; drain on paper towels. Crumble; set aside.

3. In same Dutch oven, combine milk and flour; blend well. Cook over medium heat for about 15 minutes or until bubbly and thickened, stirring frequently.

4. Cut cooked potatoes in half. Scoop out cooked potato from skins; place in medium bowl. Discard skins. Mash potatoes well.

5. Add potatoes, bacon, 2 tablespoons of the onions, 1 cup of the cheese, salt and pepper to milk mixture. Cook and stir until cheese is melted. Add sour cream; cook and stir until soup is thoroughly heated.

6. To serve, ladle soup into bowls; sprinkle with remaining onions and ¼ cup cheese.

Nutrition Information Per Serving: Calories 400 • Total Fat 20g • Saturated Fat 12g • Cholesterol 55mg • Sodium 540mg • Total Carbohydrate 38g • Dietary Fiber 2g • Sugars 13g • Protein 17g. **Dietary Exchanges:** 2½ Starch • 1½ High-Fat Meat • 1 Fat OR 2½ Carbohydrate • 1½ High-Fat Meat • 1 Fat.

sausage tortellini soup

* meal-in-one

½ lb. bulk turkey Italian sausage

½ cup chopped onion

1 cup sliced carrots

1 (28-oz.) can tomato puree

1 (14½-oz.) can ready-to-serve chicken broth

2 cups water

1 teaspoon dried basil leaves

1 (9-oz.) pkg. refrigerated cheese-filled tortellini

3 cups frozen cut broccoli

1. In Dutch oven, combine sausage and onion; cook over medium heat 8 minutes or until sausage is no longer pink. Drain.

2. Add carrots; cook and stir 1 minute. Add tomato puree, broth, water and basil. Bring to a boil. Add tortellini; return to a boil. Add broccoli. Cook 6 to 8 minutes or until tortellini is tender.

Nutrition Information Per Serving: Calories 280 • Total Fat 7g • Saturated Fat 3g • Cholesterol 45mg • Sodium 650mg • Total Carbohydrate 37g • Dietary Fiber 5g • Sugars 10g • Protein 17g. **Dietary Exchanges:** 2 Starch • 1½ Vegetable • 1 Medium-Fat Meat OR 2 Carbohydrate • 1½ Vegetable • 1 Medium-Fat Meat.

minute minestrone

READY TO SERVE: 30 MINUTES
SERVINGS: 5

2 tablespoons margarine or butter

¼ cup chopped onion

1 medium zucchini, sliced

1 (10-oz.) pkg. frozen baby lima beans in a pouch with butter sauce

2 (10½-oz.) cans condensed beef broth

1 (14.5 or 16-oz.) can whole tomatoes, undrained, cut up

1 cup water

2 oz. uncooked vermicelli, broken into pieces (½ cup)

1 tablespoon grated Parmesan cheese

¼ teaspoon dried basil leaves

¼ teaspoon pepper

⅛ teaspoon garlic salt

Dash ground red pepper (cayenne)

1. Melt margarine in large saucepan over medium heat. Add onion and zucchini; cook and stir until vegetables are crisp-tender.

2. Remove frozen lima beans from pouch; add to cooked vegetables. Stir in all remaining ingredients. Simmer about 15 minutes or until vermicelli is tender, stirring occasionally.

Nutrition Information Per Serving: Calories 220 • Total Fat 7g • Saturated Fat 2g • Cholesterol 3mg • Sodium 1040mg • Total Carbohydrate 26g • Dietary Fiber 5g • Sugars 4g • Protein 12g. Dietary Exchanges: 1½ Starch • 1 Vegetable • 1 Very Lean Meat • 1 Fat OR 1½ Carbohydrate • 1 Vegetable • 1 Very Lean Meat • 1 Fat.

BROTH OR CONSOMMÉ?

Broth (or stock) is the thin liquid that remains after simmering and straining vegetables, meat or poultry. Available in cans, it's also easy to make on your own if you have time to slow simmer the ingredients to bring out the flavor.

Consommé, on the other hand, is simply broth that is made from beef, poultry or even veal. It is clarified, which means that the liquid is no longer cloudy and all sediment has been removed.

monterey chicken fillet sandwiches

READY TO SERVE: 25 MINUTES
SERVINGS: 4

✳ super fast

4 boneless skinless chicken breast halves

½ cup plain bread crumbs

½ teaspoon garlic salt

¼ cup all purpose flour

1 egg, beaten

3 tablespoons oil

4 (5½ to 6-inch) French rolls, ranch rolls or hoagie buns, halved lengthwise

8 teaspoons mayonnaise or salad dressing

1 cup shredded lettuce

4 medium tomato slices

4 (1-oz.) slices Monterey Jack cheese

1. Place 1 chicken breast half between 2 pieces of plastic wrap or waxed paper. Working from center, gently pound chicken with flat side of meat mallet or rolling pin until about ¼ inch thick; remove wrap. Repeat with remaining chicken breast halves.

2. In small shallow bowl, combine bread crumbs and garlic salt. Coat both sides of chicken breast halves with flour. Dip each in egg; coat both sides with crumb mixture.

3. Heat oil in large skillet over medium-high heat until hot. Add chicken; cook 6 to 8 minutes on each side or until lightly browned and juices run clear.

4. Meanwhile, place French rolls, cut side up, on ungreased cookie sheet. Broil 4 to 6 inches from heat for 1 to 2 minutes or until toasted; remove top halves of rolls from cookie sheet. Spread bottom halves of rolls with mayonnaise; top with lettuce, tomato, chicken and cheese. Broil 4 to 6 inches from heat for 1 minute or until cheese is melted; cover with top halves of rolls.

Nutrition Information Per Serving: Calories 780 • Total Fat 36g • Saturated Fat 10g • Cholesterol 155mg • Sodium 1240mg • Total Carbohydrate 67g • Dietary Fiber 3g • Sugars 4g • Protein 47g. Dietary Exchanges: 4 Starch • 1 Vegetable • 4 Medium-Fat Meat • 3 Fat OR 4 Carbohydrate • 1 Vegetable • 4 Medium-Fat Meat • 3 Fat.

minute minestrone

mandarin chicken pockets

READY TO SERVE: 15 MINUTES
SERVINGS: 6

* super fast

1 cup chopped cooked chicken

1 (11-oz.) can mandarin orange segments, well drained

½ cup chopped celery

¼ cup sliced almonds, if desired

2 green onions, sliced

3 tablespoons mayonnaise or salad dressing

¼ teaspoon salt

   Dash pepper

3 (6-inch) pita (pocket) breads, cut in half

6 lettuce leaves

1. In medium bowl, combine all of the ingredients except pita breads and lettuce leaves; mix well.

2. Line each pita bread half with lettuce leaf; fill with ⅓ cup chicken mixture.

Nutrition Information Per Serving: Calories 230 • Total Fat 10g • Saturated Fat 2g • Cholesterol 25mg • Sodium 320mg • Total Carbohydrate 23g • Dietary Fiber 2g • Sugars 5g • Protein 11g. **Dietary Exchanges:** 1 Starch • ½ Fruit • 1 Lean Meat • 1½ Fat OR 1½ Carbohydrate • 1 Lean Meat • 1½ Fat.

grands!® roast beef sandwiches

PREP TIME: 15 MINUTES
READY TO SERVE: 40 MINUTES
SERVINGS: 8

1 (16.3-oz.) can Pillsbury® Grands!® Refrigerated Buttermilk Biscuits

2 tablespoons margarine or butter, melted

¼ cup garlic herb dry bread crumbs

⅓ cup mayonnaise or salad dressing

1 (4.5-oz.) can chopped green chiles

8 (1-oz.) slices cooked roast beef

4 oz. finely shredded Monterey Jack cheese (1 cup)

1. Heat oven to 375°F. Separate dough into 8 biscuits. Brush top and sides of each biscuit with margarine; coat with bread crumbs. Place 2 inches apart, crumb side up, on ungreased cookie sheet. Sprinkle any remaining bread crumbs over biscuits.

2. Bake at 375°F for 14 to 16 minutes or until golden brown. Cool 5 minutes. Set oven to broil.

3. Meanwhile, in small bowl, combine mayonnaise and green chiles; mix well.

4. Split biscuits; place tops and bottoms, cut side up, on same cookie sheet. Spread mayonnaise mixture evenly on top halves of biscuits. Arrange roast beef slices on bottom halves, folding to fit. Top beef with cheese.

5. Broil 4 to 6 inches from heat for 2 to 3 minutes or until cheese is melted and mayonnaise mixture is bubbly. Place top halves of biscuits over bottom halves.

Nutrition Information Per Serving: Calories 395 • Total Fat 24g • Saturated Fat 7g • Cholesterol 30mg • Sodium 1250mg • Total Carbohydrate 32g • Dietary Fiber 1g • Sugars 10g • Protein 13g. **Dietary Exchanges:** 2 Starch • 1 Lean Meat • 4 Fat OR 2 Carbohydrate • 1 Lean Meat • 4 Fat.

zesty black and white bean chili

READY TO SERVE: 35 MINUTES
SERVINGS: 5

* meal-in-one

1 cup chopped onions

1 garlic clove, minced

¼ cup all-purpose flour

1 to 2 teaspoons chili powder

½ teaspoon cumin

1½ cups milk

2 (9-oz.) pkg. frozen shoepeg white corn in a pouch

1 (15.5-oz.) can great northern beans, drained, rinsed

1 (15-oz.) can black beans, drained, rinsed

1 (14½-oz.) can ready-to-serve chicken broth

1 (4.5-oz.) can chopped green chiles, undrained

2 tablespoons chopped fresh cilantro

2 tablespoons finely chopped red bell pepper

1. Spray Dutch oven or large saucepan with cooking spray. Heat over medium-high heat until hot. Add onions and garlic; cook until onions are tender.

2. Stir in flour, chili powder and cumin. Gradually stir in milk. Add all remaining ingredients except cilantro and bell pepper; stir to combine.

3. Bring to a boil, stirring constantly. Reduce heat to low; simmer 15 minutes or until thickened, stirring occasionally. Stir in cilantro. If desired, add salt and pepper to taste.

4. To serve, ladle chili into serving bowls; sprinkle with bell pepper.

Nutrition Information Per Serving: Calories 320 • Total Fat 4g • Saturated Fat 1g • Cholesterol 5mg • Sodium 750mg • Total Carbohydrate 56g • Dietary Fiber 12g • Sugars 10g • Protein 16g. **Dietary Exchanges:** 3½ Starch • 1 Very Lean Meat OR 3½ Carbohydrate • 1 Very Lean Meat.

STORING SOUP

Soup and chili should be refrigerated in a tightly covered container for up to three days. For longer storage, freeze in tightly sealed containers, allowing 1½ inches of headroom for expansion. Recipes featuring beans, vegetables and meat retain flavor and texture well. Avoid freezing items with seafood, eggs or dairy products. Try freezing chili and soup in single-serving containers so each of your family members can grab a meal in a hurry.

vegetable calzones

READY TO SERVE: 45 MINUTES
SERVINGS: 4

1 (10-oz.) can Pillsbury®
 Refrigerated Pizza Crust

⅓ cup ricotta cheese

2 tablespoons prepared ranch
 salad dressing

4 oz. shredded Monterey Jack
 cheese (1 cup)

1 cup chopped fresh broccoli

½ cup chopped tomato

¼ cup chopped green bell
 pepper

1 egg white, beaten

1. Heat oven to 425°F. Spray cookie sheet with cooking spray. Unroll dough; cut into fourths. Place dough on sprayed cookie sheet; press each section to form 6-inch square.

2. In small bowl, combine ricotta cheese and salad dressing; mix well. Spoon about 1 heaping tablespoonful cheese mixture onto half of each dough square to within ½ inch of edge. Top each with ¼ cup Monterey Jack cheese.

3. In medium bowl, combine broccoli, tomato and bell pepper; mix well. Spoon scant 1/2 cup vegetable mixture on top of cheese on each square. Bring remaining half of each dough square over filling; press edges with fork to seal. Brush calzones with beaten egg white. Cut 2 or 3 slits in top of each for steam to escape.

4. Bake at 425°F for 12 to 14 minutes or until golden brown.

Nutrition Information Per Serving: Calories 365 • Total Fat 16g • Saturated Fat 7g • Cholesterol 35mg • Sodium 810mg • Total Carbohydrate 38g • Dietary Fiber 2g • Sugars 7g • Protein 17g. **Dietary Exchanges:** 2 Starch • 1 Vegetable • 1½ High-Fat Meat OR 2 Carbohydrate • 1 Vegetable • 1½ High-Fat Meat • 2½ Carb Choices.

easy crescent dogs™

READY TO SERVE: 25 MINUTES
SERVINGS: 8

* super fast

8 hot dogs

4 (¾-oz.) slices American
 cheese, each cut into 6 strips

1 (8-oz.) can Pillsbury®
 Refrigerated Crescent
 Dinner Rolls

1. Heat oven to 375°F. Slit hot dogs to within ½ inch of ends. Insert 3 strips of cheese into each slit.

2. Separate dough into 8 triangles. Wrap dough triangle around each hot dog. Place on ungreased cookie sheet, cheese side up.

3. Bake at 375°F for 12 to 15 minutes or until golden brown.

Nutrition Information Per Serving: Calories 275 • Total Fat 20g • Saturated Fat 8g • Cholesterol 35mg • Sodium 1020mg • Total Carbohydrate 15g • Dietary Fiber 0g • Sugars 6g • Protein 9g. **Dietary Exchanges:** 1 Starch • 1 High-Fat Meat • 2½ Fat OR 1 Carbohydrate • 1 High-Fat Meat • 2½ Fat • 1 Carb Choice.

ADDING FUSS-FREE FLAIR

Easy Crescent Dogs™ are scrumptious on their own; however, a little flair always goes a long way at the dinner table. Serve the savory bites with your favorite condiment such as mustard, ketchup, relish or even sauerkraut. Pop open a can of chili for a fast yet tasty addition to the dogs, or pile a few nacho chips on individual plates topped with jarred cheese sauce. Wedges of watermelon or pineapple also make fine additions as do cubes of cheese.

vegetarian fajitas

READY TO SERVE: 15 MINUTES
SERVINGS: 8

* super fast

2 tablespoons oil

1 green bell pepper, sliced

1 yellow bell pepper, sliced

1 medium onion, sliced

1 (11-oz.) can vacuum-packed whole kernel corn, drained

1 large tomato, chopped

¼ teaspoon salt

⅛ teaspoon pepper

8 (8-inch) flour tortillas, heated

Guacamole, sour cream and/or salsa, if desired

1. Heat oil in large skillet or wok over medium-high heat until hot. Add bell peppers and onion; cook and stir 2 to 3 minutes or until vegetables are crisp-tender. Add corn, tomato, salt and pepper; cook until thoroughly heated.

2. To serve, place ½ cup vegetable mixture in center of each warm tortilla. Top with desired toppings; roll up.

Nutrition Information Per Serving: Calories 260 • Total Fat 11g • Saturated Fat 4g • Cholesterol 5mg • Sodium 540mg • Total Carbohydrate 34g • Dietary Fiber 3g • Sugars 6g • Protein 6g. **Dietary Exchanges:** 2 Starch • ½ Vegetable • 2 Fat OR 2 Carbohydrate • ½ Vegetable • 2 Fat.

curried chicken salad waffle sandwiches

READY TO SERVE: 30 MINUTES
SERVINGS: 4

CORVILIA CARRINGTON THYKKUTTATHIL ✱ RENTON, WASHINGTON
BAKE-OFF® CONTEST 42, 2006

Pillsbury
Bake-Off®

3 cups cubed cooked chicken (about 1 lb.)

½ cup finely chopped, peeled jicama

½ cup finely chopped celery

½ cup chopped cashews

⅓ cup mayonnaise or salad dressing

2 teaspoons Dijon mustard

1 teaspoon curry powder

1 (6-oz.) container lemon burst low-fat yogurt

Salt and pepper, if desired

1 (16.3-oz) can large refrigerated butter flavor flaky biscuits

4 cups mixed salad greens

1. In large bowl, mix chicken, jicama, celery and cashews. In small bowl, mix mayonnaise, mustard, curry powder and yogurt. Pour mayonnaise mixture over chicken mixture; gently toss to coat. Add salt and pepper to taste.

2. Heat Belgian or regular waffle maker (to make 2 or 4 waffle sections at a time). Separate dough into 8 biscuits; press or roll each into 4-inch round. Depending on size of waffle maker, place 2 to 4 biscuit rounds at a time in hot waffle maker. Bake 2 minutes or until golden brown. Cool 1 to 2 minutes.

3. Spoon and spread 1 cup chicken mixture onto each of 4 waffles; top with remaining waffles. Cut sandwiches in half; place 2 halves on each individual plate. Serve with mixed salad greens.

Nutrition Information Per Serving: Calories 860 • Total Fat 48g • Saturated Fat 10g • Trans Fat 7g • Cholesterol 100mg • Sodium 1410mg • Total Carbohydrate 64g • Dietary Fiber 3g • Sugars 19g • Protein 43g. **Dietary Exchanges:** 3 Starch • 1 Other Carbohydrate • 1 Vegetable • 4½ Lean Meat • 6½ Fat.

philly beef steak sandwiches

* super fast

½ lb. boneless beef sirloin steak, cut into thin strips

1 large onion, halved lengthwise, sliced (1½ cups)

1 green, red or yellow bell pepper, cut into bite-sized strips

2 tablespoons lite soy sauce

1½ teaspoons Worcestershire sauce

¼ teaspoon cornstarch

2 oz. shredded sharp Cheddar cheese (½ cup)

4 hoagie buns, split, heated

1. Spray large nonstick skillet with cooking spray. Heat over medium-high heat until hot. Add beef and onion; cook 3 to 4 minutes or until beef is browned, stirring occasionally.

2. Add bell pepper; cook 1 to 2 minutes or until crisp-tender. In small bowl, combine soy sauce, Worcestershire sauce and cornstarch; blend well. Stir into mixture in skillet; cook until thickened.

3. Sprinkle cheese evenly onto bottom halves of buns. Top each with beef mixture and top halves of buns.

Nutrition Information Per Serving: Calories 430 • Total Fat 12g • Saturated Fat 5g • Cholesterol 45mg • Sodium 1060mg • Total Carbohydrate 57g • Dietary Fiber 4g • Sugars 5g • Protein 24g. Dietary Exchanges: 3½ Starch • 1 Vegetable • 1½ Medium-Fat Meat • ½ Fat OR 3½ Carbohydrate • 1 Vegetable • 1½ Medium-Fat Meat • ½ Fat.

grands!® grilled cheese sandwiches

* super fast

1 (16.3-oz.) can Pillsbury® Grands!® Refrigerated Buttermilk Biscuits

2 teaspoons oil

8 (⅔-oz.) slices American cheese

1. Separate dough into 8 biscuits. Press or roll each to form 5½-inch round.

2. Heat oil in large skillet over medium heat until hot. Add biscuit rounds, a few at a time; cook 3 minutes. Turn; cook an additional 3 minutes or until light golden brown. Remove from skillet.

3. Place 2 slices of cheese on each of 4 biscuit rounds. Top with remaining biscuit rounds.

4. Return sandwiches to skillet; cook 2 to 3 minutes. Turn; cook an additional 2 minutes or until cheese is melted.

Nutrition Information Per Serving: Calories 550 • Total Fat 32g • Saturated Fat 13g • Cholesterol 40mg • Sodium 1730mg • Total Carbohydrate 49g • Dietary Fiber 1g • Sugars 9g • Protein 16g. Dietary Exchanges: 3 Starch • ½ Fruit • 1 High-Fat Meat • 4 Fat OR 3 Carbohydrate • 1 High-Fat Meat • 4 Fat.

ham 'n cheese breadstick wraps

* super fast

1 (7-oz.) can Pillsbury® Refrigerated Breadsticks (6 breadsticks)

6 leaf lettuce leaves

6 thin slices baby Swiss cheese

6 thin slices cooked ham

1 tablespoon prepared mustard

1. Heat oven to 375°F. Prepare and bake breadsticks as directed on can. Cool 10 minutes or until completely cooled.

2. Meanwhile, place lettuce leaves on work surface. Top each with cheese slice and ham slice. Spread mustard over ham.

3. Place cooled breadstick over ham in center of each. Wrap lettuce, cheese and ham around breadsticks. Secure each with toothpick.

Nutrition Information Per Serving: Calories 230 • Total Fat 10g • Saturated Fat 6g • Cholesterol 40mg • Sodium 590mg • Total Carbohydrate 18g • Dietary Fiber 1g • Sugars 3g • Protein 15g. Dietary Exchanges: 1 Starch • 1½ High-Fat Meat OR 1 Carbohydrate • 1½ High-Fat Meat • 1 Carb Choice.

chicken pita taquitos

chicken pita taquitos

READY TO SERVE: 20 MINUTES
SERVINGS: 3

* super fast

2 (4-oz.) marinated mesquite barbecue-flavored chicken breast fillets or 1 (8.25-oz.) pkg. frozen mesquite-grilled chicken fillets

1 small zucchini, halved lengthwise, sliced crosswise

1 small onion, sliced

½ medium green bell pepper, thinly sliced

1 cup Green Giant® Niblets® Frozen Corn (from 16-oz. pkg.)

1 large tomato, chopped

½ jalapeno chile pepper, seeded, finely chopped

1 tablespoon chopped fresh cilantro

3 (6-inch) whole wheat pocket (pita) breads, halved

1. Prepare chicken according to package directions (sauteed, broiled or microwaved) until fork-tender and juices run clear.

2. Meanwhile, spray large nonstick skillet with cooking spray. Heat over medium-high heat until hot. Add zucchini, onion and bell pepper; cook and stir 4 minutes. Stir in corn, tomato, chile pepper and cilantro; simmer 3 minutes or until vegetables are tender and mixture is thoroughly heated.

3. Thinly slice cooked chicken; stir into vegetable mixture. Fill each pocket bread half with about ⅔ cup chicken and vegetable mixture.

Nutrition Information Per Serving: Calories 360 • Total Fat 6g • Saturated Fat 1g • Cholesterol 35mg • Sodium 750mg • Total Carbohydrate 54g • Dietary Fiber 8g • Sugars 7g • Protein 22g. **Dietary Exchanges:** 3 Starch • 1½ Lean Meat • 2 Vegetable.

EASY VARIATIONS

If you don't have any pita breads on hand, you can easily swap them out for flour tortillas. And if you're looking for a savory summer salad, try preparing the chicken, vegetables and herbs as directed above. Let everything cool.

Then, toss the chicken-and-vegetable mixture with torn lettuce or spinach leaves and your favorite vinaigrette or salad dressing. Serve the Southwestern salad with a few tortilla chips and tomato wedges on the side.

hot corned beef and slaw sandwiches

READY TO SERVE: 25 MINUTES
SERVINGS: 5

* super fast

1 (10.2-oz.) can Pillsbury® Grands!® Refrigerated Buttermilk Biscuits (5 biscuits)

1 egg white, beaten

½ teaspoon caraway seed

1½ cups purchased coleslaw blend (from 16-oz. pkg.)

¼ cup purchased Thousand Island salad dressing

10 oz. cooked corned beef, thinly sliced

5 (¾-oz.) slices Swiss cheese

1. Heat oven to 375°F. Separate dough into 5 biscuits; place on ungreased cookie sheet. Brush tops with egg white. Sprinkle with caraway seed. Bake at 375°F for 11 to 13 minutes or until golden brown.

2. Meanwhile, in small bowl, combine coleslaw blend and salad dressing; mix well.

3. Remove biscuits from oven. Split warm biscuits; place bottom halves on same cookie sheet. Set top halves aside. Top each bottom half with coleslaw mixture, beef and cheese.

4. Return to oven; bake an additional 3 to 5 minutes or until cheese is melted and sandwiches are hot. Cover with top halves of biscuits.

Nutrition Information Per Serving: Calories 390 • Total Fat 21g • Saturated Fat 8g • Cholesterol 65mg • Sodium 1140mg • Total Carbohydrate 28g • Dietary Fiber 1g • Sugars 7g • Protein 23g. **Dietary Exchanges:** 1½ Starch • ½ Fruit • 2½ Lean Meat • 2½ Fat OR 2 Carbohydrate • 2½ Lean Meat • 2½ Fat • 2 Carb Choices.

italian chicken orzo soup

PREP TIME: 10 MINUTES
READY TO SERVE: 45 MINUTES
SERVINGS: 5

1 tablespoon oil

½ cup chopped onion

1 cup sliced carrot

1½ cups cubed cooked chicken

7 oz. (1 cup) uncooked orzo or rosamarina (rice-shaped pasta)

½ teaspoon dried Italian seasoning

3 (14½-oz.) cans ready-to-serve chicken broth

1½ cups milk

2 tablespoons all-purpose flour

1 cup frozen cut green beans, thawed

1. Heat oil in Dutch oven over medium-high heat until hot. Add onion and carrot; cook and stir 3 to 5 minutes or until onion is tender, stirring occasionally.

2. Add chicken, orzo, Italian seasoning and broth; mix well. Bring to a boil. Reduce heat to low; simmer 15 minutes or until orzo is tender, stirring occasionally.

3. In small bowl, combine milk and flour; beat with wire whisk until smooth. Add flour mixture and green beans to soup; blend well. Simmer 10 minutes or until soup is thickened, stirring occasionally.

Nutrition Information Per Serving: Calories 350 • Total Fat 9g • Saturated Fat 3g • Cholesterol 45mg • Sodium 870mg • Total Carbohydrate 42g • Dietary Fiber 3g • Sugars 8g • Protein 26g. Dietary Exchanges: 2½ Starch • 1 Vegetable • 2½ Lean Meat OR 2½ Carbohydrate • 1 Vegetable • 2½ Lean Meat.

chili con carne

PREP TIME: 30 MINUTES
READY TO SERVE: 2 HOURS
SERVINGS: 6

✳ plan ahead

1 lb. ground beef

½ cup chopped onion

¾ cup water

½ cup chopped green bell pepper

3 teaspoons chili powder

¼ teaspoon pepper

¼ teaspoon hot pepper sauce

1 to 2 garlic cloves, minced

1 (28-oz.) can whole tomatoes, undrained, cut up

1 (10¾-oz.) can condensed tomato soup

1 (6-oz.) can tomato paste

1 (4.5-oz.) can diced green chiles, drained

1 (15.5 or 15-oz.) can red kidney or pinto beans, drained, rinsed

1. In medium skillet, combine ground beef and onion. Cook over medium heat for 8 to 10 minutes or until beef is thoroughly cooked.

2. In large saucepan, combine ground beef mixture and all remaining ingredients except kidney beans. Bring to a boil. Reduce heat; cover and simmer 1½ to 2 hours, stirring occasionally.

3. Stir in kidney beans; simmer until thoroughly heated.

Nutrition Information Per Serving: Calories 310 • Total Fat 12g • Saturated Fat 5g • Cholesterol 45mg • Sodium 920mg • Total Carbohydrate 31g • Dietary Fiber 7g • Sugars 8g • Protein 19g. Dietary Exchanges: 2 Starch • 2 Medium-Fat Meat OR 2 Carbohydrate • 2 Medium-Fat Meat.

SLOW COOKERS TO THE RESCUE

Many soups that need to simmer for long periods of time can be set in a slow cooker to simmer on their own as long as the meat is thoroughly cooked on the stovetop first. Make sure the slow cooker is three-quarters full and avoid lifting the lid as much as possible. While it may take several hours for the soup to simmer, the slow cooker allows you to tend to other things as the ingredients blend on their own. Before you know it, dinner will be served.

italian chicken orzo soup

chicken and pepper sandwiches

READY TO SERVE: 30 MINUTES
SERVINGS: 4

4 boneless skinless chicken breast halves

½ teaspoon salt

½ teaspoon dried oregano leaves

¼ teaspoon pepper

1 tablespoon oil

1 poblano chile pepper or green bell pepper, seeded, cut into strips

1 medium onion, sliced, separated into rings

¾ cup refried beans

4 kaiser rolls, split

4 teaspoons margarine or butter

1 medium tomato, sliced

4 leaves lettuce

1. Place 1 chicken breast half between 2 pieces of plastic wrap or waxed paper. Working from center, gently pound chicken with flat side of meat mallet or rolling pin until about ¼ inch thick; remove wrap. Repeat with remaining chicken breast halves. Sprinkle chicken with salt, oregano and pepper.

2. Heat oil in large skillet over medium-high heat until hot. Add chicken; cook 6 to 8 minutes on each side or until lightly browned and juices run clear. Remove from skillet; cover to keep warm.

3. In same skillet, cook chile pepper and onion 5 to 7 minutes or until chile pepper is crisp-tender, stirring occasionally. Meanwhile, in medium saucepan, heat refried beans as directed on can.

4. Remove chile pepper mixture from skillet; keep warm. Heat same skillet over medium-high heat. Spread cut sides of rolls with margarine. Place rolls, margarine side down, in hot skillet. Cook 1 to 2 minutes or until golden brown.

5. To assemble sandwiches, place 2 to 3 tablespoons of the refried beans on bottom half of each bun. Top with chicken breast half, pepper mixture, tomato and lettuce; cover with top half of rolls.

Nutrition Information Per Serving: Calories 440 • Total Fat 13g • Saturated Fat 3g • Cholesterol 75mg • Sodium 890mg • Total Carbohydrate 45g • Dietary Fiber 5g • Sugars 5g • Protein 36g. **Dietary Exchanges:** 3 Starch • 4 Lean Meat OR 3 Carbohydrate • 4 Lean Meat.

italian super sub

PREP TIME: 15 MINUTES
READY TO SERVE: 1 HOUR 5 MINUTES
SERVINGS: 4

bread

1 (11-oz.) can Pillsbury® Refrigerated Crusty French Loaf

2 tablespoons shredded fresh Parmesan cheese

¼ teaspoon garlic salt

¼ teaspoon dried oregano leaves

filling

3 tablespoons purchased creamy Italian salad dressing

2 (1-oz.) slices Swiss cheese

¼ lb. thinly sliced cooked ham

1 small green bell pepper, sliced

2 (1-oz.) slices Cheddar cheese

¼ lb. sliced salami

1 medium tomato, sliced

1 cup shredded lettuce

1. Heat oven to 350°F. Spray cookie sheet with cooking spray. Remove dough from can; place seam side down on cookie sheet. With sharp or serrated knife, make 4 or 5 (¼-inch-deep) diagonal cuts on top of dough.

2. In small bowl, combine Parmesan cheese, garlic salt and oregano; mix well. Spray dough with cooking spray. Sprinkle with cheese mixture.

3. Bake at 350°F for 26 to 30 minutes or until light golden brown. Cool 20 minutes or until completely cooled.

4. Cut bread in half lengthwise. Brush cut sides of bread with salad dressing. Layer bottom half with Swiss cheese, ham, bell pepper, Cheddar cheese, salami, tomato and lettuce. Cover with top half of bread. Secure sandwich with toothpicks. Cut into 4 pieces.

Nutrition Information Per Serving: Calories 530 • Total Fat 28g • Saturated Fat 12g • Cholesterol 65mg • Sodium 1770mg • Total Carbohydrate 40g • Dietary Fiber 2g • Sugars 6g • Protein 28g. **Dietary Exchanges:** 2½ Starch • 3 High-Fat Meat • ½ Fat OR 2½ Carbohydrate • 3 High-Fat Meat • ½ Fat • 2½ Carb Choices.

southwest burrito burgers

READY TO SERVE: 30 MINUTES
SERVINGS: 4

1 lb. ground chicken

½ cup finely crushed tortilla chips or corn chips

¼ cup purchased salsa

4 (10-inch) flour tortillas

1 cup shredded lettuce

½ cup purchased guacamole

2 oz. shredded taco-flavored Cheddar cheese (½ cup)

½ cup purchased salsa

1. Heat grill. In medium bowl, combine ground chicken, tortilla chips and ¼ cup salsa; mix well. Shape mixture into four 4-inch-long oval patties. Wrap tortillas in 24x12-inch piece of heavy-duty foil; set aside.

2. When ready to grill, place patties on gas grill over medium-high heat or on charcoal grill 4 to 6 inches from medium-high coals. Cook 10 to 15 minutes or until no longer pink in center, turning once. During last 1 to 2 minutes of cooking, place foil packet on grill. Heat until tortillas are softened.

3. Place lettuce in center of each tortilla; top each with burger, guacamole and cheese. Fold ends of tortilla toward center; overlap sides to cover burger. Serve with ½ cup salsa.

Nutrition Information Per Serving: Calories 450 • Total Fat 20g • Saturated Fat 8g • Cholesterol 55mg • Sodium 1200mg • Total Carbohydrate 44g • Dietary Fiber 4g • Sugars 4g • Protein 23g. **Dietary Exchanges:** 3 Starch • 2 Medium-Fat Meat • 1 Fat OR 3 Carbohydrate • 2 Medium-Fat Meat • 1 Fat.

chicken and apricot bagel sandwiches

READY TO SERVE: 15 MINUTES
SERVINGS: 4

* super fast

1 (5-oz.) can chunk white chicken breast in water, drained

⅓ cup chopped dried apricots

¼ cup chopped celery

2 tablespoons sliced green onions

2 teaspoons shelled sunflower seeds

Dash pepper

¼ cup fat-free mayonnaise or salad dressing

4 bagels, split

1. In small bowl, combine all ingredients except bagels; mix well.

2. Fill each bagel with about ⅓ cup chicken mixture.

Nutrition Information Per Serving: Calories 290 • Total Fat 3g • Saturated Fat 0g • Cholesterol 15mg • Sodium 660mg • Total Carbohydrate 47g • Dietary Fiber 3g • Sugars 5g • Protein 18g. **Dietary Exchanges:** 2 Starch • 1 Fruit • 1½ Lean Meat OR 3 Carbohydrate • 1½ Lean Meat.

MAKE-AHEAD EASE

Beat the clock by preparing this fruited chicken salad a day or two in advance so mealtime isn't so rushed. Just be sure to stir in the sunflower seeds right before serving so they don't get too soggy. For a change of pace, try the recipe using whole wheat or raisin bagels, and if you don't keep canned white chicken breast in your cupboard, feel free to replace it with boiled chicken or any leftover roasted poultry you may have in the refrigerator.

chunky chicken chili

READY TO SERVE: 45 MINUTES
SERVINGS: 6

* meal-in-one

4 boneless skinless chicken breast halves, cut into bite-sized pieces

1 cup chopped onions

½ cup chopped celery

½ cup chopped carrot

2 garlic cloves, minced

1 cup salsa

1 (28-oz.) can whole tomatoes, undrained, cut up

1 (8-oz.) can tomato sauce

3 teaspoons chili powder

½ teaspoon cumin

1 (15-oz.) can garbanzo beans, drained

1 green bell pepper, chopped

1. Spray large nonstick saucepan with cooking spray. Heat over medium-high heat until hot. Add chicken, onions, celery, carrot and garlic; cook and stir until chicken is no longer pink.

2. Stir in salsa, tomatoes, tomato sauce, chili powder and cumin. Bring to a boil. Reduce heat to low; cover and simmer 30 minutes, stirring occasionally. Stir in garbanzo beans and bell pepper; simmer until thoroughly heated.

Nutrition Information Per Serving: Calories 240 • Total Fat 4g • Saturated Fat 1g • Cholesterol 45mg • Sodium 900mg • Total Carbohydrate 27g • Dietary Fiber 7g • Sugars 8g • Protein 23g. **Dietary Exchanges:** 1½ Starch • 1 Vegetable • 2½ Very Lean Meat OR 1½ Carbohydrate • 1 Vegetable • 2 Very Lean Meat.

IMPRESS WITH SOUTHWEST

With its south-of-the-border flavor and colorful flair, Chunky Chicken Chili is a great addition to suppers featuring tacos, burritos or enchiladas. Garnish individual bowls with dollops of sour cream, chopped green onion or chives, slices of spicy peppers, shredded cheese or even tortilla chips. When serving the chili as a main course, consider a simple spinach salad or wedges of warm cornbread for quick dinner accompaniments.

chicken and apricot bagel sandwiches

black bean and ham soup

PREP TIME: 15 MINUTES
READY TO SERVE: 2 HOURS 45 MINUTES
SERVINGS: 6

✳ plan ahead

8 oz. dried black beans, sorted, rinsed (1¼ cups)

5½ oz. cooked ham, cubed (1 cup)

½ cup chopped onion

½ cup thin green bell pepper strips

1 (15-oz.) can chunky tomato sauce with onions, celery and green bell peppers

1 (10¾-oz.) can condensed tomato soup

3 cups water

1 teaspoon cumin

3 teaspoons chili powder

1. Place beans in Dutch oven; add water until about 1 inch above beans. Bring to a boil. Boil 2 minutes. Remove from heat; cover and let stand 1 hour.

2. Drain and discard water. Add all remaining ingredients to beans; mix well. Bring to a boil. Reduce heat to low; simmer 1½ to 2 hours or until beans are tender, stirring occasionally.

Nutrition Information Per Serving: Calories: 240 • Total Fat 3g • Saturated Fat 1g • Cholesterol 10mg • Sodium 1050 mg • Total Carbohydrate 39g • Dietary Fiber 8g • Sugars 9g • Protein 15g. **Dietary Exchanges:** 2 Starch • 2 Vegetable • 1 Very Lean Meat OR 2 Carbohydrate • 2 Vegetable • 1 Very Lean Meat.

italian roast beef focaccia sandwiches

READY TO SERVE: 25 MINUTES
SERVINGS: 4

* **super fast**

1 (10-oz.) can Pillsbury® Refrigerated Pizza Crust

¼ cup purchased Italian salad dressing

¼ lb. thinly sliced cooked roast beef

3 thin slices provolone cheese (about 4½ oz.)

2 Italian plum tomatoes, thinly sliced

1 cup coarsely shredded lettuce

1. Heat oven to 425°F. Grease cookie sheet or spray with cooking spray. Unroll dough; place on a greased cookie sheet. Starting in center, press out the dough to form 13x9-inch rectangle.

2. With fingers or end of wooden spoon handle, make indentations on surface of dough. Drizzle with 4 teaspoons of the salad dressing.

3. Bake at 425°F for 9 to 12 minutes or until golden brown. Cool 5 minutes.

4. Place bread on cutting board or serving platter. Cut in half lengthwise. On 1 long rectangle, layer beef, cheese, tomato and lettuce. Drizzle with remaining salad dressing. Top with remaining rectangle, top side up; press down gently. Cut into 4 pieces.

Nutrition Information Per Serving: Calories 400 • Total Fat 19g • Saturated Fat 7g • Cholesterol 35mg • Sodium 1160mg • Total Carbohydrate 37g • Dietary Fiber 1g • Sugars 6g • Protein 20g. **Dietary Exchanges:** 2½ Starch • 1½ Lean Meat • 2½ Fat OR 2½ Carbohydrate • 1½ Lean Meat • 2½ Fat • 2½ Carb Choices.

sausage and black bean chili

PREP TIME: 30 MINUTES
READY TO SERVE: 1 HOUR 15 MINUTES
SERVINGS: 6

* **meal-in-one**

⅔ cup uncooked regular long-grain white rice.

1⅓ cups water

1 lb. bulk chorizo or Italian sausage

1 cup chopped onions

2 garlic cloves, crushed

2 jalapeño chiles, seeded, chopped

2 (15-oz.) cans black beans, drained, rinsed

1 (28-oz.) can Italian plum tomatoes, undrained, cut up

1 cup beer or tomato juice

1 tablespoon chopped fresh cilantro

1 teaspoon cumin

4 oz. shredded Cheddar cheese (1 cup)

1. Cook rice in water as directed on package.

2. Meanwhile, in large saucepan or Dutch oven, combine sausage, onions, garlic and chiles. Cook 8 to 10 minutes or until sausage is well browned. Drain. Stir in all remaining ingredients except rice and cheese. Cook over medium heat 30 to 45 minutes or until slightly thickened.

3. To serve, ladle chili over cooked rice in individual serving bowls; sprinkle with cheese.

Nutrition Information Per Serving: Calories 580 • Total Fat 29g • Saturated Fat 12g • Cholesterol 70mg • Sodium 1010mg • Total Carbohydrate 49g • Dietary Fiber 10g • Sugars 7g • Protein 29g. **Dietary Exchanges:** 3 Starch • 1 Vegetable • 2½ High-Fat Meat • 1½ Fat OR 3 Carbohydrate • 1 Vegetable • 2½ High-Fat Meat • 1½ Fat.

MIX THINGS UP WITH CHORIZO

Chorizo is a spicy sausage that can be found in most large grocery stores. Easy to cook with, chorizo makes a perfect addition to full-flavored dishes such as Sausage and Black Bean Chili. Look for chorizo in refrigerated cases in the ethnic aisle of the supermarket or ask the butcher where it can be found. After cooking with it once, you'll find plenty of family favorites that could benefit from the robust addition of this change-of-pace sausage.

pastrami stromboli

PREP TIME: 15 MINUTES
READY TO SERVE: 45 MINUTES
SERVINGS: 4

1   (11-oz.) can Pillsbury®
    Refrigerated Crusty French
    Loaf

2   tablespoons mayonnaise

1   teaspoon Dijon mustard

½   lb. thinly sliced pastrami

1   (6-oz.) pkg. sliced provolone
    cheese

1   cup french fried onions
    (from 2.8-oz. can)

1. Heat oven to 350°F. Spray cookie sheet with cooking spray. Carefully unroll dough onto sprayed cookie sheet. Press or roll to form 14x12-inch rectangle.

2. In small bowl, combine mayonnaise and mustard; blend well. Spread over dough to within 1 inch of all edges. Layer half each of the pastrami and cheese lengthwise in 5-inch-wide strip down center of dough to within 1 inch of each short side, overlapping pastrami and cheese. Repeat layering with remaining pastrami and cheese. Sprinkle with onions.

3. Fold long sides of dough over filling; pinch edges in center to seal. Fold ends under 1 inch; seal. Cut several slits in top for steam to escape.

4. Bake at 350°F for 26 to 30 minutes or until deep golden brown. Cool 5 minutes. Cut into crosswise slices.

Nutrition Information Per Serving: Calories 575 • Total Fat 31g • Saturated Fat 12g • Cholesterol 70mg • Sodium 1810mg • Total Carbohydrate 46g • Dietary Fiber 2g • Sugars 2g • Protein 30g. **Dietary Exchanges:** 3 Starch • 3 High-Fat Meat • 1 Fat OR 3 Carbohydrate • 3 High-Fat Meat • 1 Fat • 3 Carb Choices.

tomato-corn chowder with cilantro pesto

PREP TIME: 15 MINUTES
READY TO SERVE: 30 MINUTES
SERVINGS: 4

JENNIFER MOHN ✳ AUSTIN, TEXAS
BAKE-OFF® CONTEST 42, 2006

chowder

- 2 tablespoons extra-virgin olive oil
- 1 cup chopped white onions (2 medium)
- ¼ cup chopped fresh poblano chile (about ½ chile)
- ½ teaspoon freshly ground black pepper
- ¼ teaspoon salt
- 1½ cups organic frozen whole kernel sweet corn (from 16-oz. bag)
- 1 (14.5-oz.) can organic fire-roasted diced tomatoes
- 1 (14-oz.) can fat-free chicken broth with 33% less sodium
- ½ cup half-and-half

pesto

- 1 cup firmly packed fresh cilantro
- 2 tablespoons freshly grated Parmesan cheese
- 2 tablespoons roasted salted hulled pumpkin seeds (pepitas)
- ⅛ teaspoon salt
- ¼ teaspoon freshly ground black pepper
- 2 tablespoons extra-virgin olive oil

1. In 3-quart saucepan, heat 2 tablespoons oil over medium-high heat. Add onions and chile; sprinkle with ½ teaspoon pepper and ¼ teaspoon salt. Cook, stirring frequently, 5 minutes. Stir in frozen corn, tomatoes and broth. Heat to boiling over high heat, stirring occasionally. Reduce heat to low; cover and simmer 10 to 15 minutes.

2. Meanwhile, in small food processor, place all pesto ingredients except oil; process with on-and-off motions 2 or 3 times to mix. With processor running, slowly drizzle 2 tablespoons oil into mixture, processing about 30 seconds or until well blended. Set pesto aside.

3. In blender or with immersion blender, blend chowder in 2 batches, if necessary, about 30 to 60 seconds or until almost smooth. Stir in half-and-half. Heat chowder just until warm.

4. Ladle chowder into individual bowls. Top each with 1 heaping tablespoon pesto to be swirled in before eating.

Nutrition Information Per Serving: Calories 320 • Total Fat 21g • Saturated Fat 5g • Trans Fat 0g • Cholesterol 15mg • Sodium 780mg • Total Carbohydrate 24g • Dietary Fiber 4g • Sugars 8g • Protein 9g. **Dietary Exchanges:** 1 Starch • ½ Other Carbohydrate • 1 Vegetable • ½ High-Fat Meat • 3 Fat.

tarragon chicken burgers

READY TO SERVE: 30 MINUTES
SERVINGS: 4

- 1 lb. ground chicken
- 1 tablespoon chopped fresh tarragon or 1 teaspoon dried tarragon leaves
- 1 tablespoon finely chopped onion
- 1 tablespoon sour cream
- ⅛ teaspoon salt
- 4 burger buns, split

1. Heat grill. In large bowl, combine all ingredients except buns; mix gently. (Mixture will be moist.) Shape mixture into 4 patties.

2. When ready to grill, oil grill rack. Place patties on gas grill over medium-low heat or on charcoal grill 4 to 6 inches from medium coals. Cook 9 to 13 minutes or until no longer pink in center, turning once. Serve in burger buns.

Nutrition Information Per Serving: Calories 310 • Total Fat 13g • Saturated Fat 4g • Cholesterol 90mg • Sodium 390mg • Total Carbohydrate 22g • Dietary Fiber 1g • Sugars 5g • Protein 25g. **Dietary Exchanges:** 1½ Starch • 2½ Medium-Fat Meat OR 1½ Carbohydrate • 2½ Medium-Fat Meat.

salads & breads

chinese-style salad ✻ p. 76

cornmeal sage scones ✻ p. 70

quick tortellini salad ✻ p. 82

parmesan herb biscuits ✻ p. 78

basil and havarti cheese pinwheels ✳ p. 84

curry wild rice salad

READY TO SERVE: 10 MINUTES
SERVINGS: 4

* super fast

dressing

- ¼ cup nonfat plain yogurt
- 2 tablespoons light mayonnaise
- ½ teaspoon curry powder
- ⅛ teaspoon pepper

salad

- 1 (15-oz.) can cooked wild rice, drained
- ¼ cup chopped red bell pepper
- ¼ cup chopped celery
- 2 tablespoons raisins

1. In small bowl, combine all dressing ingredients; blend well.

2. In large bowl, combine all salad ingredients; mix well. Add dressing; toss gently to mix thoroughly. Serve immediately, or cover and refrigerate until serving time.

Nutrition Information Per Serving: Calories 120 • Total Fat 3g • Saturated Fat 1g • Cholesterol 3 mg • Sodium 320 mg • Total Carbohydrate 19g • Dietary Fiber 2g • Sugars 6g • Protein 3g. **Dietary Exchanges:** 1 Starch • ½ Fruit • ½ Fat OR 1½ Carbohydrate • ½ Fat.

SIMPLE SUBSTITUTION

If you don't usually keep a can of cooked wild rice on hand, you can still prepare Curry Wild Rice Salad for dinner tonight. Just substitute the canned rice with 2 cups cooked instant wild or brown rice.

cheddar and canadian bacon muffins

PREP TIME: 15 MINUTES
READY TO SERVE: 35 MINUTES
SERVINGS: 6 MUFFINS

1 cup all-purpose flour

2 teaspoons freeze-dried
 chopped chives

1 teaspoon baking powder

¼ teaspoon garlic powder

⅓ cup milk

¼ cup sour cream

2 tablespoons oil

1 egg

2 oz. shredded Cheddar
 cheese (½ cup)

¼ cup finely chopped
 Canadian bacon or ham

1. Heat oven to 400°F. Grease 6 muffin cups, or line with paper baking cups and spray with cooking spray. In large bowl, combine flour, chives, baking powder and garlic powder; mix well.

2. In small bowl, combine milk, sour cream, oil and egg; beat well. Add to flour mixture; stir just until dry ingredients are moistened. Fold in cheese and bacon. Divide batter evenly into greased muffin cups.

3. Bake at 400°F for 17 to 20 minutes or until toothpick inserted in center comes out clean. Immediately remove from pan. Serve warm.

Nutrition Information Per Serving: Calories 200 • Total Fat 11g • Saturated Fat 4g • Cholesterol 55mg • Sodium 250mg • Dietary Fiber 1g. **Dietary Exchanges:** 1 Starch • ½ Lean Meat • 2 Fat OR 1 Carbohydrate • ½ Lean Meat • 2 Fat.

mixed potato salad

PREP TIME: 25 MINUTES
READY TO SERVE: 1 HOUR
SERVINGS: 24

salad

3 lb. red potatoes

2 lb. sweet potatoes

1 cup chopped celery

1 medium cucumber, peeled,
 seeded and chopped

dressing

1 (8-oz.) container nonfat
 plain yogurt

¼ cup chopped fresh dill or
 1 tablespoon dried dill
 weed

¼ cup light mayonnaise or
 salad dressing

1 tablespoon lemon juice

¼ teaspoon salt

1. Place whole red and sweet potatoes separately in 2 Dutch ovens or large saucepans; cover with water. Bring to a boil. Reduce heat; simmer until tender. Simmer red potatoes 20 to 25 minutes; simmer sweet potatoes 30 to 35 minutes.

2. Drain potatoes; rinse with cold water to cool. Peel potatoes; cut into cubes. Place in large serving bowl. Add celery and cucumber; mix well.

3. In medium bowl, combine all dressing ingredients; blend well. Pour dressing over salad; toss gently. Serve immediately, or cover and refrigerate until serving time.

Nutrition Information Per Serving: Calories 90 • Total Fat 1g • Saturated Fat 0g • Cholesterol 0 mg • Sodium 60 mg • Total Carbohydrate 19g • Dietary Fiber 2g • Sugars 6g • Protein 2g. **Dietary Exchange:** 1 Starch OR 1 Carbohydrate.

cheddar and bacon biscuits

PREP TIME: 5 MINUTES
READY TO SERVE: 30 MINUTES
SERVINGS: 4

4 frozen buttermilk biscuits
 (from 25-oz. bag)

2 teaspoons cooked real
 bacon pieces (from 3-oz. jar
 or pkg.)

2 tablespoons finely shredded
 Cheddar cheese

1. Heat oven to 375°F. Place frozen biscuits on ungreased cookie sheet, sides touching. Bake 10 minutes.

2. Top biscuits with bacon and cheese. Bake 10 to 14 minutes longer or until golden brown. Serve warm.

Nutrition Information Per Serving: Calories 200 • Total Fat 11g • Saturated Fat 3.5g • Trans Fat 4g • Cholesterol 0mg • Sodium 620mg • Total Carbohydrate 22g • Dietary Fiber 0g • Sugars 3g • Protein 5g. **Dietary Exchanges:** 1½ Starch • 2 Fat.

cornmeal sage scones

PREP TIME: 15 MINUTES
READY TO SERVE: 45 MINUTES
SERVINGS: 8

1¼ cups all-purpose flour
½ cup yellow cornmeal
¼ cup grated Parmesan cheese
2 teaspoons baking powder
½ teaspoon baking soda
½ teaspoon salt
¾ teaspoon dried sage leaves, crumbled
¼ cup margarine or butter
¾ cup buttermilk

1. Heat oven to 425°F. Spray cookie sheet with cooking spray. In large bowl, combine flour, cornmeal, cheese, baking powder, baking soda, salt and sage; mix well. With pastry blender or fork, cut in margarine until mixture resembles coarse crumbs. Add buttermilk; stir just until dry ingredients are moistened.

2. On lightly floured surface, gently knead dough 10 times. Place on sprayed cookie sheet; roll or pat dough into 6½-inch round. Cut into 8 wedges; do not separate.

3. Bake at 425°F for 20 to 25 minutes or until light golden brown. Remove from cookie sheet; cool 5 minutes. Cut into wedges. Serve warm.

Nutrition Information Per Serving: Calories 170 • Total Fat 7g • Saturated Fat 2g • Cholesterol 3mg • Sodium 490mg • Dietary Fiber 1g. Dietary Exchanges: 1½ Starch • 1 Fat OR 1½ Carbohydrate • 1 Fat.

tomato-mozzarella platter

READY TO SERVE: 10 MINUTES
SERVINGS: 4

* super fast

2 large beefsteak tomatoes, sliced
¼ teaspoon salt
5 oz. fresh mozzarella cheese (8 slices)
2 teaspoons olive or vegetable oil
2 tablespoons torn fresh basil leaves
¼ teaspoon coarse ground black pepper

1. Sprinkle tomato slices with salt. Arrange tomato and cheese slices alternately on serving platter, overlapping slices.

2. Drizzle with oil; sprinkle with basil and pepper.

Nutrition Information Per Serving: Calories 150 • Total Fat 10g • Saturated Fat 5g • Cholesterol 30mg • Sodium 280mg • Total Carbohydrate 6g • Dietary Fiber 1g • Sugars 3g • Protein 8g. Dietary Exchanges: 1 Vegetable • 1 Medium-Fat Meat • 1 Fat.

lemony herb muffins

READY TO SERVE: 30 MINUTES
SERVINGS: 12 MUFFINS

1 cup all-purpose flour
1 cup whole wheat flour
¼ cup sugar
¼ cup chopped fresh chives
3 teaspoons baking powder
2 teaspoons grated lemon peel
¾ teaspoon dried basil or oregano leaves
½ teaspoon salt
1 cup milk
⅓ cup margarine or butter, melted
1 egg, slightly beaten

1. Heat oven to 400°F. Grease 12 muffin cups or line with paper baking cups. In large bowl, combine all-purpose flour, whole wheat flour, sugar, chives, baking powder, lemon peel, basil and salt; mix well.

2. Add milk, margarine and egg; stir just until dry ingredients are moistened. Fill greased muffin cups ⅔ full.

3. Bake at 400°F for 13 to 18 minutes or until toothpick inserted in center comes out clean. Immediately remove from pan. Serve warm.

Nutrition Information Per Serving: Calories 150 • Total Fat 6g • Saturated Fat 1g • Cholesterol 20mg • Sodium 290mg • Dietary Fiber 2g. Dietary Exchanges: 1 Starch • ½ Fruit • 1 Fat OR 1½ Carbohydrate • 1 Fat.

cornmeal sage scones

zucchini bread with dried cranberries

PREP TIME: 15 MINUTES
READY TO SERVE: 35 MINUTES
SERVINGS: 12

½ cup sugar

½ cup shredded unpeeled zucchini

⅓ cup milk

1 tablespoon oil

1 egg

1 cup all-purpose flour

2 teaspoons baking powder

½ teaspoon cinnamon

¼ teaspoon cloves

½ cup sweetened dried cranberries

1 tablespoon sugar, if desired

1. Heat oven to 400°F. Spray 8 or 9-inch round cake pan with cooking spray.

2. In large bowl, combine ½ cup sugar, zucchini, milk, oil and egg; mix well. Add flour, baking powder, cinnamon, cloves and dried cranberries; mix just until combined. Pour into sprayed pan. Sprinkle with 1 tablespoon sugar.

3. Bake at 400°F for 12 to 19 minutes or until light golden brown. Cool 5 minutes. Cut into wedges. Serve warm.

Nutrition Information Per Serving: Calories 120 • Total Fat 2g • Saturated Fat 0g • Cholesterol 20mg • Sodium 90mg • Dietary Fiber 1g. Dietary Exchanges: 1 Starch • ½ Fruit OR 1½ Carbohydrate.

BEST FREEZER FLAVOR

To retain maximum flavor in frozen breads, wrap them tightly in plastic wrap, then put the wrapped loaves into resealable plastic freezer bags. Or, wrap individual slices before freezing, to make it easy to thaw them quickly in the microwave for an afternoon snack or a quick treat when visitors stop by.

---

plump carrot muffins

PREP TIME: 20 MINUTES
READY TO SERVE: 40 MINUTES
SERVINGS: 12 MUFFINS

1¾ cups all-purpose flour

⅓ cup firmly packed brown sugar

1 teaspoon baking powder

1 teaspoon baking soda

1 teaspoon cinnamon

¼ teaspoon salt

½ cup shredded carrot

¾ cup orange juice

2 tablespoons oil

1½ teaspoons grated orange peel

1 teaspoon vanilla

1 egg

⅓ cup golden raisins

1. Heat oven to 375°F. Spray bottoms only of 12 muffin cups with cooking spray or line with paper baking cups. In large bowl, combine flour, brown sugar, baking powder, baking soda, cinnamon and salt; mix well.

2. In small bowl, combine carrot, orange juice, oil, orange peel, vanilla and egg; blend well. Add to flour mixture; stir just until dry ingredients are moistened. Stir in raisins. Fill sprayed muffin cups ¾ full.

3. Bake at 375°F for 15 to 18 minutes or until toothpick inserted in center comes out clean. Cool 1 minute; remove from pan. Serve warm.

Nutrition Information Per Serving: Calories 140 • Total Fat 3g • Saturated Fat 0g • Cholesterol 20mg • Sodium 200mg • Dietary Fiber 1g. Dietary Exchanges: 1 Starch • ½ Fruit • ½ Fat OR 1½ Carbohydrate • ½ Fat.

onion-chive muffins

READY TO SERVE: 30 MINUTES
SERVINGS: 12 MUFFINS

¾ cup chopped onions

1½ cups all-purpose flour

¼ cup chopped fresh chives

2 tablespoons sugar

2 teaspoons baking powder

½ teaspoon salt

¼ teaspoon baking soda

1 cup buttermilk

¼ cup oil

¼ cup refrigerated or frozen fat-free egg product, thawed, or 1 egg, slightly beaten

1. Heat oven to 375°F. Grease bottoms only of 12 muffin cups or line with paper baking cups. Spray small skillet with cooking spray. Add onions; cook and stir over medium heat until crisp-tender. Set aside.

2. In large bowl, combine flour, chives, sugar, baking powder, salt and baking soda; mix well. In small bowl, combine cooked onions, buttermilk, oil and egg product; blend well. Add to flour mixture; stir just until dry ingredients are moistened. Fill greased muffin cups about ¾ full.

3. Bake at 375°F for 12 to 14 minutes or until toothpick inserted in center comes out clean. (Muffins will be very light in color.) Immediately remove from pan. Serve warm.

Nutrition Information Per Serving: Calories 120 • Total Fat 5g • Saturated Fat 1g • Cholesterol 0mg • Sodium 230mg • Dietary Fiber 1g. **Dietary Exchanges:** 1 Starch • 1 Fat OR 1 Carbohydrate • 1 Fat.

waldorf coleslaw

READY TO SERVE: 20 MINUTES
SERVINGS: 16

✱ super fast

1 red apple, chopped

Lemon juice

6 cups shredded cabbage

1 cup seedless red grapes

1 (20-oz.) can pineapple chunks in unsweetened juice, drained

1 cup sour cream

1 tablespoon sugar

1 teaspoon lemon juice

½ teaspoon salt

⅓ cup chopped walnuts, toasted

1. In large bowl, sprinkle chopped apple with lemon juice. Add cabbage, grapes and pineapple; toss gently.

2. In small bowl, combine sour cream, sugar, 1 teaspoon lemon juice and salt; blend well. Pour sour cream mixture over cabbage mixture; toss until well coated. Serve immediately, or cover and refrigerate until serving time.

3. Just before serving, sprinkle with walnuts.

Nutrition Information Per Serving: Calories 90 • Total Fat 5g • Saturated Fat 2g • Cholesterol 5mg • Sodium 80mg • Total Carbohydrate 9g • Dietary Fiber 1g • Sugars 8g • Protein 1g. **Dietary Exchanges:** 1½ Fruit • 1 Vegetable • 1 Fat OR ½ Carbohydrate • 1 Vegetable • 1 Fat.

TOASTING WALNUTS

To toast walnuts, spread them on a cookie sheet; bake at 350°F for 5 to 7 minutes or until golden brown, stirring occasionally. Or, spread the nuts in a thin layer in a microwave-safe pie pan. Microwave on high for 4 to 7 minutes or until the walnuts are golden brown, stirring frequently.

antipasto salad

PREP TIME: 20 MINUTES
READY TO SERVE: 50 MINUTES
SERVINGS: 6

dressing
- 1/3 cup red wine vinegar
- 1/2 cup olive or vegetable oil
- 1 teaspoon Dijon mustard
- 1 teaspoon dried Italian seasoning
- 1/2 teaspoon salt
- 1/4 teaspoon sugar
- 1/8 teaspoon pepper
- 2 garlic cloves, minced, or 1 teaspoon chopped garlic in water (from 4.5-oz. jar)

salad
- 6 cups torn leaf lettuce
- 12 thin slices provolone cheese
- 1 (3.5-oz.) pkg. giant-sized sliced pepperoni
- 2 large tomatoes, cut into wedges
- 8 large fresh mushrooms, sliced
- 8 large pitted ripe olives

1. In small jar with tight-fitting lid, combine all dressing ingredients; shake well. Let stand at room temperature for 30 minutes to blend flavors.

2. To serve, place lettuce on large serving platter. Cut cheese slices in half. Roll cheese and pepperoni slices into cones. Arrange cheese and pepperoni cones, tomatoes, mushrooms and olives over lettuce. Drizzle with dressing.

Nutrition Information Per Serving: Calories 390 • Total Fat 34g • Saturated Fat 10g • Cholesterol 35mg • Sodium 850mg • Total Carbohydrate 8g • Dietary Fiber 2g • Sugars 4g • Protein 13g. **Dietary Exchanges:** 1½ Vegetable • 1½ High-Fat Meat • 4½ Fat.

CHANGE-OF-PACE DELIGHT

Antipasto Salad is a wonderful addition to Italian menus, whether they feature lasagna, spaghetti or even something as casual as pizza. However, the full-flavored dish also makes a colorful contribution to potlucks. Consider this fun salad the next time you are asked to bring something to a party. The festive buffet addition is sure to have guests asking for your secret. Best of all, it is a tasty contribution that no one else is likely to think of.

fresh green bean-walnut salad

PREP TIME: 25 MINUTES
READY TO SERVE: 1 HOUR 25 MINUTES
SERVINGS: 8

salad
- 1 lb. fresh green beans, trimmed
- 1/2 cup roasted red bell peppers (from 7.25-oz. jar), drained, cut into strips
- 1 small onion, cut into wedges
- 1/4 cup coarsely chopped walnuts

dressing
- 1/4 cup olive oil
- 2 tablespoons balsamic vinegar
- 1 teaspoon dry mustard
- 1/8 teaspoon salt

1. Place green beans in medium saucepan; add just enough water to cover. Bring to a boil over medium-high heat. Cook 8 to 10 minutes or until beans are crisp-tender, stirring occasionally. Drain; rinse with cold water to cool.

2. In medium bowl, combine green beans and all remaining salad ingredients.

3. In jar with tight-fitting lid, combine all dressing ingredients; shake well. Pour over salad; toss gently to coat. Cover; refrigerate at least 1 hour to blend flavors.

Nutrition Information Per Serving: Calories 110 • Total Fat 9g • Saturated Fat 1g • Cholesterol 0mg • Sodium 35mg • Total Carbohydrate 6g • Dietary Fiber 2g • Sugars 2g • Protein 2g. **Dietary Exchanges:** 1 Vegetable • 2 Fat.

black bean and corn salad

READY TO SERVE: 15 MINUTES
SERVINGS: 7

✳ super fast

salad

- 1 medium zucchini, halved, sliced (1 cup)
- 1 (15-oz.) can black beans, drained, rinsed
- 1 (7-oz.) can whole kernel corn, drained
- ¼ cup chopped red onion
- ¼ cup chopped fresh parsley

dressing

- ½ cup purchased oil and vinegar salad dressing
- 3 tablespoons sugar
- ¼ teaspoon seasoned salt

1. In medium bowl, combine all salad ingredients.

2. In small bowl, combine all dressing ingredients; blend well. Spoon dressing over salad; stir to coat.

Nutrition Information Per Serving: Calories 190 • Total Fat 10g • Saturated Fat 2g • Cholesterol 0mg • Sodium 350mg • Total Carbohydrate 21g • Dietary Fiber 4g • Sugars 9g • Protein 4g. **Dietary Exchanges:** 1½ Starch • 2 Fat OR 1½ Carbohydrate • 2 Fat.

sour cream drop biscuits

READY TO SERVE: 25 MINUTES
SERVINGS: 12 BISCUITS

✳ super fast

- 2 cups all-purpose flour
- 1 tablespoon sugar
- 3 teaspoons baking powder
- ½ teaspoon salt
- ¼ cup shortening
- ⅔ cup milk
- ⅔ cup sour cream

1. Heat oven to 450°F. Grease cookie sheet. In medium bowl, combine flour, sugar, baking powder and salt; mix well. With pastry blender or fork, cut in shortening until mixture is crumbly.

2. In small bowl, combine milk and sour cream; blend well. Add all at once to flour mixture; stir just until dry ingredients are moistened. Drop dough by tablespoonfuls onto greased cookie sheet.

3. Bake at 450°F for 10 to 12 minutes or until golden brown. Serve warm.

Nutrition Information Per Serving: Calories 150 • Total Fat 7g • Saturated Fat 3g • Cholesterol 5mg • Sodium 230mg • Dietary Fiber 1g. **Dietary Exchanges:** 1 Starch • 1½ Fat OR 1 Carbohydrate • 1½ Fat.

mini cheese 'n chive popovers

PREP TIME: 10 MINUTES
READY TO SERVE: 40 MINUTES
SERVINGS: 18 MINI-POPOVERS

- 2 eggs, room temperature
- ⅔ cup milk, room temperature
- ⅔ cup all-purpose flour
- 3 tablespoons finely shredded Cheddar cheese
- 1 tablespoon chopped fresh chives or 1 teaspoon freeze-dried chopped chives
- ⅛ teaspoon garlic powder
- ⅛ teaspoon salt

1. Heat oven to 450°F. Generously spray 18 miniature muffin cups with cooking spray. In small bowl, beat eggs with wire whisk or eggbeater until lemon-colored and foamy. Add milk; blend well.

2. Add all remaining ingredients; beat with wire whisk just until batter is smooth and foamy on top. Pour batter into sprayed cups, filling to within ¼ inch of top.

3. Bake at 450°F for 10 minutes. (Do not open oven.) Reduce oven temperature to 350°F; bake an additional 10 to 20 minutes or until popovers are high and deep golden brown. Remove from oven; insert sharp knife into each popover to allow steam to escape. Remove from pan. Serve warm.

Nutrition Information Per Serving: Calories 70 • Total Fat 2g • Saturated Fat 1g • Cholesterol 50mg • Sodium 70mg • Dietary Fiber 0g. **Dietary Exchanges:** ½ Starch • ½ Fat OR ½ Carbohydrate • ½ Fat.

chinese-style salad

READY TO SERVE: 40 MINUTES
SERVINGS: 4

* meal-in-one

⅓ cup purchased teriyaki sauce

3 tablespoons rice vinegar

1 teaspoon sesame seed

¼ teaspoon coarse ground black pepper

4 boneless skinless chicken breast halves

1 large head romaine lettuce, thinly sliced (about 8 cups)

2 medium carrots, cut into julienne strips (2x¼x¼-inch)

1 small red bell pepper, cut into julienne strips (2x¼x¼-inch)

4 oz. fresh pea pods, cut diagonally in half (1 cup)

1. Heat grill. In medium bowl, combine teriyaki sauce, vinegar, sesame seed and pepper; mix well. Reserve ¼ cup for dressing. Add chicken to remaining mixture; toss to coat. Let stand 5 to 10 minutes at room temperature to marinate.

2. When ready to grill, remove chicken from marinade; discard marinade. Place chicken on gas grill over medium heat or on charcoal grill 4 to 6 inches from medium coals. Cook 10 to 15 minutes or until chicken is fork tender and juices run clear, turning once.

3. Meanwhile, in large bowl combine lettuce, carrots, bell pepper and pea pods. Add reserved ¼ cup dressing; toss to coat. Arrange on 4 individual plates.

4. Slice each chicken breast half crosswise into slices; do not separate slices. Fan chicken slices; arrange 1 breast half on lettuce mixture on each plate.

Nutrition Information Per Serving: Calories 210 • Total Fat 4g • Saturated Fat 1g • Cholesterol 75mg • Sodium 630mg • Total Carbohydrate 13g • Dietary Fiber 5g • Sugars 8g • Protein 31g. **DIETARY EXCHANGES:** 2½ Vegetable • 4 Very Lean Meat.

banana snack muffins

PREP TIME: 15 MINUTES
READY TO SERVE: 40 MINUTES
SERVINGS: 12 MUFFINS

muffins

- ¾ cup all-purpose flour
- ½ cup whole wheat flour
- 1½ teaspoons baking powder
- ¼ teaspoon salt
- ½ cup sugar
- 3 tablespoons margarine or butter, softened
- ¾ cup (about 1 large) mashed ripe banana
- 1 (8-oz.) container low-fat vanilla yogurt
- 2 egg whites

topping

- 1 tablespoon sugar
- 2 teaspoons finely chopped walnuts
- ¼ teaspoon nutmeg

1. Heat oven to 375°F. Spray bottoms only of 12 muffin cups with cooking spray. In large bowl, combine all-purpose flour, whole wheat flour, baking powder and salt; mix well.

2. In medium bowl, combine ½ cup sugar and margarine; beat at low speed until well blended. Add banana, yogurt and egg whites; beat well. Add to flour mixture; stir with spoon just until dry ingredients are moistened. Divide batter evenly into muffin cups.

3. In small bowl, combine all topping ingredients; mix well. Sprinkle evenly over batter in cups.

4. Bake at 375°F for 20 to 25 minutes or until toothpick inserted in center comes out clean. Immediately remove from pan; cool slightly. Serve warm.

Nutrition Information Per Serving: Calories 150 • Total Fat 4g • Saturated Fat 1g • Cholesterol 0mg • Sodium 160mg • Dietary Fiber 1g. **Dietary Exchanges:** 1½ Starch • ½ Fat OR 1½ Carbohydrate • ½ Fat.

light caesar chicken salad

READY TO SERVE: 25 MINUTES
SERVINGS: 4

* super fast

dressing

- 2 tablespoons grated Parmesan cheese
- 2 tablespoons olive oil
- 2 tablespoons lemon juice
- 2 tablespoons water
- 1 tablespoon reduced-fat sour cream
- 1 teaspoon Worcestershire sauce
- 1 teaspoon Dijon mustard
- ½ teaspoon anchovy paste or ¼ teaspoon salt
- ¼ teaspoon pepper
- 2 garlic cloves, minced

salad

- 4 boneless skinless chicken breast halves
- 1 teaspoon salt-free garlic-herb blend
- 10 cups torn romaine lettuce
- 1 tomato, cut into 8 wedges

1. Heat grill. In medium bowl, combine all dressing ingredients; blend well.

2. Place 1 chicken breast half between 2 pieces of plastic wrap or waxed paper. Working from center, gently pound chicken with flat side of meat mallet or rolling pin until about ¼ inch thick; remove wrap. Repeat with remaining chicken breast halves.

3. When ready to grill, lightly sprinkle both sides of each chicken breast half with herb blend. Place chicken on gas grill over medium heat or on charcoal grill 4 to 6 inches from medium coals. Cook 8 to 10 minutes or until chicken is fork tender and juices run clear, turning once.

4. Meanwhile, in large bowl combine lettuce and dressing; toss to coat. Arrange salad on 4 individual plates.

5. Cut each chicken breast half crosswise into slices; do not separate slices. Fan 1 chicken breast half over lettuce mixture on each plate. Top each salad with 2 tomato wedges.

Nutrition Information Per Serving: Calories 250 • Total Fat 11g • Saturated Fat 3g • Cholesterol 75mg • Sodium 210mg • Total Carbohydrate 7g • Dietary Fiber 4g • Sugars 4g • Protein 31g. **Dietary Exchanges:** 1 Vegetable • 4 Lean Meat.

parmesan herb biscuits

READY TO SERVE: 30 MINUTES
SERVINGS: 12 BISCUITS

2 cups all-purpose flour

¼ cup chopped fresh parsley

3 tablespoons grated Parmesan cheese

1 tablespoon sugar

3 teaspoons baking powder

½ teaspoon salt

½ teaspoon dried sage leaves

¾ to 1 cup half-and-half

1 tablespoon margarine or butter, melted

1. Heat oven to 425°F. In large bowl, combine flour, parsley, 2 tablespoons of the cheese, sugar, baking powder, salt and sage; mix well. Add ¾ cup half-and-half; stir with fork just until dry ingredients are moistened, adding additional half-and-half 1 tablespoon at a time, if necessary to form a soft dough.

2. On floured surface, gently knead dough to form a smooth ball. Pat dough into ½-inch-thick square. Using knife, cut into 12 squares; place on ungreased cookie sheet. Brush with melted margarine; sprinkle with remaining 1 tablespoon cheese.

3. Bake at 425°F for 8 to 14 minutes or until light golden brown. Serve warm.

Nutrition Information Per Serving: Calories 120 • Total Fat 4g • Saturated Fat 2g • Cholesterol 10mg • Sodium 260mg • Dietary Fiber 1g. **Dietary Exchanges:** 1 Starch • 1 Fat OR 1 Carbohydrate • 1 Fat.

mexicali corn muffins

PREP TIME: 10 MINUTES
READY TO SERVE: 35 MINUTES
SERVINGS: 12 MUFFINS

1¼ cups all-purpose flour

¾ cup cornmeal

2 tablespoons sugar

4 teaspoons baking powder

½ teaspoon salt

¾ cup milk

¼ cup sour cream

¼ cup oil

1 egg

1 (4-oz.) can chopped green chiles, drained

1. Heat oven to 400°F. Line 12 muffin cups with paper baking cups or grease. In large bowl, combine flour, cornmeal, sugar, baking powder and salt; mix well.

2. In medium bowl, combine milk, sour cream, oil, egg and chiles; beat well. Add to flour mixture; stir just until dry ingredients are moistened. Fill paper-lined muffin cups ⅔ full.

3. Bake at 400°F for 18 to 22 minutes or until toothpick inserted in center comes out clean. Immediately remove from pan. Serve warm.

Nutrition Information Per Serving: Calories 160 • Total Fat 7g • Saturated Fat 2g • Cholesterol 20mg • Sodium 270mg • Dietary Fiber 1g. **Dietary Exchanges:** 1 Starch • ½ Fruit • 1 Fat OR 1½ Carbohydrate • 1 Fat.

bacon-cheddar pinwheels

PREP TIME: 15 MINUTES
READY TO SERVE: 35 MINUTES
SERVINGS: 16 PINWHEELS

1 (8-oz.) can refrigerated crescent dinner rolls

2 tablespoons ranch dressing

¼ cup cooked real bacon pieces or 4 slices bacon, crisply cooked, crumbled

½ cup finely shredded Cheddar cheese (2 oz.)

¼ cup chopped green onions (4 medium)

1. Heat oven to 350°F. Unroll dough and separate into 2 long rectangles; press each into 12x4-inch rectangle, firmly pressing perforations to seal.

2. Spread dressing over each rectangle to edges. Sprinkle each with bacon, cheese and onions.

3. Starting with one short side, roll up each rectangle; press edge to seal. With serrated knife, cut each roll into 8 slices; place cut side down on ungreased cookie sheet.

4. Bake 12 to 17 minutes or until edges are golden brown. Immediately remove from cookie sheet. Serve warm.

Nutrition Information Per Serving: Calories 80 • Total Fat 6g • Saturated Fat 2g • Trans Fat 1g • Cholesterol 5mg • Sodium 180mg • Total Carbohydrate 6g • Dietary Fiber 0g • Sugars 1g • Protein 2g.

parmesan herb biscuits

quick and easy onion rolls

PREP TIME: 20 MINUTES
READY TO SERVE: 40 MINUTES
SERVINGS: 12 ROLLS

¼ cup finely chopped onion

3 tablespoons chopped pine nuts

3 tablespoons finely chopped sun-dried tomatoes in oil, drained, 1 tablespoon oil reserved

1 tablespoon poppy seed

1 (11-oz.) can refrigerated original breadsticks

¼ cup shredded fresh Parmesan cheese (1 oz.)

1. Heat oven to 375°F. Grease cookie sheet with shortening. In small skillet, cook and stir onion, pine nuts and tomatoes over medium heat 1 to 2 minutes or until onion is tender and nuts are toasted. Remove from heat. Stir in poppy seed.

2. Unroll dough; separate into 2 sections (6 breadsticks each). Spread onion mixture over dough. Reroll dough sections; pinch edges to seal. Cut each section into 6 rolls. Place rolls cut side up on cookie sheet. Brush with reserved 1 tablespoon tomato oil. Sprinkle with cheese.

3. Bake 13 to 17 minutes or until golden brown. Serve warm.

Nutrition Information Per Serving: Calories 110 • Total Fat 5g • Saturated Fat 1g • Cholesterol 0mg • Sodium 230mg • Total Carbohydrate 14g • Dietary Fiber 0g • Sugars 2g • Protein 3g. **Dietary Exchanges:** 1 Starch • 1 Fat.

PINE NUT POINTERS

Pine nuts, also called piñon, pignoli and pignolia are the high-fat nuts found inside the pine cone of several types of pine tree. They have a very tender texture and very mild flavor. Look for them in small bottles in your produce department, but if you can't find them, use slivered almonds instead.

---

waldorf chicken salad

READY TO SERVE: 20 MINUTES
SERVINGS: 4

✳ super fast

dressing

1 (8-oz.) container low-fat plain yogurt

2 tablespoons honey

¼ teaspoon ginger

salad

2 cups cubed cooked chicken

1 cup chopped apple

1 cup seedless red grapes, halved

½ cup thinly sliced celery

½ cup raisins

4 leaves lettuce, if desired

2 tablespoons chopped walnuts

1. In small bowl, combine all dressing ingredients; blend well. In large bowl, combine all salad ingredients except lettuce and walnuts.

2. Pour dressing over salad; toss gently to coat. Arrange lettuce on 4 individual plates. Spoon salad over lettuce; sprinkle with walnuts.

Nutrition Information Per Serving: Calories 350 • Total Fat 9g • Saturated Fat 2g • Cholesterol 65mg • Sodium 115mg • Total Carbohydrate 41g • Dietary Fiber 3g • Sugars 35g • Protein 25g. **Dietary Exchanges:** 2½ Fruit • 3½ Lean Meat OR 2½ Carbohydrate • 3½ Lean Meat.

chicken gazpacho salad

READY TO SERVE: 30 MINUTES
SERVINGS: 4

* meal-in-one

3 tablespoons lemon juice

3 tablespoons olive oil or vegetable oil

1½ teaspoons chopped fresh basil or ½ teaspoon dried basil leaves

¼ teaspoon salt

3 to 4 drops hot pepper sauce

1 garlic clove, minced, or ½ teaspoon chopped garlic in water

3 green onions, sliced

2 medium tomatoes, seeded, chopped

1 small cucumber, halved lengthwise, thinly sliced

1 medium green bell pepper, chopped

4 boneless skinless chicken breast halves

4 cups torn salad greens

1. Heat grill. In medium bowl, combine all ingredients except chicken and salad greens; mix well.

2. Place 1 chicken breast half between 2 pieces of plastic wrap or waxed paper. Working from center, gently pound chicken with flat side of meat mallet or rolling pin until about ¼ inch thick; remove wrap. Repeat with remaining chicken breast halves.

3. When ready to grill, place chicken breast halves on gas grill over medium heat or on charcoal grill 4 to 6 inches from medium coals. Cook 8 to 10 minutes or until chicken is fork tender and juices run clear, turning once. Cut chicken crosswise into ½-inch slices.

4. Arrange greens on 4 individual plates. Stir vegetable mixture. Using slotted spoon, arrange vegetable mixture over greens. Arrange chicken slices over vegetable mixture; spoon liquid from vegetable mixture over chicken.

Nutrition Information Per Serving: Calories 280 • Total Fat 14g • Saturated Fat 2g • Cholesterol 75mg • Sodium 220mg • Total Carbohydrate 9g • Dietary Fiber 3g • Sugars 3g • Protein 29g. **Dietary Exchanges:** 2 Vegetable • 2 Lean Meat • 1 Fat.

bruschetta appetizer tart

PREP TIME: 15 MINUTES
READY TO SERVE: 25 MINUTES
SERVINGS: 16 TARTS

* super fast

1 refrigerated pie crust (from 15-oz. box), softened as directed on box

1 cup chopped plum (Roma) tomatoes

⅓ cup chopped fresh basil leaves

2 teaspoons olive oil

1 clove garlic, finely chopped or ¼ teaspoon garlic powder

½ cup shredded Parmesan cheese (2 oz.)

1. Heat oven to 425°F. Remove crust from pouch; unroll on ungreased cookie sheet. Bake 6 to 8 minutes or until light golden brown.

2. In medium bowl, mix remaining ingredients except cheese. Spread over partially baked crust. Sprinkle with cheese.

3. Bake 7 to 10 minutes longer or until cheese is melted and crust is golden brown. Cut into wedges.

Nutrition Information Per Serving: Calories 80 • Total Fat 5g • Saturated Fat 2g • Cholesterol 0mg • Sodium 110mg • Total Carbohydrate 7g • Dietary Fiber 0g • Sugars 0g • Protein 1g. **Dietary Exchanges:** ½ Starch • 1 Fat.

EASY AS PIE CRUST!

Refrigerated pie crust creates a thin, flaky, crisp crust to hold the traditional bruschetta toppings. Add some flair to the baked tart by scattering small fresh basil leaves over the top, or garnish individual wedges with the basil leaves.

quick tortellini salad

READY TO SERVE: 25 MINUTES
SERVINGS: 3

* **super fast**

dressing

- ⅓ cup olive oil
- 3 tablespoons red wine vinegar
- 1 teaspoon lemon juice
- ½ teaspoon sugar
- ½ teaspoon salt
- ¼ teaspoon garlic powder
- ¼ teaspoon dried oregano leaves

salad

- 1 (9-oz.) pkg. refrigerated cheese-filled tortellini
- 1 cup sliced carrots
- 1½ cups frozen cut green beans
- 2 tablespoons sliced green onions

1. In jar with tight-fitting lid, combine all dressing ingredients; shake well. Set aside.

2. Cook tortellini, carrots and green beans as directed on tortellini package until tortellini is tender and vegetables are crisp-tender. Drain; return to saucepan. Cover with cold water; let stand 5 minutes. Drain well.

3. Place tortellini, carrots and green beans in medium bowl; add onions. Pour dressing over salad; toss gently to coat.

Nutrition Information Per Serving: Calories 450 • Total Fat 24g • Saturated Fat 5g • Cholesterol 40mg • Sodium 720mg • Total Carbohydrate 48g • Dietary Fiber 6g • Sugars 7g • Protein 11g. **Dietary Exchanges:** 3 Starch • 1 Vegetable • 4½ Fat OR 3 Carbohydrate • 1 Vegetable • 4½ Fat.

sweet potato muffins

PREP TIME: 20 MINUTES
READY TO SERVE: 40 MINUTES
SERVINGS: 12 MUFFINS

1½ cups all-purpose flour

½ cup firmly packed brown sugar

2 teaspoons baking powder

1 teaspoon baking soda

1 teaspoon pumpkin pie spice

½ teaspoon salt

2 teaspoons grated orange peel

1 cup mashed canned sweet potatoes (drained, if necessary)

½ cup buttermilk

1 tablespoon molasses

2 eggs

topping

1 tablespoon sugar

¼ teaspoon cinnamon

1. Heat oven to 375°F. Spray 12 muffin cups with cooking spray, or line with paper baking cups and lightly spray paper cups. In large bowl, combine flour, brown sugar, baking powder, baking soda, pumpkin pie spice, salt and orange peel; mix well.

2. In medium bowl, combine all remaining muffin ingredients; blend well. Add to flour mixture; stir just until dry ingredients are moistened. Divide batter evenly into sprayed muffin cups.

3. In small bowl, combine sugar and cinnamon; mix well. Sprinkle evenly over the batter in the cups.

4. Bake at 375°F for 15 to 20 minutes or until toothpick inserted in center comes out clean. Immediately remove from pan. Serve warm.

Nutrition Information Per Serving: Calories 140 • Total Fat 1g • Saturated Fat 0g • Cholesterol 35mg • Sodium 320mg • Dietary Fiber 1g. **Dietary Exchanges:** 1 Starch • 1 Fruit OR 2 Carbohydrate.

french potato salad with green beans

READY TO SERVE: 25 MINUTES
SERVINGS: 6

✳ super fast

salad

6 medium potatoes (about 2 lb.), peeled, sliced

1 (8-oz.) pkg. frozen cut green beans

2 tablespoons chopped red bell pepper

dressing

½ cup dry white wine or chicken broth

¼ cup tarragon vinegar

2 tablespoons chopped fresh parsley

1 tablespoon chopped fresh chives or ¼ cup thinly sliced green onions

1 teaspoon salt

¼ teaspoon pepper

1. In medium saucepan, cook potatoes in boiling water until tender, about 10 minutes. Drain. Cook green beans as directed on package. Drain.

2. Meanwhile, in jar with tight-fitting lid, combine all dressing ingredients; shake well.

3. To serve, spoon warm green beans into center of shallow serving bowl or deep platter. Arrange warm potato slices around beans. Drizzle dressing over vegetables. Sprinkle with bell pepper.

Nutrition Information Per Serving: Calories 120 • Total Fat 0g • Saturated Fat 0g • Cholesterol 0mg • Sodium 360mg • Total Carbohydrate 24g • Dietary Fiber 3g • Sugars 2g • Protein 3g. **Dietary Exchanges:** 1½ Starch OR 1½ Carbohydrate.

FRESH FOR FROZEN

Two cups fresh green beans, cut into 1-inch pieces (about ¾ lb.), can be substituted for the frozen beans in this recipe. Simmer, covered, in a small amount of water for 15 to 20 minutes or until tender.

basil and havarti cheese pinwheels

PREP TIME: 20 MINUTES
READY TO SERVE: 40 MINUTES
SERVINGS: 16 PINWHEELS

1 (8-oz.) can refrigerated crescent dinner rolls

2 tablespoons drained finely chopped sun-dried tomatoes in oil (from 7-oz. jar)

1 (2/3-oz.) pkg. fresh basil leaves (30 to 35 leaves)

1/2 cup shredded Havarti cheese (2 oz.)

1. Heat oven to 350°F. Spray cookie sheet with cooking spray. Unroll dough and separate into 2 long rectangles; press each into 12x4-inch rectangle, firmly pressing perforations to seal.

2. Sprinkle the tomatoes over each rectangle, spreading evenly. Sprinkle each with the basil and cheese.

3. Starting with one short side, roll up each rectangle; press edge to seal. With serrated knife, cut each roll into 8 slices; place cut side down on cookie sheet.

4. Bake 15 to 20 minutes or until edges are golden brown. Immediately remove from cookie sheet. Serve warm.

Nutrition Information Per Serving: Calories 70 • Total Fat 4.5g • Saturated Fat 2g • Trans Fat 1g • Cholesterol 0mg • Sodium 140mg • Total Carbohydrate 6g • Dietary Fiber 0g • Sugars 1g • Protein 2g. **Dietary Exchanges:** 1/2 Starch • 1 Fat.

southern citrus salad

READY TO SERVE: 20 MINUTES
SERVINGS: 8

* super fast

3 cups torn leaf lettuce

3 cups torn iceberg lettuce

2 grapefruit, peeled, sectioned

3 oranges, peeled, sectioned

1 avocado, peeled, pitted and sliced

1/4 cup slivered almonds, toasted if desired

1 cup purchased poppy seed salad dressing

1. In large serving bowl, combine leaf and iceberg lettuce; toss to mix.

2. Arrange grapefruit, oranges, avocado and almonds over greens. Serve with dressing.

Nutrition Information Per Serving: Calories 290 • Total Fat 20g • Saturated Fat 3g • Cholesterol 10mg • Sodium 230mg • Total Carbohydrate 24g • Dietary Fiber 4g • Sugars 17g • Protein 3g. **Dietary Exchanges:** 1 1/2 Fruit • 1 Vegetable • 4 Fat OR 1 1/2 Carbohydrate • 1 Vegetable • 4 Fat.

summer fruit combo

READY TO SERVE: 30 MINUTES
SERVINGS: 16

dressing

1/4 cup frozen lemonade concentrate, thawed

1/4 cup honey

1/2 teaspoon poppy seed

Dash salt

salad

2 cups seedless red grapes, halved

2 cups watermelon cubes

2 medium nectarines or peeled peaches, sliced

2 medium pears, cubed

1. In small jar with tight-fitting lid, combine all dressing ingredients; shake well.

2. In large bowl, combine all salad ingredients. Pour dressing over salad; toss gently to coat.

Nutrition Information Per Serving: Calories 70 • Total Fat 0g • Saturated Fat 0g • Cholesterol 0mg • Sodium 10mg • Total Carbohydrate 17g • Dietary Fiber 1g • Sugars 15g • Protein 1g. **Dietary Exchange:** 1 Fruit OR 1 Carbohydrate.

basil and havarti cheese pinwheels

coleslaw deluxe

READY TO SERVE: 20 MINUTES
SERVINGS: 12

* super fast

salad

6 cups shredded cabbage

1½ cups shredded carrots (3 medium)

½ cup chopped green onions

dressing

1 cup salad dressing or mayonnaise

2 tablespoons cider vinegar

2 tablespoons sugar

1 to 2 tablespoons dill seed, if desired

½ teaspoon salt

1. In large bowl, combine all salad ingredients.

2. In small bowl, combine all dressing ingredients; blend well. Spoon dressing over salad; toss gently. Serve immediately, or cover and refrigerate until serving time.

Nutrition Information Per Serving: Calories 170 • Total Fat 15g • Saturated Fat 2g • Cholesterol 10mg • Sodium 210mg • Total Carbohydrate 7g • Dietary Fiber 2g • Sugars 5g • Protein 1g. **Dietary Exchanges:** 1 Vegetable • 3 Fat.

parmesan-spinach roll-ups

PREP TIME: 20 MINUTES
READY TO SERVE: 45 MINUTES
SERVINGS: 20 ROLL-UPS

1 egg

2 (10.6-oz.) boxes Pillsbury™ refrigerated Parmesan breadsticks

1 (1-lb.) bag Green Giant™ frozen cut leaf spinach, thawed, squeezed to drain

½ cup shredded mozzarella cheese (2 oz.)

1 teaspoon lemon juice

1 tablespoon all-purpose flour

1. Heat oven to 350°F. Lightly spray cookie sheets with cooking spray. In medium bowl, beat egg and contents of both containers of Parmesan spread from breadsticks with wire whisk until well-blended. Stir in spinach, cheese and lemon juice.

2. Sprinkle work surface with flour. Unroll dough onto floured surface; separate into 20 breadsticks. Press or roll each into 7x1½-inch strip.

3. Spread each strip with about 1 tablespoon spinach mixture. Starting with one short side, roll up; pinch end of dough to seal. Place the rolls, cut side up, 3 inches apart on the cookie sheets.

4. Bake 20 to 25 minutes or until golden brown. Serve warm.

Nutrition Information Per Serving: Calories 100 • Total Fat 4g • Saturated Fat 1g • Cholesterol 10 mg • Sodium 310 mg • Total Carbohydrate 13g • Dietary Fiber 0g • Sugars 2g • Protein 4g. **Dietary Exchanges:** 1 Starch • ½ Fat.

waldorf salad

READY TO SERVE: 15 MINUTES
SERVINGS: 8

* super fast

¼ cup chopped nuts

¼ cup chopped dates or raisins

2 tablespoons sugar

4 medium apples, cubed

1 stalk celery, chopped

⅔ cup mayonnaise or salad dressing

1 teaspoon lemon juice

1. In large bowl, combine all ingredients; mix well.

2. Serve immediately, or cover and refrigerate until serving time.

Nutrition Information Per Serving: Calories 230 • Total Fat 17g • Saturated Fat 2g • Cholesterol 10mg • Sodium 110mg • Total Carbohydrate 19g • Dietary Fiber 3g • Sugars 17g • Protein 1g. **Dietary Exchanges:** 1½ Fruit • 3 Fat OR 1½ Carbohydrate • 3 Fat.

garden vegetable drop biscuits

PREP TIME: 15 MINUTES
READY TO SERVE: 35 MINUTES
SERVINGS: 10 BISCUITS

1³⁄₄ cups all-purpose flour

2 teaspoons baking powder

¹⁄₂ teaspoon garlic salt

¹⁄₈ teaspoon pepper

²⁄₃ cup milk

1 (5-oz.) container garden vegetable or herb-flavored soft spreadable cheese

1 egg, beaten

³⁄₄ cup shredded unpeeled zucchini

1. Heat oven to 400°F. Grease cookie sheet. In large bowl, combine flour, baking powder, garlic salt and pepper; mix well.

2. In small bowl, combine milk, cheese and egg; blend well with wire whisk. Stir in zucchini. Add to flour mixture; stir just until dry ingredients are moistened. To form each biscuit, drop ¹⁄₄ cup dough onto greased cookie sheet.

3. Bake at 400°F for 15 to 20 minutes or until golden brown. Serve warm.

Nutrition Information Per Serving: Calories 150 • Total Fat 6g • Saturated Fat 4g • Cholesterol 35mg • Sodium 300mg • Dietary Fiber 1g. **Dietary Exchanges:** 1¹⁄₂ Starch • 1 Fat OR 1¹⁄₂ Carbohydrate • 1 Fat.

apple-cranberry tossed salad

READY TO SERVE: 10 MINUTES
SERVINGS: 12

* super fast

4 cups torn romaine lettuce

¹⁄₄ cup dried cranberries

¹⁄₄ cup chopped walnuts

1 red-skinned apple, unpeeled, cored and cubed

4 green onions, sliced (¹⁄₄ cup)

¹⁄₄ cup orange marmalade

2 tablespoons olive oil

1 tablespoon lemon juice

1. In large bowl, mix lettuce, cranberries, walnuts, apple and onions.

2. In small bowl, mix marmalade, oil and lemon juice until well blended. Drizzle over salad; toss to mix.

FRUITY FIXINGS

Feel free to get creative when preparing the Apple-Cranberry Tossed Salad. Drain a can of mandarin oranges and mix them in with the apple, or leave the apple out altogether and add a cubed pear. The options are endless!

onion rye muffins

PREP TIME: 15 MINUTES
READY TO SERVE: 35 MINUTES
SERVINGS: 12 MUFFINS

³⁄₄ cup chopped onions

¹⁄₂ cup margarine or butter

1¹⁄₄ cups all-purpose flour

³⁄₄ cup medium rye flour

2 tablespoons sugar

3 teaspoons baking powder

³⁄₄ teaspoon salt

¹⁄₂ teaspoon caraway seed, crushed

¹⁄₂ cup milk

2 eggs

1. Heat oven to 400°F. Line 12 muffin cups with paper baking cups or grease. In small skillet, cook onions in margarine until tender. Set aside.

2. In large bowl, combine all-purpose flour, rye flour, sugar, baking powder, salt and caraway seed; mix well. Add milk, eggs and cooked onions; stir just until dry ingredients are moistened. Fill paper-lined muffin cups ²⁄₃ full.

3. Bake at 400°F for 15 to 20 minutes or until toothpick inserted in center comes out clean. Immediately remove from pan. Serve warm.

Nutrition Information Per Serving: Calories 170 • Total Fat 9g • Saturated Fat 2g • Cholesterol 35mg • Sodium 360mg • Dietary Fiber 1g. **Dietary Exchanges:** 1 Starch • 1/2 Fruit • 1¹⁄₂ Fat OR 1¹⁄₂ Carbohydrate • 1¹⁄₂ Fat.

southwest salsa cornbread

PREP TIME: 10 MINUTES
READY TO SERVE: 35 MINUTES
SERVINGS: 12

1¼ cups all-purpose flour

¾ cup cornmeal

2 teaspoons baking powder

¼ teaspoon salt

1 cup frozen whole kernel corn or 7-oz. can vacuum-packed whole kernel corn, drained

¾ cup skim milk

½ cup chunky style salsa

3 tablespoons oil

1 egg

1. Heat oven to 400°F. Spray 9-inch square pan with cooking spray.

2. In large bowl, combine flour, cornmeal, baking powder and salt; mix well. Add all remaining ingredients; stir just until dry ingredients are moistened. Spoon batter evenly into sprayed pan.

3. Bake at 400°F for 18 to 23 minutes or until toothpick inserted in center comes out clean. Cut into squares. Serve warm.

Nutrition Information Per Serving: Calories 130 • Total Fat 4g • Saturated Fat 1g • Cholesterol 20mg • Sodium 220mg • Dietary Fiber 1g. **Dietary Exchanges:** 1½ Starch • ½ Fat OR 1½ Carbohydrate • ½ Fat.

rosemary-bell pepper bread

PREP TIME: 10 MINUTES
READY TO SERVE: 35 MINUTES
SERVINGS: 12

1¾ cups all-purpose flour

1½ teaspoons baking powder

½ teaspoon baking soda

¼ teaspoon salt

2 tablespoons margarine or butter

⅔ cup skim milk

½ cup chopped red, yellow or green bell pepper

1 teaspoon chopped fresh rosemary or ½ teaspoon dried rosemary leaves, crushed

1 egg or 2 egg whites

2 tablespoons grated Parmesan cheese

1. Heat oven to 400°F. Spray 8 or 9-inch round cake pan with cooking spray. In large bowl, combine flour, baking powder, baking soda and salt; mix well. With pastry blender or fork, cut in margarine until well mixed.

2. Stir in milk, bell pepper, rosemary and egg until soft dough forms. Spread dough evenly in sprayed pan. Sprinkle with Parmesan cheese.

3. Bake at 400°F for 16 to 22 minutes or until center is firm to the touch and cheese is golden brown. Cut into wedges. Serve warm or cool.

Nutrition Information Per Serving: Calories 100 • Total Fat 3g • Saturated Fat 1g • Cholesterol 20mg • Sodium 210mg • Dietary Fiber 1g. **Dietary Exchanges:** 1 Starch • ½ Fat OR 1 Carbohydrate • ½ Fat.

jalapeño corn biscuits

READY TO SERVE: 25 MINUTES
SERVINGS: 18 BISCUITS

✳ super fast

1½ cups all-purpose flour

¾ cup cornmeal

3 teaspoons baking powder

¼ teaspoon salt

½ cup shortening

1 cup milk

4 oz. shredded Monterey Jack cheese with jalapeño chiles (1 cup)

1. Heat oven to 450°F. Grease 2 cookie sheets. In large bowl, combine flour, cornmeal, baking powder and salt; mix well. With pastry blender or fork, cut in shortening until mixture resembles coarse crumbs.

2. Add milk and cheese; stir just until dry ingredients are moistened. Drop dough by generous tablespoonfuls onto greased cookie sheets.

3. Bake at 450°F for 8 to 12 minutes or until light golden brown. Serve warm.

Nutrition Information Per Serving: Calories 130 • Total Fat 8g • Saturated Fat 3g • Cholesterol 5mg • Sodium 180mg • Dietary Fiber 1g. **Dietary Exchanges:** ½ Starch • 2 Fat OR ½ Carbohydrate • 2 Fat.

rosemary-bell pepper bread
southwest salsa cornbread

cheesy corn muffins

PREP TIME: 10 MINUTES
READY TO SERVE: 35 MINUTES
SERVINGS: 12 MUFFINS

1½ cups all-purpose flour

½ cup yellow cornmeal

¼ cup sugar

3 teaspoons baking powder

¼ teaspoon salt

1 cup milk

¼ cup oil

1 egg, slightly beaten

1 cup frozen whole kernel corn or 7-oz. can vacuum-packed whole kernel corn, drained

4 oz. shredded Cheddar cheese (1 cup)

1. Heat oven to 400°F. Grease bottoms only of 12 muffin cups. In medium bowl, combine flour, cornmeal, sugar, baking powder and salt; blend well.

2. Add milk, oil and egg; stir just until dry ingredients are moistened. Fold in corn and cheese. Divide batter evenly into greased muffin cups.

3. Bake at 400°F for 20 to 25 minutes or until golden brown. Immediately remove from pan. Serve warm.

Nutrition Information Per Serving: Calories 210 • Total Fat 9g • Saturated Fat 3g • Cholesterol 30mg • Sodium 240mg • Dietary Fiber 1g. **Dietary Exchanges:** 1½ Starch • 2 Fat OR 1½ Carbohydrate • 2 Fat.

sugar-crusted sweet potato biscuits

PREP TIME: 15 MINUTES
READY TO SERVE: 35 MINUTES
SERVINGS: 12 BISCUITS

2 cups all-purpose flour

3 teaspoons baking powder

1/2 teaspoon salt

4 tablespoons brown sugar

3 tablespoons shortening

2/3 cup skim milk

1/2 cup mashed canned or cooked sweet potato

1/3 cup light sour cream

1. Heat oven to 400°F. Spray cookie sheet with cooking spray.

2. In medium bowl, combine flour, baking powder, salt and 2 tablespoons of the brown sugar; mix well. With pastry blender or fork, cut in shortening until mixture is crumbly.

3. In small bowl, combine milk, sweet potato and sour cream; blend well. Add to flour mixture all at once; stir just until dry ingredients are moistened. (If dough is too dry, add additional milk 1 teaspoon at a time, until all dry ingredients are moistened.) To form each biscuit, drop 1/4 cup dough onto sprayed cookie sheet. Sprinkle with remaining 2 tablespoons brown sugar.

4. Bake at 400°F for 15 to 20 minutes or until peaks and bottoms of biscuits are golden brown. Serve warm.

Nutrition Information Per Serving: Calories 150 • Total Fat 4g • Saturated Fat 1g • Cholesterol 2mg • Sodium 230mg • Dietary Fiber 1g. **Dietary Exchanges:** 1 Starch • 1/2 Fruit • 1 Fat OR 1 1/2 Carbohydrate • 1 Fat.

couscous chicken salad

PREP TIME: 20 MINUTES
READY TO SERVE: 1 HOUR 40 MINUTES
SERVINGS: 7

* plan ahead

salad

1 cup uncooked couscous

2 cups shredded cooked chicken

1 cup chopped green bell pepper

1 cup sliced celery

1/2 cup shredded carrot

2 green onions, sliced

dressing

1/3 cup orange juice

1/3 cup oil

1/4 cup chopped fresh parsley

2 tablespoons lemon juice

2 tablespoons soy sauce

1 teaspoon finely chopped gingerroot or 1/4 teaspoon ground ginger

Dash salt

1/8 teaspoon pepper

1. Cook couscous as directed on package. Uncover; cool 20 minutes.

2. In large bowl, combine couscous and all remaining salad ingredients; toss gently.

3. In small jar with tight-fitting lid, combine all dressing ingredients; shake well. Pour dressing over salad; toss gently. Cover; refrigerate 1 to 2 hours to blend flavors. If desired, serve on lettuce-lined plates.

Nutrition Information Per Serving: Calories 290 • Total Fat 14g • Saturated Fat 2g • Cholesterol 35mg • Sodium 370mg • Total Carbohydrate 25g • Dietary Fiber 2g • Sugars 3g • Protein 16g. **Dietary Exchanges:** 1 Starch • 2 Vegetable • 1 1/2 Lean Meat • 2 Fat OR 1 Carbohydrate • 2 Vegetable • 1 1/2 Lean Meat • 2 Fat.

MEET COUSCOUS

Couscous is a North African staple pasta that strongly resembles grain. It is available in a quick-to-prepare version that cooks in just 5 minutes. If you prefer, you can use rice instead of couscous in this chicken salad recipe. Just cook the rice according to the package directions.

tomato-basil dinner bread

PREP TIME: 10 MINUTES
READY TO SERVE: 40 MINUTES
SERVINGS: 12

2 cups all-purpose flour
1½ teaspoons baking powder
½ teaspoon baking soda
¼ teaspoon salt
1 cup chopped Italian plum tomatoes (3 medium)
¾ cup plain yogurt
¼ cup chopped fresh basil
2 tablespoons margarine or butter, softened
1 egg

1. Heat oven to 400°F. Spray 9-inch round cake pan with cooking spray. In large bowl, combine flour, baking powder, baking soda and salt; mix well.

2. In small bowl, combine tomatoes, yogurt, basil, margarine and egg; blend well. Add to flour mixture; stir just until dry ingredients are moistened. Spoon dough evenly into sprayed pan.

3. Bake at 400°F for 22 to 28 minutes or until bread is golden brown and center is firm to the touch. Cut into wedges. Serve warm.

Nutrition Information Per Serving: Calories 120 • Total Fat 3g • Saturated Fat 1g • Cholesterol 20mg • Sodium 200mg • Dietary Fiber 1g. Dietary Exchanges: 1 Starch • 1/2 Fat OR 1 Carbohydrate • 1/2 Fat.

wilted spinach salad

READY TO SERVE: 25 MINUTES
SERVINGS: 6

* super fast

2 eggs
6 cups torn fresh spinach
2 tablespoons chopped green onions
3 slices bacon, cut into ½-inch pieces
¼ cup cider vinegar
2 teaspoons sugar
¼ teaspoon salt
¼ teaspoon dry mustard
⅛ teaspoon pepper

1. Place eggs in small saucepan; cover with cold water. Bring to a boil. Reduce heat; simmer about 15 minutes. Immediately drain; run cold water over eggs to stop cooking. Peel eggs; chop.

2. In large bowl, combine spinach, onions and eggs. Set aside.

3. In small skillet, cook bacon until crisp. Add all remaining ingredients; heat until sugar is dissolved. Pour over spinach mixture; toss gently. Serve immediately.

Nutrition Information Per Serving: Calories 60 • Total Fat 3g • Saturated Fat 1g • Cholesterol 75mg • Sodium 210mg • Total Carbohydrate 4g • Dietary Fiber 2g • Sugars 2g • Protein 5g. Dietary Exchanges: 1 Vegetable • 1/2 Medium-Fat Meat.

carrot and herb dinner biscuits

READY TO SERVE: 25 MINUTES
SERVINGS: 12 BISCUITS

* super fast

1¼ cups all-purpose flour
¾ cup cornmeal
¼ cup sugar
3 teaspoons baking powder
1 teaspoon dried basil leaves
1 teaspoon dried parsley flakes
½ teaspoon salt
¾ cup margarine or butter
½ cup shredded carrot
⅓ cup milk
1 egg, slightly beaten

1. Heat oven to 400°F. In medium bowl, combine flour, cornmeal, sugar, baking powder, basil, parsley flakes and salt; mix well. With pastry blender or fork, cut in margarine until mixture resembles coarse crumbs. Stir in carrot.

2. Add milk and egg; stir just until dry ingredients are moistened. To form each biscuit, drop ¼ cup of dough onto ungreased cookie sheet.

3. Bake at 400°F for 12 to 14 minutes or until light golden brown. Serve warm.

Nutrition Information Per Serving: Calories 200 • Total Fat 12g • Saturated Fat 2g • Cholesterol 20mg • Sodium 360mg • Dietary Fiber 1g. Dietary Exchanges: 1 Starch • 1/2 Fruit • 2 Fat OR 1 1/2 Carbohydrate • 2 Fat.

mini focaccia rounds

PREP TIME: 10 MINUTES
READY TO SERVE: 25 MINUTES
SERVINGS: 8

* super fast

1 (11-oz.) can refrigerated original breadsticks

2 tablespoons olive or vegetable oil

1 tablespoon grated Parmesan cheese

1 teaspoon dried rosemary leaves, crushed

1 teaspoon dried basil leaves

1 teaspoon instant dried minced or chopped onion

1. Heat oven to 375°F. Lightly grease cookie sheets with shortening. Remove dough from can. Separate into 8 coils. Do not unroll breadsticks. Place coils on cookie sheets. Press each coil into 4-inch round. Drizzle with oil.

2. In small bowl, mix cheese, rosemary, basil and onion; sprinkle over dough.

3. Bake 8 to 15 minutes or until golden brown.

Nutrition Information Per Serving: Calories 140 • Total Fat 6g • Saturated Fat 1g • Cholesterol 0mg • Sodium 290mg • Total Carbohydrate 19g • Dietary Fiber 0g • Sugars 2g • Protein 3g. **Dietary Exchanges:** 1 Starch • 1/2 Other Carbohydrate • 1 Fat.

summer fruit and chicken salad

READY TO SERVE: 15 MINUTES
SERVINGS: 4

* super fast

dressing

1/2 cup low-fat raspberry yogurt

1/4 cup mayonnaise or salad dressing

2 tablespoons honey

salad

4 leaves leaf lettuce

1/2 lb. thinly sliced cooked chicken

1/2 medium cantaloupe, seeds removed, peeled, cut into very thin slices

1 cup fresh raspberries

1/2 cup fresh blueberries

1. In small bowl, combine all dressing ingredients; blend well. Refrigerate until serving time.

2. To serve, arrange lettuce on large platter or on 4 individual plates. Arrange chicken, cantaloupe, raspberries and blueberries over lettuce. Drizzle with dressing.

Nutrition Information Per Serving: Calories 300 • Total Fat 13g • Saturated Fat 2g • Cholesterol 35mg • Sodium 590mg • Total Carbohydrate 31g • Dietary Fiber 4g • Sugars 28g • Protein 14g. **Dietary Exchanges:** 2 Fruit • 2 Lean Meat • 1 1/2 Fat OR 2 Carbohydrate • 2 Lean Meat • 1 1/2 Fat.

spoon bread

PREP TIME: 25 MINUTES
READY TO SERVE: 1 HOUR 15 MINUTES
SERVINGS: 8

2 cups water

1 cup white cornmeal

1 teaspoon seasoned salt

1 cup buttermilk

2 tablespoons margarine or butter, melted

2 teaspoons baking powder

3 eggs, separated

1. Heat oven to 375°F. Grease 2-quart casserole. In medium saucepan, bring water to a boil. Slowly stir in cornmeal and salt. Reduce heat to medium; cook about 5 minutes or until very thick, stirring constantly. Remove from heat; stir in buttermilk. Cool 5 minutes.

2. Gradually beat in 2 tablespoons margarine, baking powder and egg yolks. In small bowl, beat egg whites until stiff but not dry. Fold into cornmeal mixture. Pour batter into greased casserole.

3. Bake at 375°F for 40 to 50 minutes or until bread is golden brown and knife inserted near center comes out clean. Serve immediately with margarine, if desired.

Nutrition Information Per Serving: Calories 130 • Total Fat 6g • Saturated Fat 1g • Cholesterol 80mg • Sodium 410mg • Dietary Fiber 1g. **Dietary Exchanges:** 1 Starch • 1 Fat OR 1 Carbohydrate • 1 Fat.

cheddar-pepper cornbread

PREP TIME: 15 MINUTES
READY TO SERVE: 40 MINUTES
SERVINGS: 12

- 1 cup all-purpose flour
- 1 cup yellow cornmeal
- 3 teaspoons baking powder
- ½ teaspoon salt
- ½ teaspoon cumin
- 1 cup skim milk
- ¼ cup honey
- ¼ cup nonfat plain yogurt
- 3 egg whites
- ½ cup chopped red bell pepper
- 4 oz. shredded Cheddar cheese (1 cup)

1. Heat oven to 425°F. Spray 9-inch square pan with cooking spray. In large bowl, combine flour, cornmeal, baking powder, salt and cumin; mix well.

2. In medium bowl, combine milk, honey, yogurt and egg whites; blend well. Stir in bell pepper and ½ cup of the cheese. Add to flour mixture; stir just until dry ingredients are moistened. (Batter will be lumpy.) Pour into sprayed pan. Sprinkle with remaining ½ cup cheese.

3. Bake at 425°F for 18 to 22 minutes or until toothpick inserted in center comes out clean. Cut into squares. Serve warm.

Nutrition Information Per Serving: Calories 160 • Total Fat 4g • Saturated Fat 2g • Cholesterol 10mg • Sodium 300mg • Dietary Fiber 1g. **Dietary Exchanges:** 1½ Starch • 1 Fat OR 1½ Carbohydrate • 1 Fat.

CORNBREAD ACCOMPANIMENTS

Serve savory cornbread squares with chili and a tossed salad. Leftover cornbread can be crumbled and used in place of bread crumbs or oatmeal in your favorite meat loaf, meatballs or poultry dressing.

summer squash bread with lemon and dill

PREP TIME: 15 MINUTES
READY TO SERVE: 45 MINUTES
SERVINGS: 1 (18-SLICE) LOAF

- 2½ cups all-purpose flour
- 2 tablespoons chopped fresh dill or 2 teaspoons dried dill weed
- 2 teaspoons grated lemon peel
- 1 teaspoon baking soda
- ½ teaspoon baking powder
- ¼ teaspoon salt
- 2 tablespoons margarine or butter
- 1 cup skim milk
- ½ cup finely shredded yellow summer squash or zucchini
- 1 tablespoon skim milk

1. Heat oven to 400°F. Spray cookie sheet with cooking spray. In large bowl, combine flour, dill, lemon peel, baking soda, baking powder and salt; mix well. With pastry blender or fork, cut in margarine until well mixed.

2. Stir in 1 cup milk and squash until mixture forms a stiff dough. With sprayed hands, shape dough into a 7-inch round on sprayed cookie sheet. Brush top with 1 tablespoon milk.

3. Bake at 400°F for 20 to 30 minutes or until golden brown. Cut into slices. Serve warm or cool.

Nutrition Information Per Serving: Calories 70 • Total Fat 1g • Saturated Fat 0g • Cholesterol 0mg • Sodium 135mg • Dietary Fiber 1g. **Dietary Exchanges:** 1 Starch OR 1 Carbohydrate.

spicy sweet potato bread

READY TO SERVE: 30 MINUTES
SERVINGS: 12

½ cup sugar

½ cup mashed canned or cooked sweet potatoes

⅓ cup milk

1 tablespoon oil

1 egg

1 cup all-purpose flour

2 teaspoons baking powder

¼ teaspoon nutmeg

¼ teaspoon allspice

½ cup dried currants

1. Heat oven to 400°F. Spray 8- or 9-inch square pan with cooking spray.

2. In large bowl, combine sugar and sweet potatoes; blend well. Add milk, oil and egg; mix well. Add flour, baking powder, nutmeg and allspice; stir just until dry ingredients are moistened. Stir in currants. Pour batter into sprayed pan.

3. Bake at 400°F for 12 to 19 minutes or until bread is light golden brown and center is firm to the touch. Cut into squares. Serve warm or cool.

Nutrition Information Per Serving: Calories 120 • Total Fat 2g • Saturated Fat 0g • Cholesterol 20mg • Sodium 95mg • Dietary Fiber 1g. **Dietary Exchanges:** 1 Starch • ½ Fruit OR 1½ Carbohydrate.

seven-layer vegetable salad

PREP TIME: 20 MINUTES
READY TO SERVE: 4 HOURS 20 MINUTES
SERVINGS: 12

✱ plan ahead

½ lb. sliced bacon

3 cups torn iceberg lettuce

3 cups torn romaine lettuce

1 cup mayonnaise or salad dressing

4 teaspoons sugar

1 (1-lb.) pkg. frozen sweet peas, cooked, drained

½ cup sliced green onions

½ cup sliced celery

6 oz. shredded Cheddar cheese (1½ cups)

1. Cook bacon until crisp. Drain; set aside.

2. In 13x9-inch (3-quart) baking dish, toss iceberg and romaine lettuce. Spread with ½ cup of the mayonnaise; sprinkle with 2 teaspoons of the sugar.

3. Layer with peas, onions and celery. Spread with remaining ½ cup mayonnaise; sprinkle with remaining 2 teaspoons sugar. Sprinkle with cheese. Cover; refrigerate at least 4 hours or overnight.

4. Just before serving, crumble bacon; sprinkle over top.

Nutrition Information Per Serving: Calories 260 • Total Fat 22g • Saturated Fat 6g • Cholesterol 30 mg • Sodium 330mg • Total Carbohydrate 8g • Dietary Fiber 2g • Sugars 5g • Protein 8g. **Dietary Exchanges:** 1 Vegetable • 1 High-Fat Meat • 3 Fat.

banana-blueberry mini-loaves

PREP TIME: 15 MINUTES
READY TO SERVE: 1 HOUR 40 MINUTES
SERVINGS: 3 (12-SLICE) LOAVES

✱ plan ahead

1 cup sugar

½ cup oil

1 cup (2 medium) mashed ripe bananas

½ cup low-fat plain yogurt

1 teaspoon vanilla

2 eggs

2 cups all-purpose flour

1 teaspoon baking soda

½ teaspoon salt

1 cup fresh or frozen blueberries (do not thaw)

1. Heat oven to 350°F. Grease and flour bottoms only of three 6x3½-inch loaf pans. In large bowl, combine sugar and oil; beat well. Add bananas, yogurt, vanilla and eggs; blend well.

2. Add flour, baking soda and salt; stir just until dry ingredients are moistened. Gently stir in blueberries. Pour into greased and floured pans.

3. Bake at 350°F for 40 to 50 minutes or until toothpick inserted in center comes out clean. Cool 5 minutes; remove from pans. Cool 30 minutes or until completely cooled. Wrap tightly and store in refrigerator.

Nutrition Information Per Serving: Calories 80 • Total Fat 3g • Saturated Fat 1g • Cholesterol 10mg • Sodium 70mg • Dietary Fiber 0g. **Dietary Exchanges:** ½ Starch • ½ Fruit • ½ Fat OR 1 Carbohydrate • ½ Fat.

chicken and spinach salad with orange dressing

READY TO SERVE: 25 MINUTES
SERVINGS: 4

* super fast

1 (10-oz.) pkg. prewashed fresh spinach, torn

1/2 cup orange juice

3 tablespoons brown sugar

3 tablespoons vinegar

1 teaspoon grated orange peel

1/8 teaspoon salt

2 medium shallots, minced

4 boneless skinless chicken breast halves

1/4 teaspoon black and red pepper blend or black pepper

6 orange slices, halved

1 1/2 cups fresh strawberry halves

1. Heat grill. Place spinach in large bowl. In small saucepan, combine orange juice, brown sugar, vinegar, orange peel, salt and shallots; mix well. Bring to a boil over medium heat, stirring occasionally. Immediately pour over spinach; toss to combine. Arrange on 4 individual plates.

2. Place 1 chicken breast half between 2 pieces of plastic wrap or waxed paper. Working from center, gently pound chicken with flat side of meat mallet or rolling pin until about 1/4 inch thick; remove wrap. Repeat with remaining chicken breast halves.

3. When ready to grill, sprinkle 1 side of each chicken breast half with 1/8 teaspoon of the pepper blend. Place chicken, peppered side down, on gas grill over medium heat or on charcoal grill 4 to 6 inches from medium coals. Cook 5 minutes. Sprinkle chicken with remaining pepper blend; turn chicken. Cook an additional 3 to 5 minutes or until chicken is fork tender and juices run clear.

4. Cut chicken breasts crosswise into slices; do not separate slices. Fan 1 chicken breast half over spinach mixture on each plate. Arrange orange slices and strawberries around chicken.

Nutrition Information Per Serving: Calories 260 • Total Fat 4g • Saturated Fat 1g • Cholesterol 75mg • Sodium 190mg • Total Carbohydrate 25g • Dietary Fiber 4g • Sugars 19g • Protein 30g. **Dietary Exchanges:** 1 1/2 Fruit • 1 Vegetable • 4 Very Lean Meat OR 1 1/2 Carbohydrate • 1 Vegetable • 4 Very Lean Meat.

irish soda bread

PREP TIME: 15 MINUTES
READY TO SERVE: 1 HOUR
SERVINGS: 1 (16-SLICE) LOAF

2 1/4 cups all-purpose flour

2 tablespoons sugar

1 teaspoon baking powder

1 teaspoon baking soda

1/2 teaspoon salt

1/4 cup margarine or butter

1/2 cup raisins

2 teaspoons caraway seed, if desired

1 cup buttermilk

1 tablespoon margarine or butter, melted

1. Heat oven to 375°F. Grease 8-inch round cake pan. In large bowl, combine flour, sugar, baking powder, baking soda and salt; blend well. With pastry blender or fork, cut in 1/4 cup margarine until mixture is crumbly. Stir in raisins and caraway seed. Add milk all at once; blend well.

2. On well-floured surface, knead dough 5 or 6 times or until no longer sticky. Press dough in greased pan. With sharp knife, cut an "X" 1/4 inch deep on top of loaf. Brush with melted margarine.

3. Bake at 375°F for 25 to 35 minutes or until golden brown. Immediately remove from pan. Cool on wire rack for 10 minutes. Serve warm.

Nutrition Information Per Serving: Calories 130 • Total Fat 4g • Saturated Fat 1g • Cholesterol 0mg • Sodium 230mg • Dietary Fiber 1g. **Dietary Exchanges:** 1 1/2 Starch • 1/2 Fat OR 1 1/2 Carbohydrate • 1/2 Fat.

chicken and spinach salad with orange dressing

chicken, corn and black bean salad

READY TO SERVE: 20 MINUTES
SERVINGS: 5

* super fast

dressing

- ½ cup apricot preserves (chop large pieces)
- ¼ cup lime juice
- 1 tablespoon oil
- 1 teaspoon chili powder
- ⅛ to ¼ teaspoon ground red pepper (cayenne)

salad

- 2 cups cubed cooked chicken
- 1 medium red or green bell pepper, chopped
- 2 cups frozen whole kernel corn, thawed
- 1 (15-oz.) can black beans, drained, rinsed
- 5 to 6 leaves Boston lettuce

1. In small bowl, combine all dressing ingredients; blend well.

2. In large bowl, combine all salad ingredients except lettuce. Add dressing; blend well. Arrange lettuce on 5 individual plates. Spoon salad over lettuce.

Nutrition Information Per Serving: Calories 360 • Total Fat 8g • Saturated Fat 2g • Cholesterol 50mg • Sodium 75mg • Total Carbohydrate 50g • Dietary Fiber 7g • Sugars 19g • Protein 23g. **Dietary Exchanges:** 2 Starch • 1 Fruit • 1 Vegetable • 2 Lean Meat • ½ Fat OR 3 Carbohydrate • 1 Vegetable • 2 Lean Meat • ½ Fat.

chicken wild rice salad

PREP TIME: 15 MINUTES
READY TO SERVE: 3 HOURS 30 MINUTES
SERVINGS: 6

* plan ahead

- 1 cup uncooked wild rice
- ½ cup salad dressing or mayonnaise
- ⅓ cup sour cream
- ½ teaspoon salt
- ¼ teaspoon dried marjoram leaves, crushed
- ⅛ teaspoon white pepper
- 2 cups cubed cooked chicken
- ½ cup diagonally sliced celery
- ½ cup chopped red bell pepper
- ½ cup sliced fresh mushrooms
- ¼ cup diagonally sliced green onions
- 6 leaves lettuce
- 1 large tomato, cut into wedges
- ¼ cup slivered almonds, toasted

1. Cook wild rice according to package directions. Drain; refrigerate 30 minutes or until chilled.

2. Meanwhile, in small bowl combine salad dressing, sour cream, salt, marjoram and pepper; blend well.

3. In large bowl, combine cooked rice, chicken, celery, bell pepper, mushrooms and green onions. Add mayonnaise mixture; toss gently. Cover; refrigerate 2 to 3 hours to blend flavors.

4. Arrange lettuce on 4 individual plates. Spoon salad over lettuce. Garnish with tomato wedges and toasted almonds.

Nutrition Information Per Serving: Calories 330 • Total Fat 16g • Saturated Fat 4g • Cholesterol 55mg • Sodium 380mg • Total Carbohydrate 27g • Dietary Fiber 3g • Sugars 6g • Protein 19g. **Dietary Exchanges:** 2 Starch • 2 Very Lean Meat • 2 Fat OR 2 Carbohydrate • 2 Very Lean Meat • 2 Fat.

LIGHTEN IT UP!

To lower the fat by 3 grams per serving in this recipe, substitute nonfat sour cream or nonfat plain yogurt for the sour cream.

lemony fruit salad

PREP TIME: 25 MINUTES
READY TO SERVE: 1 HOUR 10 MINUTES
SERVINGS: 20

1 (2.9-oz.) pkg. lemon pudding and pie filling mix (not instant)

½ cup sugar

¼ cup water

2 egg yolks

2 cups water

1 cup whipping cream, whipped

1 (29-oz.) can sliced peaches, drained

1 (20-oz.) can pineapple chunks, drained

1 (16-oz.) can mandarin orange segments, drained

1 (16-oz.) can sliced pears, drained

1. In medium saucepan, combine pudding mix, sugar and ¼ cup water. Stir in egg yolks. Add 2 cups water; mix well. Cook over medium heat until mixture comes to a full boil, stirring constantly. Cool about 45 minutes or until completely cooled, stirring occasionally.

2. Fold in whipped cream. Gently fold in drained fruits. Serve immediately, or cover and refrigerate several hours or overnight.

Nutrition Information Per Serving: Calories 120 • Total Fat 5g • Saturated Fat 3g • Cholesterol 40mg • Sodium 30mg • Total Carbohydrate 18g • Dietary Fiber 1g • Sugars 16g • Protein 1g. **Dietary Exchanges:** 1 Fruit • 1 Fat OR 1 Carbohydrate • 1 Fat.

pumpernickel muffins

PREP TIME: 15 MINUTES
READY TO SERVE: 35 MINUTES
SERVINGS: 12 MUFFINS

1 cup all-purpose flour

1 cup medium rye flour

⅓ cup firmly packed dark brown or regular brown sugar

2 tablespoons unsweetened cocoa

3 teaspoons baking powder

½ teaspoon salt

½ cup raisins, if desired

½ teaspoon caraway seed, if desired

1¼ cups buttermilk

¼ cup oil

1 tablespoon molasses

1 egg, beaten

1. Heat oven to 400°F. Grease bottoms only of 12 muffin cups or line with paper baking cups. In medium bowl, combine all-purpose flour, rye flour, brown sugar, cocoa, baking powder, salt, raisins and caraway seed; mix well.

2. In small bowl, combine buttermilk, oil, molasses and egg; blend well. Add to flour mixture; stir just until dry ingredients are moistened. Fill greased muffin cups ¾ full.

3. Bake at 400°F for 15 to 20 minutes or until toothpick inserted in center comes out clean. Cool 1 minute; remove from pan. Serve warm.

Nutrition Information Per Serving: Calories 190 • Total Fat 6g • Saturated Fat 1g • Cholesterol 20mg • Sodium 250mg • Dietary Fiber 2g. **Dietary Exchanges:** 1½ Starch • ½ Fruit • 1 Fat OR 2 Carbohydrate • 1 Fat.

tuscan panzanella salad

READY TO SERVE: 25 MINUTES
SERVINGS: 6

* **super fast**

3 cups cubed dry (day-old) Italian bread

¼ cup balsamic vinegar

2 teaspoons olive oil

⅛ teaspoon coarse ground black pepper

2 medium tomatoes, seeded, diced

2 medium cucumbers, halved, seeded and chopped

1 red bell pepper, chopped

¼ cup sliced ripe olives

¼ cup thinly sliced fresh basil leaves

1. Heat oven to 350°F. Place bread cubes on ungreased cookie sheet. Toast bread at 350°F for 5 to 10 minutes or until lightly browned.

2. Meanwhile, in small bowl, combine vinegar, oil and pepper; blend well.

3. In large bowl, combine tomatoes, cucumbers, bell pepper, olives and toasted bread cubes. Pour vinegar mixture over salad; toss gently to coat. Sprinkle with basil.

Nutrition Information Per Serving: Calories 100 • Total Fat 3g • Saturated Fat 0g • Cholesterol 0mg • Sodium 160mg • Total Carbohydrate 14g • Dietary Fiber 2g • Sugars 4g • Protein 3g. **Dietary Exchanges:** ½ Starch • 1 Vegetable • ½ Fat OR ½ Carbohydrate • 1 Vegetable • ½ Fat.

brown bread muffin gems

PREP TIME: 10 MINUTES
READY TO SERVE: 35 MINUTES
SERVINGS: 12 MUFFINS

1½ cups whole wheat flour
½ cup cornmeal
½ cup chopped dates, if desired
⅓ cup sugar
¼ cup chopped nuts
1 teaspoon baking soda
½ teaspoon salt
1 cup buttermilk
¼ cup molasses

1. Heat oven to 375°F. Grease bottoms only of 12 muffin cups. In medium bowl, combine flour, cornmeal, dates, sugar, nuts, baking soda and salt; mix well.

2. Add buttermilk and molasses; stir just until dry ingredients are moistened. Fill greased muffin cups about ¾ full.

3. Bake at 375°F for 16 to 25 minutes or until toothpick inserted in center comes out clean. Cool 1 minute; remove from pan. Serve warm.

Nutrition Information Per Serving: Calories 160 • Total Fat 2g • Saturated Fat 0g • Cholesterol 0mg • Sodium 220mg • Dietary Fiber 3g. **Dietary Exchanges:** 1 Starch • 1 Fruit • ½ Fat OR 2 Carbohydrate • ½ Fat.

german potato salad

READY TO SERVE: 25 MINUTES
SERVINGS: 8

✳ **super fast**

2 lb. small new red potatoes (10 to 16)
4 slices bacon
½ cup chopped onion
¼ cup sugar
2 tablespoons all-purpose flour
½ teaspoon salt
Dash pepper
1 cup water
⅓ cup vinegar
Fresh parsley, if desired

1. In medium saucepan, cook potatoes in boiling water for 15 to 20 minutes or until tender. Drain. Peel potatoes; slice.

2. Meanwhile, in large skillet, cook bacon until crisp. Remove bacon from skillet; drain on paper towels. Reserve 2 tablespoons drippings in skillet. Add onion; cook and stir until crisp-tender.

3. Add sugar, flour, salt and pepper; blend well. Gradually add water and vinegar. Cook over medium-high heat until bubbly and thickened, stirring constantly.

4. Stir in potatoes; cook until thoroughly heated. Crumble bacon; sprinkle over top. Garnish with parsley.

Nutrition Information Per Serving: Calories 160 • Total Fat 5g • Saturated Fat 2g • Cholesterol 5mg • Sodium 190mg • Total Carbohydrate 25g • Dietary Fiber 2g • Sugars 7g • Protein 3g. **Dietary Exchanges:** 1 Starch • ½ Fruit • 1 Fat OR 1½ Carbohydrate • 1 Fat.

strawberry mini-muffins

PREP TIME: 15 MINUTES
READY TO SERVE: 40 MINUTES
SERVINGS: 36 MINI-MUFFINS

2 cups all-purpose flour
½ cup sugar
3 teaspoons baking powder
½ teaspoon salt
¾ cup milk
⅓ cup oil
1 egg
1 cup chopped fresh strawberries
2 tablespoons sugar

1. Heat oven to 375°F. Spray 36 miniature muffin cups with cooking spray. In large bowl, combine flour, ½ cup sugar, baking powder and salt; mix well.

2. In small bowl, combine milk, oil and egg; blend well. Add to flour mixture; stir just until dry ingredients are moistened. Gently stir in strawberries. Spoon rounded tablespoonful batter into each sprayed muffin cup. Sprinkle 2 tablespoons sugar evenly over batter in cups.

3. Bake for 12 to 16 minutes or until edges are light golden brown and toothpick inserted in center comes out clean. Cool 3 minutes; remove from pan. Serve warm.

Nutrition Information Per Serving: Calories 60 • Total Fat 2g • Saturated Fat 0g • Cholesterol 5mg • Sodium 75mg • Dietary Fiber 0g. **Dietary Exchanges:** ½ Starch • ½ Fat OR ½ Carbohydrate • ½ Fat.

cobb salad

READY TO SERVE: 45 MINUTES
SERVINGS: 6

* meal-in-one

1½ cups cubed cooked chicken

2 eggs, hard-cooked, coarsely chopped

6 slices bacon, crisply cooked, crumbled

4 cups torn salad greens

1 large tomato, chopped

¼ cup sliced green onions

1 avocado, peeled, sliced or cubed, tossed in lemon juice

4 oz. crumbled blue cheese (1 cup)

½ to 1 cup purchased fat-free or reduced-calorie thousand island salad dressing

1. On large serving platter or in 13x9-inch (3-quart) baking dish, arrange all ingredients except dressing in rows.

2. Or, arrange each serving on lettuce-lined plate. Serve salad with dressing or spoon dressing over each salad.

Nutrition Information Per Serving: Calories 320 • Total Fat 18g • Saturated Fat 7g • Cholesterol 120mg • Sodium 850mg • Total Carbohydrate 19g • Dietary Fiber 4g • Sugars 11g • Protein 20g. **Dietary Exchanges:** 1 Starch • 1 Vegetable • 2 Lean Meat • 2½ Fat OR 1 Carbohydrate • 1 Vegetable • 2 Lean Meat • 2½ Fat.

perfect popovers

PREP TIME: 10 MINUTES
READY TO SERVE: 1 HOUR
SERVINGS: 10 POPOVERS

3 eggs, room temperature

1¼ cups milk, room temperature

1¼ cups all-purpose flour

¼ teaspoon salt

1. Heat oven to 450°F. Generously grease 10 popover cups or 6-oz. custard cups. In small bowl, beat eggs with eggbeater or wire whisk until lemon-colored and foamy. Add milk; blend well. Add flour and salt; beat with eggbeater just until batter is smooth and foamy on top. Pour batter into greased cups, filling about ⅔ full.

2. Bake at 450°F for 15 minutes. (Do not open oven.) Reduce oven temperature to 350°F; bake an additional 25 to 35 minutes or until popovers are high, hollow and deep golden brown. Remove from oven; insert sharp knife into each popover to allow steam to escape. Remove from cups. Serve warm.

Nutrition Information Per Serving: Calories 90 • Total Fat 2g • Saturated Fat 1g • Cholesterol 65mg • Sodium 90mg • Dietary Fiber 0g. **Dietary Exchanges:** 1 Starch • ½ Fat OR 1 Carbohydrate • ½ Fat.

cucumbers in sour cream

PREP TIME: 15 MINUTES
READY TO SERVE: 45 MINUTES
SERVINGS: 8

4 medium cucumbers, sliced

1½ teaspoons salt

¾ cup white vinegar

¾ cup water

1 cup sour cream

1 teaspoon chopped fresh dill or ¼ teaspoon dill weed

1 teaspoon sugar

Dash pepper

1. Place cucumbers in medium bowl; sprinkle with salt. Add vinegar and water; stir. Let stand 30 minutes, stirring occasionally. Drain well; return to bowl.

2. In small bowl, combine sour cream, dill, sugar and pepper; blend well. Add to cucumbers; mix gently. Serve immediately, or cover and refrigerate until serving time.

Nutrition Information Per Serving: Calories 70 • Total Fat 6g • Saturated Fat 4g • Cholesterol 15mg • Sodium 420mg • Total Carbohydrate 4g • Dietary Fiber 0g • Sugars 3g • Protein 1g. **Dietary Exchanges:** 1 Vegetable • 1 Fat.

cobb salad

asian noodle and vegetable salad

PREP TIME: 25 MINUTES
READY TO SERVE   1 HOUR 25 MINUTES
SERVINGS: 6

salad

- 1 (1-lb.) pkg. frozen broccoli, carrots and water chestnuts
- 3 cups shredded cabbage
- ¼ cup sliced green onions

dressing

- 2 tablespoons oil
- 1 tablespoon cider vinegar
- 4 teaspoons sugar
- 1 (3-oz.) pkg. oriental-flavor instant ramen noodle soup mix
- 1 tablespoon sesame seed, toasted

1. Cook vegetables as directed on package until crisp-tender. Drain; rinse with cold water to cool. In large bowl, combine vegetables, cabbage and onions.

2. In small jar with tight-fitting lid, combine oil, vinegar, sugar and seasoning packet from soup mix; shake well. Pour over vegetable mixture; toss to coat. Cover; refrigerate at least 1 hour to blend flavors.

3. Just before serving, break noodles into pieces. Add noodle pieces and sesame seed to salad; toss to combine.

Nutrition Information Per Serving: Calories 160 • Total Fat 8g • Saturated Fat 2g • Cholesterol 0mg • Sodium 330mg • Total Carbohydrate 19g • Dietary Fiber 3g • Sugars 7g • Protein 4g. **Dietary Exchanges:** ½ Starch • 2 Vegetable • 1½ Fat OR ½ Carbohydrate • 2 Vegetable • 1½ Fat.

savory biscuit monkey bread

PREP TIME: 15 MINUTES
READY TO SERVE: 55 MINUTES
SERVINGS: 10

- ¼ cup margarine or butter, melted
- ½ teaspoon dry mustard
- 1 garlic clove, minced, or ¼ teaspoon garlic powder
- 1 (12-oz.) can Pillsbury® Golden Layers™ Refrigerated Buttermilk Biscuits (10 biscuits)
- ¼ cup grated Parmesan cheese

1. Heat oven to 400°F. In small bowl, combine margarine, dry mustard and garlic; mix well. Coat bottom of 8- or 9-inch round cake pan with 2 tablespoons of the margarine mixture.

2. Separate dough into 10 biscuits; cut each into quarters. Arrange biscuit pieces evenly in prepared pan. Drizzle reserved margarine mixture over biscuit pieces. Sprinkle with cheese.

3. Bake at 400°F for 30 to 40 minutes or until golden brown. Invert bread onto wire rack; invert again onto serving plate. Serve warm.

Nutrition Information Per Serving: Calories 235 • Total Fat 13g • Saturated Fat 3g • Cholesterol 0mg • Sodium 710mg • Total Carbohydrate 25g • Dietary Fiber 1g • Sugars 7g • Protein 5g. **Dietary Exchanges:** 1½ Starch • 2½ Fat OR 1½ Carbohydrate • 2½ Fat.

tangy carrot-raisin salad

READY TO SERVE: 20 MINUTES
SERVINGS: 7

* super fast

- 3 cups shredded carrots
- 1 cup raisins
- 3 tablespoons oil
- 2 tablespoons honey
- 2 tablespoons lemon juice
- ¼ teaspoon salt
- ⅛ teaspoon nutmeg

1. In medium bowl, combine carrots and raisins.

2. In small bowl, combine all remaining ingredients; mix well. Pour over carrot mixture; toss until well blended. Serve immediately, or cover and refrigerate until serving time.

Nutrition Information Per Serving: Calories 170 • Total Fat 6g • Saturated Fat 1g • Cholesterol 0mg • Sodium 95mg • Total Carbohydrate 29g • Dietary Fiber 2g • Sugars 23g • Protein 1g. **Dietary Exchanges:** 2 Fruit • ½ Vegetable • 1 Fat OR 2 Carbohydrate • ½ Vegetable • 1 Fat.

orange-carrot bread

PREP TIME: 20 MINUTES
READY TO SERVE: 40 MINUTES
SERVINGS: 12

bread

¾ cup finely shredded carrots

½ cup sugar

¼ cup orange juice

1 tablespoon oil

1 egg or 2 egg whites

¾ cup all-purpose flour

2 teaspoons baking powder

topping

2 tablespoons sugar

1 tablespoon orange peel

1. Heat oven to 400°F. Spray 8- or 9-inch round cake pan with cooking spray. In large bowl, combine carrots, ½ cup sugar, orange juice, oil and egg; mix well.

2. Add flour and baking powder; stir just until combined. Pour into sprayed pan.

3. In small bowl, combine topping ingredients; mix well. Sprinkle evenly over batter.

4. Bake at 400°F for 14 to 19 minutes or until bread is golden brown and springs back when touched lightly in center. Cut into wedges. Serve warm or cool.

Nutrition Information Per Serving: Calories 90 • Total Fat 2g • Saturated Fat 0g • Cholesterol 20mg • Sodium 90mg • Dietary Fiber 0g. **Dietary Exchanges:** 1 Starch OR 1 Carbohydrate.

refrigerated fruit salad

PREP TIME: 10 MINUTES
READY TO SERVE: 4 HOURS 10 MINUTES
SERVINGS: 12

* plan ahead

1 (21-oz.) can peach pie filling

1 (20-oz.) can pineapple chunks in unsweetened juice, drained

1 (11-oz.) can mandarin orange segments, drained

1 cup seedless red grapes, halved, or 1 cup fresh blueberries

1 cup miniature marshmallows

2 bananas, sliced

1. In large bowl, combine all ingredients; mix well.

2. Cover; refrigerate at least 4 hours or overnight.

Nutrition Information Per Serving: Calories 110 • Total Fat 0g • Saturated Fat 0g • Cholesterol 0mg • Sodium 10 mg • Total Carbohydrate 27g • Dietary Fiber 2g • Sugars 22g • Protein 1g. **Dietary Exchanges:** 2 Fruit OR 2 Carbohydrate.

gorgonzola cheese biscuits

READY TO SERVE: 35 MINUTES
SERVINGS: 18 BISCUITS

2 cups all-purpose flour

3 teaspoons baking powder

½ teaspoon sugar

¼ teaspoon salt

¼ teaspoon baking soda

¼ teaspoon nutmeg

⅓ cup margarine or butter

4 oz. crumbled gorgonzola cheese

¾ to 1 cup buttermilk

1. Heat oven to 425°F. Grease cookie sheet. In large bowl, combine flour, baking powder, sugar, salt, baking soda and nutmeg; mix well. With pastry blender or fork, cut in margarine and cheese until mixture resembles coarse crumbs.

2. Add ¾ cup buttermilk; stir with fork until mixture leaves sides of bowl and forms a soft, moist dough, adding additional buttermilk if necessary.

3. On floured surface, toss dough lightly until no longer sticky. Roll out to ½-inch thickness; cut with floured 2-inch round cutter. Place on greased cookie sheet with sides touching.

4. Bake at 425°F for 10 to 15 minutes or until light golden brown. Serve warm.

Nutrition Information Per Serving: Calories 110 • Total Fat 5g • Saturated Fat 2g • Cholesterol 5mg • Sodium 270mg • Dietary Fiber 0g. **Dietary Exchanges:** 1 Starch • ½ Fat OR 1 Carbohydrate • ½ Fat.

beef & ground beef

picadillo wraps * p.129

wrapped tenderloin with gravy * p. 124

pan-broiled steak * p. 114

easy beef pot pie * p. 119

beef stew casserole ✳ p. 131

beef and bean burritos

READY TO SERVE: 25 MINUTES
SERVINGS: 10 BURRITOS

✳ super fast

1 lb. ground beef

1 medium onion, chopped

1 cup refried beans (from 16-oz. can)

¼ cup taco sauce

1½ teaspoons chili powder

½ teaspoon salt

¼ teaspoon pepper

10 (7- or 8-inch) flour tortillas, heated

1 cup shredded lettuce

4 oz. shredded Cheddar cheese (1 cup)

1 tomato, chopped

½ cup salsa, if desired

1. In large skillet, combine ground beef and onion; cook over medium heat for 8 to 10 minutes or until beef is thoroughly cooked, stirring frequently. Drain.

2. Stir in beans, taco sauce, chili powder, salt and pepper; mix well. Reduce heat to low; simmer 5 minutes.

3. Spoon about ¼ cup beef mixture onto center of each tortilla. Top each with lettuce, cheese and tomato. Fold bottom ⅓ of each tortilla over filling; fold sides in toward center, leaving top open. Serve with salsa.

Nutrition Information Per Serving: Calories 290 • Total Fat 13g • Saturated Fat 5g • Cholesterol 40mg • Sodium 580mg • Total Carbohydrate 27g • Dietary Fiber 3g • Sugars 3g • Protein 15g. **Dietary Exchanges:** 2 Starch • 1½ Medium-Fat Meat • 0 Fat OR 2 Carbohydrate • 1 Medium-Fat Meat • 0 Fat.

parmesan chicken-fried steak

READY TO SERVE: 30 MINUTES
SERVINGS: 4

steak

⅓ cup all-purpose flour

½ teaspoon salt

½ teaspoon garlic powder

¼ teaspoon pepper

⅓ cup milk

⅓ cup unseasoned dry bread crumbs

⅓ cup grated Parmesan cheese

½ teaspoon dried oregano leaves

1 lb. boneless beef round steak (½ inch thick), cut into 4 pieces

3 tablespoons oil

gravy

1 tablespoon butter

1 tablespoon all-purpose flour

1 cup half-and-half or milk

¼ teaspoon salt

¼ teaspoon coarse ground black pepper

1. In shallow dish, combine ⅓ cup flour, ½ teaspoon salt, garlic powder and ¼ teaspoon pepper; mix well. Place milk in second shallow dish. In third shallow dish, combine bread crumbs, cheese and oregano; mix well.

2. Place 1 steak piece between 2 pieces of plastic wrap or waxed paper. Working from center, pound steak pieces with flat side of meat mallet or rolling pin until about ¼ inch thick; remove wrap. Repeat with remaining steak pieces. Dip each in flour mixture to coat. Dip in milk; dip in bread crumb mixture to coat.

3. Heat oil in large skillet over medium heat until hot. Add steak; cook 10 to 15 minutes or until tender, turning once. Remove steak from skillet; cover to keep warm.

4. To make gravy, melt butter in same skillet. With wire whisk, stir in 1 tablespoon flour; cook until light brown. Add all remaining gravy ingredients; cook and stir over medium heat until bubbly and thickened. Serve gravy over steak.

Nutrition Information Per Serving: Calories 450 • Total Fat 28g • Saturated Fat 11g • Cholesterol 95mg • Sodium 700mg • Total Carbohydrate 20g • Dietary Fiber 1g • Sugars 4g • Protein 30g. **Dietary Exchanges:** 1 Starch • 3½ Lean Meat • 3 Fat OR 1 Carbohydrate • 3 Lean Meat • 3 Fat.

mexican beef 'n bean pizza

READY TO SERVE: 35 MINUTES
SERVINGS: 6

✳ meal-in-one

1 (10-oz.) can Pillsbury®
Refrigerated Pizza Crust

½ lb. lean ground beef

¼ teaspoon salt

⅛ teaspoon pepper

1 (16-oz.) can refried beans

1 cup taco sauce or chunky-
style salsa

1 (11-oz.) can vacuum-packed
whole kernel corn with red
and green peppers, well
drained

4 oz. shredded Cheddar
cheese (1 cup)

1 cup shredded lettuce

1 medium tomato, chopped

½ cup sliced green onions, if
desired

1. Heat oven to 400°F. Grease 12-inch pizza pan. Unroll dough; place in greased pan. Starting at center, press out dough to edge of pan. Bake at 400°F for 9 to 11 minutes or until crust begins to brown.

2. Meanwhile, in medium skillet, brown ground beef with salt and pepper over medium-high heat for 5 to 7 minutes or until thoroughly cooked, stirring frequently. Drain.

3. Remove partially baked crust from oven. Spread refried beans evenly over crust. Spread 1/2 cup of the taco sauce over beans. Top with ground beef mixture, corn and cheese.

4. Return to oven; bake an additional 12 to 15 minutes or until crust is golden brown and cheese is melted. Top with lettuce, tomatoes and green onions. Serve with remaining 1/2 cup taco sauce.

Nutrition Information Per Serving: Calories 410 • Total Fat 14g • Saturated Fat 6g • Cholesterol 45mg • Sodium 1460mg • Total Carbohydrate 49g • Dietary Fiber 7g • Sugars 10g • Protein 21g. **Dietary Exchanges:** 3 Starch • 1 Vegetable • 1½ Medium-Fat Meat • 1 Fat OR 3 Carbohydrate • 1 Vegetable • 1½ Medium-Fat Meat • 1 Fat.

pepper steaks with blackberry glaze

READY TO SERVE: 25 MINUTES
SERVINGS: 4

✳ **super fast**

glaze
½ cup blackberry jam

¼ cup red wine vinegar

steaks
3 teaspoons coarse ground black pepper

4 (4-oz.) boneless beef strip steaks

½ cup fresh or frozen blackberries, thawed

1. Heat grill. In small saucepan, combine jam and vinegar. Cook over medium heat until jam is melted, stirring constantly. Remove from heat.

2. Rub pepper on both sides of each steak. When ready to grill, place steaks on gas grill over medium heat or on charcoal grill 4 to 6 inches from medium-high coals. Cook 8 to 12 minutes or until of desired doneness, turning once.

3. To serve, spread steaks with glaze; top with berries.

Nutrition Information Per Serving: Calories 250 • Total Fat 4g • Saturated Fat 1g • Cholesterol 60mg • Sodium 45mg • Total Carbohydrate 30g • Dietary Fiber 2g • Sugars 21g • Protein 24g. **Dietary Exchanges:** 2 Fruit • 3 Very Lean Meat OR 2 Carbohydrate • 3 Very Lean Meat.

veal parmigiana with vermicelli

PREP TIME: 30 MINUTES
READY TO SERVE: 1 HOUR
SERVINGS: 6

* meal-in-one

parmigiana

- 6 veal cutlets (¼ inch thick)
- ½ cup grated Parmesan cheese
- ¼ cup unseasoned dry bread crumbs
- ½ teaspoon dried oregano leaves
- ¼ teaspoon pepper
- ¼ cup all-purpose flour
- 2 eggs, slightly beaten
- 2 to 3 tablespoons oil
- 1 (2.5-oz.) jar sliced mushrooms, drained
- 1 (28-oz.) jar spaghetti sauce

vermicelli

- 8 oz. uncooked vermicelli or spaghetti
- 1 to 2 tablespoons butter
- ¼ cup grated Parmesan cheese, if desired
- 4 oz. shredded mozzarella cheese (1 cup)

1. Place 1 veal cutlet between 2 pieces of plastic wrap or waxed paper. Working from center, gently pound cutlet with flat side of meat mallet or rolling pin until about ⅛ inch thick; remove wrap. Repeat with remaining cutlets.

2. Heat oven to 350°F. In pie pan or shallow dish, combine ½ cup Parmesan cheese, bread crumbs, oregano and pepper; mix well. Coat each cutlet with flour; dip in eggs. Coat with Parmesan cheese mixture.

3. Heat oil in large skillet over medium-high heat until hot. Add cutlets; cook 6 to 7 minutes or until golden brown on both sides. Remove from skillet. Arrange cutlets in ungreased 13x9-inch (3-quart) baking dish; sprinkle with mushrooms. Spoon spaghetti sauce over mushrooms. Bake at 350°F for 25 to 30 minutes or until bubbly.

4. Meanwhile, cook vermicelli to desired doneness as directed on package. Drain; toss with butter and ¼ cup Parmesan cheese. Cover to keep warm.

5. Remove baking dish from oven; sprinkle veal with mozzarella cheese. Serve veal over vermicelli.

Nutrition Information Per Serving: Calories 610 • Total Fat 26g • Saturated Fat 10g • Cholesterol 195mg • Sodium 1030mg • Total Carbohydrate 48g • Dietary Fiber 4g • Sugars 2g • Protein 46g. Dietary Exchanges: 3 Starch • 5 Medium-Fat Meat OR 3 Carbohydrate • 5 Medium-Fat Meat.

cheeseburger foldovers

PREP TIME: 20 MINUTES
READY TO SERVE: 45 MINUTES
SERVINGS: 8

- ¾ lb. lean ground beef
- ½ cup chopped onion
- 2 tablespoons ketchup
- 1 tablespoon prepared mustard
- 1 (16.3-oz.) can Pillsbury® Grands!® Refrigerated Flaky Biscuits
- 4 oz. shredded Cheddar and American cheese blend (1 cup)
- 16 dill pickle slices
- 1 egg, beaten
- 1 teaspoon sesame seed, if desired

1. Heat oven to 375°F. In large skillet, cook ground beef and onion over medium-high heat for 5 to 7 minutes or until beef is thoroughly cooked, stirring frequently. Drain. Stir in ketchup and mustard.

2. Separate dough into 8 biscuits. On ungreased large cookie sheet, press or roll each biscuit to form 6-inch round. Spoon beef mixture onto one side of each biscuit. Sprinkle each with cheese. Top each with 2 pickles. Fold dough in half over filling; press edges with fork to seal. Make 2 or 3 small slits in top of each for steam to escape. Brush each with beaten egg. Sprinkle with sesame seed.

3. Bake at 375°F for 18 to 22 minutes or until deep golden brown.

Nutrition Information Per Serving: Calories 360 • Total Fat 20g • Saturated Fat 7g • Cholesterol 65mg • Sodium 980mg • Total Carbohydrate 28g • Dietary Fiber 1g • Sugars 5g • Protein 16g. Dietary Exchanges: 2 Starch • 1½ Medium-Fat Meat • 2 Fat OR 2 Carbohydrate • 1½ Medium-Fat Meat • 2 Fat.

beef and spinach deep-dish pizza

PREP TIME: 25 MINUTES
READY TO SERVE: 1 HOUR 15 MINUTES
SERVINGS: 8

* meal-in-one

- 1 (9-oz.) pkg. frozen spinach in a pouch
- 1 lb. lean ground beef
- 1 small onion, chopped
- 1 (8-oz.) can pizza sauce
- 1 (11-oz.) can Pillsbury® Refrigerated Crusty French Loaf
- 4 oz. sliced pepperoni
- 8 oz. shredded Italian cheese blend (2 cups)
- 1 egg
- 1 teaspoon olive oil

1. Heat oven to 350°F. Spray 9½-inch deep-dish glass pie pan with cooking spray. Cook spinach as directed on package. Drain well; set aside to cool.

2. Meanwhile, in medium skillet, cook ground beef and onion over medium-high heat for 5 to 7 minutes or until beef is thoroughly cooked, stirring frequently. Drain. Stir in pizza sauce until well mixed.

3. Carefully unroll dough. Place in sprayed pie pan so edges extend over sides of pan. Pat dough in bottom and up sides of pan, leaving dough extended over sides. Spoon ground beef mixture into crust. Top with pepperoni slices and half of the cheese.

4. Squeeze spinach to remove moisture. Slightly beat egg in small bowl. Add spinach; mix well. Spoon spinach mixture over cheese. Top with remaining half of cheese.

5. Fold extended edges of dough up and over filling; seal all edges. Cut several slits in top for steam to escape. Brush crust with oil.

6. Bake at 350°F for 38 to 48 minutes or until deep golden brown. Let stand 10 minutes before serving.

Nutrition Information Per Serving: Calories 425 • Total Fat 26g • Saturated Fat 11g • Cholesterol 95mg • Sodium 960mg • Total Carbohydrate 24g • Dietary Fiber 2g • Sugars 2g • Protein 26g. **Dietary Exchanges:** 1½ Starch • 3 High-Fat Meat OR 1½ Carbohydrate • 3 High-Fat Meat.

italian spaghetti with meat sauce

READY TO SERVE: 40 MINUTES
SERVINGS: 8

* meal-in-one

- 1 (16-oz.) pkg. uncooked spaghetti
- 1 lb. extra-lean ground beef
- 1 cup chopped onions
- 1 cup sliced fresh mushrooms
- ½ cup chopped green bell pepper
- 2 garlic cloves, minced
- 2 (6-oz.) cans tomato paste
- 1 (15-oz.) can tomato sauce
- 2 cups water
- 3 teaspoons dried parsley flakes
- 3 teaspoons dried Italian seasoning
- 1½ teaspoons dried basil leaves
- ½ teaspoon sugar
- ½ teaspoon pepper
- ¾ teaspoon Worcestershire sauce
- ¼ cup grated Parmesan cheese, if desired

1. Cook spaghetti to desired doneness as directed on package. Drain; cover to keep warm.

2. Meanwhile, spray large skillet with cooking spray. Heat over medium heat until hot. Add ground beef, onions, mushrooms, bell pepper and garlic; cook 8 to 10 minutes or until beef is thoroughly cooked, stirring frequently. Drain well.

3. Stir in tomato paste and tomato sauce; mix well. Gradually stir in water. Stir in parsley, Italian seasoning, basil, sugar, pepper and Worcestershire sauce. Bring to a boil. Reduce heat to low; cover and simmer 15 minutes, stirring occasionally.

4. Serve sauce over spaghetti; sprinkle with Parmesan cheese.

Nutrition Information Per Serving: Calories 400 • Total Fat 9g • Saturated Fat 3g • Cholesterol 40mg • Sodium 760mg • Total Carbohydrate 58g • Dietary Fiber 5g • Sugars 6g • Protein 22g. **Dietary Exchanges:** 3 Starch • 2 Vegetable • 1 Lean Meat • ½ Fat OR 3 Carbohydrate • 2 Vegetable • 1 Lean Meat • 0 Fat.

beef and spinach deep-dish pizza

pan-broiled steak smothered in mushrooms

READY TO SERVE: 30 MINUTES
SERVINGS: 4

1 tablespoon olive or vegetable oil

4 (4-oz.) beef tenderloin steaks

¼ teaspoon salt

¼ teaspoon coarse ground black pepper

1 tablespoon butter

2 large shallots, minced

1 (8-oz.) pkg. sliced fresh mushrooms (3 cups)

¼ cup red wine

¼ cup beef broth

1. Heat oil in large skillet over medium-high heat until hot. Add steaks; sprinkle with salt and pepper. Cook steaks until of desired doneness, turning once. Remove steaks from skillet; cover to keep warm.

2. Add butter and shallots to skillet; cook and stir until shallots are tender. Add mushrooms and wine; cook 3 to 5 minutes, stirring occasionally. Add broth; cook until thoroughly heated. Serve over steaks.

Nutrition Information Per Serving: Calories 230 • Total Fat 14g • Saturated Fat 5g • Cholesterol 60mg • Sodium 250mg • Total Carbohydrate 4g • Dietary Fiber 1g • Sugars 1g • Protein 19g. **Dietary Exchanges:** 1 Vegetable • 2 Medium-Fat Meat • 1 Fat.

beef with chili rub and sour cream

READY TO SERVE: 25 MINUTES
SERVINGS: 4

* super fast

- 2 tablespoons chili powder
- 3 teaspoons dried oregano leaves
- 1 teaspoon cumin
- 1/2 teaspoon salt
- 1/2 teaspoon pepper
- 1/4 teaspoon onion powder
- 1/4 teaspoon ground red pepper (cayenne)
- 1 lb. boneless beef top sirloin steak (1/2 to 3/4 inch thick)
- 1/4 cup sour cream

1. Heat grill. In small bowl, combine all ingredients except beef and sour cream; mix well. Brush both sides of beef with water. Sprinkle seasoning mixture over both sides; with fingers, rub into beef.

2. When ready to grill, place beef on gas grill over medium-high heat or on charcoal grill 4 to 6 inches from medium-high coals; cover grill. Cook 9 to 12 minutes or until beef is of desired doneness, turning once. Let stand 5 minutes before serving.

3. To serve, cut beef diagonally into thin slices. Top each serving with 1 tablespoon sour cream.

Nutrition Information Per Serving: Calories 190 • Total Fat 9g • Saturated Fat 4g • Cholesterol 65mg • Sodium 360mg • Total Carbohydrate 4g • Dietary Fiber 2g • Sugars 1g • Protein 22g. **Dietary Exchanges:** 1 Vegetable • 3 Lean Meat.

grilled steak with charred sweet onions

PREP TIME: 25 MINUTES
READY TO SERVE: 40 MINUTES
SERVINGS: 4

1. In small bowl, combine all steak ingredients except steak; mix well. Place steak in shallow glass dish or resealable food storage plastic bag. Pour oil mixture over steak; turn steak to coat. Cover dish or seal bag. Let stand at room temperature for 15 to 30 minutes to marinate.

2. Meanwhile, heat grill. Brush onions lightly with 1 tablespoon oil; sprinkle with paprika.

3. When ready to grill, if desired, sprinkle steak with salt and pepper. (Steak can be cut into 4 servings before grilling, if desired.) Place steak and onions on gas grill over medium heat or on charcoal grill 4 to 6 inches from medium coals. Cook 10 to 15 minutes or until steak is of desired doneness and onions are tender, turning once.

Nutrition Information Per Serving: Calories 190 • Total Fat 9g • Saturated Fat 2g • Cholesterol 60mg • Sodium 65mg • Total Carbohydrate 5g • Dietary Fiber 1g • Sugars 3g • Protein 21g. **Dietary Exchanges:** 1 Vegetable • 3 Lean Meat.

steak

- 2 tablespoons Worcestershire sauce
- 1 tablespoon olive or vegetable oil
- 1 teaspoon dried thyme leaves
- 1 teaspoon dried rosemary leaves
- 1 large garlic clove, minced
- 1 lb. boneless beef sirloin steak (3/4 inch thick)

onions

- 2 sweet onions, cut into 1/2-inch-thick slices
- 1 tablespoon olive or vegetable oil
- 1/2 teaspoon paprika

SOME LIKE IT RARE

While pink-centered burgers are a food safety hazard, a rare steak will likely be all right. That's because a solid cut of meat, such as a steak or roast, is essentially sterile on the inside. Grinding and mixing beef, on the other hand, can contaminate the whole batch with surface bacteria.

Check the doneness of relatively thin cuts of beef, such as steak, by cutting into the center with a steak knife. The meat can be slightly pink if you like rare or medium, but it should not appear translucent or raw in the middle. For roasts, check the temperature with a meat thermometer.

swedish meatball and biscuit casserole

PREP TIME: 15 MINUTES
READY TO SERVE: 45 MINUTES
SERVINGS: 4

* meal-in-one

1 (12-oz.) pkg. frozen Swedish-style meatballs, thawed

1 (12-oz.) jar beef gravy

1 (4.5-oz.) jar sliced mushrooms, drained

1/2 cup frozen pearl onions, thawed

1/2 cup sour cream

2 teaspoons Worcestershire sauce

4 Pillsbury® Home Baked Classics™ Frozen Buttermilk Biscuits (from 25-oz. pkg.)

1 tablespoon chopped fresh parsley, if desired

1. Heat oven to 375°F. Spray 8-inch square (2-quart) glass baking dish with cooking spray.

2. In medium saucepan, combine all ingredients except biscuits and parsley; mix well. Cook over medium-high heat for 5 to 8 minutes or until mixture is bubbly and thoroughly heated, stirring frequently. Pour mixture into sprayed baking dish. Arrange frozen biscuits over top.

3. Bake at 375°F for 25 to 30 minutes or until biscuits are deep golden brown and filling is bubbly. Serve meatball mixture over biscuits. Sprinkle each serving with parsley.

Nutrition Information Per Serving: Calories 535 • Total Fat 31g • Saturated Fat 13g • Cholesterol 115mg • Sodium 1720mg • Total Carbohydrate 40g • Dietary Fiber 2g • Sugars 7g • Protein 26g. **Dietary Exchanges:** 2 Starch • 1/2 Fruit • 3 High-Fat Meat • 1 Fat OR 2 1/2 Carbohydrate • 3 High-Fat Meat • 1 Fat.

FROM-SCRATCH MEATBALLS

Want to prepare Swedish Meatball and Biscuit Casserole but don't happen to have a package of frozen meatballs on hand? Use your favorite meatball recipe instead! Add a little bit of ground allspice or nutmeg with the salt and pepper your recipe calls for.

You can also use just about any meat loaf recipe you like. Simply add the seasonings and shape the meat mixture into balls instead of putting it in a loaf pan. Cook the meatballs, then add them to the gravy as noted in Step 2 of the recipe above.

---

main dish spanish rice

PREP TIME: 20 MINUTES
READY TO SERVE: 1 HOUR
SERVINGS: 5

* meal-in-one

1 lb. ground beef

6 slices bacon, cut into small pieces

1 medium onion, thinly sliced

1/4 cup chopped green bell pepper

3/4 cup uncooked regular long-grain white rice

1/4 cup ketchup

1 (14.5 to 16-oz.) can whole tomatoes, undrained, cut up

1 (8-oz.) can tomato sauce

1/2 teaspoon salt

1/8 teaspoon pepper

2 drops hot pepper sauce

1. In large skillet, cook ground beef over medium heat for 8 to 10 minutes or until thoroughly cooked, stirring frequently. Drain well. Remove beef from skillet; set aside.

2. In same skillet, cook bacon until crisp. Remove bacon; drain on paper towel, reserving 2 tablespoons drippings in skillet.

3. Add onion and bell pepper to reserved drippings in skillet; cook and stir until crisp-tender. Add cooked ground beef, bacon and all remaining ingredients; mix well. Bring to a boil. Reduce heat to low; cover and simmer 30 to 40 minutes or until rice is tender.

Nutrition Information Per Serving: Calories 380 • Total Fat 17g • Saturated Fat 6g • Cholesterol 60mg • Sodium 940mg • Total Carbohydrate 35g • Dietary Fiber 3g • Sugars 6g • Protein 21g. **Dietary Exchanges:** 2 Starch • 1 Vegetable • 2 Medium-Fat Meat • 1 Fat OR 2 Carbohydrate • 1 Vegetable • 2 Medium-Fat Meat • 1 Fat.

beef pepper steak casserole

PREP TIME: 25 MINUTES
READY TO SERVE: 45 MINUTES
SERVINGS: 6

* meal-in-one

- 2 tablespoons oil
- 1 medium green bell pepper, cut into bite-sized strips
- 1 medium red bell pepper, cut into bite-sized strips
- 1 medium onion, cut into thin wedges
- 1 lb. beef strips for stir-frying
- 1 (12-oz.) jar beef gravy
- 1 (10-oz.) can diced tomatoes and green chiles, undrained
- 1 egg
- 1 tablespoon water
- 1 (7-oz.) can Pillsbury® Refrigerated Breadsticks (6 breadsticks)

1. Heat oven to 375°F. Heat oil in 12-inch skillet over medium-high heat until hot. Add bell peppers and onion; cook and stir 3 minutes. Add beef strips; cook and stir 3 to 5 minutes or until beef is lightly browned and vegetables are softened.

2. Add gravy and tomatoes; mix well. Cook until mixture is hot and bubbly, stirring occasionally. Remove from heat. Pour mixture into ungreased 8-inch square (2-quart) glass baking dish.

3. In small bowl, beat egg and water until well blended. Separate dough into 6 breadsticks. Tie each into loose knot. Arrange knots on top of hot beef mixture. Brush knots with egg mixture. Discard any remaining egg mixture.

4. Bake at 375°F for 15 to 20 minutes or until breadsticks are deep golden brown.

Nutrition Information Per Serving: Calories 290 • Total Fat 12g • Saturated Fat 3g • Cholesterol 75mg • Sodium 700mg • Total Carbohydrate 25g • Dietary Fiber 2g • Sugars 5g • Protein 20g. **Dietary Exchanges:** 1½ Starch • 2 Lean Meat • 1 Fat OR 1½ Carbohydrate • 2 Lean Meat • 1 Fat.

pepper corned beef hash

READY TO SERVE: 30 MINUTES
SERVINGS: 4

* meal-in-one

- 1 tablespoon oil
- 2 cups cubed cooked corned beef
- 2 cups frozen hash-brown potatoes
- ½ cup chopped green bell pepper
- ½ cup chopped red bell pepper
- ½ cup chopped onion
- ¼ teaspoon pepper

1. Heat oil in large skillet over medium heat until hot. Add all remaining ingredients; mix well.

2. Cook 10 to 15 minutes or until bell peppers are tender and mixture is thoroughly heated, stirring occasionally.

Nutrition Information Per Serving: Calories 300 • Total Fat 17g • Saturated Fat 5g • Cholesterol 70mg • Sodium 820mg • Total Carbohydrate 22g • Dietary Fiber 2g • Sugars 2g • Protein 15g. **Dietary Exchanges:** 1 Starch • 2 Medium-Fat Meat • 1 Fat OR 1 Carbohydrate • 2 Medium-Fat Meat • 1 Fat.

bbq beef biscuit bake

PREP TIME: 10 MINUTES
READY TO SERVE: 1 HOUR 15 MINUTES
SERVINGS: 5

1 (32-oz.) container refrigerated barbecue sauce with sliced fully cooked beef

1 (8.3-oz.) can baked beans, undrained (3/4 cup)

1 (10.2-oz.) can Pillsbury® Grands!® Refrigerated Buttermilk Biscuits (5 biscuits)

1. Heat oven to 375°F. In ungreased 11x7-inch (2-quart) glass baking dish, combine beef and beans; mix well. Cover with foil. Bake at 375°F for 40 minutes or until bubbly.

2. Meanwhile, separate dough into 5 biscuits; cut each into 8 pieces.

3. Remove baking dish from oven. Uncover; place biscuit pieces evenly over hot mixture in baking dish.

4. Return to oven; bake, uncovered, an additional 12 to 15 minutes or until biscuits are deep golden brown.

Nutrition Information Per Serving: Calories 430 • Total Fat 13g • Saturated Fat 3g • Cholesterol 30mg • Sodium 1990mg • Total Carbohydrate 61g • Dietary Fiber 3g • Sugars 32g • Protein 20g. **Dietary Exchanges:** 4 Starch • 1 High-Fat Meat OR 4 Carbohydrate • 1 High-Fat Meat.

biscuit-topped green bean and beef casserole

PREP TIME: 25 MINUTES
READY TO SERVE: 55 MINUTES
SERVINGS: 5

* meal-in-one

1 lb. lean ground beef

2 cups frozen cut green beans

1 (10³/₄-oz.) can condensed cream of mushroom soup

1 (8-oz.) can sliced water chestnuts, drained

½ cup milk

1 (2.8-oz.) can french-fried onions

1 (12-oz.) can Pillsbury® Golden Layers™ Refrigerated Flaky Biscuits

1. Heat oven to 350°F. Spray 8-inch square (2-quart) glass baking dish with cooking spray. Brown ground beef in large skillet over medium-high heat until thoroughly cooked, stirring frequently. Drain.

2. Add beans, soup, water chestnuts and milk; mix well. Reduce heat to medium; cover and cook 8 to 10 minutes or until bubbly, stirring occasionally. Stir in half of onions. Spoon mixture into sprayed baking dish.

3. Separate dough into 10 biscuits; cut each into quarters. Place biscuit pieces, points up, over beef mixture.

4. Bake at 350°F for 15 minutes. Slightly crush remaining half of onions; sprinkle over biscuits. Bake an additional 10 to 15 minutes or until biscuits are deep golden brown.

Nutrition Information Per Serving: Calories 600 • Total Fat 34g • Saturated Fat 10g • Cholesterol 60mg • Sodium 1310mg • Total Carbohydrate 50g • Dietary Fiber 3g • Sugars 8g • Protein 24g. **Dietary Exchanges:** 3 Starch • 1 Vegetable • 2 Medium-Fat Meat • 4¹/₂ Fat OR 3 Carbohydrate • 1 Vegetable • 2 Medium-Fat Meat • 4¹/₂ Fat.

MENU SUGGESTION

This hearty, satisfying main course is based on the very popular green bean-mushroom soup side dish. Serve it with steamed baby carrots. If you wish, sprinkle the carrots with dried dill weed or tarragon.

easy beef pot pie

PREP TIME: 15 MINUTES
READY TO SERVE: 1 HOUR
SERVINGS: 8

✳ meal-in-one

1 (15-oz.) pkg. Pillsbury®
Refrigerated Pie Crusts,
softened as directed on
package

1 (12-oz.) jar beef gravy

1 tablespoon cornstarch

2 cups frozen mixed
vegetables

1 (4.5-oz.) jar sliced
mushrooms, drained

1 tablespoon Worcestershire
sauce

1 lb. thickly sliced cooked
roast beef, cubed

1. Heat oven to 425°F. Prepare pie crust as directed on package for two-crust pie using 9-inch glass pie pan.

2. In large saucepan, combine gravy and cornstarch; blend well. Add frozen mixed vegetables, mushrooms and Worcestershire sauce; mix well. Cook over medium-high heat until bubbly. Stir in roast beef. Pour into crust-lined pan. Top with second crust; seal edges and flute. Cut decorative slits in several places in top crust.

3. Bake at 425°F for 30 to 45 minutes or until crust is golden brown and filling is bubbly. Cover edge of crust with strips of foil after first 15 minutes of baking to prevent excessive browning.

Nutrition Information Per Serving: Calories 350 • Total Fat 16g • Saturated Fat 7g • Cholesterol 40mg • Sodium 1100mg • Total Carbohydrate 35g • Dietary Fiber 2g • Sugars 2g • Protein 16g. **Dietary Exchanges:** 2½ Starch • 1 Lean Meat • 2 Fat OR 2½ Carbohydrate • 1 Lean Meat • 2 Fat.

grilled steak and potato salad

grilled steak and potato salad

READY TO SERVE: 30 MINUTES
SERVINGS: 4

✳ meal-in-one

½ lb. new red potatoes, halved

⅔ cup purchased fat-free honey Dijon salad dressing

¾ lb. boneless beef sirloin steak (¾ inch thick)

¼ teaspoon salt

¼ teaspoon coarse ground black pepper

4 cups torn romaine lettuce

2 tomatoes, cut into thin wedges

½ cup thinly sliced red onion

1. Heat grill. Place potatoes in medium saucepan; add enough water to cover. Bring to a boil. Reduce heat to medium; cook 5 to 8 minutes or just until potatoes are fork-tender.

2. Drain potatoes; place in medium bowl. Add 2 tablespoons of the salad dressing; toss to coat evenly. Brush steak with 1 tablespoon of the salad dressing; sprinkle with salt and pepper.

3. When ready to grill, place steak and potatoes on gas grill over medium heat or on charcoal grill 4 to 6 inches from medium coals; cover grill. Cook 8 to 15 minutes or until steak is of desired doneness and potatoes are golden brown, turning once.

4. Meanwhile, arrange lettuce, tomatoes and onion on large serving platter. Slice steak into thin slices; arrange on platter. Top with potatoes. Drizzle salad with remaining salad dressing. If desired, sprinkle with additional pepper.

Nutrition Information Per Serving: Calories 250 • Total Fat 4g • Saturated Fat 1g • Cholesterol 45mg • Sodium 660mg • Total Carbohydrate 35g • Dietary Fiber 4g • Sugars 13g • Protein 18g. **Dietary Exchanges:** 1½ Starch • ½ Fruit • 1 Vegetable • 1½ Lean Meat OR 2 Carbohydrate • 1 Vegetable • 1½ Lean Meat.

southwest steak kabobs

READY TO SERVE: 30 MINUTES
SERVINGS: 4 KABOBS

✳ meal-in-one

¼ cup margarine or butter, melted

¼ cup chopped fresh cilantro

½ teaspoon cumin

¼ teaspoon garlic salt

½ teaspoon hot pepper sauce

2 ears fresh sweet corn, husked, each cut into 4 pieces

8 pickled sweet red cherry peppers

1 lb. boneless beef sirloin steak, cut into 1-inch cubes

1. Heat grill. In small bowl, combine margarine, cilantro, cumin, garlic salt and hot pepper sauce; mix well. Alternately thread corn, peppers and beef cubes onto four 12 to 14-inch metal skewers.

2. When ready to grill, place kabobs on gas grill over medium heat or on charcoal grill 4 to 6 inches from medium coals. Cook 7 to 8 minutes or until corn is tender and beef is of desired doneness, turning once and brushing frequently with margarine mixture.

Nutrition Information Per Serving: Calories 230 • Total Fat 9g • Saturated Fat 2g • Cholesterol 60mg • Sodium 340mg • Total Carbohydrate 13g • Dietary Fiber 2g • Sugars 2g • Protein 23g. **Dietary Exchanges:** 1 Starch • 3 Lean Meat OR 1 Carbohydrate • 3 Lean Meat.

BROILER KABOBS

To broil Southwest Steak Kabobs, place them on a broiler pan. Broil 4 to 6 inches from the heat using the times in the recipe above as a guide, turning and brushing with the margarine mixture as directed in the recipe.

seasoned ground beef and sausage

READY TO SERVE: 20 MINUTES
YIELD: 2 CUPS

* super fast

2 lb. lean (at least 80%) ground beef

¾ lb. bulk pork sausage

1 cup chopped onions

1. In 4-quart Dutch oven, cook ground beef, sausage and onions over medium-high heat 10 to 15 minutes, stirring frequently, until browned.

2. Cover; reduce heat to medium-low. Cook 5 to 6 minutes, stirring occasionally, until meat is thoroughly cooked; drain.

Nutrition Information Per Serving: Calories 270 • Total Fat 18g • Saturated Fat 7g • Trans Fat 1g • Cholesterol 85mg • Sodium 200mg • Total Carbohydrate 2g • Dietary Fiber 0g • Sugars 0g • Protein 24g. **Dietary Exchange:** 3½ Medium-Fat Meat.

cheesy stuffed peppers

READY TO SERVE: 40 MINUTES
SERVINGS: 6

* meal-in-one

2 cups Seasoned Ground Beef and Sausage (recipe above)

½ cup uncooked instant white rice

¼ cup tomato paste

1 (19-oz.) can Progresso® Vegetable Classics hearty tomato soup

1 (4.5-oz.) can Old El Paso® chopped green chiles, undrained

1½ cups shredded Cheddar cheese (6 oz.)

3 large green bell peppers, halved lengthwise, seeds removed

2 tablespoons water

1. In 12-inch skillet, mix Seasoned Ground Beef and Sausage, uncooked rice, tomato paste, ¾ cup of the soup and the green chiles. Cook over medium heat until thoroughly heated, stirring occasionally. Remove from heat; stir in 1 cup of the cheese. Spoon mixture evenly into pepper halves.

2. Place filled peppers in same skillet. Pour remaining soup and the water over peppers. Cover tightly with foil or domed lid. Cook over medium-low heat 20 to 25 minutes or until peppers are fork-tender. Remove from heat. Sprinkle peppers with remaining ½ cup cheese. Cover; let stand 2 minutes or until cheese is melted. To serve, spoon sauce mixture from skillet over peppers.

Nutrition Information Per Serving: Calories 580 • Total Fat 35g • Saturated Fat 15g • Trans Fat 1.5g • Cholesterol 145mg • Sodium 1210mg • Total Carbohydrate 26g • Dietary Fiber 4g • Sugars 9g • Protein 42g. **Dietary Exchanges:** 1 Starch • ½ Other Carbohydrate • 1 Vegetable • 5½ Medium-Fat Meat • 1 Fat.

PEPPER POINTERS

If the lid on the skillet doesn't fit over the peppers, use foil instead. Red, yellow, orange or green bell peppers can be used in this recipe. A melon baller works well to remove the seeds from the bell peppers.

garden vegetable spaghetti

READY TO SERVE: 25 MINUTES
SERVINGS: 6

* super fast

12 oz. uncooked spaghetti

1 tablespoon olive oil

2 cups cubed zucchini
(¾ inch)

1 small onion, chopped
(¼ cup)

½ red bell pepper, chopped
(½ cup)

1 clove garlic, minced

2 cups Seasoned Ground Beef
and Sausage (recipe at left)

1 (26-oz.) jar tomato pasta
sauce

Salt and pepper, if desired

⅓ cup shredded Parmesan
cheese

1. Cook and drain spaghetti as directed on package; cover to keep warm.

2. Meanwhile, in 12-inch skillet, heat oil over medium heat. Cook zucchini, onion, pepper and garlic in oil 10 minutes, stirring occasionally, until vegetables are crisp-tender. Stir in Seasoned Ground Beef and Sausage, and pasta sauce. Cook 5 to 8 minutes, stirring frequently, until thoroughly heated. Season to taste with salt and pepper.

3. Serve sauce over cooked spaghetti; top with shredded cheese.

Nutrition Information Per Serving: Calories 780 • Total Fat 34g • Saturated Fat 11g • Trans Fat 1g • Cholesterol 120mg • Sodium 1200mg • Total Carbohydrate 74g • Dietary Fiber 6g • Sugars 15g • Protein 44g. **Dietary Exchanges:** 3 Starch • 1½ Other Carbohydrate • 1 Vegetable • 4½ Medium-Fat Meat • 2 Fat.

smoky bbq chili

READY TO SERVE: 25 MINUTES
SERVINGS: 8

* super fast

2 cups Seasoned Ground Beef
and Sausage (recipe above,
left)

1 cup hickory smoke flavor
barbecue sauce

1 (16-oz.) can Old El Paso®
refried beans

1 (15-oz.) can spicy chili beans,
undrained

1 (14.5-oz.) can diced
tomatoes, undrained

½ cup water

3 green onions, chopped, if
desired

1. In 4-quart Dutch oven, mix all ingredients; cover.

2. Cook over medium-low heat 15 to 20 minutes, stirring occasionally, until thoroughly heated. Sprinkle individual servings with onions.

Nutrition Information Per Serving: Calories 420 • Total Fat 19g • Saturated Fat 7g • Trans Fat 1g • Cholesterol 90mg • Sodium 1120mg • Total Carbohydrate 32g • Dietary Fiber 6g • Sugars 12g • Protein 30g. **Dietary Exchanges:** 1 Starch • 1 Other Carbohydrate • 4 Medium-Fat Meat.

CHILI CHOICE

The refried beans give this distinctive chili a smooth, thick texture. If you prefer a thinner chili, simply add a little more water.

Most of the ingredients in this recipe are common pantry items. Keep the ingredients on hand, and you'll have an instant meal.

wrapped tenderloin with gravy

PREP TIME: 20 MINUTES
READY TO SERVE: 35 MINUTES
SERVINGS: 2

KELLY LYNNE BAXTER ✳ OLYMPIA, WASHINGTON
BAKE-OFF® CONTEST 42, 2006

- 2 tablespoons olive oil
- 2 beef tenderloin steaks, about 1 inch thick (4 oz. each)
- ½ teaspoon Montreal steak seasoning
- 4 refrigerated buttermilk biscuits (2 twin-packs from 21-oz. pkg.)
- 1 egg yolk
- 1 tablespoon water
- 1 cup crumbled Gorgonzola cheese (4 oz.)
- ⅛ teaspoon pepper
- ½ cup whipping cream
- ½ teaspoon Worcestershire sauce
- 1 (4.5 oz.) jar sliced mushrooms, drained
- 1½ teaspoons chopped fresh parsley

1. Heat oven to 400°F. In 8-inch skillet, heat oil over medium-high heat. Pat steaks dry with paper towel; sprinkle both sides with steak seasoning. Add steaks to skillet; cook 1 to 2 minutes on each side or until browned. Remove steaks from skillet; place on plate.

2. Spray cookie sheet or 13x9-inch baking dish with cooking spray. On cookie sheet or in baking dish, roll or press 2 of the biscuits into 5- to 6-inch rounds. Place 1 steak on center of each flattened biscuit. Press remaining 2 biscuits into 5- to 6-inch rounds; place over steaks. Flute or crimp edges with fork to seal. In small bowl, beat egg yolk and water with fork until blended; brush over top biscuits. Bake 14 to 18 minutes or until golden brown.

3. Meanwhile, in 1-quart saucepan, mix cheese, pepper, whipping cream and Worcestershire sauce. Heat to boiling. Reduce heat to medium-low; simmer uncovered, stirring constantly, until cheese is melted. Stir in mushrooms. Keep warm over low heat.

4. Serve half of mushroom gravy over each wrapped steak; sprinkle with parsley.

Nutrition Information Per Serving: Calories 1130 • Total Fat 78g • Saturated Fat 34g • Trans Fat 9g • Cholesterol 260mg • Sodium 2300mg • Total Carbohydrate 57g • Dietary Fiber 1g • Sugars 14g • Protein 50g. **Dietary Exchanges:** 3 Starch • 1 Other Carbohydrate • 6 Medium-Fat Meat • 9 Fat.

beef 'n pepperoni pizza pie

PREP TIME: 35 MINUTES
READY TO SERVE: 55 MINUTES
SERVINGS: 6

* meal-in-one

¾ lb. lean ground beef

½ cup pizza sauce

2 tablespoons ketchup

2½ oz. sliced pepperoni, quartered (1/2 cup)

¼ cup grated Parmesan cheese

1 (10-oz.) can Pillsbury® Refrigerated Pizza Crust

1 (4.5-oz.) jar sliced mushrooms, drained

⅓ cup chopped green bell pepper

¼ cup sliced ripe olives

6 oz. shredded mozzarella cheese (1½ cups)

1. Heat oven to 400°F. Spray 9-inch pie pan with cooking spray. Brown ground beef in medium skillet over medium-high heat for 5 to 7 minutes or until thoroughly cooked, stirring frequently. Drain.

2. Stir pizza sauce, ketchup, pepperoni and Parmesan cheese into beef. Cook 3 to 5 minutes or until thoroughly heated, stirring occasionally.

3. Unroll dough into sprayed pan, stretching dough while pressing firmly in bottom and up sides of pan. Spoon hot beef mixture into crust. Top with mushrooms, bell pepper, olives and cheese.

4. Bake at 400°F for 15 to 20 minutes or until crust is golden brown. Let stand 10 minutes before serving.

Nutrition Information Per Serving: Calories 410 • Total Fat 21g • Saturated Fat 9g • Cholesterol 65mg • Sodium 1100mg • Total Carbohydrate 28g • Dietary Fiber 2g • Sugars 5g • Protein 27g. **Dietary Exchanges:** 2 Starch • 3 Medium-Fat Meat • 1 Fat OR 2 Carbohydrate • 3 Medium-Fat Meat • 1 Fat.

veal scaloppine with marsala sauce

READY TO SERVE: 20 MINUTES
SERVINGS: 6

* super fast

6 veal cutlets (about 1½ lb.)

2 tablespoons all-purpose flour

2 tablespoons unseasoned dry bread crumbs

¼ teaspoon salt

2 teaspoons oil

½ cup sweet Marsala wine

2 tablespoons chopped fresh parsley

1. Place 1 veal cutlet between 2 pieces of plastic wrap or waxed paper. Working from center, gently pound cutlet with flat side of meat mallet or rolling pin until about ¼ inch thick; remove wrap. Repeat with remaining cutlets.

2. In pie pan or shallow dish, combine flour, bread crumbs and salt; mix well. Lightly coat cutlets with flour mixture.

3. Heat oil in large skillet over medium-high heat until hot. Add cutlets; cook about 1 minute on each side or until browned. Remove from skillet; cover to keep warm.

4. Add wine to skillet; bring to a boil. Cook 1 to 2 minutes or until the wine is slightly reduced.

5. Serve wine sauce over veal; sprinkle with parsley.

Nutrition Information Per Serving: Calories 170 • Total Fat 5g • Saturated Fat 2g • Cholesterol 95mg • Sodium 270mg • Total Carbohydrate 5g • Dietary Fiber 0g • Sugars 1g • Protein 26g. **Dietary Exchange:** 3 Lean Meat.

barbecue beef pizza

READY TO SERVE: 30 MINUTES
SERVINGS: 4

✻ meal-in-one

1 (10-oz.) can Pillsbury® Refrigerated Pizza Crust

2 cups refrigerated barbecue sauce with sliced fully cooked beef (from 32-oz. container)

6 oz. shredded Monterey Jack cheese (1½ cups)

½ medium red onion, thinly sliced

1 green bell pepper, cut into thin strips

1. Heat oven to 425°F. Spray cookie sheet with cooking spray. Unroll dough; place on sprayed cookie sheet. Starting at center, press out dough to form 13x9-inch rectangle. Bake at 425°F for 7 to 9 minutes or until light golden brown.

2. Remove partially baked crust from oven. Top with beef in sauce, cheese, onion and bell pepper.

3. Return to oven; bake an additional 10 to 12 minutes or until crust is golden brown and cheese is melted.

Nutrition Information Per Serving: Calories 520 • Total Fat 19g • Saturated Fat 11g • Cholesterol 70mg • Sodium 1410mg • Total Carbohydrate 54g • Dietary Fiber 4g • Sugars 17g • 34g Protein. **Dietary Exchanges:** 2½ Starch • 1 Fruit • 4 Lean Meat • 1 Fat OR 3½ Carbohydrate • 4 Lean Meat • 1 Fat.

speedy swedish meatballs

READY TO SERVE: 30 MINUTES
SERVINGS: 4

1 lb. ground beef

¼ cup unseasoned dry bread or cracker crumbs

½ teaspoon salt

⅛ teaspoon pepper

1 small onion, chopped

1 egg

1 tablespoon oil

1 (10¾-oz.) can cream of mushroom soup

¼ cup water or milk

⅛ teaspoon nutmeg or allspice

1. In medium bowl, combine all ingredients except oil; mix well. Shape into 1½ to 2-inch meatballs.

2. Heat oil in large skillet over medium-high heat until hot. Add meatballs; cook 10 to 12 minutes or until thoroughly cooked, turning occasionally. Drain.

3. In the same skillet, add the soup, water or milk and nutmeg or allspice; combine. Cover; simmer meatballs and gravy 15 minutes, stirring occasionally.

EASY APPETIZER

Use this same recipe for fuss-free cocktail meatballs. Simply shape the meat mixture into two dozen 1-inch meatballs, and cook them as directed above. Prepare the gravy as directed, or leave the gravy out and pair the balls with a prepared barbecue sauce from the grocery store.

sloppy joes

READY TO SERVE: 40 MINUTES
SERVINGS: 6

1 lb. lean ground beef

½ cup chopped green bell pepper or celery

½ cup chopped onion

1 tablespoon brown sugar

1 teaspoon dry mustard

¼ teaspoon salt

⅛ teaspoon pepper

½ cup ketchup

1 tablespoon vinegar

1 tablespoon Worcestershire sauce

1 (8-oz.) can tomato sauce

6 sandwich buns, split

1. In large skillet, combine ground beef, bell pepper and onion; cook over medium heat for 8 to 10 minutes or until beef is thoroughly cooked, stirring frequently. Drain well.

2. Add all remaining ingredients except buns; mix well. Cover; simmer 15 to 20 minutes, stirring occasionally. Serve in buns.

Nutrition Information Per Serving: Calories 320 • Total Fat 12g • Saturated Fat 4g • Cholesterol 45mg • Sodium 900mg • Total Carbohydrate 35g • Dietary Fiber 2g • Sugars 12g • Protein 18g. **Dietary Exchanges:** 1½ Starch • 1 Fruit • 2 Medium-Fat Meat OR 2½ Carbohydrate • 2 Medium-Fat Meat.

beef and pepper stromboli

PREP TIME: 15 MINUTES
READY TO SERVE: 35 MINUTES
SERVINGS: 6

½ lb. lean ground beef

1 (10-oz.) can Pillsbury® Refrigerated Pizza Crust

¼ cup pizza sauce

4 oz. shredded mozzarella cheese (1 cup)

¼ cup chopped green and/or red bell pepper

¼ teaspoon dried Italian seasoning

1. Heat oven to 400°F. Spray cookie sheet with cooking spray. Brown ground beef in medium skillet over medium-high heat for 5 to 7 minutes or until thoroughly cooked, stirring frequently. Drain. Set aside.

2. Unroll dough; place on sprayed cookie sheet. Starting at center, press out dough to form 12x8-inch rectangle.

3. Spread pizza sauce over dough to within 2 inches of long sides and ½ inch of short sides. Spoon cooked ground beef lengthwise in 3-inch-wide strip down center of dough to within ½ inch of each short side. Top with cheese, bell pepper and Italian seasoning. Fold long sides of dough over filling; press edges to seal.

4. Bake at 400°F for 15 to 20 minutes or until crust is golden brown.

Nutrition Information Per Serving: Calories 250 • Total Fat 10g • Saturated Fat 4g • Cholesterol 35mg • Sodium 500mg • Total Carbohydrate 24g • Dietary Fiber 1g • Sugars 3g • Protein 16g. **Dietary Exchanges:** 1½ Starch • 1½ Medium-Fat Meat • ½ Fat OR 1½ Carbohydrate • 1½ Medium-Fat Meat • ½ Fat.

pepper steak

2 cups uncooked instant rice, if desired

2 cups water

1 cup beef broth

¼ cup hoisin sauce

1 tablespoon cornstarch

¼ to ½ teaspoon coarse ground black pepper

3 tablespoons ketchup

1 tablespoon rice vinegar

½ teaspoon Worcestershire sauce

1 tablespoon oil

1 lb. beef flank or boneless top sirloin steak, thinly sliced

1 medium onion, cut into 8 pieces

1 medium green bell pepper, cut into strips

1 medium red bell pepper, cut into strips

1 medium yellow bell pepper, cut into strips

1. Cook rice in water as directed on package.

2. Meanwhile, in small bowl, combine broth, hoisin sauce, cornstarch, pepper, ketchup, vinegar and Worcestershire sauce; blend well. Set aside.

3. Heat oil in large skillet or wok over medium-high heat until hot. Add beef and onion; cook and stir 2 to 3 minutes or until beef is no longer pink. Add bell peppers and cornstarch mixture; cook and stir 2 to 3 minutes or until vegetables are crisp-tender and sauce is bubbly and thickened. Serve over rice.

Nutrition Information Per Serving: Calories 480 • Total Fat 13g • Saturated Fat 4g • Cholesterol 45mg • Sodium 690mg • Total Carbohydrate 66g • Dietary Fiber 3g • Sugars 13g • Protein 24g. **Dietary Exchanges:** 3 Starch • 1 Fruit • 1 Vegetable • 2 Medium-Fat Meat OR 4 Carbohydrate • 1 Vegetable • 2 Medium-Fat Meat.

LIGHTEN UP

If you love beef but are cutting back on dietary fat, try to choose leaner cuts and use lower-fat techniques such as marinating or moist cooking methods to improve tenderness and flavor. Also, look for recipes that combine beef with plenty of pasta, rice or veggies, which will fill you up with less meat.

---

mexican beef melts

1 lb. lean ground beef

1 (1.25-oz.) pkg. taco seasoning mix

⅔ cup water

1½ cups chunky-style salsa

1 (16.3-oz.) can Pillsbury® Grands!® Refrigerated Southern Style or Buttermilk Biscuits

4 oz. shredded Monterey Jack cheese or Mexican cheese blend (1 cup)

1 cup sour cream, if desired

1. Heat oven to 375°F. Lightly spray large cookie sheet with cooking spray. Brown ground beef in large skillet over medium-high heat for 5 to 7 minutes or until thoroughly cooked, stirring frequently. Drain.

2. Add taco seasoning mix, water and ½ cup of the salsa; cook 2 to 4 minutes or until mixture has thickened, stirring occasionally.

3. Separate dough into 8 biscuits. Press or roll each to form a 6-inch round. Spoon about ¼ cup beef mixture onto center of each round. Top each with 1 tablespoon of the cheese. Fold dough over filling; press edges firmly with fork to seal. Place on sprayed cookie sheet.

4. Bake at 375°F for 9 to 14 minutes or until golden brown. To serve, top each sandwich with 1 heaping tablespoon remaining salsa and 1 tablespoon remaining cheese. Serve with sour cream.

Nutrition Information Per Serving: Calories 440 • Total Fat 27g • Saturated Fat 12g • Cholesterol 60mg • Sodium 1470mg • Total Carbohydrate 31g • Dietary Fiber 2g • Sugars 8g • Protein 19g. **Dietary Exchanges:** 2 Starch • 2 Medium-Fat Meat • 3 Fat OR 2 Carbohydrate • 2 Medium-Fat Meat • 3 Fat.

picadillo wraps

READY TO SERVE: 30 MINUTES
SERVINGS: 8 WRAPS

CAROL MCLAUGHLIN ✻ OMAHA, NEBRASKA
BAKE-OFF® CONTEST 42, 2006

1 lb. lean (at least 80%) ground beef

1 (9.2-oz.) box cheesy enchilada skillet-meal mix for hamburger

2 cups water

1 tablespoon red or white wine vinegar

½ to 1 teaspoon ground cinnamon

1 (16-oz.) jar chunky-style salsa

3 tablespoons milk

½ cup raisins

½ cup slivered almonds

1 (2.25-oz.) can sliced ripe olives, drained

1 (11.5-oz.) pkg. flour tortillas for burritos, 8 inch (8 tortillas), heated

Lime wedges, if desired

Fresh cilantro sprigs, if desired

1. In 12-inch skillet, cook ground beef over medium-high heat, stirring frequently, until thoroughly cooked; drain and return to skillet. Stir in uncooked Rice and Seasoning Mix from enchilada mix, water, vinegar, cinnamon and salsa. Heat to boiling. Reduce heat to medium-low; cover and simmer 10 to 12 minutes, stirring occasionally, until rice is tender.

2. Meanwhile, in small bowl, stir milk and Topping Mix from enchilada mix 30 seconds until blended; set aside.

3. Stir raisins, almonds and olives into beef mixture. Spoon about ¾ cup mixture down center of each warm tortilla; roll up. Serve wraps drizzled with topping; garnish plates with lime wedges and cilantro sprigs.

Nutrition Information Per Serving: Calories 470 • Total Fat 18g • Saturated Fat 4.5g • Trans Fat 1g • Cholesterol 35mg • Sodium 1260mg • Total Carbohydrate 59g • Dietary Fiber 2g • Sugars 10g • Protein 18g. **Dietary Exchanges:** 3 Starch • 1 Other Carbohydrate • 1½ Medium-Fat Meat • 1½ Fat.

beef stew casserole

beef stew casserole

PREP TIME: 20 MINUTES
READY TO SERVE: 1 HOUR 10 MINUTES
SERVINGS: 6

* meal-in-one

2 tablespoons olive or vegetable oil

1 lb. boneless lean beef round steak (1/2 inch thick), cut into 1-inch pieces

1/2 teaspoon dried thyme leaves

1/8 teaspoon pepper

2 cups Green Giant® frozen mixed vegetables (from 1-lb. bag)

2 cups refrigerated diced cooked potatoes with onions (from 20-oz. bag)

1 (14.5-oz.) can diced tomatoes with roasted garlic and onion, undrained

1 (12-oz.) jar beef gravy

1 (4.5-oz.) jar Green Giant® sliced mushrooms, drained

1 (12-oz.) can Pillsbury® Golden Layers® refrigerated buttermilk flaky biscuits

Chopped fresh parsley, if desired

1. Heat oven to 375°F. In 10-inch skillet, heat oil over medium-high heat. Add beef; sprinkle with thyme and pepper. Cook 5 to 7 minutes, stirring occasionally, until beef is browned.

2. Meanwhile, in large bowl, mix remaining ingredients except biscuits and parsley.

3. Stir beef into vegetable mixture. Pour into ungreased 13x9-inch (3-quart) glass baking dish.

4. Cover dish with foil. Bake 28 to 30 minutes or until bubbly around edges.

5. Cut each biscuit into 4 pieces. Place biscuit pieces evenly on beef mixture, leaving space between pieces. Bake, uncovered, 14 to 18 minutes longer or until biscuits are golden brown. Sprinkle with parsley.

Nutrition Information Per Serving: Calories 440 • Total Fat 16g • Saturated Fat 4g • Trans Fat 2.5g • Cholesterol 45mg • Sodium 1210mg • Total Carbohydrate 47g • Dietary Fiber 5g • Sugars 7g • Protein 26g. **Dietary Exchanges:** 2 Starch • 1 Other Carbohydrate • 1 Vegetable • 2 1/2 Lean Meat • 1 1/2 Fat.

paprika beef

READY TO SERVE: 35 MINUTES
SERVINGS: 4

* meal-in-one

8 oz. uncooked wide egg noodles (5 cups)

1 tablespoon olive or vegetable oil

1 lb. boneless beef sirloin steak, cut into thin bite-sized strips

1 (8-oz.) pkg. sliced fresh mushrooms (3 cups)

1 large onion, sliced

2 garlic cloves, minced

3 teaspoons paprika

1 (8-oz.) can tomato sauce

1/4 cup sour cream

1 teaspoon all-purpose flour

2 tablespoons chopped fresh parsley

1. Cook noodles to desired doneness as directed on package. Drain; cover to keep warm.

2. Meanwhile, heat oil in large skillet over medium-high heat until hot. If desired, sprinkle beef strips with salt and pepper. Add half of beef to skillet; cook and stir 3 to 4 minutes or until browned. Remove beef; set aside. Repeat with remaining beef strips; remove from skillet.

3. Add mushrooms, onion and garlic to skillet; cook and stir over medium heat for 2 to 3 minutes or until vegetables are tender. Return beef to skillet. Add paprika; mix well. Cook 1 minute. Stir in tomato sauce.

4. In small bowl, combine sour cream and flour. Add to beef mixture; cook 1 minute or until thoroughly heated. If mixture becomes too thick, stir in 1 to 2 tablespoons water.

5. Add parsley to cooked noodles; toss well. Serve beef mixture over noodles.

Nutrition Information Per Serving: Calories 470 • Total Fat 14g • Saturated Fat 5g • Cholesterol 120mg • Sodium 410mg • Total Carbohydrate 54g • Dietary Fiber 4g • Sugars 8g • Protein 32g. **Dietary Exchanges:** 3 Starch • 2 Vegetable • 2 1/2 Lean Meat • 1 Fat OR 3 Carbohydrate • 2 Vegetable • 2 1/2 Lean Meat • 1 Fat.

basic meatballs

READY TO SERVE: 30 MINUTES
SERVINGS: 4

1 lb. ground beef
¼ cup unseasoned dry bread or cracker crumbs
½ teaspoon salt
⅛ teaspoon pepper
1 small onion, chopped
1 egg
1 tablespoon oil

1. In medium bowl, combine all of the ingredients except oil; mix well. Shape into 1 to 2-inch meatballs.

2. Heat oil in large skillet over medium-high heat until hot. Add meatballs; cook 10 to 12 minutes or until thoroughly cooked, turning occasionally. Drain.

Nutrition Information Per Serving: Calories 300 • Total Fat 21g • Saturated Fat 7g • Cholesterol 120mg • Sodium 400mg • Total Carbohydrate 6g • Dietary Fiber 0g • Sugars 1g • Protein 21g. Dietary Exchanges: ½ Starch • 3 Medium-Fat Meat • 1 Fat OR ½ Carbohydrate • 3 Medium-Fat Meat • 1 Fat.

french dip sandwiches

READY TO SERVE: 15 MINUTES
SERVINGS: 6

* super fast

1½ lb. sliced cooked roast beef
1½ cups water
2 beef-flavored bouillon cubes or ½ cup beef pan drippings
1 teaspoon instant minced onion
½ teaspoon soy sauce
12 slices crusty French bread or 6 sandwich buns, split

1. In medium saucepan, combine beef, water and bouillon. Cook over medium heat until thoroughly heated, stirring occasionally. Add onion and soy sauce. Cook 1 to 3 minutes.

2. Serve between slices of crusty French bread or in sandwich buns. Individual portions of bouillon mixture (au jus) can be served for dipping sandwiches.

Nutrition Information Per Serving: Calories 270 • Total Fat 7g • Saturated Fat 2g • Cholesterol 65mg • Sodium 660mg • Total Carbohydrate 26g • Dietary Fiber 2g • Sugars 2g • Protein 25g. Dietary Exchanges: 1 Starch • 3 Lean Meat OR 1 Carbohydrate • 3 Lean Meat.

taco salad

READY TO SERVE: 25 MINUTES
SERVINGS: 6

* super fast

1 lb. extra-lean ground beef
1 medium onion, chopped
1 (1¼-oz.) pkg. taco seasoning mix
½ cup water
½ head lettuce, torn into bite-sized pieces
6 oz. corn chips (4 cups)
3 oz. shredded Cheddar or American cheese (¾ cup)
2 medium tomatoes, cut into wedges
¼ cup purchased French or Russian salad dressing

1. In large skillet, brown ground beef and onion until beef is thoroughly cooked. Drain. Stir in taco seasoning mix and water; simmer 10 minutes over low heat, stirring occasionally.

2. Line individual salad bowls or plates with lettuce. Sprinkle with corn chips. Spoon beef mixture in center of each. Sprinkle with cheese. Garnish with tomatoes. Serve with salad dressing.

Nutrition Information Per Serving: Calories 530 • Total Fat 36g • Saturated Fat 11g • Cholesterol 60mg • Sodium 1280mg • Total Carbohydrate 31g • Dietary Fiber 3g • Sugars 7g • Protein 21g. Dietary Exchanges: 1½ Starch • 1 Vegetable • 2 Lean Meat • 6 Fat OR 1½ Carbohydrate • 1 Vegetable • 2 Lean Meat • 6 Fat.

porterhouse steaks with grilled vegetables

READY TO SERVE: 35 MINUTES
SERVINGS: 4

1. Heat grill. Place mushrooms, bell peppers and chile in disposable foil pan or in center of 18x12-inch sheet of heavy-duty foil. In small bowl, combine butter and garlic; mix well. Pour butter mixture over vegetables. Cover pan with foil or seal packet securely using double-fold seals.

2. In small bowl, combine oil, peppercorns and salt; mix well. Brush each steak with the oil mixture.

3. When ready to grill, place steaks and vegetables on gas grill over medium-high heat or on charcoal grill 4 to 6 inches from medium-high coals. Cook 10 to 20 minutes or until steaks are of desired doneness and bell peppers are crisp-tender, turning steaks once. Serve vegetables with steaks.

Nutrition Information Per Serving: Calories 390 • Total Fat 28g • Saturated Fat 10g • Cholesterol 95mg • Sodium 300mg • Total Carbohydrate 6g • Dietary Fiber 2g • Sugars 3g • Protein 29g. Dietary Exchanges: 1 Vegetable • 4 Lean Meat • 3 Fat.

vegetables

- 8 oz. purchased assorted fresh wild mushrooms or mushrooms, cut in half
- 1 red bell pepper, cut into strips
- 1 yellow bell pepper, cut into strips
- 1 poblano chile, seeded, cut into strips
- 3 tablespoons butter; melted
- 2 garlic cloves, minced

steak

- 2 tablespoons olive oil
- ½ teaspoon coarsely ground assorted peppercorns or black peppercorns
- ¼ teaspoon salt
- 4 (6 to 8-oz.) beef porterhouse steaks (¾ inch thick)

> ### OVEN–BROILED STEAKS
>
> To broil steaks, place them on a broiler pan; broil 4 to 6 inches from the heat using the times above as a guide, turning once. Cook the vegetables in the skillet over medium-high heat for 6 to 8 minutes, stirring occasionally.

liver, bacon and onions

READY TO SERVE: 25 MINUTES
SERVINGS: 4

* super fast

- 1 lb. beef liver
- ¼ cup all-purpose flour
- ½ teaspoon salt
- ⅛ teaspoon pepper
- 4 slices bacon
- 2 medium onions, sliced

1. Cut liver into serving-sized pieces. In shallow bowl, combine flour, salt and pepper; mix well. Coat liver with flour mixture.

2. In large skillet, cook bacon over medium heat until crisp. Remove bacon; drain on paper towel, reserving drippings in skillet.

3. Add liver and onions to skillet; cook 2 to 3 minutes on each side or until thoroughly cooked. Serve topped with crisp bacon.

Nutrition Information Per Serving: Calories 220 • Total Fat 7g • Saturated Fat 3g • Cholesterol 330mg • Sodium 430mg • Total Carbohydrate 14g • Dietary Fiber 1g • Sugars 3g • Protein 24g. Dietary Exchanges: ½ Starch • 1 Vegetable • 3 Lean Meat OR ½ Carbohydrate • 1 Vegetable • 3 Lean Meat.

chicken & turkey

grilled chicken taco salad ✳ p. 165

chicken curry stuffed potatoes ✳ p. 168

teriyaki grilled chicken kabobs ✳ p. 163

tuscan roasted potato-chicken salad ✳ p. 150

chicken pot pie with flaky crust ✳ p. 138

grilled turkey tenderloins

PREP TIME: 45 MINUTES
READY TO SERVE: 4 HOURS 45 MINUTES
SERVINGS: 4

* plan ahead

¼ cup oil

¼ cup soy sauce

¼ teaspoon dried basil leaves

¼ teaspoon dried marjoram leaves

¼ teaspoon dried thyme leaves

1 lb. fresh turkey tenderloins

1. In 8-inch square (2-quart) glass baking dish or resealable food storage plastic bag, combine all ingredients except turkey; mix well. Add turkey; turn to coat. Cover dish or seal bag. Refrigerate 2 to 4 hours to marinate, turning occasionally.

2. Heat grill. When ready to grill, remove turkey from marinade; reserve marinade. Place turkey on gas grill over low heat or on charcoal grill 4 to 6 inches from medium coals. Cook 20 to 30 minutes or until turkey is fork-tender and juices run clear, turning once and brushing frequently with reserved marinade. Discard any remaining marinade.

Nutrition Information Per Serving: Calories 140 • Total Fat 4g • Saturated Fat 1g • Cholesterol 75mg • Sodium 300mg • Total Carbohydrate 0g • Dietary Fiber 0g • Sugars 0g • Protein 27g. **Dietary Exchange: 4 Very Lean Meat.**

TURKEY TIP

To broil turkey, place the meat on an oiled broiler pan. Broil 4 to 6 inches from heat using the times indicated in the recipe instructions above as a guide, turning once and brushing frequently with the reserved marinade.

apricot-glazed chicken with almond couscous

READY TO SERVE: 25 MINUTES
SERVINGS: 4

* super fast

chicken

- 4 boneless skinless chicken breast halves
- ½ teaspoon garlic powder
- ¼ teaspoon pepper
- ⅛ teaspoon ground red pepper (cayenne)
- 2 tablespoons apricot preserves

couscous

- 1 cup chicken broth
- 1 tablespoon margarine or butter
- 1 cup uncooked couscous
- 2 tablespoons slivered almonds, toasted

1. Place 1 chicken breast half between 2 pieces of plastic wrap or waxed paper. Working from center, gently pound chicken with flat side of meat mallet or rolling pin until about ¼ inch thick; remove wrap. Repeat with remaining chicken breast halves.

2. In small bowl, combine garlic powder, pepper and ground red pepper; mix well. Sprinkle on both sides of chicken. Arrange chicken on broiler pan.

3. Broil 4 to 6 inches from heat for 6 to 10 minutes or until chicken is fork-tender and juices run clear. Brush with half of apricot preserves. Broil 1 minute or until bubbly. Brush with remaining preserves.

4. Meanwhile, in medium saucepan bring broth and margarine to a boil. Stir in couscous and almonds. Remove from heat; cover. Let stand 5 minutes. Fluff with fork; serve with chicken.

Nutrition Information Per Serving: Calories 390 • Total Fat 8g • Saturated Fat 2g • Cholesterol 75mg • Sodium 300mg • Total Carbohydrate 44g • Dietary Fiber 3g • Sugars 6g • Protein 35g. **Dietary Exchanges:** 2 Starch • 1 Fruit • 4 Very Lean Meat • 1 Fat OR 3 Carbohydrate • 4 Very Lean Meat • 1 Fat.

citrus chicken with peppers

READY TO SERVE: 20 MINUTES
SERVINGS: 4

* super fast

- 4 boneless skinless chicken breast halves
- 1 medium red bell pepper, cut into strips
- 1 medium green bell pepper, cut into strips
- ⅓ cup orange juice
- 2 tablespoons lime juice
- 2 tablespoons honey
- ½ teaspoon paprika
- ¼ teaspoon salt

Dash pepper

- 1 tablespoon cornstarch
- 2 tablespoons water

1. Place chicken breast halves in large skillet. Arrange bell pepper strips around chicken. In small bowl, combine orange juice, lime juice, honey, paprika, salt and pepper; blend well. Pour over chicken and peppers. Bring to a boil; reduce heat. Cover; simmer 8 to 10 minutes or until chicken is fork-tender and juices run clear. Using slotted spoon, transfer chicken and peppers to serving plate; cover to keep warm.

2. In small bowl, combine cornstarch and water; blend until smooth. Stir into hot liquid in skillet. Cook over medium heat until mixture thickens and boils, stirring constantly. Spoon over chicken and peppers.

Nutrition Information Per Serving: Calories 200 • Total Fat 3g • Saturated Fat 1g • Cholesterol 75mg • Sodium 200mg • Total Carbohydrate 16g • Dietary Fiber 1g • Sugars 12g • Protein 27g. **Dietary Exchanges:** 1 Fruit • 4 Very Lean Meat OR 1 Carbohydrate • 4 Very Lean Meat.

LIVELY LEFTOVERS

A fantastic lunch is always at hand when you have an extra helping of Citrus Chicken with Peppers in the refrigerator. Cut the chicken into strips, dice the peppers and mix everything together. Set a lettuce leaf or a handful of baby spinach leaves over a flour tortilla or into a pita. Next, add the chicken mixture. Paired with an apple and a snack-sized bag of tortilla chips, this no-fuss wrap or colorful pita make brown-bagging it a snap.

chicken pot pie with flaky crust

PREP TIME: 40 MINUTES
READY TO SERVE: 1 HOUR 35 MINUTES
SERVINGS: 4

∗ meal-in-one

1 sheet frozen puff pastry
  (from 17.3-oz. package),
  thawed

1 tablespoon olive or
  vegetable oil

¾ lb. boneless skinless chicken
  breasts, cut into ½-inch
  pieces

1 large onion, coarsely
  chopped (1 cup)

1 cup quartered ready-to-eat
  baby-cut carrots (5 to 6 oz.)

¾ cup Green Giant® frozen
  sweet peas (from 1-lb. bag)

½ cup sour cream

1 (12-oz.) jar chicken gravy

2 tablespoons cornstarch

¼ teaspoon dried thyme
  leaves

¼ teaspoon pepper

1 egg, beaten, if desired

1. Heat oven to 375°F. On lightly floured surface, unroll puff pastry. With rolling pin, roll out into 11-inch square. Cut off corners to make an 11-inch round. Cut slits or small designs in several places in pastry; set aside.

2. In 10-inch skillet, heat oil over medium-high heat. Add chicken; cook about 4 minutes, stirring frequently, until no longer pink in center. Add onion and carrots; cook 5 minutes, stirring frequently, until vegetables are crisp-tender. Remove from heat; stir in peas.

3. In medium bowl, beat remaining ingredients except egg with wire whisk until well blended. Stir into chicken mixture in skillet. Spoon into 9-inch deep-dish glass pie plate. Place pastry over filling, allowing to hang over edge.

4. Bake 20 minutes. Brush crust with beaten egg. Cover edge of crust with strips of foil to prevent excessive browning.

5. Bake 20 to 25 minutes longer or until crust is golden brown. Let stand 10 minutes before serving.

Nutrition Information Per Serving: Calories 610 • Total Fat 37g • Saturated Fat 13g • Trans Fat 2.5g • Cholesterol 135mg • Sodium 720mg • Total Carbohydrate 44g • Dietary Fiber 3g • Sugars 7g • Protein 27g. Dietary Exchanges: 1 Starch • 1½ Other Carbohydrate • 1 Vegetable • 3 Very Lean Meat • 7 Fat.

POT PIE POINTERS

You can use 2¾ cups Green Giant® frozen mixed vegetables instead of the onion, carrots and frozen peas. Just stir them into the cooked chicken before adding the gravy mixture.

Use a miniature cookie or canapé cutter to make steam holes in the pastry. Save the pastry cutouts and place on top of the pastry after brushing it with egg. Bake as directed.

---

spicy chicken vegetable pizzas

READY TO SERVE: 20 MINUTES
SERVINGS: 2

∗ super fast

1 cup frozen corn, broccoli
  and red peppers, cooked,
  well drained

4 oz. shredded hot pepper
  Monterey Jack cheese
  (1 cup)

¾ cup shredded or chopped
  cooked chicken

½ cup chopped green onions

½ teaspoon dried oregano
  leaves

2 (6-inch) prebaked Italian
  bread shells

1. Heat oven to 425°F. In medium bowl, combine vegetables, cheese, chicken, green onions and oregano; toss to combine. Place bread shells on ungreased cookie sheet. Spoon vegetable mixture evenly on bread shells.

2. Bake at 425°F for 5 to 6 minutes or until thoroughly heated and cheese is melted.

Nutrition Information Per Serving: Calories 680 • Total Fat 26g • Saturated Fat 13g • Cholesterol 105mg • Sodium 970mg • Total Carbohydrate 66g • Dietary Fiber 4g • Sugars 8g • Protein 45g. Dietary Exchanges: 4 Starch • 1 Vegetable • 4½ Lean Meat • 2½ Fat OR 4 Carbohydrate • 1 Vegetable • 4½ Lean Meat • 2½ Fat.

chicken pot pie with flaky crust

quick caribbean cassoulet

READY TO SERVE: 30 MINUTES
SERVINGS: 4

DEBORAH BIGGS ✳ OMAHA, NEBRASKA
BAKE-OFF® CONTEST 42, 2006

2½ teaspoons olive oil

½ cup Italian-style dry bread crumbs

½ lb. bulk chorizo sausage

1 teaspoon minced garlic in water (from a jar) or finely chopped fresh garlic

2 cups chopped skinned deli rotisserie chicken (from 2 to 2½-lb. chicken)

1 cup organic sun-dried tomato pasta sauce

½ cup reduced-fat (lite) coconut milk (from 14-oz. can), stirred well to blend

1 teaspoon mild taco seasoning mix (from 1.25-oz. package)

½ teaspoon salt, if desired

¼ teaspoon pepper

1 (15-oz.) can cannellini (white kidney) beans, undrained

2 to 3 tablespoons finely chopped fresh cilantro

4 sprigs fresh cilantro

1. In 10-inch skillet, mix oil and bread crumbs. Cook over medium heat 3 to 5 minutes, stirring frequently, just until crumb mixture begins to brown. Place crumbs in bowl; set aside for topping.

2. In same skillet, cook chorizo over medium heat 5 to 8 minutes, stirring frequently, until thoroughly cooked and browned. Add garlic; cook and stir 1 minute. Drain drippings from skillet. Stir in chicken, pasta sauce, coconut milk, taco seasoning mix, salt, pepper and beans. Heat to boiling. Reduce heat to medium-low; simmer uncovered 6 to 10 minutes, stirring frequently, until slightly thickened.

3. Stir in chopped cilantro. Ladle cassoulet into individual bowls. Sprinkle about 2 tablespoons bread crumb mixture over each serving and garnish with cilantro sprig.

Nutrition Information Per Serving: Calories 640 • Total Fat 33g • Saturated Fat 12g • Trans Fat 0g • Cholesterol 110mg • Sodium 1820mg • Total Carbohydrate 42g • Dietary Fiber 8g • Sugars 5g • Protein 45g. **Dietary Exchanges:** 2 Starch • 1 Other Carbohydrate • 5½ Lean Meat • 3 Fat.

turkey stew with biscuits

PREP TIME: 30 MINUTES
READY TO SERVE: 50 MINUTES
SERVINGS: 6

✳ meal-in-one

4 slices bacon, cut into
½-inch pieces

1 (¾ to 1-lb.) fresh turkey
breast tenderloin, cut into
½-inch pieces

2 (10¾-oz.) cans condensed
cream of chicken soup

1 (1-lb.) pkg. frozen broccoli,
carrots and cauliflower

¼ to ½ teaspoon poultry
seasoning

¾ cup sour cream

1 (6-oz.) can Pillsbury® Golden
Layers™ Refrigerated
Buttermilk Biscuits
(5 biscuits)

1. Heat oven to 375°F. Cook bacon in large skillet over medium heat until crisp. Reserve bacon and 1 tablespoon drippings in skillet. Add turkey to skillet; cook and stir until browned and no longer pink.

2. Stir in soup, vegetables and poultry seasoning. Cook until bubbly, stirring frequently. Reduce heat; cover and simmer 5 to 7 minutes or until vegetables are crisp-tender.

3. Stir in sour cream. Spoon mixture into ungreased 2½-quart oval casserole or 12x8-inch (2-quart) glass baking dish.

4. Separate dough into 5 biscuits; cut each in half. Arrange cut side down over hot mixture around outer edges of casserole.

5. Bake at 375°F for 14 to 18 minutes or until biscuits are deep golden brown and bottoms are no longer doughy.

Nutrition Information Per Serving: Calories 360 • Total Fat 19g • Saturated Fat 7g • Cholesterol 70mg • Sodium 1190mg • Total Carbohydrate 27g • Dietary Fiber 3g • Sugars 6g • Protein 21g. **Dietary Exchanges:** 1½ Starch • 1 Vegetable • 2 Lean Meat • 2½ Fat OR 1½ Carbohydrate • 1 Vegetable • 2 Lean Meat • 2½ Fat.

baked chicken peanut kabobs

READY TO SERVE: 35 MINUTES
SERVINGS: 6

4 boneless skinless chicken
breast halves, cut into 1-inch
pieces

12 fresh whole mushrooms

6 green onions, cut into
2-inch pieces

½ cup purchased teriyaki
sauce

1 tablespoon oil

¼ cup creamy peanut butter

¼ teaspoon hot pepper sauce

1. Heat oven to 450°F. Spray broiler pan with cooking spray. Alternately thread chicken, mushrooms and green onions on six 8 to 12-inch metal skewers. Place on sprayed broiler pan.

2. In small bowl, combine 2 tablespoons of the teriyaki sauce and oil; mix well. Brush on kabobs.

3. Bake at 450°F for 18 to 20 minutes or until chicken is no longer pink, turning once and brushing with teriyaki and oil mixture. Discard any remaining teriyaki and oil mixture.

4. To prepare sauce, in medium bowl combine remaining teriyaki sauce, peanut butter and hot pepper sauce; mix well. Using a clean brush, brush sauce on kabobs before serving. Serve with remaining sauce.

Nutrition Information Per Serving: Calories 200 • Total Fat 8g • Saturated Fat 2g • Cholesterol 50mg • Sodium 850mg • Total Carbohydrate 8g • Dietary Fiber 1g • Sugars 4g • Protein 23g. **Dietary Exchanges:** ½ Fruit • 2 Lean Meat OR ½ Carbohydrate • 2 Lean Meat.

easy oriental chicken salad

easy oriental chicken salad

PREP TIME: 20 MINUTES
READY TO SERVE: 35 MINUTES
SERVINGS: 4

✳ meal-in-one

¼ cup soy sauce

¼ cup water

2 boneless skinless chicken breast halves, cut into thin crosswise strips

1 (8-oz.) can sliced water chestnuts, drained

1 cup julienne-cut (1x¼x¼-inch) carrots

½ cup diagonally sliced green onions

¼ cup sugar

½ cup oil

⅓ cup white wine vinegar

½ teaspoon ginger

1½ cups finely chopped red cabbage

1 cup chow mein noodles

1. In large skillet, bring soy sauce and water to a boil. Add chicken. Reduce heat; cover and simmer 5 to 8 minutes or until chicken is no longer pink. Drain; cool 15 minutes.

2. In medium bowl, combine water chestnuts, carrots, green onions and chicken.

3. In small jar with tight-fitting lid, combine sugar, oil, vinegar and ginger; shake well. Pour over salad; toss to coat. Just before serving, add cabbage and chow mein noodles to salad; toss gently.

Nutrition Information Per Serving: Calories 480 • Total Fat 32g • Saturated Fat 4g • Cholesterol 35mg • Sodium 360mg • Total Carbohydrate 33g • Dietary Fiber 3g • Sugars 18g • Protein 16g. **Dietary Exchanges:** 1 Starch • 1 Fruit • 2 Lean Meat • 5½ Fat OR 2 Carbohydrate • 2 Lean Meat • 5½ Fat.

lemon chicken

READY TO SERVE: 30 MINUTES
SERVINGS: 4

chicken

¾ cup finely crushed corn flakes cereal

½ teaspoon ginger

⅛ teaspoon pepper

1 egg white

1 teaspoon water

1 teaspoon soy sauce

4 boneless skinless chicken breast halves

sauce

½ cup chicken broth

1 tablespoon cornstarch

⅓ cup honey

3 tablespoons fresh lemon juice

1 teaspoon ketchup

⅛ teaspoon garlic powder

1 teaspoon grated lemon peel

2 green onions, cut into ½-inch pieces, including tops

1. Line cookie sheet with foil; place in oven. Heat oven to 450°F. In pie pan, combine crushed cereal, ginger and pepper; mix well. In small bowl, beat egg white, water and soy sauce until frothy. Brush both sides of chicken with egg white mixture. Place in pie pan; spoon cereal mixture over chicken to coat evenly.

2. Remove hot foil-lined cookie sheet from oven; arrange coated chicken on sheet. Bake at 450°F for 15 to 20 minutes or until chicken is fork-tender and juices run clear.

3. Meanwhile, in medium saucepan, combine broth and cornstarch; blend until smooth. Add honey, lemon juice, ketchup and garlic powder; mix well. Bring to a boil over medium-high heat, stirring constantly. Remove from heat; stir in lemon peel.

4. To serve, cut each chicken breast half crosswise into 6 or 7 pieces; arrange on 4 individual plates. Spoon sauce over chicken; sprinkle with green onions.

Nutrition Information Per Serving: Calories 310 • Total Fat 3g • Saturated Fat 1g • Cholesterol 75mg • Sodium 440mg • Total Carbohydrate 41g • Dietary Fiber 1g • Sugars 24 g • Protein 30g. **Dietary Exchanges:** 1 Starch • 1½ Fruit • 4 Very Lean Meat OR 2½ Carbohydrate • 4 Very Lean Meat.

chicken marengo

1 tablespoon olive oil or vegetable oil

4 bone-in chicken breast halves, skin removed

1 tablespoon all-purpose flour

1/2 teaspoon dried basil leaves

1/4 teaspoon garlic powder

1/8 teaspoon pepper

1/2 cup dry white wine or chicken broth

2 tablespoons tomato paste

2 (14.5 or 16-oz.) cans regular or Italian whole tomatoes, well drained, cut up

1/2 cup coarsely chopped green bell pepper

1 medium onion, cut into 8 thin wedges

1/4 cup halved or sliced pitted ripe olives

1. Heat oil in large skillet over medium-high heat until hot. Add chicken breast halves; cook until browned on all sides.

2. In medium bowl, combine flour, basil, garlic powder, pepper, wine and tomato paste; blend until smooth. Stir in tomatoes. Move chicken to side of skillet; add tomato mixture. Place chicken, meaty side up, in tomato mixture. Bring to a boil. Reduce heat to medium-low; cover and cook 10 minutes, stirring occasionally.

3. Turn chicken; stir in bell pepper and onion. Cover; cook an additional 8 to 10 minutes or until chicken is fork-tender and juices run clear, stirring occasionally. Stir in the olives.

Nutrition Information Per Serving: Calories 280 • Total Fat 8g • Saturated Fat 1g • Cholesterol 75mg • Sodium 230mg • Total Carbohydrate 17g • Dietary Fiber 3g • Sugars 7g • Protein 30g. **Dietary Exchanges:** 1/2 Starch • 2 Vegetable • 3 1/2 Lean Meat OR 1/2 Carbohydrate • 2 Vegetable • 3 1/2 Lean Meat.

deluxe turkey club pizza

✳ meal-in-one

crust

1 (10-oz.) can Pillsbury® Refrigerated Pizza Crust

2 teaspoons sesame seed

topping

6 slices bacon, cut into 1-inch pieces

1/4 cup light or regular mayonnaise

1/2 to 1 teaspoon grated lemon peel

4 oz. shredded Monterey Jack cheese (1 cup)

1 tablespoon thinly sliced fresh basil or 1 teaspoon dried basil leaves

1/4 lb. cooked turkey breast slices, cut into 1-inch strips

2 small Italian plum tomatoes or 1 small tomato, thinly sliced

2 oz. shredded Swiss cheese (1/2 cup)

Fresh basil leaves, if desired

1. Heat oven to 425°F. Lightly spray 12-inch pizza pan or 13x9-inch pan with cooking spray. Unroll dough; place in sprayed pan. Starting at center, press out dough to edge of pan. Sprinkle sesame seed evenly over dough. Bake at 425°F for 10 to 12 minutes or until crust is light golden brown.

2. Meanwhile, cook bacon in large skillet over medium heat until crisp. Drain on paper towels. Discard drippings. In small bowl, combine mayonnaise and lemon peel; blend well.

3. Remove partially baked crust from oven. Spread mayonnaise mixture over crust. Top with Monterey Jack cheese, sliced basil, turkey strips, cooked bacon and tomatoes. Sprinkle with Swiss cheese.

4. Return to oven; bake an additional 7 to 9 minutes or until crust is golden brown and cheese is melted. Garnish with fresh basil leaves.

Nutrition Information Per Serving: Calories 320 • Total Fat 17g • Saturated Fat 8g • Cholesterol 40mg • Sodium 920mg • Total Carbohydrate 24g • Dietary Fiber 1g • Sugars 3g • Protein 18g. **Dietary Exchanges:** 1 1/2 Starch • 2 Lean Meat • 2 Fat OR 1 1/2 Carbohydrate • 2 Lean Meat • 2 Fat.

bacon cheddar chicken fillet melt

READY TO SERVE: 30 MINUTES
SERVINGS: 4

4 boneless skinless chicken breast halves

8 slices bacon

1 small red onion, sliced

4 slices pumpernickel bread, toasted

4 teaspoons steak sauce

4 oz. shredded Cheddar cheese (1 cup)

1. Place 1 chicken breast half between 2 pieces of plastic wrap or waxed paper. Working from center, gently pound chicken with flat side of meat mallet or rolling pin until about $\frac{1}{4}$ inch thick; remove wrap. Repeat with remaining chicken breast halves.

2. Cook bacon in large skillet over medium heat until crisp. Remove bacon; drain on paper towels. Reserve 1 tablespoon drippings in skillet. Add onion to drippings; cook and stir 2 to 4 minutes or until tender. Remove onion from skillet. Add chicken to skillet; cook 6 to 8 minutes on each side or until lightly browned and juices run clear.

3. Place toasted bread slices on cookie sheet; spread each slice with 1 teaspoon steak sauce. Top with chicken, bacon slices, onion and cheese. Broil 4 to 6 inches from heat for 1 to 2 minutes or until cheese is melted.

Nutrition Information Per Serving: Calories 440 • Total Fat 23g • Saturated Fat 10g • Cholesterol 15mg • Sodium 760mg • Total Carbohydrate 18g • Dietary Fiber 2g • Sugars 3g • Protein 40g.
Dietary Exchanges: 1 Starch • 5 Lean Meat • 2 Fat OR 1 Carbohydrate • 5 Lean Meat • 2 Fat.

double-dipped chicken nuggets

PREP TIME: 10 MINUTES
READY TO SERVE: 30 MINUTES
SERVINGS: 6

¼ cup all-purpose flour

½ teaspoon seasoned salt

1 cup finely crushed corn flakes cereal

4 boneless skinless chicken breast halves, cut into 1-inch pieces

¼ cup margarine or butter, melted

1. Heat oven to 400°F. In plastic bag, combine flour and seasoned salt; shake to mix. Place crushed cereal in another plastic bag.

2. Add chicken pieces to flour mixture in bag; shake to coat. Dip floured pieces in margarine; coat with crushed cereal. Place in ungreased 15x10x1-inch baking pan.

3. Bake at 400°F for 15 to 20 minutes or until chicken is no longer pink.

Nutrition Information Per Serving: Calories 230 • Total Fat 10g • Saturated Fat 2g • Cholesterol 50mg • Sodium 410mg • Total Carbohydrate 16g • Dietary Fiber 1g • Sugars 1g • Protein 19g. **Dietary Exchanges:** 1 Starch • 2 Lean Meat • 1 Fat OR 1 Carbohydrate • 2 Lean Meat • 1 Fat.

"IS IT READY YET?"

To test for doneness on cut pieces of chicken or turkey, use a small, sharp knife to slice into the center of a large piece of meat. The center of the meat should still look juicy and moist, but any juices you see should be clear—not pink. The poultry meat itself should not look pink either, with the exception of dark meat nearest the bone. For proper food safety you should practice this doneness test no matter how you prepare poultry.

---

chicken breasts florentine

READY TO SERVE: 20 MINUTES
SERVINGS: 4

* super fast

1 (9-oz.) pkg. frozen spinach in a pouch

3 tablespoons butter, melted

4 boneless skinless chicken breast halves

⅓ cup plain bread crumbs

¼ teaspoon dried basil leaves

2 tablespoons oil

2 oz. shredded mozzarella cheese (½ cup)

1. Cook spinach as directed on package; squeeze to drain. Stir in butter; set aside.

2. Meanwhile, place 1 chicken breast half between two pieces of plastic wrap or waxed paper. Working from center, gently pound chicken with flat side of meat mallet or rolling pin until about ¼ inch thick; remove wrap. Repeat with remaining chicken breast halves. In shallow bowl, combine bread crumbs and basil. Coat chicken breasts with crumb mixture.

3. Heat oil in large skillet over medium-high heat until hot. Add chicken breasts; cook 5 to 7 minutes on each side or until lightly browned, fork-tender and juices run clear. Reduce heat to low. Spoon cooked spinach evenly over each chicken breast half; sprinkle with cheese. Cover; cook until cheese is melted.

Nutrition Information Per Serving: Calories 370 • Total Fat 22g • Saturated Fat 9g • Cholesterol 105mg • Sodium 450mg • Total Carbohydrate 9g • Dietary Fiber 1g • Sugars 1g • Protein 34g. **Dietary Exchanges:** 2 Vegetable • 4 Lean Meat • 2 Fat.

chicken and bean skillet supper

READY TO SERVE: 30 MINUTES
SERVINGS: 6

✳ meal-in-one

4 slices bacon, cut into
½-inch pieces

2 boneless skinless chicken
breast halves, cut into 1-inch
pieces

4 boneless skinless chicken
thighs, cut into 1-inch pieces

1 cup chopped onions

1 cup chopped green bell
pepper

½ cup purchased thick and
chunky salsa

½ teaspoon dried thyme
leaves

1 (16-oz.) can baked beans,
undrained

1 (15.5-oz.) can dark red
kidney beans, drained

1 (15.5-oz.) can great
northern beans, drained

1. In large skillet or Dutch oven, cook bacon over medium heat until crisp. Drain, reserving 3 tablespoons drippings in skillet. Add chicken, onions and bell pepper; cook and stir until chicken is browned.

2. Stir in remaining ingredients. Bring to a boil. Reduce heat to low; simmer 15 to 20 minutes or until chicken is no longer pink, stirring occasionally.

Nutrition Information Per Serving: Calories 390 • Total Fat 15g • Saturated Fat 5g • Cholesterol 70mg • Sodium 890mg • Total Carbohydrate 36g • Dietary Fiber 9g • Sugars 10g • Protein 28g. **Dietary Exchanges:** 2 Starch • 1 Vegetable • 3 Lean Meat • 1 Fat OR 2 Carbohydrate • 1 Vegetable • 3 Lean Meat • 1 Fat.

one-pan crispy chicken and biscuits

PREP TIME: 5 MINUTES
READY TO SERVE: 40 MINUTES
SERVINGS: 4

✳ meal-in-one

⅔ cup corn flake crumbs

1 teaspoon seasoned salt

¼ cup milk

4 boneless skinless chicken
breast halves

1 (16.3-oz.) can Pillsbury®
Grands!® Refrigerated
Buttermilk Biscuits

1. Heat oven to 375°F. Line 15x10x1-inch baking pan with foil.

2. In shallow dish, combine corn flake crumbs and seasoned salt; mix well. Place milk in another shallow dish. Dip chicken in milk; coat with crumb mixture. Arrange chicken in center of foil-lined pan.

3. Bake at 375°F for 15 minutes. Remove chicken from oven. Separate dough into 8 biscuits. Place biscuits in pan around chicken.

4. Return to oven; bake an additional 15 to 17 minutes or until biscuits are golden brown and chicken is fork-tender and juices run clear.

Nutrition Information Per Serving: Calories 605 • Total Fat 21g • Saturated Fat 6g • Cholesterol 75mg • Sodium 1960mg • Total Carbohydrate 68g • Dietary Fiber 2g • Sugars 18g • Protein 36g. **Dietary Exchanges:** 4½ Starch • 3 Medium-Fat Meat • 1 Fat OR 4½ Carbohydrate • 3 Medium-Fat Meat • 1 Fat.

CORN FLAKE CRUMBLES

It's easy to make your own corn flake crumbs. You'll need about 1½ cups corn flake cereal to get ⅔ cup crumbs. Place the cereal in a resealable food storage plastic bag and crush with a rolling pin. You could also use a small saucepan or your hands. This is a job the kids will love to help you with.

chicken and vegetables with dijon vinaigrette

READY TO SERVE: 30 MINUTES
SERVINGS: 4

* meal-in-one

salad

- 4 boneless skinless chicken breast halves
- 1/2 teaspoon peppered seasoned salt or seasoned salt
- 4 medium new red potatoes, quartered
- 1/4 teaspoon salt
- 1/2 lb. whole green beans
- 1 medium red bell pepper, cut into thin strips
- 1 medium yellow summer squash, cut into 2-inch thin strips

dressing

- 1/3 cup chopped walnuts, toasted
- 1/4 cup olive oil or vegetable oil
- 1/3 cup white wine vinegar
- 2 tablespoons Dijon mustard
- 2 teaspoons sugar

1. Heat grill. Sprinkle chicken with peppered seasoned salt. When ready to grill, place chicken on gas grill over medium heat or on charcoal grill 4 to 6 inches from medium-high coals. Cook 10 to 15 minutes or until chicken is fork-tender and juices run clear, turning once.

2. Meanwhile, place potatoes in large skillet; add 1/2 inch of water and the salt. Bring to a boil. Reduce heat to medium; cover and cook 5 minutes. Add green beans; cover and cook an additional 6 to 8 minutes or until vegetables are crisp-tender. Add bell pepper and squash; cook 2 to 4 minutes or until all vegetables are just tender. Drain.

3. In small jar with tight-fitting lid, combine all dressing ingredients; shake well. Cut warm chicken crosswise into slices. Arrange chicken and vegetables on large platter; drizzle with dressing.

Nutrition Information Per Serving: Calories 460 • Total Fat 24g • Saturated Fat 3g • Cholesterol 75mg • Sodium 450mg • Total Carbohydrate 28g • Dietary Fiber 6g • Sugars 8g • Protein 32g. **Dietary Exchanges:** 1 Starch • 2 Vegetable • 4 Lean Meat • 2 1/2 Fat OR 1 Carbohydrate • 2 Vegetable • 4 Lean Meat • 2 1/2 Fat.

chicken and fettuccine primavera

READY TO SERVE: 25 MINUTES
SERVINGS: 4

* super fast

- 6 oz. uncooked fettuccine
- 1 tablespoon olive oil or vegetable oil
- 4 boneless skinless chicken breast halves, cut into thin strips
- 1 (14.5-oz.) can Italian-style tomatoes with olive oil, garlic and spices, undrained
- 1/2 teaspoon fennel seed
- 1/4 teaspoon salt
- 1/8 teaspoon ground red pepper (cayenne)
- 1 cup coarsely chopped green bell pepper
- 2 cups sliced yellow summer squash
- 1 oz. shredded fresh Parmesan cheese, if desired (1/4 cup)

1. Cook fettuccine to desired doneness as directed on package. Drain; cover to keep warm.

2. Meanwhile, heat oil in large skillet or Dutch oven over medium-high heat until hot. Add chicken strips; cook and stir until browned. Stir in tomatoes, fennel seed, salt and ground red pepper. Bring to a boil. Reduce heat to medium; cook 2 to 3 minutes.

3. Stir in bell pepper and summer squash; cook an additional 4 to 6 minutes or until vegetables are crisp-tender and chicken is no longer pink, stirring occasionally. Stir in fettuccine; cook an additional 2 to 4 minutes or until thoroughly heated, stirring frequently. Sprinkle with Parmesan cheese.

Nutrition Information Per Serving: Calories 410 • Total Fat 12g • Saturated Fat 3g • Cholesterol 110mg • Sodium 760mg • Total Carbohydrate 41g • Dietary Fiber 4g • Sugars 7g • Protein 35g. **Dietary Exchanges:** 2 Starch • 2 Vegetable • 3 1/2 Lean Meat OR 2 Carbohydrate • 2 Vegetable • 3 1/2 Lean Meat.

chicken and vegetables
with dijon vinaigrette

tuscan roasted potato-chicken salad

READY TO SERVE: 30 MINUTES
SERVINGS: 4

KAREN TEDESCO ✳ WEBSTER GROVES, MISSOURI
BAKE-OFF® CONTEST 42, 2006

- 1 (19-oz.) bag frozen roasted potatoes with garlic and herb sauce
- 1 cup diced fresh mozzarella cheese (6 oz.)
- ⅓ cup oil-packed sun-dried tomatoes, drained, cut into strips
- 2 to 3 teaspoons chopped fresh rosemary
- 1 (15-oz.) can cannellini (white kidney) beans, drained, rinsed
- 1 (6-oz.) pkg. refrigerated grilled chicken breast strips, heated in microwave as directed on package, coarsely chopped
- ⅓ cup basil pesto
- 2 teaspoons fresh lemon juice
  Salt and pepper, if desired
- 3 cups mixed baby salad greens
- ¼ cup pine nuts, toasted

1. In 2-quart microwavable bowl or casserole, microwave frozen potatoes and sauce chips, covered, on high 9 to 13 minutes, stirring once halfway through microwaving, until potatoes are tender. Stir potatoes to mix with sauce. Pour potato mixture into large bowl.

2. Stir in cheese, tomatoes, rosemary, beans and warm chicken. Add pesto and lemon juice; gently toss to coat. Season to taste with salt and pepper.

3. Arrange salad greens on large serving platter. Spoon potato salad over lettuce; sprinkle with pine nuts. Serve warm or at room temperature.

Nutrition Information Per Serving: Calories 610 • Total Fat 30g • Saturated Fat 10g • Trans Fat 1g • Cholesterol 55mg • Sodium 1290mg • Total Carbohydrate 48g • Dietary Fiber 10g • Sugars 4g • Protein 36g. **Dietary Exchanges:** 3 Starch • 1 Vegetable • 3½ Lean Meat • 3½ Fat.

PINE NUTS POINTER

To toast pine nuts, place them in a single layer on a cookie sheet; bake them at 350°F for 8 minutes, stirring once until they are golden brown.

herb cheese-stuffed chicken breasts

PREP TIME: 10 MINUTES
READY TO SERVE: 45 MINUTES
SERVINGS: 4

4 boneless skinless chicken breast halves

2 oz. feta cheese, crumbled (¼ cup)

¼ cup chopped fresh parsley

2 teaspoons chopped fresh oregano or ¼ teaspoon dried oregano leaves

2 tablespoons olive or vegetable oil

2 (14.5-oz.) cans Italian-style diced tomatoes, undrained

¼ cup sliced ripe olives

4 teaspoons cornstarch

1. Heat oven to 350°F. Using sharp knife, cut 3-inch slit in meaty side of each chicken breast half to form pocket.

2. In small bowl, combine feta cheese, parsley, oregano and oil; mix well. Gently spoon ¼ of mixture into each pocket. Place chicken in ungreased 13x9-inch (3-quart) baking dish.

3. In medium bowl, combine tomatoes, olives and cornstarch; mix well. Pour over the chicken.

4. Bake at 350°F for 35 to 40 minutes or until the chicken is fork-tender and the juices run clear.

Nutrition Information Per Serving: Calories 320 • Total Fat 14g • Saturated Fat 4g • Cholesterol 85mg • Sodium 750mg • Total Carbohydrate 18g • Dietary Fiber 3g • Sugars 5g • Protein 31g. **Dietary Exchanges:** ½ Starch • 2 Vegetable • 4 Very Lean Meat • 2 Fat OR ½ Carbohydrate • 2 Vegetable • 4 Very Lean Meat • 2 Fat.

chicken with pasta and pesto

READY TO SERVE: 20 MINUTES
SERVINGS: 4

* super fast

5 oz. uncooked medium shell pasta (2 cups)

1 tablespoon oil

4 boneless skinless chicken breast halves, cut into 1-inch pieces

1 (14-oz.) can artichoke hearts, drained, quartered

½ cup purchased pesto

½ cup chopped tomato

1 oz. shredded fresh Parmesan cheese (¼ cup)

1. Cook pasta to desired doneness as directed on package. Drain; cover to keep warm.

2. Meanwhile, heat oil in large skillet over medium-high heat until hot. Add chicken; cook and stir 4 to 5 minutes or until browned and no longer pink. Stir in artichoke hearts, pesto and pasta. Cook an additional 1 to 2 minutes or until thoroughly heated, stirring constantly. Sprinkle with tomato and Parmesan cheese.

Nutrition Information Per Serving: Calories 440 • Total Fat 16g • Saturated Fat 4g • Cholesterol 80mg • Sodium 340mg • Total Carbohydrate 36g • Dietary Fiber 5g • Sugars 3g • Protein 37g. **Dietary Exchanges:** 2 Starch • 1 Vegetable • 4 Lean Meat • 1 Fat OR 2 Carbohydrate • 1 Vegetable • 4 Lean Meat • 1 Fat.

sage and rosemary chicken strips

READY TO SERVE: 20 MINUTES
SERVINGS: 4

* super fast

⅓ cup all-purpose flour

½ teaspoon onion powder

¼ teaspoon salt

¼ teaspoon dried rosemary leaves, crushed

⅛ teaspoon ground sage

4 boneless skinless chicken breast halves, cut into long, thin strips

1 tablespoon oil

1. In shallow bowl, combine flour, onion powder, salt, rosemary and sage; mix well. Generously coat chicken pieces with flour mixture.

2. Heat oil in large skillet over medium-high heat until hot. Add chicken; reduce heat to medium. Cook and stir 8 to 10 minutes, or until lightly browned on all sides and no longer pink.

Nutrition Information Per Serving: Calories 210 • Total Fat 7g • Saturated Fat 1g • Cholesterol 75mg • Sodium 200mg • Total Carbohydrate 8g • Dietary Fiber 0g • Sugars 0g • Protein 28g. **Dietary Exchanges:** ½ Starch • 4 Very Lean Meat • ½ Fat OR ½ Carbohydrate • 4 Very Lean Meat • ½ Fat.

chicken spinach pizza

READY TO SERVE: 30 MINUTES
SERVINGS: 8

✳ meal-in-one

1 (10-oz.) can refrigerated pizza crust

2 cups frozen cut leaf spinach, cooked, well drained

1½ cups chopped cooked chicken

3 to 4 thinly sliced Italian plum tomatoes

¼ teaspoon garlic powder

¼ teaspoon dried marjoram leaves

6 oz. shredded Swiss cheese (1½ cups)

1. Heat oven to 400°F. Grease 12-inch pizza pan. Unroll dough; place in greased pan. Starting at center, press out with hands. Bake at 400°F for 7 to 9 minutes or until light golden brown.

2. Top partially baked crust with remaining ingredients. Bake an additional 12 to 15 minutes or until cheese is melted and crust is golden brown.

Nutrition Information Per Serving: Calories 240 • Total Fat 9g • Saturated Fat 5g • Cholesterol 45mg • Sodium 320mg • Total Carbohydrate 20g • Dietary Fiber 2g • Sugars 2g • Protein 19g. **Dietary Exchanges:** 1 Starch • 1 Vegetable • 2 Medium-Fat Meat OR 1 Carbohydrate • 1 Vegetable • 2 Medium-Fat Meat.

grilled barbecue chicken pizza

READY TO SERVE: 20 MINUTES
SERVINGS: 8

✳ super fast

2 cups cubed cooked chicken

½ cup barbecue sauce

1 teaspoon chili powder

1 (16-oz.) prebaked Italian bread shell

8 oz. shredded Monterey Jack cheese (2 cups)

¼ cup finely chopped onion

¼ cup chopped green bell pepper

1. Heat grill. In small bowl, combine chicken, barbecue sauce and chili powder; spread evenly on bread shell. Sprinkle with cheese, onion and bell pepper.

2. When ready to grill, place pizza directly on gas grill over medium heat or on charcoal grill 4 to 6 inches from medium coals. Cover grill; cook 10 minutes or until bottom of pizza is crisp and cheese is melted.

Nutrition Information Per Serving: Calories 340 • Total Fat 15g • Saturated Fat 7g • Cholesterol 60mg • Sodium 610mg • Total Carbohydrate 28g • Dietary Fiber 1g • Sugars 2g • Protein 24g. **Dietary Exchanges:** 2 Starch • 2½ Lean Meat • 2 Fat OR 2 Carbohydrate • 2½ Lean Meat • 2 Fat.

pesto, turkey and pasta salad

READY TO SERVE: 30 MINUTES
SERVINGS: 6

✳ meal-in-one

8 oz. uncooked bow tie pasta (3 cups)

2 cups diced cooked turkey

½ cup sliced marinated sun-dried tomatoes

1 (2¼-oz.) can sliced ripe olives, drained

½ cup mayonnaise

½ cup purchased pesto

4 leaves leaf lettuce

1 oz. shredded fresh Parmesan cheese (¼ cup)

1. Cook pasta to desired doneness as directed on package. Drain; rinse with cold water to cool.

2. In large bowl, combine cooked pasta, turkey, tomatoes and olives.

3. In small bowl, combine mayonnaise and pesto; blend well. Add to turkey mixture; toss to coat.

4. Line 4 individual plates with lettuce. Spoon turkey mixture over lettuce. Sprinkle with cheese.

Nutrition Information Per Serving: Calories 510 • Total Fat 31g • Saturated Fat 6g • Cholesterol 55mg • Sodium 480mg • Total Carbohydrate 34g • Dietary Fiber 2g • Sugars 4g • Protein 23g. **Dietary Exchanges:** 2½ Starch • 2 Lean Meat • 4½ Fat OR 2½ Carbohydrate • 2 Lean Meat • 4½ Fat.

chicken almond ding

READY TO SERVE: 25 MINUTES
SERVINGS: 4

* **super fast**

- 1 cup chicken broth
- 2 tablespoons cornstarch
- 2 tablespoons soy sauce
- 1 tablespoon rice vinegar
- 1 teaspoon sugar
- ¼ teaspoon salt, if desired
- 1 tablespoon oil
- 2 garlic cloves, minced
- ½ cup slivered almonds
- 4 boneless skinless chicken breast halves, cut into ½-inch pieces
- 1 medium red bell pepper, cut into ¾-inch pieces
- 1 cup fresh pea pods, trimmed, cut diagonally in half
- 1 (8-oz.) can sliced water chestnuts, drained
- 2 cups chopped Chinese (napa) cabbage
- 4 cups hot cooked rice

1. In small bowl combine broth, cornstarch, soy sauce, vinegar, sugar and salt; mix well. Set aside.

2. Heat oil in large skillet or wok over medium-high heat until hot. Add garlic, almonds and chicken; cook and stir 3 to 4 minutes or until chicken is no longer pink and almonds are golden brown.

3. Add bell pepper; cook and stir 2 to 3 minutes. Add pea pods and water chestnuts; cook and stir 3 to 4 minutes or until vegetables are crisp-tender. Add cabbage and cornstarch mixture; cook and stir until sauce is thickened and bubbly. Serve over rice.

Nutrition Information Per Serving: Calories 560 • Total Fat 15g • Saturated Fat 2g • Cholesterol 70mg • Sodium 940mg • Total Carbohydrate 68g • Dietary Fiber 5g • Sugars 6g • Protein 37g. **Dietary Exchanges:** 4 Starch • 1 Vegetable • 3 Lean Meat • 1 Fat OR 4 Carbohydrate • 1 Vegetable • 3 Lean Meat • 1 Fat.

ABOUT WATER CHESTNUTS

Water chestnuts…edible tubers that grow underwater…make great kitchen staples. You can add the crunchy little bites to cold salads, easy stir-fries and even hearty dinner casseroles. They are available canned, either whole or sliced, so they're easy to keep on hand. Fresh water chestnuts are available in some Chinese and ethnic markets, but they must be peeled before using and are much sweeter and crisper than the canned variety.

no-bake salad pizza

READY TO SERVE: 15 MINUTES
SERVINGS: 8

✻ super fast

1 cup purchased spinach dip

1 (10-oz.) thin crust Italian bread shell

1 cup chopped broccoli

1 cup cubed cooked chicken

1/3 cup sliced green onions

1 small tomato, seeded, chopped

1. Spread spinach dip evenly over bread shell to within 1/2 inch of edge. Top with remaining ingredients.

2. To serve, cut into 8 wedges.

Nutrition Information Per Serving: Calories 230 • Total Fat 12g • Saturated Fat 4g • Cholesterol 30mg • Sodium 330mg • Total Carbohydrate 19g • Dietary Fiber 1g • Sugars 3g • Protein 11g. **Dietary Exchanges:** 1 Starch • 1 Vegetable • 1 Lean Meat • 1 1/2 Fat OR 1 Carbohydrate • 1 Vegetable • 1 Lean Meat • 1 1/2 Fat.

chicken and black bean burritos

READY TO SERVE: 30 MINUTES
SERVINGS: 6

✻ meal-in-one

1 tablespoon oil

3 boneless skinless chicken breast halves, cut into thin strips

1 (15-oz.) can black beans, drained, rinsed

3 tablespoons water

1/2 teaspoon cumin

1 garlic clove, minced

2 to 3 drops hot pepper sauce

6 (8 to 10-inch) flour tortillas

6 lettuce leaves

1 small tomato, seeded, chopped

1/4 cup sliced green onions

2 tablespoons chopped fresh cilantro

1. Heat oven to 350°F. Heat oil in large skillet over medium-high heat until hot. Add chicken; cook and stir 5 minutes or until chicken is no longer pink. Remove from skillet; cover to keep warm.

2. In same skillet, combine beans, water, cumin, garlic and hot pepper sauce; mix well. Cook over medium-high heat until thoroughly heated, stirring occasionally and mashing beans slightly.

3. Meanwhile, wrap tortillas in foil. Bake at 350°F for 10 minutes or until warm.

4. Place 1 lettuce leaf on each warm tortilla; spoon about 2 tablespoons bean mixture down center of each. Top each with 1/3 cup cooked chicken; sprinkle with tomato, onions and cilantro. Fold in sides of each tortilla over filling, overlapping to form triangle.

Nutrition Information Per Serving: Calories 330 • Total Fat 8g • Saturated Fat 2g • Cholesterol 35mg • Sodium 440mg • Total Carbohydrate 42g • Dietary Fiber 5g • Sugars 1g • Protein 22g. **Dietary Exchanges:** 3 Starch • 2 Very Lean Meat • 1/2 Fat OR 3 Carbohydrate • 2 Very Lean Meat • 1/2 Fat.

grilled caribbean chicken

READY TO SERVE: 30 MINUTES
SERVINGS: 4

1 teaspoon allspice

½ teaspoon dried thyme leaves

½ teaspoon paprika

¼ teaspoon hot pepper sauce

2 teaspoons olive or vegetable oil

2 teaspoons lime juice

4 boneless skinless chicken breast halves

1. Heat grill. In small bowl, combine all ingredients except chicken; mix well. Rub mixture on chicken breast halves. Let stand at room temperature for 15 minutes to marinate.

2. When ready to grill, place chicken on gas grill over medium heat or on charcoal grill 4 to 6 inches from medium coals. Cook 8 to 10 minutes or until chicken is fork-tender and juices run clear, turning once.

Nutrition Information Per Serving: Calories 160 • Total Fat 5g • Saturated Fat 1g • Cholesterol 75mg • Sodium 65mg • Total Carbohydrate 1g • Dietary Fiber 0g • Sugars 0g • Protein 27g. **Dietary Exchanges:** 4 Very Lean Meat • ½ Fat.

saucy chicken and peaches

READY TO SERVE: 20 MINUTES
SERVINGS: 4

✳ super fast

1 teaspoon oil

4 boneless skinless chicken breast halves

1 (16-oz.) can sliced peaches in light syrup, undrained

1 tablespoon cornstarch

2 tablespoons brown sugar

1 tablespoon cider vinegar

1 tablespoon soy sauce

½ to 1 teaspoon dried basil leaves

1. Heat oil in large skillet over medium heat until hot. Add chicken; cook 4 to 5 minutes, or until lightly browned. Turn chicken; cover and cook an additional 4 to 5 minutes, or until chicken is fork-tender and juices run clear. Remove from skillet; cover to keep warm.

2. Meanwhile, drain peach syrup into glass measuring cup; add water to make 1 cup liquid. Stir in cornstarch, brown sugar, vinegar, soy sauce and basil.

3. Pour liquid into hot skillet; cook and stir until thickened and bubbly. Gently stir in peach slices and chicken. If desired, serve with hot cooked rice.

Nutrition Information Per Serving: Calories 250 • Total Fat 4g • Saturated Fat 1g • Cholesterol 75mg • Sodium 330mg • Total Carbohydrate 26g • Dietary Fiber 1g • Sugars 21g • Protein 27g. **Dietary Exchanges:** 2 Fruit • 4 Very Lean Meat OR 2 Carbohydrate • 4 Very Lean Meat.

peppered chicken

READY TO SERVE: 25 MINUTES
SERVINGS: 4

✳ super fast

8 boneless skinless chicken thighs

1 teaspoon dried thyme leaves

¼ teaspoon garlic powder

¼ teaspoon onion salt

¼ teaspoon white pepper

¼ teaspoon ground red pepper (cayenne)

¼ teaspoon black pepper

1 tablespoon oil

1. Heat grill. Place 2 chicken thighs between 2 pieces of plastic wrap or waxed paper. Working from center, gently pound chicken with flat side of meat mallet or rolling pin until about ¼ inch thick; remove wrap. Repeat with remaining chicken thighs.

2. In small bowl, combine all remaining ingredients except oil. Brush both sides of chicken thighs with oil; coat with pepper mixture.

3. When ready to grill, place chicken thighs on gas grill over medium heat or on charcoal grill 4 to 6 inches from medium coals. Cook 8 to 10 minutes or until chicken is fork-tender and juices run clear, turning once.

Nutrition Information Per Serving: Calories 240 • Total Fat 15g • Saturated Fat 4g • Cholesterol 100mg • Sodium 200mg • Total Carbohydrate 0g • Dietary Fiber 0g • Sugars 0g • Protein 27g. **Dietary Exchanges:** 4 Lean Meat • ½ Fat.

light chicken chop suey

READY TO SERVE: 20 MINUTES
SERVINGS: 4

✳ super fast

1 tablespoon cornstarch

½ teaspoon sugar

⅛ teaspoon garlic powder

½ cup chicken broth

1 to 2 tablespoons soy sauce

1 tablespoon dry sherry, if desired

1 teaspoon oil

4 boneless skinless chicken breast halves, cut into ½-inch pieces

1 cup coarsely chopped red or green bell pepper

1 cup coarsely chopped celery

1 cup diagonally cut green onions (½-inch pieces)

1 (8-oz.) pkg. fresh bean sprouts

1. In small bowl, combine cornstarch, sugar, garlic powder, broth, soy sauce and sherry; blend well.

2. Heat oil in large skillet over medium-high heat until hot. Add chicken; cook and stir 3 to 4 minutes or until chicken is no longer pink. Add bell pepper, celery and onions; cover and cook 3 to 5 minutes or until vegetables are crisp-tender, stirring occasionally.

3. Stir in bean sprouts; cook about 1 minute or until sprouts are thoroughly heated. Add cornstarch mixture to skillet; cook and stir until mixture thickens. If desired, serve with hot cooked rice; garnish with lettuce.

Nutrition Information Per Serving: Calories 220 • Total Fat 7g • Saturated Fat 1g • Cholesterol 70mg • Sodium 730mg • Total Carbohydrate 11g • Dietary Fiber 3g • Sugars 5g • Protein 29g. Dietary Exchanges: 2 Vegetable • 3½ Very Lean Meat • 1 Fat.

oven chicken cordon bleu

PREP TIME: 20 MINUTES
READY TO SERVE: 50 MINUTES
SERVINGS: 4

4 boneless skinless chicken breast halves

2 teaspoons Dijon mustard

4 teaspoons chopped fresh chives

4 very thin slices cooked lean ham (about ¾ oz. each)

4 very thin slices reduced-fat Swiss cheese (about ¾ oz. each)

1 egg white

1 tablespoon water

⅓ cup finely crushed corn flakes or bran flakes cereal

¼ teaspoon paprika

1. Heat oven to 375°F. Spray 8-inch square (1½-quart) baking dish with cooking spray. Place 1 chicken breast half between 2 pieces of plastic wrap or waxed paper. Working from center, gently pound chicken with flat side of meat mallet or rolling pin until about ¼ inch thick; remove wrap. Repeat with remaining chicken breast halves.

2. Spread each chicken breast half with ½ teaspoon mustard; sprinkle each with 1 teaspoon chives. Cut ham and cheese slices to fit chicken. Top each chicken breast half with ham and cheese slice. Roll up, tucking ends inside.

3. In shallow bowl, combine egg white and water; beat slightly. Place cereal crumbs in shallow dish. Coat chicken rolls with egg white mixture; roll in crumbs. Place in sprayed dish; sprinkle with paprika.

4. Bake at 375°F for 25 to 30 minutes or until chicken is fork-tender and juices run clear.

Nutrition Information Per Serving: Calories 250 • Total Fat 7g • Saturated Fat 3g • Cholesterol 95mg • Sodium 790mg • Total Carbohydrate 9g • Dietary Fiber 0g • Sugars 2g • Protein 38g. Dietary Exchanges: ½ Starch • 5 Very Lean Meat OR ½ Carbohydrate • 5 Very Lean Meat.

turkey philly loaf

READY TO SERVE: 30 MINUTES
SERVINGS: 4

1 (11-oz.) can Pillsbury®
  Refrigerated Crusty French
  Loaf

½ medium green bell pepper,
  thinly sliced

¼ cup sliced onion

1 (4.5-oz.) jar sliced
  mushrooms, drained

2 teaspoons olive oil

¼ teaspoon dried rosemary
  leaves, crushed

2 oz. fat-free cream cheese,
  softened

4 oz. thinly sliced cooked
  turkey

4 oz. sliced mozzarella cheese

1. Heat oven to 350°F. Bake loaf as directed on can. Cool 10 minutes.

2. Set oven to broil. On ungreased broiler pan, combine bell pepper, onion and mushrooms. Brush with oil. Sprinkle with rosemary. Broil 4 to 6 inches from heat for 8 to 10 minutes or until bell pepper and onion are fork-tender, stirring occasionally.

3. Return oven temperature to 350°F. Cut loaf in half lengthwise. Spread bottom half with cream cheese. Layer with turkey, bell pepper mixture, cheese and top half of loaf. Place filled loaf on ungreased cookie sheet.

4. Bake at 350°F for 2 to 3 minutes or until cheese is melted. Cut into 4 pieces.

Nutrition Information Per Serving: Calories 390 • Total Fat 12g • Saturated Fat 5g • Cholesterol 35mg • Sodium 830mg • Total Carbohydrate 45g • Dietary Fiber 4g • Sugars 3g • Protein 25g. **Dietary Exchanges:** 3 Starch • 2 Medium-Fat Meat OR 3 Carbohydrate • 2 Medium-Fat Meat.

quick chicken divan

PREP TIME: 15 MINUTES
READY TO SERVE: 50 MINUTES
SERVINGS: 6

* **meal-in-one**

1 (1-lb.) pkg. frozen cut broccoli

2 cups cubed cooked chicken

1 (10¾-oz.) can condensed cream of chicken soup

½ cup mayonnaise or salad dressing

1 teaspoon lemon juice

2 oz. shredded Cheddar cheese (½ cup)

½ cup soft bread crumbs

2 tablespoons margarine or butter, melted

1. Heat oven to 350°F. Grease 12x8-inch (2-quart) baking dish. Cook broccoli as directed on package; drain.

2. Arrange broccoli in greased baking dish. Layer chicken over broccoli. In small bowl, combine soup, mayonnaise and lemon juice; mix well. Spread over chicken; sprinkle with cheese.

3. In small bowl, combine bread crumbs and margarine; sprinkle over top. Bake at 350°F for 30 to 35 minutes or until thoroughly heated.

Nutrition Information Per Serving: Calories 370 • Total Fat 28g • Saturated Fat 7g • Cholesterol 65mg • Sodium 680mg • Total Carbohydrate 10g • Dietary Fiber 2g • Sugars 2g • Protein 20g. **Dietary Exchanges:** ½ Starch • 1 Vegetable • 2½ Lean Meat • 4 Fat OR ½ Carbohydrate • 1 Vegetable • 2½ Lean Meat • 4 Fat.

salsa chicken cacciatore

READY TO SERVE: 55 MINUTES
SERVINGS: 5

2 tablespoons oil

3 to 3½ lb. cut-up frying chicken, skin removed

¼ cup all-purpose flour

1 (14.5-oz.) can salsa-style chunky tomatoes, undrained

1 teaspoon chili powder

½ teaspoon dried oregano leaves

1 cup frozen whole kernel corn

1. Heat oil in large skillet over medium-high heat until hot. Coat chicken pieces with flour; add to skillet. Cook 4 to 5 minutes on each side, or until browned; drain. Stir in tomatoes, chili powder and oregano. Bring to a boil.

2. Reduce heat to low; cover and simmer 30 minutes. Stir in corn; cover and cook an additional 10 to 15 minutes or until chicken is fork-tender and juices run clear, stirring occasionally.

Nutrition Information Per Serving: Calories 320 • Total Fat 13g • Saturated Fat 3g • Cholesterol 90mg • Sodium 240mg • Total Carbohydrate 19g • Dietary Fiber 2g • Sugars 4g • Protein 32g. **Dietary Exchanges:** 1 Starch • 1 Vegetable • 4 Lean Meat OR 1 Carbohydrate • 1 Vegetable • 4 Lean Meat.

skillet arroz con pollo

READY TO SERVE: 40 MINUTES
SERVINGS: 4

✳ meal-in-one

2 teaspoons olive oil

4 chicken legs, skin removed

4 chicken thighs, skin removed

1 (14½-oz.) can ready-to-serve chicken broth

1 cup uncooked converted or regular long-grain white rice

½ cup sliced green onions

½ cup chopped red or green bell pepper

¼ teaspoon turmeric or saffron

⅛ teaspoon garlic powder

⅛ to ¼ teaspoon ground red pepper (cayenne)

1. Heat oil in large skillet over medium-high heat until hot. Add chicken; cook until browned on all sides. Move chicken to side of skillet. Add remaining ingredients; blend well. Place chicken in rice mixture. Bring to a boil. Reduce heat to low; cover and simmer 15 minutes, stirring occasionally.

2. Turn chicken; cover and simmer an additional 5 to 10 minutes, or until chicken is fork-tender and juices run clear.

Nutrition Information Per Serving: Calories 390 • Total Fat 11g • Saturated Fat 3g • Cholesterol 90mg • Sodium 420mg • Total Carbohydrate 40g • Dietary Fiber 1g • Sugars 1g • Protein 32g. **Dietary Exchanges:** 2 Starch • 2 Vegetable • 3 Lean Meat • ½ Fat OR 2 Carbohydrate • 2 Vegetable • 3 Lean Meat • ½ Fat.

grilled turkey drumsticks

PREP TIME: 45 MINUTES
READY TO SERVE: 1 HOUR 5 MINUTES
SERVINGS: 4

4 turkey drumsticks (about 2 lb.)

6 cups water

1½ cups beer

1 medium onion, sliced

¾ cup chili sauce

1 teaspoon dry mustard

1. In Dutch oven or large saucepan, combine turkey drumsticks, water, 1¼ cups of the beer and onion. Bring to a boil. Reduce heat; cover and simmer 30 minutes. Drain; discard liquid.

2. Meanwhile, heat grill. In small bowl, combine remaining ¼ cup beer, chili sauce and dry mustard; mix well. Set aside.

3. When ready to grill, place drumsticks on gas grill over medium heat or on charcoal grill 4 to 6 inches from medium-high coals; brush with sauce. Cover grill; cook 20 to 30 minutes or until turkey is fork-tender and juices run clear, turning and brushing frequently with sauce. Bring any remaining sauce to a boil; serve with turkey drumsticks.

Nutrition Information Per Serving: Calories 260 • Total Fat 7g • Saturated Fat 2g • Cholesterol 85 mg • Sodium 780mg • Total Carbohydrate 13g • Dietary Fiber 0g • Sugars 9g • Protein 35g. **Dietary Exchanges:** 1 Fruit • 5 Very Lean Meat • ½ Fat OR 1 Carbohydrate • 5 Very Lean Meat • ½ Fat.

BROILER OPTION

To broil the turkey drumsticks, place them on a foil-lined broiler pan; broil 4 to 6 inches from the heat using the times in the recipe above as a guide. Be sure to turn and brush the drumsticks frequently with the sauce.

mediterranean chicken and bow ties

READY TO SERVE: 25 MINUTES
SERVINGS: 4

* super fast

pasta

- 4 quarts water
- 1 tablespoon chopped fresh basil or 1 teaspoon dried basil leaves
- 1 teaspoon chicken-flavor instant bouillon
- 8 oz. uncooked bow tie pasta (3½ cups)

chicken

- 2 tablespoons olive oil or vegetable oil
- 4 boneless skinless chicken breast halves, cut into ½-inch strips
- 1 garlic clove, minced
- ½ cup water
- 1 teaspoon cornstarch
- ½ cup diagonally cut green onions (½-inch pieces)
- 1 (2¼-oz.) can sliced pitted ripe olives, drained
- ¼ cup chopped fresh basil or 1 teaspoon dried basil leaves
- ½ teaspoon chicken-flavor instant bouillon
- 1 cup cherry tomato halves

1. Bring water, 1 tablespoon basil and 1 teaspoon bouillon to a boil. Add pasta; cook to desired doneness as directed on package. Drain; cover to keep warm.

2. Meanwhile, heat oil in large skillet over medium-high heat. Add chicken and garlic; cook and stir 6 to 9 minutes or until chicken is no longer pink. In small bowl, combine ½ cup water and cornstarch; blend well. Stir into chicken.

3. Add onions, olives, ¼ cup basil and ½ teaspoon bouillon; cook and stir 2 to 3 minutes or until mixture is slightly thickened and glazed. Pour over pasta; add tomatoes and toss to coat. Garnish with fresh basil, if desired.

Nutrition Information Per Serving: Calories 440 • Total Fat 13g • Saturated Fat 2g • Cholesterol 70mg • Sodium 460mg • Total Carbohydrate 47g • Dietary Fiber 3g • Sugars 3g • Protein 34g. **Dietary Exchanges:** 3 Starch • 3½ Lean Meat OR 3 Carbohydrate • 3½ Lean Meat.

FUN WITH FOCACCIA

For a simple accompaniment to the chicken, roll out purchased pizza dough and brush it with olive oil. Next, sprinkle on a little salt, pepper and dried herbs (or try minced fresh herbs). Bake the focaccia bread at 450°F for 15 minutes or until it is golden brown and baked through. Round out the easy meal with a green salad and a fresh fruit cup. Or, if time permits, complete the dinner with a berry tart, fruit crisp or tiramisu.

chicken risotto

READY TO SERVE: 25 MINUTES
SERVINGS: 4

* meal-in-one

- 2 tablespoons olive oil or vegetable oil
- 4 boneless skinless chicken breast halves, cut into ¾-inch pieces
- ½ cup chicken broth
- ⅓ cup dry white wine
- ⅛ teaspoon pepper
- 1 (9-oz.) pkg. frozen mixed vegetables in a pouch
- 1 cup uncooked instant white rice
- ½ cup sliced green onions
- 2 to 4 tablespoons grated Parmesan cheese

1. Heat oil in large skillet over medium-high heat until hot. Add chicken; cook and stir 2 to 4 minutes or until lightly browned. Drain. Add broth, wine, pepper and vegetables. Bring to a boil.

2. Reduce heat to low; cover and simmer 5 minutes, or until chicken is no longer pink and vegetables are crisp-tender. Stir in rice and green onions. Remove from heat. Cover; let stand 5 minutes. Sprinkle with Parmesan cheese.

Nutrition Information Per Serving: Calories 370 • Total Fat 12g • Saturated Fat 3g • Cholesterol 75mg • Sodium 350mg • Total Carbohydrate 29g • Dietary Fiber 3g • Sugars 3g • Protein 33g. **Dietary Exchanges:** 2 Starch • 4 Lean Meat OR 2 Carbohydrate • 4 Lean Meat.

light lemon chicken

READY TO SERVE: 20 MINUTES
SERVINGS: 4

* super fast

2 lemons

2 teaspoons cornstarch

1 teaspoon sugar

½ cup chicken broth

2 tablespoons dry sherry

2 tablespoons soy sauce

1 tablespoon oil

4 boneless skinless chicken breast halves, cut into ¼-inch strips

½ teaspoon salt

⅛ teaspoon pepper

6 to 8 green onions, cut diagonally into 1½-inch pieces

1 medium red bell pepper, cut into ¼-inch strips

1 (4.5-oz.) jar sliced mushrooms, drained

4 cups hot cooked rice

1. Meanwhile, cut ⅛-inch thin strips of lemon peel from half of 1 lemon. Set aside. Slice other half and reserve for garnish. Squeeze juice from second lemon. In small bowl, combine cornstarch and sugar. Add 2 tablespoons lemon juice, broth, sherry and soy sauce; blend well. Set aside.

2. Heat oil in large skillet or wok over medium-high heat until hot. Add chicken; sprinkle with salt and pepper. Cook and stir 3 to 4 minutes or until chicken is no longer pink. Remove from skillet; cover to keep warm.

3. Add green onions, bell pepper and mushrooms to skillet. Cook and stir 1 minute. Add lemon juice mixture to vegetables; cook and stir 1 to 2 minutes or until thickened. Return chicken to skillet; add lemon strips. Cook and stir 1 minute. Serve with rice. Garnish with lemon slices.

Nutrition Information Per Serving: Calories 430 • Total Fat 7g • Saturated Fat 2g • Cholesterol 75mg • Sodium 1090mg • Total Carbohydrate 57g • Dietary Fiber 3g • Sugars 4g • Protein 34g. **Dietary Exchanges:** 3 Starch • 2 Vegetable • 2½ Lean Meat OR 3 Carbohydrate • 2 Vegetable • 2½ Lean Meat.

teriyaki grilled chicken kabobs

teriyaki grilled chicken kabobs

PREP TIME: 30 MINUTES
READY TO SERVE: 2 HOURS 30 MINUTES
SERVINGS: 4 KABOBS

* plan ahead

marinade

- 2 tablespoons brown sugar
- 3 tablespoons soy sauce
- 2 tablespoons dry sherry
- 1 tablespoon oil
- ¼ teaspoon ginger
- ⅛ teaspoon garlic powder

kabobs

- 8 boneless skinless chicken thighs
- 1 large red bell pepper, cut into 8 pieces
- 1 medium zucchini, cut into 8 pieces
- 8 (1 to 2-inch) chunks fresh pineapple or 8 canned pineapple chunks

1. In 12x8-inch (2-quart) baking dish or resealable food storage plastic bag, combine all marinade ingredients; mix well. Cut chicken thighs in half; add to marinade. Cover dish or seal bag. Refrigerate at least 2 hours to marinate, turning chicken once.

2. Heat grill. Remove chicken from marinade; reserve marinade. Alternately thread chicken, bell pepper, zucchini and pineapple onto four 12-inch metal skewers.

3. When ready to grill, place kabobs on gas grill over medium heat or on charcoal grill 4 to 6 inches from medium-high coals. Cook 15 to 20 minutes or until chicken is no longer pink, turning often and brushing frequently with reserved marinade. Discard any remaining marinade.

Nutrition Information Per Serving: Calories 280 • Total Fat 13g • Saturated Fat 3g • Cholesterol 100mg • Sodium 300mg • Total Carbohydrate 12g • Dietary Fiber 2g • Sugars 8g • Protein 29g. Dietary Exchanges: ½ Fruit • 1 Vegetable • 4 Lean Meat OR ½ Carbohydrate • 1 Vegetable • 4 Lean Meat.

BROILER KABOBS

To broil these chicken kabobs, place them on a broiler pan; broil 4 to 6 inches from the heat using the times listed above in the recipe as a guide. Turn them often and brush them frequently with the reserved marinade.

---

fajita chicken salad

READY TO SERVE: 30 MINUTES
SERVINGS: 4

* meal-in-one

- 2 (8-inch) flour tortillas

salad

- 1 tablespoon oil
- 1 tablespoon red wine vinegar
- 1 teaspoon chopped fresh cilantro
- 1 teaspoon fresh lime juice
- ½ teaspoon sugar
- ⅛ teaspoon garlic powder
- 4 cups shredded leaf lettuce

chicken

- 2 boneless skinless chicken breast halves, thinly sliced
- 1 small onion, cut into thin wedges
- 1 medium red or green bell pepper, cut into 1x¼x¼-inch strips
- ½ teaspoon chili powder
- ½ teaspoon coarse ground black pepper
- ¼ teaspoon cumin

1. Heat oven to 375°F. Cut tortillas into ¼-inch strips; cut strips into 2-inch pieces. Place in single layer on ungreased cookie sheet. Bake at 375°F for 6 to 8 minutes or until lightly browned and crisp.

2. Meanwhile, in small jar with tight-fitting lid, combine all salad ingredients except lettuce; shake well. In medium bowl, combine lettuce and dressing; toss gently to coat. Arrange on 4 individual plates.

3. Spray large skillet with cooking spray. Heat over medium-high heat until hot. Add all chicken ingredients; cook and stir 5 to 7 minutes or until chicken is no longer pink and vegetables are tender. Place ¼ of warm chicken mixture on each lettuce-lined plate; top with tortilla strips.

Nutrition Information Per Serving: Calories 200 • Total Fat 7g • Saturated Fat 1g • Cholesterol 50mg • Sodium 135mg • Total Carbohydrate 15g • Dietary Fiber 2g • Sugars 4g • Protein 20g. Dietary Exchanges: ½ Starch • 2 Vegetable • 2 Lean Meat OR ½ Carbohydrate • 2 Vegetable • 2 Lean Meat.

greek marinated turkey slices

READY TO SERVE: 30 MINUTES
SERVINGS: 4

2 tablespoons lemon juice

1 tablespoon olive or vegetable oil

2 garlic cloves, minced

½ teaspoon dried oregano leaves

¼ teaspoon salt

⅛ teaspoon pepper

4 (3-oz.) fresh turkey breast slices

1. In shallow glass dish, combine all ingredients except turkey; mix well. Add turkey breast slices; turn to coat. Refrigerate 15 minutes to marinate.

2. Spray broiler pan with cooking spray. Remove turkey from marinade; place on sprayed pan. Discard marinade.

3. Broil 4 to 6 inches from heat for 6 to 8 minutes or until turkey is fork-tender and juices run clear, turning once.

Nutrition Information Per Serving: Calories 90 • Total Fat 1g • Saturated Fat 0g • Cholesterol 55mg • Sodium 70mg • Total Carbohydrate 0g • Dietary Fiber 0g • Sugars 0g • Protein 20g. **Dietary Exchange:** 3 Very Lean Meat.

smoked turkey waldorf salad

READY TO SERVE: 10 MINUTES
SERVINGS: 4

＊ super fast

2 medium red apples, chopped

½ cup chopped celery

½ lb. smoked turkey, cubed (1½ cups)

⅓ cup light mayonnaise or salad dressing

4 cups torn Bibb or Boston lettuce

¼ cup chopped walnuts, toasted if desired

1. In medium bowl, combine apples, celery, turkey and mayonnaise; mix well.

2. Arrange lettuce on individual plates. Spoon apple mixture onto lettuce. Sprinkle with walnuts.

Nutrition Information Per Serving: Calories 230 • Total Fat 13g • Saturated Fat 2g • Cholesterol 25mg • Sodium 690mg • Total Carbohydrate 15g • Dietary Fiber 3g • Sugars 10g • Protein 12g. **Dietary Exchanges:** ½ Fruit • 1 Vegetable • 1½ Lean Meat • 2 Fat OR ½ Carbohydrate • 1 Vegetable • 1½ Lean Meat • 2 Fat.

BIBB OR BOSTON?

What's the difference between Bibb and Boston lettuce? It's all in the head! Bibb lettuce has small heads of tender, buttery-feeling leaves with a slightly sweet, mild flavor. Boston lettuce heads are somewhat larger and looser, but the leaves are also buttery-feeling and have similar flavor to Bibb lettuce.

grilled chicken taco salad

READY TO SERVE: 30 MINUTES
SERVINGS: 4

✳ meal-in-one

dressing

- ⅓ cup purchased reduced-calorie French salad dressing
- ⅓ cup purchased thick and chunky salsa
- ¼ cup sliced green onions

salad

- 4 boneless skinless chicken breast halves
- ½ teaspoon chili powder
- ¼ teaspoon garlic powder
- 4 cups shredded lettuce
- 2 medium tomatoes, chopped
- 4 oz. shredded reduced-fat Cheddar cheese (1 cup)
- ½ cup tortilla chips (1 oz.)
- ¼ cup nonfat sour cream

1. In small bowl, combine all dressing ingredients; blend well. Refrigerate until serving time.

2. Heat grill. Place 1 chicken breast half between 2 pieces of plastic wrap or waxed paper. Working from center, gently pound chicken with flat side of meat mallet or rolling pin until about ¼ inch thick; remove wrap. Repeat with remaining chicken breast halves. Sprinkle chicken with chili powder and garlic powder.

3. When ready to grill, place chicken on gas grill over medium heat or on charcoal grill 4 to 6 inches from medium-high coals. Cook 8 to 10 minutes, or until chicken is fork-tender and juices run clear, turning once.

4. Arrange lettuce, tomatoes and cheese on 4 individual plates. Cut chicken crosswise into slices; place over lettuce mixture. Arrange tortilla chips around edge of each plate. Drizzle dressing over each salad; top with sour cream.

Nutrition Information Per Serving: Calories 340 • Total Fat 12g • Saturated Fat 5g • Cholesterol 95mg • Sodium 710mg • Total Carbohydrate 9g • Dietary Fiber 3g • Sugars 9g • Protein 38g. **Dietary Exchanges:** ½ Starch • 2 Vegetable • 4½ Lean Meat OR ½ Carbohydrate • 2 Vegetable • 4½ Lean Meat.

grilled raspberry chicken spinach salad

READY TO SERVE: 25 MINUTES
SERVINGS: 4

* super fast

glaze and dressing
- 1 cup red raspberry preserves
- ⅓ cup red wine vinegar

salad
- 4 boneless skinless chicken breast halves
- 8 cups torn prewashed spinach
- 2 cups melon balls or cubes
- 1 cup fresh raspberries or halved small strawberries
- 1 small red onion, thinly sliced

1. Heat grill. In small bowl, combine preserves and vinegar; blend well. Reserve ⅓ cup for glaze. Set remaining mixture aside for dressing.

2. When ready to grill, oil grill rack. Place chicken on gas grill over medium heat or on charcoal grill 4 to 6 inches from medium coals. Brush chicken with reserved glaze; cook 5 minutes. Turn chicken over; brush with glaze. Cook an additional 3 to 7 minutes or until chicken is fork-tender and juices run clear, brushing occasionally with glaze.

3. Meanwhile, arrange spinach, melon, raspberries and onion on 4 individual plates. Slice each chicken breast crosswise; Arrange over spinach mixture. Drizzle with dressing.

Nutrition Information Per Serving: Calories 420 • Total Fat 4g • Saturated Fat 1g • Cholesterol 75mg • Sodium 190mg • Total Carbohydrate 65g • Dietary Fiber 7g • Sugars 47g • Protein 32g. **Dietary Exchanges:** 4 Fruit • 2 Vegetable • 4 Very Lean Meat OR 4 Carbohydrate • 2 Vegetable • 4 Very Lean Meat.

subgum chicken stir-fry

READY TO SERVE: 20 MINUTES
SERVINGS: 4

* super fast

4 cups hot cooked rice

1 cup chicken broth

2 tablespoons cornstarch

3 tablespoons oyster sauce

2 teaspoons soy sauce

1 tablespoon oil

¼ cup chopped onion

1 garlic clove, minced

4 boneless skinless chicken breast halves, cut into 1-inch pieces

1 cup thinly sliced bok choy

1 cup fresh bean sprouts

1 medium green bell pepper, cut into ¼-inch strips

1 (8-oz.) can sliced bamboo shoots, drained

1. Cook rice as directed on package. Cover to keep warm.

2. In small bowl, combine chicken broth, cornstarch, oyster sauce and soy sauce.

3. Heat oil in large skillet or wok over medium-high heat until hot. Add onion, garlic and chicken; cook and stir 3 to 4 minutes, or until chicken is no longer pink. Add bok choy, bean sprouts, bell pepper and bamboo shoots; cook and stir 3 to 4 minutes, or until vegetables are crisp-tender. Gradually add cornstarch mixture; cook until thickened and bubbly, stirring constantly. Serve over rice.

Nutrition Information Per Serving: Calories 430 • Total Fat 7g • Saturated Fat 2g • Cholesterol 70mg • Sodium 1040mg • Total Carbohydrate 58g • Dietary Fiber 3g • Sugars 5g • Protein 33g. **Dietary Exchanges:** 3 Starch • 2 Vegetable • 2½ Lean Meat OR 3 Carbohydrate • 2 Vegetable • 2½ Lean Meat.

easy chicken pot pies

PREP TIME: 15 MINUTES
READY TO SERVE: 35 MINUTES
SERVINGS: 8

* meal-in-one

1 (16.3-oz.) can Pillsbury® Grands!® Refrigerated Flaky Biscuits

1 (19-oz.) can ready-to-serve roasted white meat chicken, pasta and Italian garden vegetables or chicken noodle soup

1 to 2 tablespoons margarine or butter, melted

1 teaspoon dried Italian seasoning

½ teaspoon garlic powder

1 oz. shredded mozzarella cheese (¼ cup)

1. Heat oven to 375°F. Lightly spray 8 (2¼x1¼-inch) muffin cups with cooking spray. Separate dough into 8 biscuits; separate each biscuit into 2 layers. Place 8 biscuit halves in sprayed muffin cups, pressing in bottom and up sides to cover.

2. Drain soup; discard liquid or freeze for a later use. Spoon drained soup evenly into biscuit-lined cups. Place remaining biscuit halves over soup; gently seal each biscuit.

3. Brush biscuit tops with margarine. Sprinkle with Italian seasoning and garlic powder. Top each with ½ tablespoon cheese.

4. Bake at 375°F for 15 to 18 minutes or until edges are golden brown.

Nutrition Information Per Serving: Calories 260 • Total Fat 13g • Saturated Fat 4g • Cholesterol 15mg • Sodium 890mg • Total Carbohydrate 28g • Dietary Fiber 1g • Sugars 4g • Protein 8g. **Dietary Exchanges:** 2 Starch • ½ Medium-Fat Meat • 1½ Fat OR 2 Carbohydrate • ½ Medium-Fat Meat • 1½ Fat.

INSTANT FLAVOR

The liquid, or broth, drained from the canned soup can be frozen in ice-cube trays. Remove the frozen cubes from the trays and place in a resealable storage bag or freezer container. Add a few cubes to the water when cooking vegetables, pasta or rice. Or use several cubes to enhance soup or stew.

chicken curry stuffed potatoes

PREP TIME: 20 MINUTES
READY TO SERVE: 55 MINUTES
SERVINGS: 4

✴ meal-in-one

- 4 medium baking potatoes
- 1 cup chicken broth
- 2 tablespoons all-purpose flour
- ½ teaspoon curry powder
- ¼ teaspoon onion salt
- 1 tablespoon oil
- 2 cups fresh broccoli florets or frozen cut broccoli
- ¼ cup chopped red bell pepper
- 1 cup sour cream
- 2 teaspoons lemon juice
- 1 cup chopped cooked chicken
- 2 oz. shredded Cheddar cheese (½ cup)

1. Heat oven to 400°F. Pierce potatoes with fork. Bake at 400°F for 45 to 55 minutes or until tender.

2. Meanwhile, in small bowl using wire whisk, blend broth, flour, curry powder and onion salt. Heat 1 tablespoon oil in large skillet over medium-high heat until hot. Gradually add frozen broccoli and bell pepper; cook and stir 5 to 7 minutes or until broccoli is crisp-tender. Reduce heat to medium.

3. Gradually stir in chicken broth mixture; cook and stir until sauce is thickened and bubbly. Remove from heat. Stir in sour cream, lemon juice and chicken. Cook over low heat 2 minutes or until thoroughly heated.

4. To serve, cut potatoes in half lengthwise, cutting to but not through bottom of potatoes. Mash slightly with fork. Place potatoes on 4 individual plates; spoon chicken mixture over hot potatoes. Sprinkle with cheese.

Nutrition Information Per Serving: Calories 430 • Total Fat 21g • Saturated Fat 12g • Cholesterol 75mg • Sodium 480mg • Total Carbohydrate 39g • Dietary Fiber 4g • Sugars 5g • Protein 21g. **Dietary Exchanges:** 2 Starch • 2 Vegetable • 2 Lean Meat • 3 Fat OR 2 Carbohydrate • 2 Vegetable • 2 Lean Meat • 3 Fat.

chicken salad italiana

READY TO SERVE: 35 MINUTES
SERVINGS: 4

✴ meal-in-one

- ⅓ cup balsamic vinegar
- 2 tablespoons water
- 2 teaspoons dried Italian seasoning
- 4 boneless skinless chicken breast halves
- 1 tablespoon oil
- ½ teaspoon sugar
- ½ lb. asparagus
- 8 cups torn Bibb lettuce
- 1 (15-oz.) can garbanzo beans, drained, rinsed
- 1 small red onion, sliced, separated into rings
- 1 medium tomato, cut into 8 wedges

1. Heat grill. In small bowl, combine vinegar, water and Italian seasoning; mix well. Place 2 to 3 tablespoons vinegar mixture in medium bowl. Add chicken; toss to coat. Let stand 5 to 10 minutes at room temperature to marinate. To prepare dressing, add oil and sugar to remaining vinegar mixture in small bowl; mix well. Set aside.

2. Place 1 chicken breast half between 2 pieces of plastic wrap or waxed paper. Working from center, gently pound chicken with flat side of meat mallet or rolling pin until about ¼ inch thick; remove wrap. Repeat with remaining chicken breast halves.

3. When ready to grill, remove chicken from marinade; discard marinade. Place chicken on gas grill over medium heat or on charcoal grill 4 to 6 inches from medium coals. Cook 8 to 10 minutes or until chicken is fork-tender and juices run clear, turning once.

4. Meanwhile, place asparagus in large skillet; add ½ inch water. Bring to a boil. Reduce heat; cover and simmer 2 to 4 minutes, or until asparagus is bright green and crisp-tender.

5. Arrange lettuce on 4 individual plates; sprinkle each with garbanzo beans. Slice each chicken breast half crosswise into slices; do not separate slices. Fan chicken slices; arrange 1 breast half on lettuce mixture on each plate. Arrange steamed asparagus, onion rings and tomato wedges around chicken. Serve with dressing.

Nutrition Information Per Serving: Calories 320 • Total Fat 9g • Saturated Fat 2g • Cholesterol 75mg • Sodium 230mg • Total Carbohydrate 24g • Dietary Fiber 7g • Sugars 5g • Protein 35g. **Dietary Exchanges:** 1 Starch • 2 Vegetable • 4 Very Lean Meat • 1 Fat OR 1 Carbohydrate • 2 Vegetable • 4 Very Lean Meat • 1 Fat.

chicken curry stuffed potatoes

chicken broccoli potato salad

READY TO SERVE: 15 MINUTES
SERVINGS: 5

✻ super fast

dressing
- ¾ cup mayonnaise
- 2 tablespoons grated Parmesan cheese
- ½ teaspoon sugar
- ½ teaspoon dried oregano leaves
- ¼ teaspoon onion powder

salad
- 2 cups diced cooked potatoes
- 2 cups frozen cut broccoli, cooked crisp-tender, drained
- 2 cups cubed cooked chicken
- 1 (2-oz.) jar diced pimiento, drained

1. In small jar with tight-fitting lid, combine all dressing ingredients; shake well.

2. In large bowl, combine all salad ingredients. Add dressing; stir gently to coat.

Nutrition Information Per Serving: Calories 450 • Total Fat 32g • Saturated Fat 6g • Cholesterol 70mg • Sodium 310mg • Total Carbohydrate 19g • Dietary Fiber 3g • Sugars 3g • Protein 21g. **Dietary Exchanges:** 1 Starch • 1 Vegetable • 2 Lean Meat • 5 Fat OR 1 Carbohydrate • 1 Vegetable • 2 Lean Meat • 5 Fat.

piccata chicken

READY TO SERVE: 30 MINUTES
SERVINGS: 4

4 boneless skinless chicken breast halves

¼ cup all-purpose flour

¼ teaspoon salt

¼ teaspoon white pepper

2 tablespoons oil

½ cup chicken broth

2 teaspoons Worcestershire sauce

¼ teaspoon dried marjoram leaves

2 tablespoons fresh lemon juice

¼ cup chopped fresh parsley

1. Place 1 chicken breast half between 2 pieces of plastic wrap or waxed paper. Working from center, gently pound chicken with flat side of meat mallet or rolling pin until about ¼ inch thick; remove wrap. Repeat with remaining chicken breast halves.

2. In shallow bowl, combine flour, salt and pepper. Coat chicken breast halves with flour mixture. Heat oil in large skillet over medium-high heat until hot. Add chicken; cook 3 to 5 minutes on each side or until golden brown, fork-tender and juices run clear.

3. Remove chicken from skillet; cover to keep warm. Add broth, Worcestershire sauce and marjoram to skillet; cook and stir 1 to 2 minutes. Stir in lemon juice and parsley. Serve over chicken.

Nutrition Information Per Serving: Calories 230 • Total Fat 10g • Saturated Fat 2g • Cholesterol 75mg • Sodium 320mg • Total Carbohydrate 7g • Dietary Fiber 0g • Sugars 0g • Protein 28g. **Dietary Exchanges:** ½ Starch • 3½ Lean Meat OR ½ Carbohydrate • 3½ Lean Meat.

colorful chicken fried rice

READY TO SERVE: 25 MINUTES
SERVINGS: 6

* super fast

⅔ cup uncooked regular long-grain white rice

1⅓ cups water

¼ cup ketchup

2 tablespoons soy sauce

1 teaspoon ginger

½ teaspoon salt

⅛ teaspoon pepper

4 boneless skinless chicken breast halves, cut into thin bite-sized pieces

1 tablespoon oil or margarine

2 garlic cloves, minced

2 cups frozen mixed vegetables, thawed

¼ cup finely chopped onion

1 (8-oz.) can pineapple chunks, drained

1. Cook rice in water as directed on package.

2. Meanwhile, in medium bowl, combine ketchup, soy sauce, ginger, salt and pepper; blend well. Add chicken; stir to coat. Set aside.

3. Heat oil in large skillet over medium heat. Add garlic; cook and stir until light golden brown. Add chicken mixture; cook and stir 3 to 5 minutes or until chicken is no longer pink.

4. Add mixed vegetables, onion and pineapple; cook and stir 3 to 4 minutes or until vegetables are crisp-tender. Add rice; cook and stir 1 to 2 minutes or until rice is thoroughly heated.

Nutrition Information Per Serving: Calories 240 • Total Fat 5g • Saturated Fat 1g • Cholesterol 50mg • Sodium 700mg • Total Carbohydrate 27g • Dietary Fiber 2g • Sugars 5g • Protein 21g. **Dietary Exchanges:** 1 Starch • 1 Fruit • 2½ Very Lean Meat • ½ Fat OR 2 Carbohydrate • 2½ Very Lean Meat • ½ Fat.

pork, ham & lamb

lamb and asparagus stir-fry ✳ p. 174

chinese sweet-and-sour pork ✳ p. 182

pineapple-canadian bacon pizza rings ✳ p. 177

rosemary roasted pork tenderloin ✳ p. 178

apricot glazed lamb chops * p. 188

lamb and asparagus stir-fry

READY TO SERVE: 30 MINUTES
SERVINGS: 6

* meal-in-one

13½ oz. uncooked medium egg noodles (6 cups)

½ cup vegetable broth

2 teaspoons cornstarch

¾ teaspoon dried rosemary leaves, crushed

¼ teaspoon salt

¼ teaspoon coarse ground black pepper

2 teaspoons olive oil

1 lb. boneless lean lamb sirloin or round steak, cut into thin strips

1 large onion, halved, thinly sliced

1 lb. fresh asparagus spears, cut diagonally into 1-inch pieces

1 small red bell pepper, cut into 2x¼x¼-inch strips

1. Cook noodles to desired doneness as directed on the package. Drain; cover to keep warm.

2. Meanwhile, in small bowl or jar with tight-fitting lid, combine broth, cornstarch, rosemary, salt and pepper; blend or shake well. Set aside.

3. Heat oil in large skillet or wok over medium-high heat until hot. Add lamb; cook and stir 3 minutes. Add onion and asparagus; cook and stir an additional 3 minutes or until onion is tender and lamb is no longer pink. Add bell pepper; cook and stir 1 minute. Add broth mixture; cook and stir until thickened. Serve lamb mixture over noodles.

Nutrition Information Per Serving: Calories 380 • Total Fat 8g • Saturated Fat 2g • Cholesterol 100mg • Sodium 220mg • Total Carbohydrate 53g • Dietary Fiber 4g • Sugars 6g • Protein 23g. **Dietary Exchanges:** 3 Starch • 1 Vegetable • 1½ Lean Meat • ½ Fat OR 3 Carbohydrate • 1 Vegetable • 1½ Lean Meat • ½ Fat.

lime-marinated pork with citrus salsa

READY TO SERVE: 1 HOUR
SERVINGS: 6

salsa
- ½ cup chopped fresh orange sections
- ½ cup chopped green bell pepper
- ¼ cup sliced red onion
- 1 medium tomato, seeded, chopped
- ½ red jalapeño chile, finely chopped
- 1 tablespoon chopped fresh mint
- 1 teaspoon grated lime peel

pork
- 2 tablespoons lime juice
- 2 teaspoons olive or vegetable oil
- 4 garlic cloves, minced
- ½ teaspoon salt
- ¼ teaspoon coarse ground black pepper
- 2 (¾-lb.) pork tenderloins

1. In medium bowl, combine all salsa ingredients; mix well. Let stand at room temperature for 1 hour to blend flavors.

2. Meanwhile, heat grill. In small bowl, combine lime juice, oil, garlic, salt and pepper; mix well. Brush oil mixture over pork tenderloins, coating all sides.

3. When ready to grill, place pork on gas grill over medium heat or on charcoal grill 4 to 6 inches from medium coals. Cook 20 to 30 minutes or until pork is no longer pink in center, turning occasionally. Serve with salsa.

Nutrition Information Per Serving: Calories 170 • Total Fat 6g • Saturated Fat 2g • Cholesterol 65mg • Sodium 230mg • Total Carbohydrate 5g • Dietary Fiber 1g • Sugars 3g • Protein 24g. **Dietary Exchanges:** 1 Vegetable • 3 Lean Meat.

TENDERLOIN TIP

To broil the two pork tenderloins called for in the main course above, place them on a broiler pan. Broil 4 to 6 inches from the heat, turning the pork occasionally. Use the cook times in the instructions as a guide.

---

pork loin chops with fresh tomato relish

READY TO SERVE: 20 MINUTES
SERVINGS: 4

* super fast

pork chops
- 4 (3-oz.) boneless pork loin chops
- ¼ teaspoon salt
- Dash pepper

relish
- 2 tablespoons apple jelly
- 2 teaspoons rice vinegar
- 1 teaspoon tomato paste
- ¼ teaspoon salt
- ⅛ teaspoon dried thyme leaves
- 1 medium tomato, diced
- ¼ cup diced zucchini
- 1 teaspoon chopped fresh parsley

1. Spray broiler pan with cooking spray. Sprinkle pork chops with ¼ teaspoon salt and dash pepper; place on sprayed pan. Broil 4 to 6 inches from heat for 8 to 12 minutes or until pork is no longer pink in center, turning once.

2. Meanwhile, in small saucepan or microwave-safe bowl, combine jelly, vinegar, tomato paste, ¼ teaspoon salt and thyme; mix well. Heat over medium heat or microwave on high for 30 to 40 seconds until jelly melts, stirring occasionally.

3. In small bowl, combine tomato, zucchini and parsley. Pour hot jelly mixture over tomato mixture; mix well. Serve relish with pork chops.

Nutrition Information Per Serving: Calories 140 • Total Fat 5g • Saturated Fat 2g • Cholesterol 35mg • Sodium 310mg • Total Carbohydrate 9g • Dietary Fiber 1g • Sugars 6g • Protein 14g. **Dietary Exchanges:** ½ Fruit • 2 Lean Meat OR ½ Carbohydrate • 2 Lean Meat.

grands!® sausage gravy

READY TO SERVE: 20 MINUTES
SERVINGS: 8

✳ **super fast**

1 (16.3-oz.) can Pillsbury®
Grands!® Refrigerated
Buttermilk Biscuits

¾ lb. bulk pork sausage

⅓ cup all-purpose flour

½ teaspoon salt

¼ teaspoon coarse ground
black pepper

3 cups milk

1. Bake biscuits as directed on can.

2. Meanwhile, crumble sausage into large skillet. Cook over medium-high heat until browned and no longer pink, stirring frequently.

3. With wire whisk, stir flour, salt and pepper into sausage. Gradually stir in milk, cooking and stirring until mixture is bubbly and thickened.

4. Split warm biscuits; place on individual serving plates. Spoon sausage mixture over biscuits.

Nutrition Information Per Serving: Calories 345 • Total Fat 17g • Saturated Fat 5g • Cholesterol 25mg • Sodium 1150mg • Total Carbohydrate 36g • Dietary Fiber 1g • Sugars 13g • Protein 11g. **Dietary Exchanges:** 1½ Starch • 1 Low-Fat Milk • 3 Fat OR 2½ Carbohydrate • 3 Fat.

cheese-topped pork chops

READY TO SERVE: 20 MINUTES
SERVINGS: 4

✳ **super fast**

2 tablespoons all-purpose
flour

½ teaspoon salt

½ teaspoon paprika

⅛ teaspoon pepper

1 egg, slightly beaten

1 to 2 teaspoons
Worcestershire sauce

¼ cup unseasoned dry bread
crumbs

¼ cup grated Parmesan cheese

4 boneless pork loin chops

2 tablespoons oil

4 slices mozzarella cheese

4 slices tomato

1. In small bowl, combine flour, salt, paprika and pepper. In another small bowl, combine egg and Worcestershire sauce. In a third small bowl, combine bread crumbs and grated Parmesan cheese.

2. Coat pork chops with seasoned flour; dip in egg mixture, then coat with crumb mixture. In large skillet, heat oil over medium-high heat until hot. Add chops; cook until browned on both sides. Reduce heat to medium; cook 5 to 7 minutes or until pork is thoroughly cooked and no longer pink in center.

3. Top each chop with 1 slice of mozzarella cheese and 1 slice of tomato. Cover; heat until tomato is hot and cheese begins to melt.

lamb patties

READY TO SERVE: 30 MINUTES
SERVINGS: 4

1 lb. ground lamb

2 tablespoons chopped onion

½ teaspoon salt

⅛ teaspoon pepper

1. In medium bowl, combine all ingredients; mix well. Shape into 4 patties.

2. Broil on broiler pan or grill 3 to 4 inches from heat for 6 to 8 minutes on each side or until no longer pink in center.

Nutrition Information Per Serving: Calories 210 • Total Fat 15g • Saturated Fat 6g • Cholesterol 75mg • Sodium 330mg • Total Carbohydrate 0g • Dietary Fiber 0g • Sugars 0g • Protein 19g. **Dietary Exchange:** 3 Medium-Fat Meat.

pineapple-canadian bacon pizza ring

PREP TIME: 25 MINUTES
READY TO SERVE: 45 MINUTES
SERVINGS: 5

* meal-in-one

1 (12-oz.) can Pillsbury® Golden Layers™ Refrigerated Flaky Biscuits

3 tablespoons purchased sweet-and-sour sauce

1 (8-oz.) can pineapple tidbits in unsweetened juice, well drained

1 (5-oz.) pkg. thinly sliced Canadian bacon, chopped

4 oz. shredded Monterey Jack cheese (1 cup)

¼ cup chopped bell pepper (any color)

2 tablespoons sliced green onions

1. Heat oven to 400°F. Separate dough into 10 biscuits. Press or roll each to form a 4½-inch round. On ungreased cookie sheet, arrange biscuits, slightly overlapping, to form 12-inch-diameter ring.

2. Spread sweet-and-sour sauce evenly over biscuits. Top each biscuit with pineapple and Canadian bacon. Sprinkle with cheese. Top with bell pepper and green onions.

3. Bake at 400°F for 15 to 20 minutes or until crust is golden brown. Cool 5 minutes. To serve, pull apart into individual pizzas.

Nutrition Information Per Serving: Calories 415 • Total Fat 20g • Saturated Fat 8g • Cholesterol 40mg • Sodium 1430mg • Total Carbohydrate 43g • Dietary Fiber 1g • Sugars 19g • Protein 17g. **Dietary Exchanges:** 2 Starch • 1 Fruit • 1½ Medium-Fat Meat • 1½ Fat OR 3 Carbohydrate • 1½ Medium-Fat Meat • 1½ Fat.

roast pork with garlic pepper crust

PREP TIME: 15 MINUTES
READY TO SERVE: 1 HOUR
SERVINGS: 4

4 to 6 garlic cloves, minced

1 tablespoon chopped fresh parsley or 1 teaspoon dried parsley flakes

1 teaspoon coarse ground black pepper

½ teaspoon dried thyme leaves

1 tablespoon lime or lemon juice

1 teaspoon olive oil

2 (½ lb.) pork tenderloins

1. Heat oven to 450°F. Line shallow roasting pan with foil; spray foil with cooking spray. In small bowl, combine garlic, parsley, pepper and thyme. In small cup, combine lime juice and oil.

2. Brush pork tenderloins with lime juice mixture, coating well. Rub garlic-pepper mixture over top and sides of tenderloins, pressing lightly. Place in sprayed foil-lined pan, garlic-pepper side up.

3. Bake at 450°F for 25 to 35 minutes or until pork is no longer pink in center. Let stand 5 to 10 minutes before cutting diagonally into ½-inch slices.

Nutrition Information Per Serving: Calories 150 • Total Fat 5g • Saturated Fat 2g • Cholesterol 65mg • Sodium 50mg • Total Carbohydrate 2g • Dietary Fiber 0g • Sugars 0g • Protein 24g. **Dietary Exchange:** 3 Lean Meat.

rosemary roasted pork tenderloin

PREP TIME: 15 MINUTES
READY TO SERVE: 50 MINUTES
SERVINGS: 3

5 teaspoons olive or vegetable oil

1 (3/4-lb.) pork tenderloin

1 tablespoon chopped fresh rosemary or 1 teaspoon dried rosemary leaves

1 large garlic clove, minced

1/8 teaspoon salt

1/4 teaspoon coarse ground black pepper

1. Heat oven to 425°F. Heat 2 teaspoons of the oil in large skillet over medium-high heat until hot. Add pork tenderloin; cook until golden brown on all sides.

2. Place pork tenderloin in ungreased shallow baking pan. In small cup, combine remaining 3 teaspoons oil, rosemary and garlic; mix well. Brush rosemary mixture over pork tenderloin. Sprinkle with salt and pepper.

3. Bake at 425°F for 18 to 25 minutes or until pork is no longer pink in center. Let stand 10 minutes before cutting into slices.

Nutrition Information Per Serving: Calories 210 • Total Fat 12g • Saturated Fat 2g • Cholesterol 65mg • Sodium 135mg • Total Carbohydrate 1g • Dietary Fiber 1g • Sugars 0g • Protein 24g. **Dietary Exchanges:** 3 1/2 Lean Meat • 1/2 Fat.

broiled lamb chops with mint sauce

READY TO SERVE: 20 MINUTES
SERVINGS: 4

* super fast

mint sauce
⅓ cup apple jelly
2 tablespoons vinegar
2 tablespoons water
2 teaspoons dried mint flakes
¼ teaspoon salt

lamb
4 lamb chops (1 inch thick)

1. In small saucepan, combine all sauce ingredients. Bring to a boil. Reduce heat to low; simmer 5 minutes.

2. Meanwhile, place lamb chops on broiler pan; brush with sauce. Broil 4 to 6 inches from heat for 9 to 11 minutes or until browned and of desired doneness, turning chops and brushing with sauce once during cooking. Bring remaining sauce to a boil. Serve sauce with lamb chops.

Nutrition Information Per Serving: Calories 170 • Total Fat 5g • Saturated Fat 2g • Cholesterol 40mg • Sodium 170mg • Total Carbohydrate 18g • Dietary Fiber 0g • Sugars 12g • Protein 12g. **Dietary Exchanges:** 1 Fruit • 2 Lean Meat OR 1 Carbohydrate • 2 Lean Meat.

cheesy sausage 'n broccoli loaf

PREP TIME: 15 MINUTES
READY TO SERVE: 45 MINUTES
SERVINGS: 4

* meal-in-one

1 (12-oz.) pkg. bulk sage-flavored pork sausage
1 (11-oz.) can Pillsbury® Refrigerated Crusty French Loaf
2 cups frozen cut broccoli, cooked, drained
4 oz. shredded mozzarella cheese (1 cup)
4 oz. shredded Cheddar cheese (1 cup)

1. Heat oven to 350°F. Cook sausage in medium skillet over medium-high heat until no longer pink, stirring frequently. Drain.

2. Carefully unroll dough onto ungreased cookie sheet. Press to form 14x12-inch rectangle. Spoon sausage down center of dough. Top with cooked broccoli and cheeses. Fold long sides of dough over filling, meeting in center; press edges and ends to seal.

3. Bake at 350°F for 20 to 30 minutes or until golden brown. Cut into crosswise slices.

Nutrition Information Per Serving: Calories 540 • Total Fat 29g • Saturated Fat 14g • Cholesterol 80mg • Sodium 1320mg • Total Carbohydrate 38g • Dietary Fiber 2g • Sugars 5g • Protein 30g. **Dietary Exchanges:** 2 Starch • 1 Vegetable • 3 High-Fat Meat • 1 Fat OR 2 Carbohydrate • 1 Vegetable • 3 High-Fat Meat • 1 Fat.

hot ham and swiss on rye

PREP TIME: 10 MINUTES
READY TO SERVE: 30 MINUTES
SERVINGS: 8

½ cup margarine or butter, softened
¼ cup horseradish mustard
¼ cup chopped onion
4 teaspoons poppy seed
8 rye sandwich buns, split
8 thin slices boiled ham
8 slices (3½x3½-inch) Swiss cheese

1. Heat oven to 350°F. In small bowl, combine margarine, mustard, onion and poppy seed. Spread mixture on cut surfaces of buns. Fill each bun with 1 slice ham and 1 slice cheese.

2. Wrap each sandwich in foil; place on ungreased cookie sheet. Bake at 350°F for 15 to 20 minutes or until thoroughly heated.

Nutrition Information Per Serving: Calories 380 • Total Fat 23g • Saturated Fat 8g • Cholesterol 40mg • Sodium 980mg • Total Carbohydrate 24g • Dietary Fiber 3g • Sugars 2g • Protein 18g. **Dietary Exchanges:** 1½ Starch • 2 Medium-Fat Meat • 2½ Fat OR 1½ Carbohydrate • 2 Medium-Fat Meat • 2½ Fat.

ham and macaroni picnic salad

READY TO SERVE: 20 MINUTES
SERVINGS: 12

* super fast

salad

- 4 eggs
- 16 oz. uncooked elbow macaroni (4 cups)
- 1 cup diced cooked ham
- 1 cup sliced celery
- ½ cup chopped green onions
- ¼ cup sweet pickle relish
- 1 (2-oz.) jar diced pimientos, drained

dressing

- 1 cup salad dressing or mayonnaise
- 2 tablespoons prepared mustard
- ½ teaspoon salt
- ¼ teaspoon pepper

1. Place eggs in medium saucepan; cover with cold water. Bring to a boil. Reduce heat; simmer about 15 minutes. Immediately drain; run cold water over eggs to stop cooking. Peel eggs; chop. Set aside.

2. Meanwhile, cook macaroni to desired doneness as directed on package. Drain; rinse with cold water to cool.

3. In large bowl, combine the cooked macaroni, ham, celery, onions, pickle relish and pimientos.

4. In small bowl, combine all dressing ingredients; blend well. Add to the salad; mix well. Gently stir in the hard-cooked eggs. Serve immediately, or cover and refrigerate until serving time.

Nutrition Information Per Serving: Calories 270 • Total Fat 10g • Saturated Fat 2g • Cholesterol 80mg • Sodium 500mg • Total Carbohydrate 36g • Dietary Fiber 1g • Sugars 6g • Protein 10g. **Dietary Exchanges:** 2½ Starch • ½ Medium-Fat Meat • 1 Fat OR 2½ Carbohydrate • ½ Medium-Fat Meat • 1 Fat.

cuban-style sandwiches with au jus

PREP TIME: 15 MINUTES
READY TO SERVE: 45 MINUTES
SERVINGS: 4

ANGELA BUCHANAN ***** BOULDER, COLORADO
BAKE-OFF® CONTEST 42, 2006

- 1 (17-oz.) pkg. refrigerated fully cooked pork roast au jus
- 1 (13.2-oz.) can refrigerated country Italian loaf with pure olive oil
- 1 teaspoon ground cumin
- 2 teaspoons minced garlic in water (from a jar)
- ¼ lb. thinly sliced cooked honey ham
- 4 (1-oz.) slices pepper Jack cheese
- 1 cup beef broth
- 1 (4.5-oz.) can chopped green chiles

1. Heat oven to 350°F. Spray cookie sheet or 15x10x1-inch pan with cooking spray. Drain juice from pork roast into blender; set aside. Shred or chop pork into bite-size pieces; set aside.

2. Unroll dough into 1 large (about 14x9-inch) rectangle. With kitchen scissors or sharp knife, cut dough crosswise making 2 (9x7-inch) rectangles. Sprinkle each dough rectangle with ½ teaspoon cumin and 1 teaspoon garlic. Place half of ham and half of cheese in 3-inch-wide strip lengthwise down center of each dough rectangle. Divide pork evenly over cheese.

3. Bring long sides of dough up over filling to meet in center; pinch seam to seal. Pinch ends to seal. With pancake turner, place seam side down on cookie sheet or 15x10x1-inch pan. Cut 3 diagonal slashes in top of each sandwich.

4. Bake 25 to 30 minutes or until golden brown. Remove from cookie sheet; place on wire rack. Cool 5 minutes. Meanwhile, pour broth and undrained green chiles into blender with juice from pork; blend on medium-high speed 15 to 30 seconds or until smooth. Pour juice mixture into 2-cup microwavable measuring cup.

5. To serve, microwave juice mixture on high 2 to 3 minutes or until hot; divide mixture into 4 (6 or 8-oz.) ramekins or cups. Cut each sandwich diagonally in half. Serve sandwiches with juice mixture for dipping.

Nutrition Information Per Serving: Calories 620 • Total Fat 24g • Saturated Fat 9g • Trans Fat 0g • Cholesterol 140mg • Sodium 1720mg • Total Carbohydrate 45g • Dietary Fiber 0g • Sugars 5g • Protein 56g. **Dietary Exchanges:** 3 Starch • 7 Lean Meat.

hash-brown potato and sausage pie

PREP TIME: 15 MINUTES
READY TO SERVE: 1 HOUR
SERVINGS: 6

* meal-in-one

- 1 lb. bulk pork sausage
- 5 cups frozen shredded hash-brown potatoes
- ¼ cup chopped onion
- 8 oz. shredded Cheddar cheese (2 cups)
- 4 eggs
- ½ cup milk
- 1 Pillsbury® Refrigerated Pie Crust (from 15-oz. pkg.), softened as directed on package

1. Heat oven to 425°F. Spray 9-inch deep-dish glass pie pan with cooking spray. Cook sausage in large skillet over medium-high heat until thoroughly cooked, stirring frequently. Drain.

2. Add potatoes and onion to sausage in skillet; mix well. Cook 5 to 8 minutes or until potatoes are slightly soft, stirring occasionally. Remove from heat. Stir in cheese.

3. Beat eggs in large bowl. Add milk; blend well. Reserve 1 tablespoon egg mixture for topping. Add potato mixture to remaining egg mixture; mix well. Spoon potato-egg mixture into sprayed pie pan, keeping mixture away from the edges.

4. Remove pie crust from pouch. Unfold crust; press out fold lines. Place over potato mixture, tucking edges of crust around potato mixture. Turn edges under and press to edge of pie pan. Cut several slits in crust for steam to escape. Brush with reserved tablespoon egg mixture.

5. Bake at 425°F for 25 minutes. Cover top of pie with foil to prevent excessive browning. Bake an additional 15 to 20 minutes or until potatoes are tender and crust is deep golden brown. Cut into wedges.

Nutrition Information Per Serving: Calories 640 • Total Fat 37g • Saturated Fat 17g • Cholesterol 220mg • Sodium 930mg • Total Carbohydrate 54g • Dietary Fiber 3g • Sugars 6g • Protein 26g.
Dietary Exchanges: 3½ Starch • 2 High-Fat Meat • 3½ Fat OR 3½ Carbohydrate • 2 High-Fat Meat • 3½ Fat.

chinese sweet-and-sour pork

chinese sweet-and-sour pork

READY TO SERVE: 40 MINUTES
SERVINGS: 4

* meal-in-one

1⅓ cups uncooked regular long-grain white rice

2⅔ cups water

¼ cup cornstarch

2 tablespoons all-purpose flour

1 teaspoon sugar

¼ teaspoon baking soda

3 tablespoons water

1 egg, beaten

½ lb. boneless pork loin chops, cut into 2x½x¼-inch pieces

Oil for frying

3 tablespoons brown sugar

2 tablespoons cornstarch

½ teaspoon chicken-flavor instant bouillon

½ cup water

3 tablespoons rice vinegar

2 tablespoons ketchup

2 teaspoons soy sauce

1 (20-oz.) can pineapple chunks in unsweetened juice, drained, reserving 3 tablespoons liquid

1 garlic clove, minced

1 green bell pepper, cut into ¾-inch pieces

1. Cook rice in 2⅔ cups water as directed on package.

2. Meanwhile, in medium bowl, combine ¼ cup cornstarch, flour, sugar, baking soda, 3 tablespoons water and egg; mix well. Add pork; stir until well blended.

3. In deep fryer, heavy saucepan or wok, heat 2 to 3 inches of oil to 375°F. Fry battered pork pieces, ¼ of total amount at a time, for 2 to 3 minutes or until golden brown and no longer pink in center, turning once. Drain on paper towels. Reserve 1 tablespoon oil from deep fryer.

4. In small saucepan, combine brown sugar, 2 tablespoons cornstarch, bouillon, ½ cup water, vinegar, ketchup, soy sauce and reserved 3 tablespoons pineapple liquid; blend well. Cook over medium-high heat until bubbly and thickened, stirring constantly. Keep warm.

5. Heat reserved 1 tablespoon oil in large skillet or wok until hot. Add garlic and bell pepper; cook and stir 2 to 3 minutes or until pepper is crisp-tender. Stir in pineapple chunks, pork and sauce. Cook until thoroughly heated. Serve immediately over rice.

Nutrition Information Per Serving: Calories 640 • Total Fat 24g • Saturated Fat 4g • Cholesterol 85mg • Sodium 510mg • Total Carbohydrate 86g • Dietary Fiber 2g • Sugars 25g • Protein 19g. **Dietary Exchanges:** 2½ Starch • 3 Fruit • 1½ Medium-Fat Meat • 3 Fat OR 5½ Carbohydrate • 1½ Medium-Fat Meat • 3 Fat.

ham and swiss grands!® pizzas

READY TO SERVE: 30 MINUTES
SERVINGS: 5

* meal-in-one

1 (10.2-oz.) can Pillsbury® Grands!® Refrigerated Buttermilk Biscuits (5 biscuits)

5 teaspoons creamy mustard-mayonnaise sauce

6 oz. shredded Swiss cheese (1½ cups)

¾ cup coarsely chopped cooked ham

2 tablespoons sliced green onions

3 Italian plum tomatoes

1. Heat oven to 375°F. Spray large cookie sheet with cooking spray or lightly grease. Separate dough into 5 biscuits; place on sprayed cookie sheet. Press out each biscuit to form a 6-inch round.

2. Spread each with mustard-mayonnaise sauce. Top each with cheese, ham and onions. Cut each tomato into 5 slices. Place 3 tomato slices on each pizza.

3. Bake at 375°F for 10 to 15 minutes or until bottoms of crusts are deep golden brown and cheese is melted.

Nutrition Information Per Serving: Calories 360 • Total Fat 20g • Saturated Fat 9g • Cholesterol 40mg • Sodium 1040mg • Total Carbohydrate 28g • Dietary Fiber 1g • Sugars 5g • Protein 18g. **Dietary Exchanges:** 2 Starch • 1½ Lean Meat • 3 Fat OR 2 Carbohydrate • 1½ Lean Meat • 3 Fat.

lumpy pan pizza

PREP TIME: 10 MINUTES
READY TO SERVE: 40 MINUTES
SERVINGS: 6

✳ meal-in-one

1 (16.3-oz.) can Pillsbury® Grands!® Refrigerated Original Flaky Layers Biscuits

1 (8-oz.) can pizza sauce

8 oz. finely shredded mozzarella cheese (2 cups)

16 (1½-inch) slices pepperoni

1. Heat oven to 375°F. Separate dough into 8 biscuits. Cut each biscuit into 8 pieces; place in medium bowl. Add pizza sauce and 1 cup of the cheese; toss to coat.

2. Spoon and spread mixture in ungreased 9-inch square (2-quart) glass baking dish. Top with pepperoni and remaining 1 cup cheese.

3. Bake at 375°F for 22 to 28 minutes or until golden brown and bubbly.

Nutrition Information Per Serving: Calories 460 • Total Fat 26g • Saturated Fat 9g • Cholesterol 30mg • Sodium 1500mg • Total Carbohydrate 37g • Dietary Fiber 1g • Sugars 7g • Protein 19g. **Dietary Exchanges:** 2 Starch • ½ Fruit • 2 Medium-Fat Meat • 3 Fat OR 2½ Carbohydrate • 2 Medium-Fat Meat • 3 Fat.

ham and cheese biscuit pockets

READY TO SERVE: 40 MINUTES
SERVINGS: 5

CAROL J. GROSS ✳ FORT MORGAN, COLORADO
BAKE-OFF® CONTEST 31, 2006

1 cup cubed cooked ham

4 oz. shredded Swiss cheese (1 cup)

½ cup finely chopped peeled apple

1 (12-oz.) can refrigerated flaky biscuits

1 egg, slightly beaten

1 teaspoon water

Alfalfa sprouts, if desired

Chopped tomato, if desired

1. Heat oven to 375° F. Lightly grease large cookie sheet. In small bowl, combine ham, cheese and apple; mix gently. Separate dough into 10 biscuits. On greased cookie sheet, press or roll out 5 biscuits to 4-inch circles.

2. Place about ½ cup ham mixture onto center of each circle. Press or roll out remaining 5 biscuits to 5-inch circles. Place each over filling. Press edges with fork to seal. Combine egg and water; brush over filled biscuits.

3. Bake at 375° F for 13 to 18 minutes or until golden brown. Cut each in half to form pocket sandwiches. To serve, garnish with alfalfa sprouts and tomato. Serve warm.

Nutrition Information Per Serving: Calories 370 • Protein 17g • Carbohydrate 33g • Fat 19g • Sodium 1160mg.

peppered pork pitas with garlic sauce

READY TO SERVE: 20 MINUTES
SERVINGS: 8

✳ super fast

garlic sauce

- ⅓ cup mayonnaise or salad dressing
- 2 tablespoons milk
- 2 garlic cloves, minced

pork pitas

- 1 lb. boneless pork loin chops, cut into thin strips
- 1 tablespoon olive or vegetable oil
- 1 teaspoon coarse ground black pepper
- 1 (7.25-oz.) jar roasted red bell peppers, drained, sliced
- 4 (6-inch) pita (pocket) breads, halved

1. In small bowl, combine mayonnaise, milk and garlic; mix well. Set aside.

2. In medium bowl, combine pork, oil and pepper; mix well. Heat large skillet over medium-high heat until hot. Add pork mixture; cook 3 to 4 minutes or until pork is lightly browned and no longer pink, stirring occasionally. Stir in roasted peppers; heat until warm.

3. Lightly brush insides of pita bread halves with garlic sauce. Fill each with pork mixture. If desired, drizzle remaining garlic sauce over top.

Nutrition Information Per Serving: Calories 520 • Total Fat 27g • Saturated Fat 6g • Cholesterol 80mg • Sodium 480mg • Total Carbohydrate 38g • Dietary Fiber 2g • Sugars 2g • Protein 31g. **Dietary Exchanges:** 2 Starch • 1½ Vegetable • 3 Lean Meat • 3½ Fat OR 2 Carbohydrate • 1½ Vegetable • 3 Lean Meat • 3½ Fat.

grilled ham slice with pineapple salsa

READY TO SERVE: 30 MINUTES
SERVINGS: 6

pineapple salsa

- 1 (8-oz.) can crushed pineapple, drained
- 2 tablespoons orange marmalade
- 1 tablespoon chopped fresh cilantro
- 2 teaspoons chopped fresh jalapeño chile
- 2 teaspoons lime juice
- ¼ teaspoon salt

ham

- 1 (1½ lb.) fully cooked center-cut ham slice (¾ to 1 inch thick)

1. Heat grill. In small bowl, combine all salsa ingredients; mix well.

2. When ready to grill, place ham on gas grill over medium heat or on charcoal grill 4 to 6 inches from medium coals. Cook 10 to 20 minutes or until thoroughly heated, turning 2 or 3 times. Serve with pineapple salsa.

Nutrition Information Per Serving: Calories 140 • Total Fat 4g • Saturated Fat 1g • Cholesterol 40mg • Sodium 1310mg • Total Carbohydrate 9g • Dietary Fiber 0g • Sugars 6g • Protein 17g. **Dietary Exchanges:** ½ Fruit • 2 Lean Meat OR ½ Carbohydrate • 2 Lean Meat.

caribbean pork tenderloins

READY TO SERVE: 55 MINUTES
SERVINGS: 6

1 teaspoon garlic powder

1 teaspoon dried thyme leaves

1 teaspoon allspice

1 teaspoon nutmeg

½ teaspoon salt

½ teaspoon mace

½ teaspoon cloves

¼ teaspoon coarse ground black pepper

2 (¾-lb.) pork tenderloins

1. Heat grill. In small bowl, combine all ingredients except pork tenderloins; mix well. Rub mixture over pork, coating well.

2. When ready to grill, place pork on gas grill over medium-high heat or on charcoal grill 4 to 6 inches from medium-high coals. Cook 20 to 30 minutes or until pork is no longer pink in center, turning pork occasionally. To serve, cut pork into slices.

Nutrition Information Per Serving: Calories 140 • Total Fat 4g • Saturated Fat 2g • Cholesterol 65mg • Sodium 230mg • Total Carbohydrate 1g • Dietary Fiber 0g • Sugars 0g • Protein 24g. **Dietary Exchange:** 3 Lean Meat.

on-the-go pepperoni pizzas

READY TO SERVE: 15 MINUTES
SERVINGS: 6

* super fast

1 (8-oz.) can pizza sauce

1 (3-oz.) pkg. cream cheese, softened

1 (8-oz.) package sliced pepperoni, coarsely chopped (2½ cups)

¼ cup chopped green onions (4 medium)

¼ cup finely chopped green bell pepper

1½ cups shredded mozzarella cheese (6-oz.)

6 English muffins or bagels, split, toasted

1. In large bowl, mix pizza sauce and cream cheese until well blended. Stir in pepperoni, onions, bell pepper and 1 cup of the cheese. Cover; refrigerate up to 3 days.

2. To make 1 serving, place 2 toasted muffin halves on microwavable plate. Top each half with about ¼ cup pepperoni mixture and heaping tablespoon remaining cheese. Microwave on high about 1 minute or until hot.

Nutrition Information Per Serving: Calories 470 • Total Fat 28g • Saturated Fat 13g • Trans Fat 0g • Cholesterol 60mg • Sodium 1400mg • Total Carbohydrate 33g • Dietary Fiber 2g • Sugars 11g • Protein 22g. **Dietary Exchanges:** 1½ Starch • ½ Other Carbohydrate • 2½ High-Fat Meat • 1½ Fat.

DOUBLY GOOD!

If you have a large family or need a larger amount of pizzas, go ahead and double all of the ingredients in the above recipe. Store the pepperoni mixture in the refrigerator for no longer than 3 days.

---

pasta carbonara

READY TO SERVE: 20 MINUTES
SERVINGS: 6

* super fast

1 (16-oz.) pkg. uncooked linguine

2 teaspoons margarine or butter

1¼ cups finely chopped Canadian bacon

1 cup finely chopped onions

1 garlic clove, minced

¾ cup skim milk

½ cup refrigerated or frozen fat-free egg product, thawed

½ teaspoon cracked black pepper

¼ cup grated Parmesan cheese

1. Cook linguine to desired doneness as directed on package. Drain; cover to keep warm.

2. Meanwhile, in Dutch oven or large saucepan, melt margarine over medium heat. Add bacon, onions and garlic; cook and stir 4 minutes or until onions are tender.

3. Add cooked linguine, milk, egg product and pepper to bacon mixture; toss gently to mix. Cook 1 minute or until thoroughly heated. Remove from heat; toss gently. Sprinkle with cheese.

Nutrition Information Per Serving: Calories 390 • Total Fat 6g • Saturated Fat 2g • Cholesterol 20mg • Sodium 550mg • Total Carbohydrate 62g • Dietary Fiber 2g • Sugars 6g • Protein 21g. **Dietary Exchanges:** 4 Starch • 1½ Lean Meat OR 4 Carbohydrate • 1½ Lean Meat.

apricot-glazed lamb chops

PREP TIME: 30 MINUTES
READY TO SERVE: 1 HOUR
SERVINGS: 4

1 (16-oz.) can apricot halves, drained, reserving liquid

¼ cup oil

2 tablespoons vinegar

¼ teaspoon salt

4 lamb chops (1 inch thick)

2 tablespoons brown sugar

2 teaspoons cornstarch

Dash allspice

2 tablespoons orange juice

1. In shallow baking dish, combine ½ cup of the reserved apricot liquid, oil, vinegar and salt. (Reserve remaining apricot liquid for sauce.) Place lamb chops in apricot mixture, turning to coat all sides. Refrigerate 30 minutes.

2. Remove chops from marinade, reserving marinade. Place lamb chops on broiler pan. Broil 4 to 6 inches from heat for 9 to 11 minutes or until browned and of desired doneness, turning chops and basting occasionally with reserved marinade.

3. Meanwhile, reserve 8 apricot halves for garnish. In blender container or food processor bowl with metal blade, combine remaining apricots and reserved apricot liquid, brown sugar, cornstarch, allspice and orange juice. Blend or process 1 minute or until smooth; pour into small saucepan. Cook and stir over medium heat until thickened.

4. To serve, arrange lamb chops on serving platter; garnish with reserved apricot halves. Serve with warm apricot sauce.

Nutrition Information Per Serving: Calories 330 • Total Fat 18g • Saturated Fat 3g • Cholesterol 40mg • Sodium 170mg • Total Carbohydrate 28g • Dietary Fiber 2g • Sugars 23g • Protein 13g. Dietary Exchanges: 2 Fruit • 2 Lean Meat • 2 Fat OR 2 Carbohydrate • 2 Lean Meat • 2 Fat.

italian frittata biscuits

PREP TIME: 15 MINUTES
READY TO SERVE: 35 MINUTES
SERVINGS: 8

1 (16.3-oz.) can Pillsbury® Grands!® Refrigerated Buttermilk Biscuits

3 eggs

1¼ to 1½ teaspoons dried Italian seasoning

½ cup diced cooked ham

4 oz. shredded 6-cheese Italian blend (1 cup)

¼ cup roasted red bell peppers (from a jar), drained, chopped

½ cup diced seeded Italian plum tomatoes

2 tablespoons thinly sliced fresh basil leaves

1. Heat oven to 375°F. Spray large cookie sheet with cooking spray. Separate dough into 8 biscuits. Place 3 inches apart on sprayed cookie sheet. Press out each biscuit to form a 4-inch round with ¼-inch-high rim around outside edge,

2. Beat 1 of the eggs in small bowl. Brush over tops and sides of biscuits. Sprinkle with 1 teaspoon of the Italian seasoning.

3. In another small bowl, combine remaining 2 eggs and remaining ¼ to ½ teaspoon Italian seasoning; beat well. Spoon evenly into indentations in each biscuit. Top with the ham, ½ cup of the cheese, roasted peppers, tomatoes, basil and the remaining ½ cup cheese.

4. Bake at 375°F for 15 to 20 minutes or until the biscuits are golden brown and the eggs are set.

Nutrition Information Per Serving: Calories 290 • Total Fat 14g • Saturated Fat 5g • Cholesterol 90mg • Sodium 920mg • Total Carbohydrate 29g • Dietary Fiber 1g • Sugars 9g • Protein 12g. Dietary Exchanges: 2 Starch • 1 Medium-Fat Meat • 1 Fat OR 2 Carbohydrate • 1 Medium-Fat Meat • 1 Fat.

apricot-glazed lamb chops

peachy chipotle-pork tacos

READY TO SERVE: 30 MINUTES
SERVINGS: 5

NATALIE HVAL ✹ PORTLAND, OREGON
BAKE-OFF® CONTEST 42, 2006

1 lb. boneless pork loin chops (¾ to 1 inch thick)

Salt and pepper, if desired

1 cup organic frozen sliced peaches (from 10-oz. bag), slightly thawed, coarsely chopped

1 cup organic medium chipotle salsa

3 tablespoons honey

3 tablespoons red wine vinegar

2 tablespoons finely chopped garlic (10 to 12 medium cloves)

1 (4.7-oz.) box taco shells (10 shells)

½ small red onion, thinly sliced

2½ cups chopped romaine lettuce

2 avocados, pitted, peeled and cut into 10 wedges, if desired

2 limes, cut into 10 wedges

1 small bunch fresh cilantro, if desired

1. Heat 12-inch skillet over medium-high heat. Sprinkle pork chops with salt and pepper; add to skillet. Cook 8 to 10 minutes, turning once, until meat thermometer inserted in center of chops reads 160°F. Remove from skillet; place on cutting board to cool slightly. Remove skillet from heat.

2. To same skillet, carefully add peaches, salsa, honey, vinegar and garlic. Cook over medium-high heat about 5 minutes, stirring constantly, until mixture is thickened. Cut pork into ½-inch pieces; stir into peach mixture. Meanwhile, heat taco shells as directed on box.

3. To serve, divide pork mixture evenly among warm taco shells. Top each with onion and lettuce. Garnish each with 1 avocado wedge; squeeze juice from 1 lime wedge over each and garnish with cilantro.

Nutrition Information Per Serving: Calories 360 • Total Fat 13g • Saturated Fat 3.5g • Trans Fat 2g • Cholesterol 55mg • Sodium 370mg • Total Carbohydrate 39g • Dietary Fiber 4g • Sugars 16g • Protein 23g. Dietary Exchanges: 1½ Starch • 1 Other Carbohydrate • 2½ Lean Meat • 1 Fat.

ham and biscuit stacks

READY TO SERVE: 25 MINUTES
SERVINGS: 5

✹ **super fast**

1 (12-oz.) can Pillsbury® Golden Layers™ Refrigerated Flaky Biscuits

2 tablespoons honey

2 tablespoons prepared mustard

5 (4-inch-square) thin slices cooked ham

5 (4-inch-square) thin slices Swiss cheese

10 small lettuce leaves

1. Heat oven to 400°F. Bake biscuits as directed on can.

2. Meanwhile, in small bowl, combine honey and mustard; blend well. Place 1 ham slice on each cheese slice. Cut each stack into 4 squares.

3. Split warm biscuits. Spread each biscuit half with ½ teaspoon honey-mustard mixture. Stack 2 squares of ham and cheese on bottom half of each biscuit. Top with lettuce leaves. Cover with top halves of biscuits.

Nutrition Information Per Serving: Calories 340 • Total Fat 16g • Saturated Fat 6g • Cholesterol 30mg • Sodium 1140mg • Total Carbohydrate 36g • Dietary Fiber 1g • Sugars 10g • Protein 14g. Dietary Exchanges: 1½ Starch • 1 Fruit • 1½ Lean Meat • 2 Fat OR 2½ Carbohydrate • 1½ Lean Meat • 2 Fat.

pork and sweet potato supper

PREP TIME: 20 MINUTES
READY TO SERVE: 40 MINUTES
SERVINGS: 5

* meal-in-one

2 tablespoons oil

1 lb. pork tenderloins, cut into 1-inch pieces

2 cups cubed peeled dark-orange sweet potatoes (about 2 medium)

½ cup chopped onion

⅔ cup maple-flavored syrup

2 tablespoons all-purpose flour

½ to 1 teaspoon ginger

¼ teaspoon salt

⅛ teaspoon pepper

1 cup frozen sweet peas

1 pear, peeled, chopped, if desired

1 (12-oz.) can Pillsbury® Golden Layers™ Refrigerated Flaky Biscuits

1. Heat oven to 375°F. Heat oil in large ovenproof skillet over medium-high heat until hot. Add pork, sweet potatoes and onion; cook 8 to 10 minutes or until pork is browned and sweet potatoes are crisp-tender, stirring occasionally.

2. In small bowl, combine syrup, flour, ginger, salt and pepper; blend well. Stir syrup mixture, peas and pear into pork mixture. Cook mixture 1 to 2 minutes or until hot, stirring frequently.

3. Separate dough into 10 biscuits; cut each into quarters. Arrange biscuit pieces over pork mixture in skillet.

4. Bake at 375°F for 15 to 20 minutes or until biscuits are golden brown.

Nutrition Information Per Serving: Calories 640 • Total Fat 19g • Saturated Fat 5g • Cholesterol 55mg • Sodium 1060mg • Total Carbohydrate 94g • Dietary Fiber 5g • Sugars 41g • Protein 28g. **Dietary Exchanges:** 3½ Starch • 2½ Fruit • 2½ Lean Meat • 2 Fat OR 6 Carbohydrate • 2½ Lean Meat • 2 Fat.

SWEET-AND-SAVORY COMBO

You'll enjoy the combination of sweet and savory in this flavorful one-dish meal. Be sure to peel and cut the sweet potatoes just before using them so they don't discolor. When it comes to the pear, any type such as Bosc or Bartlett, would be delicious in this no-fuss recipe. If it suits your family's taste better, however, substitute an apple for the pear.

---

canadian bacon and potato quiche

PREP TIME: 25 MINUTES
READY TO SERVE: 1 HOUR 15 MINUTES
SERVINGS: 8

* meal-in-one

1 Pillsbury® Refrigerated Pie Crust (from 15-oz. pkg.), softened as directed on package

1 cup frozen diced hash-brown potatoes (from 30-oz. pkg.), thawed

1 cup cut (½-inch) fresh asparagus spears

1 cup diced Canadian bacon

6 oz. shredded Havarti cheese (1½ cups)

4 eggs

1 cup milk

½ teaspoon dried marjoram leaves

¼ teaspoon salt

1. Heat oven to 375°F. Prepare pie crust as directed on package for one-crust baked shell using 9-inch glass pie pan. Prick crust generously with fork. Bake at 375°F for about 8 minutes or until light golden brown.

2. Remove partially baked crust from oven. Layer potatoes, asparagus, bacon and cheese in crust. In medium bowl, beat eggs, milk, marjoram and salt until well blended. Pour over mixture in crust.

3. Bake at 375°F for 45 to 50 minutes or until knife inserted in center comes out clean. Let stand 5 minutes. Cut into wedges.

Nutrition Information Per Serving: Calories 275 • Total Fat 17g • Saturated Fat 7g • Cholesterol 140mg • Sodium 620mg • Total Carbohydrate 16g • Dietary Fiber 1g • Sugars 0g • Protein 15g. **Dietary Exchanges:** 1 Skim Milk • 1 Vegetable • 1 High-Fat Meat • 1½ Fat OR 1 Carbohydrate • 1 Vegetable • 1 High-Fat Meat • 1½ Fat.

breaded pork chops

READY TO SERVE: 20 MINUTES
SERVINGS: 4

✳ **super fast**

2 tablespoons all-purpose flour

½ teaspoon salt

½ teaspoon paprika

⅛ teaspoon pepper

1 egg, slightly beaten

1 to 2 teaspoons Worcestershire sauce

½ cup unseasoned dry bread crumbs

2 tablespoons oil

4 boneless pork loin chops

1. In small bowl, combine flour, salt, paprika and pepper; mix well. In another small bowl, combine egg and Worcestershire sauce. Coat pork chops with seasoned flour; dip in egg mixture and coat with crumbs.

2. In large skillet, heat oil over medium-high heat until hot. Add chops; cook until browned on both sides. Reduce heat to medium; cook 5 to 7 minutes or until pork is no longer pink in center.

Nutrition Information Per Serving: Calories 310 • Total Fat 17g • Saturated Fat 4g • Cholesterol 120mg • Sodium 470mg • Total Carbohydrate 13g • Dietary Fiber 1g • Sugars 1g • Protein 27g. Dietary Exchanges: 1 Starch • 3½ Lean Meat • 1 Fat OR 1 Carbohydrate • 3½ Lean Meat • 1 Fat.

golden pork chow mein

READY TO SERVE: 30 MINUTES
SERVINGS: 6

✳ **meal-in-one**

1 tablespoon oil

1½ lb. lean pork steak, bones removed, cut into ¼-inch slices

1 cup sliced carrots

½ cup diagonally sliced celery

1 cup water

2 tablespoons soy sauce

2 teaspoons sugar

1 teaspoon beef-flavor instant bouillon

½ teaspoon garlic powder

½ teaspoon grated gingerroot or ⅛ teaspoon ground ginger

8 to 9 oz. fresh bean sprouts (4 cups)

½ cup diagonally sliced green onions

1 (2-oz.) jar sliced pimientos, drained

¼ cup cold water

2 tablespoons cornstarch

Chow mein noodles

1. Heat oil in large skillet or wok over medium-high heat until hot. Add pork; cook and stir until browned. Remove pork from skillet; cover to keep warm.

2. To liquid in skillet, add carrots, celery, 1 cup water, soy sauce, sugar, bouillon, garlic powder and gingerroot; mix well. Reduce heat to medium-low. Cover; simmer 4 to 5 minutes or until vegetables are crisp-tender. Stir in cooked pork, bean sprouts, onions and pimientos; cook until thoroughly heated.

3. In small bowl, combine ¼ cup water and cornstarch; blend until smooth. Gradually stir into mixture in skillet. Cook and stir over medium-high heat until sauce is bubbly and thickened. Serve over chow mein noodles.

Nutrition Information Per Serving: Calories 310 • Total Fat 15g • Saturated Fat 3g • Cholesterol 50mg • Sodium 650mg • Total Carbohydrate 23g • Dietary Fiber 3g • Sugars 4g • Protein 21g. Dietary Exchanges: 1 Starch • 1 Vegetable • 2 Lean Meat • 2 Fat OR 1 Carbohydrate • 1 Vegetable • 2 Lean Meat • 2 Fat.

STIR-FRY TIPS

Trim off and discard all visible fat before stir-frying pieces of pork. Freezing the meat for 30 minutes or so will firm it up just enough to make it easy to cut the meat into uniform pieces. Doing so helps ensure even cooking. Stir-fry the meat in batches, if necessary, to avoid crowding the pan or wok. If the chunks of pork are crowded, they will steam instead of truly being stir-fried, and won't have an appealing browned exterior.

teriyaki veggie-pork burgers

READY TO SERVE: 30 MINUTES
SERVINGS: 4

LISA HUFF ✽ BIRMINGHAM, CALIFORNIA
BAKE-OFF® CONTEST 42, 2006

1 (9-oz.) box frozen broccoli, carrots and cauliflower in teriyaki sauce

1 green onion, coarsely chopped (1 tablespoon)

1 lb. lean ground pork

½ cup panko bread crumbs

1 teaspoon ground ginger

¼ cup mayonnaise or salad dressing

1 tablespoon teriyaki sauce

1 (6-oz.) container orange crème or mandarin orange low-fat yogurt

4 whole wheat or multi-grain burger buns (4 to 5 inch), split, toasted

16 thin slices cucumber

1. In food processor, place frozen teriyaki vegetables and onion; process with on-and-off motions until finely chopped. Place in large bowl. Stir in ground pork, bread crumbs and ginger until well blended. Shape mixture into 4 patties, about 5 inches in diameter and ½ inch thick.

2. Spray 12-inch skillet with cooking spray; heat over medium heat. Add patties; cover and cook 10 to 12 minutes, turning once, until browned and meat thermometer inserted in center of patties reads 160°F.

3. Meanwhile, in small bowl, mix mayonnaise, teriyaki sauce and yogurt with wire whisk until well blended.

4. Spread mayonnaise mixture evenly on top and bottom halves of toasted buns. Top bottom halves with patties and cucumber slices. Cover with top halves of buns.

Nutrition Information Per Serving: Calories 560 • Total Fat 31g • Saturated Fat 9g • Trans Fat 1g • Cholesterol 80mg • Sodium 840mg • Total Carbohydrate 40g • Dietary Fiber 5g • Sugars 15g • Protein 28g. **Dietary Exchanges:** 1½ Starch • 1 Other Carbohydrate • 1 Vegetable • 3 Medium-Fat Meat • 3 Fat.

grilled stuffed pork chops

READY TO SERVE: 30 MINUTES
SERVINGS: 4

stuffing

1 teaspoon dried marjoram leaves

1 teaspoon freeze-dried chopped chives

1 teaspoon dried basil leaves

2 cups herb-seasoned stuffing mix

1/3 cup finely chopped onion

1/2 cup hot water

1/4 cup margarine or butter, melted

pork chops

4 pork loin chops (1 inch thick)

1. Heat grill. In medium bowl, combine marjoram, chives and basil; mix well. Reserve 2 teaspoons herb mixture; set aside. To remaining herb mixture, add stuffing mix, onion, water and margarine; mix well.

2. Cut deep horizontal pocket in one side of each pork chop. Stuff each chop with about 1/2 cup stuffing mixture; press firmly. Sprinkle reserved herb mixture on both sides of each chop.

3. When ready to grill, place chops on gas grill over medium-high heat or on charcoal grill 4 to 6 inches from medium-high coals. Cook 15 to 20 minutes or until pork is no longer pink in center, turning once.

Nutrition Information Per Serving: Calories 460 • Total Fat 24g • Saturated Fat 6g • Cholesterol 100mg • Sodium 600mg • Total Carbohydrate 23g • Dietary Fiber 2g • Sugars 2g • Protein 38g. Dietary Exchanges: 1 1/2 Starch • 4 1/2 Lean Meat • 2 Fat OR 1 1/2 Carbohydrate • 4 1/2 Lean Meat • 2 Fat.

ham and spinach melts

READY TO SERVE: 20 MINUTES
SERVINGS: 4

ANITA L. HUNTER ✳ NEWARK, DELAWARE
BAKE-OFF® CONTEST 42, 2006

1 (9-oz.) box frozen spinach

1/2 cup reduced-fat sour cream

1 tablespoon chopped fresh basil

1 tablespoon sun-dried tomato bits or chopped sun-dried tomatoes in oil

1/8 teaspoon salt

1/2 teaspoon lemon juice

1 clove garlic, finely chopped

8 flour tortillas for soft tacos and fajitas, 6 inch (from 10.5-oz. pkg.)

1/2 lb. sliced cooked ham

1 (12-oz.) jar sliced roasted red bell peppers in water, drained (about 1 1/4 cups)

8 oz. sliced provolone cheese

1. Remove spinach from pouch; place in colander. Rinse with warm water until thawed; drain well. Squeeze spinach dry with paper towel. Meanwhile, in small bowl, mix sour cream, basil, tomatoes, salt, lemon juice and garlic.

2. On each tortilla, spread 1 tablespoon sour cream mixture. Top 4 tortillas evenly with ham, roasted peppers, spinach and cheese. Cover with remaining tortillas, sour cream mixture down.

3. Spray griddle or 12-inch skillet with cooking spray; heat over medium heat. Cook 2 sandwiches at a time 2 to 3 minutes on each side or until golden brown and thoroughly heated. Cut each sandwich in half to serve.

Nutrition Information Per Serving: Calories 520 • Total Fat 27g • Saturated Fat 14g • Trans Fat 0g • Cholesterol 80mg • Sodium 1680mg • Total Carbohydrate 36g • Dietary Fiber 2g • Sugars 8g • Protein 33g. Dietary Exchanges: 2 Starch • 1/2 Other Carbohydrate • 4 Medium-Fat Meat • 1 Fat.

ham, broccoli and rice pie

PREP TIME: 25 MINUTES
READY TO SERVE: 1 HOUR 5 MINUTES
SERVINGS: 6

1 Pillsbury® Refrigerated Pie Crust (from 15-oz. pkg.), softened as directed on package

3 eggs

¼ cup milk

1½ cups finely chopped cooked ham

2 (10-oz.) pkgs. frozen long-grain white rice and broccoli with cheese-flavored sauce, thawed

8 oz. shredded Swiss cheese (2 cups)

⅛ teaspoon pepper

1. Heat oven to 425°F. Prepare pie crust as directed on package for one-crust baked shell using 9-inch glass pie pan. Do not prick crust. Bake at 425°F for 7 to 8 minutes or until crust begins to brown.

2. Meanwhile, beat eggs in large bowl. Add milk, ham, rice and broccoli mixture, 1 cup of the Swiss cheese and pepper; mix well.

3. Remove partially baked crust from oven. Reduce oven temperature to 400°F. Pour ham mixture into crust. Top with remaining 1 cup cheese.

4. Return to oven; bake at 400°F for an additional 35 to 40 minutes or until knife inserted in center comes out clean. If necessary, cover edge of crust with strips of foil after 15 to 20 minutes of baking to prevent excessive browning. Let stand 10 minutes before serving.

Nutrition Information Per Serving: Calories 500 • Total Fat 27g • Saturated Fat 13g • Cholesterol 170mg • Sodium 1110mg • Total Carbohydrate 38g • Dietary Fiber 0g • Sugars 5g • Protein 26g. **Dietary Exchanges:** 2½ Starch • 2½ Medium-Fat Meat • 2½ Fat OR 2½ Carbohydrate • 2½ Medium-Fat Meat • 2½ Fat.

TAKE CARE WITH CUSTARD

Because Ham, Broccoli and Rice Pie is a custard dish, overbaking it may cause the egg filling to break down, giving the pie a curdled look. It will still taste great, but it just won't look as nice.

Start testing for doneness at the minimum bake time (35 minutes), and remove the pie from the oven as soon as a knife inserted in the center comes out clean.

pepperoni pizza calzone

PREP TIME: 20 MINUTES
READY TO SERVE: 55 MINUTES
SERVINGS: 8

* meal-in-one

2 (10-oz.) cans Pillsbury® Refrigerated Pizza Crust

3 oz. small pepperoni slices (42 slices)

1 (4.5-oz.) jar sliced mushrooms, well drained

½ cup sliced pimiento-stuffed green olives

8 oz. thinly sliced provolone cheese

1 tablespoon grated Parmesan cheese

1 (14 or 15-oz.) jar pizza sauce, heated

1. Heat oven to 375°F. Lightly grease 12-inch pizza pan. Unroll 1 can of dough; place in greased pan. Starting at center, press out dough to edge of pan. Layer pepperoni, mushrooms, olives and provolone cheese over dough.

2. Unroll remaining can of dough. Press out dough on work surface to form 12-inch round. Fold dough in half; place over cheese on dough in pan and unfold. Press outside edges to seal. Cut several slits in top crust for steam to escape. Sprinkle with Parmesan cheese.

3. Bake at 375°F for 30 to 35 minutes or until crust is deep golden brown. Cut pizza into wedges; serve with warm pizza sauce.

Nutrition Information Per Serving: Calories 380 • Total Fat 18g • Saturated Fat 7g • Cholesterol 35mg • Sodium 1520mg • Total Carbohydrate 39g • Dietary Fiber 2g • Sugars 7g • Protein 17g. **Dietary Exchanges:** 2 Starch • ½ Fruit • 1½ High-Fat Meat • 1 Fat OR 2½ Carbohydrate • 1½ High-Fat Meat • 1 Fat.

fish & seafood

fettuccine with pesto cream and salmon ✳ p. 198

fish fillets with california salsa ✳ p. 208

grands!® tuna melts ✳ p. 200

broiled snapper with cilantro sauce ✳ p. 214

dill-marinated salmon steaks　＊　p. 213

fettuccine with pesto cream and salmon

READY TO SERVE: 30 MINUTES
SERVINGS: 4

8 oz. uncooked fettuccine

2 teaspoons olive or vegetable oil

1 teaspoon grated lemon peel

1 garlic clove, minced

¼ teaspoon salt

Dash pepper

2 (6-oz.) salmon fillets

1 cup whipping cream

½ cup purchased pesto

1 oz. shredded fresh Parmesan cheese (¼ cup)

Freshly ground black pepper, if desired

1. Cook fettuccine to desired doneness as directed on package. Drain; cover pasta to keep warm.

2. Meanwhile, in small bowl, combine oil, lemon peel, garlic, salt and dash pepper; mix well. Spray broiler pan with cooking spray. Place salmon, skin side down, on sprayed pan. Brush top of salmon with oil mixture.

3. Broil 3 to 4 inches from heat for 10 minutes or until fish flakes easily with fork.

4. Remove skin from broiled salmon; discard skin. Break salmon into bite-sized pieces.

5. In large saucepan, bring cream just to a boil over medium heat. Add cooked fettuccine; toss to coat. Gently fold salmon and pesto into fettuccine. Sprinkle each serving with cheese and freshly ground pepper.

Nutrition Information Per Serving: Calories 700 • Total Fat 43g • Saturated Fat 18g • Cholesterol 205mg • Sodium 560mg • Total Carbohydrate 44g • Dietary Fiber 2g • Sugars 4g • Protein 33g. **Dietary Exchanges:** 3 Starch • 3½ Lean Meat • 6 Fat OR 3 Carbohydrate • 3½ Lean Meat • 6 Fat.

mini shrimp bakes

PREP TIME: 20 MINUTES
READY TO SERVE: 45 MINUTES
SERVINGS: 8

1 (8-oz.) can Pillsbury® Refrigerated Crescent Dinner Rolls

1 (8-oz.) pkg. cream cheese, softened

2 tablespoons chopped onion or 1 teaspoon instant minced onion

¼ teaspoon salt

1 teaspoon prepared horseradish

1 (6-oz.) pkg. (2 cups) frozen cooked shrimp, thawed, or 4½-oz. can shrimp, drained, rinsed

¼ cup cooked real bacon pieces

Paprika

1. Heat oven to 375°F. Separate dough into 8 triangles. Place each triangle in ungreased muffin cup; press dough in bottom and up sides to cover.

2. In medium bowl, combine cream cheese, onion, salt and horseradish; blend well. Stir in shrimp. Spoon about ¼ cup mixture into each cup. Sprinkle with bacon and paprika.

3. Bake at 375°F for 20 to 25 minutes or until crust is golden brown. Let stand 5 minutes before serving.

Nutrition Information Per Serving: Calories 240 • Total Fat 16g • Saturated Fat 8g • Cholesterol 75mg • Sodium 590mg • Total Carbohydrate 15g • Dietary Fiber 1g • Sugars 5g • Protein 9g. Dietary Exchanges: 1 Starch • 1 Medium-Fat Meat • 2 Fat OR 1 Carbohydrate • 1 Medium-Fat Meat • 2 Fat.

MAKE-AHEAD MEAL

To make these Mini Shrimp Bakes ahead of time, simply prepare the recipe through the end of Step 2. Cover the muffin cups and refrigerate for up to 2 hours, then bake as directed.

If you have any of the baked cups left over after your meal, just wrap them loosely in foil and refrigerate them for lunch or dinner the next day. Pop the wrapped mini bakes in a 375°F oven for 12 to 15 minutes or until they are warmed through.

tuna salad buns

READY TO SERVE: 25 MINUTES
SERVINGS: 6

* super fast

4 oz. cubed or shredded American or Cheddar cheese (1 cup)

¼ cup sliced pimiento-stuffed green olives

2 tablespoons chopped onion

2 tablespoons chopped green bell pepper

2 tablespoons pickle relish, drained

⅓ cup mayonnaise or salad dressing

1 (6-oz.) can water-packed tuna, drained, flaked

6 sandwich buns, split

1. Heat oven to 350°F. In medium bowl, combine all ingredients except sandwich buns; mix well. Fill buns with mixture. Wrap each in foil. Place on ungreased cookie sheet.

2. Bake at 350°F for 15 minutes or until cheese melts.

Nutrition Information Per Serving: Calories 330 • Total Fat 19g • Saturated Fat 6g • Cholesterol 35mg • Sodium 840mg • Total Carbohydrate 25g • Dietary Fiber 1g • Sugars 7g • Protein 15g. Dietary Exchanges: 1½ Starch • 1½ Very Lean Meat • 3½ Fat OR 1½ Carbohydrate • 1½ Very Lean Meat • 3½ Fat.

OPEN-FACED SANDWICHES

For open-faced tuna salad sandwiches, just spread the filling from the recipe above on bun halves or toasted bread. Broil the sandwiches for 3 to 5 minutes or until the cheese melts. Serve the sandwiches warm from the oven with your favorite pasta salad or steaming bowls of tomato soup.

grands!® tuna melts

PREP TIME: 15 MINUTES
READY TO SERVE: 35 MINUTES
SERVINGS: 8

2 (6-oz.) cans water-packed tuna, well drained

⅓ cup chopped onion

⅓ cup mayonnaise

⅛ teaspoon salt

⅛ teaspoon pepper

1 (16.3-oz.) can Pillsbury® Grands!® Refrigerated Flaky Biscuits

4 oz. shredded Cheddar cheese (1 cup)

Sour cream, if desired

Chopped tomato, if desired

Shredded lettuce, if desired

1. Heat oven to 350°F. Grease cookie sheet. In medium bowl, combine tuna, onion, mayonnaise, salt and pepper; mix well.

2. Separate dough into 8 biscuits. Place 4 biscuits on greased cookie sheet. Press or roll each to form 5-inch round. Spoon tuna mixture evenly onto center of each biscuit. Top each with cheese. Press or roll remaining 4 biscuits to form 5-inch rounds. Place over filling. Press edges to seal.

3. Bake at 350°F for 15 to 20 minutes or until golden brown. Cut each sandwich in half. Top each with sour cream, tomato and lettuce.

Nutrition Information Per Serving: Calories 380 • Total Fat 23g • Saturated Fat 7g • Cholesterol 35mg • Sodium 870mg • Total Carbohydrate 27g • Dietary Fiber 1g • Sugars 5g • Protein 17g. Dietary Exchanges: 2 Starch • 1½ Lean Meat • 3½ Fat OR 2 Carbohydrate • 1½ Lean Meat • 3½ Fat.

salmon à la king casserole

PREP TIME: 15 MINUTES
READY TO SERVE: 35 MINUTES
SERVINGS: 6

* meal-in-one

1 (1-lb.) jar Alfredo sauce

1 (9-oz.) pkg. frozen baby early peas in pouch, thawed

1 (4.5-oz.) jar sliced mushrooms, drained

2 (14¾-oz.) cans pink salmon, drained, skin and bones removed

1 (2-oz.) jar chopped pimientos, drained

1 (8-oz.) can Pillsbury® Refrigerated Crescent Dinner Rolls

1. Heat oven to 375°F. Spray 12x8-inch (2-quart) glass baking dish with cooking spray. In medium saucepan, combine Alfredo sauce, peas and mushrooms; cook over medium heat until bubbly. Remove from heat. Gently stir in salmon and pimientos. Pour into sprayed baking dish.

2. Unroll dough into 2 long rectangles. Press edges and perforations to form 1 rectangle. Place over salmon mixture in baking dish.

3. Bake at 375°F for 12 to 18 minutes or until crust is golden brown.

Nutrition Information Per Serving: Calories 470 • Total Fat 25g • Saturated Fat 10g • Cholesterol 95mg • Sodium 1670mg • Total Carbohydrate 27g • Dietary Fiber 3g • Sugars 7g • Protein 33g. Dietary Exchanges: 2 Starch • 4 Lean Meat • 2 Fat OR 2 Carbohydrate • 4 Lean Meat • 2 Fat.

DELIGHTFUL DILL

Dill is an herb that goes particularly well with salmon. Stir in 1 tablespoon chopped fresh dill or 1 teaspoon dried dill weed with the salmon in this hot bake. Garnish each serving with a sprig of feathery fresh dill. This casserole is also good made with canned tuna, drained, in place of the salmon.

grands!® tuna melts

crab and corn cobbler

PREP TIME: 15 MINUTES
READY TO SERVE: 50 MINUTES
SERVINGS: 4

❉ meal-in-one

2 cups milk

⅓ cup all-purpose flour

¼ teaspoon salt

⅛ teaspoon pepper

1 (10-oz.) pkg. frozen southwestern-style whole kernel corn with roasted red peppers

1 (8-oz.) pkg. chunk-style imitation crabmeat (surimi)

3 tablespoons chopped green onions

1 (4-oz.) can Pillsbury® Refrigerated Crescent Dinner Rolls (4 rolls)

1. Heat oven to 350°F. Spray 1½-quart casserole with cooking spray. In medium saucepan, combine milk, flour, salt and pepper; blend well. Cook over medium-high heat until bubbly and thickened, stirring constantly.

2. Add corn with peppers, imitation crabmeat and green onions. Cook and stir until thoroughly heated. Pour into sprayed casserole.

3. Remove dough from can; do not unroll. Cut into 8 slices; cut each in half crosswise. Arrange over hot mixture.

4. Bake at 350°F for 30 to 35 minutes or until casserole is bubbly and rolls are deep golden brown.

Nutrition Information Per Serving: Calories 315 • Total Fat 7g • Saturated Fat 3g • Cholesterol 25mg • Sodium 1210mg • Total Carbohydrate 45g • Dietary Fiber 3g • Sugars 12g • Protein 18g. **Dietary Exchanges:** 3 Starch • 1 Very Lean Meat • 1 Fat OR 3 Carbohydrate • 1 Very Lean Meat • 1 Fat.

COBBLE A COBBLER!

Cobblers aren't just for fruit anymore. This savory cobbler is packed with a creamy crab and corn mixture, for instance. Give it a blush of color by sprinkling the biscuits with a little paprika before baking. It's a perfect dish to serve for brunch or supper and a great way to warm up chilly nights.

---

panfried fish

READY TO SERVE: 20 MINUTES
SERVINGS: 4

❉ super fast

1 egg, slightly beaten

¼ cup milk

½ cup all-purpose flour or cornmeal

1 lb. fish fillets

¼ cup oil or shortening

1. In shallow dish, combine egg and milk; blend well. Place flour in another shallow dish. Dip fish in egg mixture; coat with flour.

2. Heat oil in large skillet over medium-high heat. Add fish; cook 5 to 7 minutes or until golden brown and fish flakes easily with fork, turning once during cooking. If desired, season with salt and pepper to taste.

Nutrition Information Per Serving: Calories 290 • Total Fat 16g • Saturated Fat 2g • Cholesterol 105mg • Sodium 95mg • Total Carbohydrate 13g • Dietary Fiber 0g • Sugars 1g • Protein 24g. **Dietary Exchanges:** 1 Starch • 3 Medium-Fat Meat OR 1 Carbohydrate • 3 Medium-Fat Meat.

batter-fried fish

READY TO SERVE: 25 MINUTES
SERVINGS: 4

* super fast

1 lb. fish fillets, cut into serving-sized pieces
Oil for frying
½ cup milk
1 egg
½ cup all-purpose flour
½ teaspoon salt
Dash hot pepper sauce

1. Heat 1 to 1½ inches oil in Dutch oven, large saucepan or deep fryer to 375°F. In medium bowl, combine milk and egg; beat well. Add flour, salt and hot pepper sauce; beat until smooth. Dip fish in batter; allow excess to drain off.

2. With slotted spoon, add fish to hot oil; fry at 375°F for 3 to 4 minutes or until fish is golden brown and flakes easily with fork, turning once. Drain on paper towels.

Nutrition Information Per Serving: Calories 300 • Total Fat 16g • Saturated Fat 3g • Cholesterol 105 mg • Sodium 370mg • Total Carbohydrate 14g • Dietary Fiber 0g • Sugars 2g • Protein 24g. Dietary Exchanges: 1 Starch • 3 Medium-Fat Meat OR 1 Carbohydrate • 3 Medium-Fat Meat.

grands!® crescent shrimp salad sandwiches

PREP TIME: 15 MINUTES
READY TO SERVE: 35 MINUTES
SERVINGS: 6

1 (15.5-oz.) can Pillsbury® Grands!® Refrigerated Crescent Dinner Rolls
2 (5-oz.) pkg. frozen cooked salad shrimp, thawed (about 1¾ cups)
¼ cup chopped celery
2 tablespoons sliced green onions
⅓ cup tartar sauce
8 to 10 drops hot pepper sauce
6 leaves leaf lettuce

1. Bake crescent dinner rolls as directed on can. Cool 15 minutes.

2. Meanwhile, in medium bowl, combine all remaining ingredients except lettuce leaves.

3. Split crescent rolls. Spoon about ¼ cup filling evenly onto bottom half of each roll. Top with lettuce leaves and top halves of rolls.

Nutrition Information Per Serving: Calories 390 • Total Fat 23g • Saturated Fat 5g • Cholesterol 100mg • Sodium 720mg • Total Carbohydrate 30g • Dietary Fiber 1g • Sugars 6g • Protein 15g. Dietary Exchanges: 2 Starch • 1½ Very Lean Meat • 4 Fat OR 2 Carbohydrate • 1½ Very Lean Meat • 4 Fat.

creamed tuna on toast

READY TO SERVE: 15 MINUTES
SERVINGS: 6

* super fast

½ cup milk
1 (10¾-oz.) can condensed cream of celery soup
½ teaspoon instant minced onion
1 (15-oz.) can sweet peas, drained
1 (6-oz.) can water-packed tuna, drained, flaked
1 tablespoon chopped pimientos
6 to 8 slices bread, toasted, buttered if desired

1. In medium saucepan, combine milk, soup and onion; cook over medium heat until smooth, stirring frequently.

2. Stir in peas, tuna and pimientos; cook until thoroughly heated, stirring occasionally. Serve over toast.

Nutrition Information Per Serving: Calories 240 • Total Fat 9g • Saturated Fat 4g • Cholesterol 30mg • Sodium 830mg • Total Carbohydrate 27g • Dietary Fiber 3g • Sugars 4g • Protein 12g. Dietary Exchanges: 2 Starch • 1 Very Lean Meat • 1 Fat OR 2 Carbohydrate • 1 Very Lean Meat • 1 Fat.

smoky shrimp with creamy grits

READY TO SERVE: 30 MINUTES
SERVINGS: 4

LILLIAN JAGENDORF ✳ NEW YORK, NEW YORK
BAKE-OFF® CONTEST 42, 2006

3 cups water

1 to 2 teaspoons salt

1 can (14.75 oz.) cream-style sweet corn

¾ cup quick-cooking grits

½ cup finely chopped green onions (8 medium)

2 oz. cream cheese

¼ cup butter

1 large clove garlic, finely chopped

1½ lb. uncooked deveined peeled large shrimp

1 teaspoon seafood seasoning (from 6-oz. container)

1 teaspoon chipotle chiles in adobo sauce (from 7-oz. can), finely chopped

1 can (14.5 oz.) organic fire-roasted diced tomatoes, drained

1. In 3-quart saucepan, heat water, salt and corn to boiling. With wire whisk, gradually beat in grits. Return to boiling, beating constantly. Reduce heat to low; cover and simmer 5 to 7 minutes, stirring occasionally, until thickened. Remove from heat. Stir in onions and cream cheese until well combined. Cover; keep warm.

2. Meanwhile, in 10-inch heavy skillet, melt butter over medium-high heat. Add garlic; cook and stir about 2 minutes or until lightly browned. Add shrimp; cook and stir 4 to 6 minutes or just until shrimp are pink. Stir in seafood seasoning, chipotle chiles and tomatoes. Reduce heat to medium; simmer uncovered 2 to 3 minutes or until tomatoes are thoroughly heated.

3. Divide grits mixture evenly among individual large soup bowls; spoon shrimp mixture evenly over top.

Nutrition Information Per Serving: Calories 480 • Total Fat 19g • Saturated Fat 11g • Trans Fat 1g • Cholesterol 290mg • Sodium 1720mg • Total Carbohydrate 45g • Dietary Fiber 2g • Sugars 11g • Protein 32g. **Dietary Exchanges:** 2 Starch • 1 Other Carbohydrate • 3½ Very Lean Meat • 3½ Fat.

mediterranean shrimp and bow ties

6 oz. uncooked bow tie pasta (3 cups)

1 tablespoon olive or vegetable oil

1 lb. shelled deveined uncooked medium or large shrimp

½ cup green onion pieces (½ inch)

2 garlic cloves, minced

½ teaspoon dried oregano leaves

¼ teaspoon salt

2 tablespoons lemon juice

½ cup sliced kalamata or ripe olives

1. Cook pasta to desired doneness as directed on package. Drain; cover to keep warm.

2. Meanwhile, heat oil in large skillet over medium-high heat until hot. Add shrimp, onions and garlic; cook and stir 3 to 5 minutes or until shrimp turn pink. Remove from the heat.

3. Add pasta to skillet with all remaining ingredients. Cook 1 to 2 minutes or until thoroughly heated.

Nutrition Information Per Serving: Calories 320 • Total Fat 10g • Saturated Fat 1g • Cholesterol 160mg • Sodium 600mg • Total Carbohydrate 35g • Dietary Fiber 1g • Sugars 2g • Protein 23g. **Dietary Exchanges:** 2 Starch • 1 Vegetable • 2 Very Lean Meat • 1½ Fat OR 2 Carbohydrate • 1 Vegetable • 2 Very Lean Meat • 1½ Fat.

fish creole

1. Heat oven to 350°F. Arrange fish fillets in ungreased 12x8-inch (2-quart) or 8-inch square baking dish.

2. Melt margarine in medium skillet over medium-high heat. Add onion, celery and bell pepper; cook and stir until tender. Stir in all remaining ingredients. Spoon mixture over fish.

3. Bake at 350°F for 15 to 20 minutes or until fish flakes easily with fork.

Nutrition Information Per Serving: Calories 160 • Total Fat 4g • Saturated Fat 1g • Cholesterol 50mg • Sodium 230mg • Total Carbohydrate 9g • Dietary Fiber 1g • Sugars 5g • Protein 21g. **Dietary Exchanges:** 2 Vegetable • 2½ Very Lean Meat • ½ Fat.

1 lb. fish fillets

1 tablespoon margarine or butter

⅓ cup chopped onion

¼ cup chopped celery

2 tablespoons finely chopped green bell pepper

2 to 3 teaspoons sugar

¼ teaspoon dried oregano leaves

⅛ teaspoon pepper

1 (8-oz.) can stewed tomatoes, undrained, cut up

EFFORTLESS ADD-ONS

Beat the dinner doldrums by serving Fish Creole with a change-of-pace side dish. Buttery breadsticks jazz up any meal without much fuss. If you have any leftover white rice from last night's supper, combine it with a little salsa and some canned kidney beans that you've rinsed and drained.

Warmed in the microwave, the instant red beans and rice make a great addition to the fish fillets, particularly when seasoned to taste with cumin.

grilled whitefish with dill tartar sauce

READY TO SERVE: 15 MINUTES
SERVINGS: 4

✱ super fast

sauce

- ⅓ cup mayonnaise or salad dressing
- 1 tablespoon sweet pickle relish
- 1 tablespoon chopped fresh dill or 1 teaspoon dried dill weed

fish

- ¼ cup butter, melted
- 1 teaspoon lemon juice
- 4 (4-oz.) whitefish, haddock or orange roughy fillets

1. Heat grill. In small bowl, combine all sauce ingredients; mix well. Set aside. In separate small bowl, combine butter and lemon juice; blend well.

2. When ready to grill, carefully oil grill rack. Place whitefish on gas grill over medium heat or on charcoal grill 4 to 6 inches from medium coals. Brush with butter mixture. Cook 6 to 9 minutes or until fish flakes easily with fork, turning once and brushing occasionally with butter mixture. Serve with sauce.

Nutrition Information Per Serving: Calories 390 • Total Fat 33g • Saturated Fat 10g • Cholesterol 110mg • Sodium 310mg • Total Carbohydrate 2g • Dietary Fiber 0g • Sugars 2g • Protein 22g. **Dietary Exchanges:** 3 Very Lean Meat • 6 Fat.

cajun-spiced grouper sandwiches

READY TO SERVE: 20 MINUTES
SERVINGS: 4

✱ super fast

- 4 (4-oz.) grouper or cod fillets
- 2 teaspoons dried Cajun seasoning
- 4 onion sandwich buns, split, toasted
- ¼ cup tartar sauce
- 4 tomato slices
- 4 lettuce leaves

1. Spray medium skillet with cooking spray. Heat over medium-high heat until hot. Pat fillets dry with paper towel; sprinkle both sides with Cajun seasoning. Cook 10 to 14 minutes or until fish flakes easily with fork, turning once.

2. To assemble sandwiches, spread sandwich bun halves with tartar sauce. Fill each with tomato slice, lettuce leaf and cooked fillet.

Nutrition Information Per Serving: Calories 340 • Total Fat 12g • Saturated Fat 2g • Cholesterol 55mg • Sodium 850mg • Total Carbohydrate 31g • Dietary Fiber 2g • Sugars 2g • Protein 26g. **Dietary Exchanges:** 2 Starch • 3 Very Lean Meat • 1½ Fat OR 2 Carbohydrate • 3 Very Lean Meat • 1½ Fat.

salmon salad crescent sandwiches

READY TO SERVE: 20 MINUTES
SERVINGS: 6

✱ super fast

- 1 (15.5-oz.) can Pillsbury® Grands!® Refrigerated Crescent Dinner Rolls
- 1 (14.75 to 16-oz.) can salmon, drained, flaked
- 2 hard-cooked eggs, peeled, chopped
- ¼ cup chopped celery
- 2 tablespoons drained dill pickle relish
- ½ teaspoon onion salt
- ⅓ cup mayonnaise or salad dressing
- 6 small leaves leaf or iceberg lettuce

1. Bake crescent rolls as directed on can.

2. Meanwhile, in medium bowl, combine salmon, eggs, celery, relish, onion salt and mayonnaise; mix well.

3. Carefully cut each warm crescent roll in half to make 2 layers. Line bottom halves of rolls with lettuce. Top each with salmon mixture. Cover with top halves of rolls.

Nutrition Information Per Serving: Calories 480 • Total Fat 31g • Saturated Fat 6g • Cholesterol 105mg • Sodium 1120mg • Total Carbohydrate 31g • Dietary Fiber 1g • Sugars 8g • Protein 20g. **Dietary Exchanges:** 1½ Starch • ½ Fruit • 2 Lean Meat • 5 Fat OR 2 Carbohydrate • 2 Lean Meat • 5 Fat.

alfredo tuna over biscuits

READY TO SERVE: 20 MINUTES
SERVINGS: 5

✳ super fast

1 (10.2-oz.) can Pillsbury®
Grands!® Refrigerated
Buttermilk Biscuits
(5 biscuits)

2 (9-oz.) pkg. frozen broccoli,
carrots and peas in a low-fat
Alfredo sauce

2 (6-oz.) cans albacore tuna,
drained

1 (10-oz.) container
refrigerated Alfredo sauce

1½ oz. shredded fresh
Parmesan cheese (⅓ cup)

1. Heat oven to 375°F. Bake biscuits as directed on can.

2. Meanwhile, cook vegetables as directed on package. Pour into medium microwave-safe bowl. Add tuna and Alfredo sauce; mix well. Microwave on high for 3 minutes or until thoroughly heated, stirring once.

3. Split warm biscuits; place bottom halves on individual serving plates. Top with half of tuna mixture. Top each serving with biscuit top and remaining tuna mixture. Sprinkle each with cheese.

Nutrition Information Per Serving: Calories 570 • Total Fat 32g • Saturated Fat 16g • Cholesterol 90mg • Sodium 1760mg • Total Carbohydrate 41g • Dietary Fiber 3g • Sugars 13g • Protein 33g. **Dietary Exchanges:** 1 Starch • 1 Fruit • 2 Vegetable • 3½ Very Lean Meat • 6 Fat OR 2 Carbohydrate • 2 Vegetable • 3½ Very Lean Meat • 6 Fat.

THE NEW TUNA

When planning on Alfredo Tuna Over Biscuits, look for the new vacuum-sealed pouches of tuna and you won't need to worry about draining the can.

You'll find this new product wherever you buy canned tuna. If refrigerated Alfredo sauce isn't available, use 1¼ cups sauce from a jar of Alfredo sauce.

fish fillets with california salsa

READY TO SERVE: 20 MINUTES
SERVINGS: 4

* super fast

salsa

1½ cups chopped tomato

1 cup chopped peeled ripe avocado

¼ cup sliced green onions

2 tablespoons chopped fresh cilantro

½ teaspoon salt

2 jalapeño chiles, chopped

fish

2 tablespoons oil

2 tablespoons lime juice

1 lb. orange roughy fillets

1. Heat grill. Cut two 12-inch-square pieces of heavy-duty foil; pierce several holes in foil. In medium bowl, combine all salsa ingredients; mix well. Set aside.

2. In small bowl, combine oil and lime juice; mix well.

3. When ready to grill, place foil pieces on gas grill over medium heat or on charcoal grill 4 to 6 inches from medium coals. Brush fish fillets with oil mixture; place on foil pieces. Cook 6 to 7 minutes or until fish flakes easily with fork, turning once. Serve salsa over grilled fish.

Nutrition Information Per Serving: Calories 230 • Total Fat 14g • Saturated Fat 2g • Cholesterol 25mg • Sodium 350mg • Total Carbohydrate 8g • Dietary Fiber 3g • Sugars 3g • Protein 18g. **Dietary Exchanges:** 2 Vegetable • 2 Very Lean Meat • 2½ Fat.

FISH BROIL

To broil fish, place it directly on the broiler pan; broil 4 to 6 inches from the heat using the times in the recipe above as a guide, turning once.

clam sauce with linguine

READY TO SERVE: 25 MINUTES
SERVINGS: 3

✳ **super fast**

6 oz. uncooked linguine

2 tablespoons olive or vegetable oil

¼ cup finely chopped onion

1 garlic clove, minced

2 tablespoons chopped fresh parsley

½ teaspoon dried oregano leaves

½ teaspoon dried basil leaves

⅛ teaspoon pepper

¼ cup dry white wine

1 (6½-oz.) can minced clams, drained, reserving liquid

2 tablespoons grated Parmesan cheese, if desired

1. Cook linguine to desired doneness as directed on package. Drain; cover to keep warm.

2. Meanwhile, heat oil in medium skillet over medium-high heat. Add onion and garlic; cook 1 to 2 minutes or until onion is tender, stirring constantly. Stir in parsley, oregano, basil, pepper, wine and reserved clam liquid. Cook 5 minutes, stirring constantly.

3. Add clams; cook until thoroughly heated. Serve sauce over cooked linguine. Sprinkle each serving with Parmesan cheese.

Nutrition Information Per Serving: Calories 370 • Total Fat 12g • Saturated Fat 2g • Cholesterol 25mg • Sodium 190mg • Total Carbohydrate 46g • Dietary Fiber 2g • Sugars 3g • Protein 17g. **Dietary Exchanges:** 3 Starch • 1 Very Lean Meat • 2 Fat OR 3 Carbohydrate • 1 Very Lean Meat • 2 Fat.

salmon loaf

PREP TIME: 15 MINUTES
READY TO SERVE: 1 HOUR 15 MINUTES
SERVINGS: 6

1 (14¾-oz.) can salmon, drained and flaked, reserving liquid

2 eggs, beaten

2 cups soft bread cubes or ⅓ cup unseasoned dry bread crumbs

2 tablespoons finely chopped fresh parsley

¼ teaspoon salt

⅛ teaspoon pepper

1 small onion, chopped

2 tablespoons lemon juice

1. Heat oven to 350°F. Generously grease 8x4-inch loaf pan or 8-inch square pan. In large bowl, combine salmon, reserved liquid and all remaining ingredients; mix well. Press in greased loaf pan or form into loaf shape in greased square pan.

2. Bake at 350°F for 50 to 60 minutes or until loaf is golden brown and knife inserted in center comes out clean. Let stand 5 minutes. Loosen edges and remove from pan. To serve, cut into slices.

Nutrition Information Per Serving: Calories 140 • Total Fat 6g • Saturated Fat 2g • Cholesterol 95mg • Sodium 490mg • Total Carbohydrate 7g • Dietary Fiber 1g • Sugars 1g • Protein 15g. **Dietary Exchanges:** ½ Starch • 2 Lean Meat OR ½ Carbohydrate • 2 Lean Meat.

batter-fried shrimp or scallops

READY TO SERVE: 25 MINUTES
SERVINGS: 4

* super fast

1 lb. shelled deveined
uncooked medium shrimp
or scallops
Oil for frying
½ cup milk
1 egg
½ cup all-purpose flour
½ teaspoon salt
Dash hot pepper sauce

1. Heat 1 to 1½ inches oil in Dutch oven, large saucepan or deep fryer to 375°F. In medium bowl, combine milk and egg; beat well. Add flour, salt and hot pepper sauce; beat until smooth. Dip shrimp in batter, allow excess to drain off.

2. With slotted spoon, add shrimp to hot oil; fry at 375°F for 3 to 4 minutes or until golden brown. Drain on paper towels.

Nutrition Information Per Serving: Calories 290 • Total Fat 17g • Saturated Fat 3g • Cholesterol 215mg • Sodium 480mg • Total Carbohydrate 14g • Dietary Fiber 0g • Sugars 2g • Protein 21g. Dietary Exchanges: 1½ Starch • 2½ Medium-Fat Meat • ½ Fat OR 1 Carbohydrate • 2½ Medium-Fat Meat • ½ Fat.

crabmeat and avocado wraps

READY TO SERVE: 15 MINUTES
SERVINGS: 4

* super fast

4 (10-inch) flour tortillas
⅔ cup purchased Alfredo
sauce
2 (6-oz.) cans crabmeat, well
drained, flaked
1 ripe avocado, pitted, peeled
and cubed
2 cups shredded lettuce
¼ cup sliced green onions

1. Heat tortillas as directed on package.

2. Meanwhile, in medium saucepan, combine Alfredo sauce and crabmeat; cook over medium heat just until thoroughly heated, stirring occasionally. Fold in avocado.

3. Spoon half of mixture across center of each tortilla; top with lettuce and onions. Fold sides over filling. Fold bottom up over filling and continue rolling to enclose filling.

Nutrition Information Per Serving: Calories 470 • Total Fat 25g • Saturated Fat 9g • Cholesterol 85mg • Sodium 660mg • Total Carbohydrate 38g • Dietary Fiber 5g • Sugars 3g • Protein 22g. Dietary Exchanges: 2½ Starch • 2 Very Lean Meat • 4½ Fat OR 2½ Carbohydrate • 2 Very Lean Meat • 4½ Fat.

tarragon grilled fish and vegetables

READY TO SERVE: 35 MINUTES
SERVINGS: 4

* meal-in-one

2 tablespoons olive or
vegetable oil
2 carrots, cut into julienne
strips (1½x¼x¼ inch)
1 zucchini, cut into julienne
strips (1½x¼x¼ inch)
1 small red bell pepper, cut
into thin strips
½ cup sliced red onion
4 (6-oz.) orange roughy fillets
4 teaspoons chopped fresh
tarragon or 1½ teaspoons
dried tarragon leaves
2 tablespoons margarine or
butter, chilled

1. Heat grill. Heat oil in medium skillet over medium-high heat until hot. Add carrots, zucchini, bell pepper and onion; cook and stir 2 to 3 minutes or until vegetables are crisp-tender.

2. Cut four 18x12-inch pieces of heavy-duty foil. Place 1 orange roughy fillet on each; sprinkle with salt and pepper, if desired. Top each fillet with ¼ of vegetable mixture, tarragon and margarine. Wrap each packet securely using double-fold seals, allowing room for heat expansion.

3. When ready to grill, place packets, seam side up, on gas grill over medium heat or on charcoal grill 4 to 6 inches from medium coals. Cook 12 to 18 minutes or until fish flakes easily with fork, rearranging packets several times during cooking. Open packets carefully to allow hot steam to escape.

Nutrition Information Per Serving: Calories 260 • Total Fat 14g • Saturated Fat 2g • Cholesterol 35mg • Sodium 190mg • Total Carbohydrate 8g • Dietary Fiber 2g • Sugars 5g • Protein 26g. Dietary Exchanges: 1½ Vegetable • 3½ Very Lean Meat • 2 Fat.

grilled walleye with pecan butter

READY TO SERVE: 25 MINUTES
SERVINGS: 4

❋ super fast

¼ cup butter, softened

2 teaspoons chopped fresh chives

2 teaspoons orange juice

½ cup chopped pecans, toasted

4 (6-oz.) walleye fillets

¼ teaspoon salt

Dash coarse ground black pepper

1. Heat grill. Cut two 12-inch-square pieces of heavy-duty foil. With tip of sharp knife, cut 2-inch slits every 2 inches across foil. Spray foil with cooking spray.

2. In small bowl, combine the butter, chives, orange juice and ¼ cup of the pecans; mix well.

3. When ready to grill, place foil pieces on gas grill over medium heat or on charcoal grill 4 to 6 inches from medium coals. Sprinkle walleye fillets with salt and pepper. Place fillets on foil; cook 8 to 12 minutes or until fish flakes easily with fork, turning once. During last minute of cooking time, top fillets with pecan butter. Remove fillets from heat; place on serving platter. Sprinkle with remaining ¼ cup pecans.

Nutrition Information Per Serving: Calories 360 • Total Fat 23g • Saturated Fat 8g • Cholesterol 175mg • Sodium 340mg • Total Carbohydrate 4g • Dietary Fiber 1g • Sugars 1g • Protein 34g. **Dietary Exchanges:** 5 Very Lean Meat • 4 Fat.

seafood salad with crab louis dressing

READY TO SERVE: 30 MINUTES
SERVINGS: 7

❋ meal-in-one

dressing

¾ cup chili sauce

¼ cup light mayonnaise

¼ cup low-fat plain yogurt

salad

1 (7-oz.) pkg. small shell macaroni (2 cups)

1 (10-oz.) pkg. frozen cooked shrimp, thawed, drained

1 (8-oz.) pkg. imitation crabmeat (surimi), cut into ½-inch pieces

½ cup sliced celery

½ cup chopped green bell pepper

Lettuce leaves, if desired

6 to 8 ripe olives, quartered

3 medium tomatoes, cut into wedges

2 tablespoons chopped fresh parsley, if desired

1. In small bowl, combine all dressing ingredients; blend well. Set aside.

2. Cook macaroni to desired doneness as directed on package. Drain; rinse with cold water to cool.

3. In large bowl, combine cooked macaroni, shrimp, imitation crabmeat, celery and bell pepper; toss gently to mix.

4. Line 7 individual salad bowls with lettuce leaves. Place about ⅔ cup crabmeat mixture in each bowl. Garnish with olives, tomatoes and parsley. Serve with dressing.

Nutrition Information Per Serving: Calories 270 • Total Fat 5g • Saturated Fat 1g • Cholesterol 90mg • Sodium 880mg • Total Carbohydrate 37g • Dietary Fiber 2g • Sugars 10g • Protein 18g. **Dietary Exchanges:** 2 Starch • 1 Vegetable • 1½ Very Lean Meat • ½ Fat OR 2 Carbohydrate • 1 Vegetable • 1½ Very Lean Meat • ½ Fat.

WHAT'S IN A NAME?

Surimi is the Japanese word for "minced fish." It has been popular in Japan and other Asian countries for hundreds of years. In the U.S., surimi is typically made from Alaska Pollock, enhanced with natural and artificial crab flavorings. The flaky, red-tinged faux crab is especially popular in seafood salad but often appears in quiche and other seafood casseroles.

dill-marinated salmon steaks

dill-marinated salmon steaks

PREP TIME: 20 MINUTES
READY TO SERVE: 2 HOURS 20 MINUTES
SERVINGS: 4

* plan ahead

2 tablespoons lemon juice

1 tablespoon oil

1 teaspoon dried dill weed

¼ teaspoon salt

⅛ teaspoon pepper

4 (4 to 6-oz.) salmon steaks
(1 inch thick)

1. In small bowl, combine all ingredients except salmon steaks; mix well. Place salmon in shallow nonmetal container or resealable food storage plastic bag. Add lemon juice mixture; turn to coat both sides. Cover; refrigerate at least 2 hours to marinate.

2. Heat grill. Cut four 18x12-inch pieces of heavy-duty foil. Remove salmon from marinade; place 1 steak on each piece of foil. Wrap each packet securely using double-fold seals, allowing room for heat expansion.

3. When ready to grill, place packets, seam side down, on gas grill over medium-high heat or on charcoal grill 4 to 6 inches from medium-high coals. Cook 10 to 15 minutes or until fish flakes easily with fork, turning once. Open packets carefully to allow hot steam to escape.

Nutrition Information Per Serving: Calories 310 • Total Fat 17g • Saturated Fat 3g • Cholesterol 125mg • Sodium 130mg • Total Carbohydrate 0g • Dietary Fiber 0g • Sugars 0g • Protein 40 g. **Dietary Exchanges:** 5½ Lean Meat.

OVEN-BAKED STEAKS

Dill-Marinated Salmon Steaks can also be baked in the oven. To bake salmon, place the fish in a 13x9-inch (3-quart) baking dish; cover with foil. Bake at 400°F for 15 to 20 minutes or until the fish flakes easily with a fork.

---

tuna casserole

PREP TIME: 20 MINUTES
READY TO SERVE: 55 MINUTES
SERVINGS: 6

* meal-in-one

1 (7-oz.) pkg. uncooked elbow macaroni (1½ cups)

1 cup milk

4 oz. shredded Cheddar cheese (1 cup)

1 (10¾-oz.) can condensed cream of mushroom soup

1 (6-oz.) can tuna, drained, flaked

1 (4-oz.) can mushroom pieces and stems, drained

2 tablespoons chopped pimientos, if desired

2 teaspoons instant minced onion

½ teaspoon dry mustard

½ cup crushed potato chips

1. Heat oven to 350°F. Grease 2-quart casserole. Cook macaroni in large saucepan or Dutch oven to desired doneness as directed on package. Drain; return to saucepan.

2. Add all remaining ingredients except potato chips to cooked macaroni; stir to combine. Pour mixture into greased casserole; sprinkle with potato chips.

3. Bake at 350°F for 25 to 35 minutes or until thoroughly heated.

Nutrition Information Per Serving: Calories 330 • Total Fat 13g • Saturated Fat 6g • Cholesterol 30mg • Sodium 660mg • Total Carbohydrate 35g • Dietary Fiber 2g • Sugars 5g • Protein 18g. **Dietary Exchanges:** 2½ Starch • 1½ Very Lean Meat • 2 Fat OR 2½ Carbohydrate • 1½ Very Lean Meat • 2 Fat.

broiled snapper with cilantro sauce

READY TO SERVE: 25 MINUTES
SERVINGS: 6

✳ super fast

sauce

- ½ cup sour cream
- ¼ cup chopped fresh cilantro
- ¼ cup mayonnaise or salad dressing
- 2 tablespoons chopped fresh parsley
- 1 teaspoon chopped shallots

snapper

- 2 tablespoons margarine or butter, melted
- 1 tablespoon chopped fresh parsley
- 1 tablespoon lemon juice
- 4 (6 to 8-oz.) red snapper fillets (¾ to 1 inch thick)

1. In blender container, combine all sauce ingredients; blend on high speed until well mixed. Set aside.

2. In small bowl, combine margarine, 1 tablespoon parsley and lemon juice; mix well. Brush margarine mixture over snapper fillets. If desired, sprinkle fillets with salt and pepper. Place fillets, skin side down, on broiler pan.

3. Broil 4 to 6 inches from heat for 8 to 10 minutes or until fish flakes easily with fork. Serve sauce with fillets.

Nutrition Information Per Serving: Calories 290 • Total Fat 17g • Saturated Fat 5g • Cholesterol 70mg • Sodium 210mg • Total Carbohydrate 2g • Dietary Fiber 0g • Sugars 1g • Protein 32g. **Dietary Exchanges:** 4½ Very Lean Meat • 3 Fat.

poached fish

READY TO SERVE: 30 MINUTES
SERVINGS: 4

- 1 tablespoon salt
- 4 peppercorns
- 2 stalks celery, cut into pieces
- 2 carrots, cut into pieces
- 2 slices lemon
- 2 bay leaves
- 1 medium onion, sliced
- 1 quart water (4 cups)
- 2 lb. dressed whole fish or fish fillets

1. In large skillet, combine all ingredients except fish. Bring to a boil. Reduce heat to low; simmer 5 minutes to blend flavors.

2. Add fish; cover and simmer 20 minutes or until fish flakes easily with fork. If liquid does not cover fish, turn fish over after 10 minutes for even cooking. With slotted spoon, remove fish from liquid; place on serving platter.

Nutrition Information Per Serving: Calories 250 • Total Fat 10g • Saturated Fat 3g • Cholesterol 125mg • Sodium 100mg • Total Carbohydrate 0g • Dietary Fiber 0g • Sugars 0g • Protein 41g. **Dietary Exchanges:** 6 Very Lean Meat • 1 Fat.

suit yourself tuna salad

READY TO SERVE: 25 MINUTES
SERVINGS: 5

* super fast

salad

- 6 oz. uncooked medium shell pasta (2¼ cups)
- 2 (6-oz.) cans water-packed tuna or 1 (14.3-oz.) can salmon, drained, flaked
- ½ cup diagonally sliced celery
- ½ cup shredded carrot

dressing

- ½ to ¾ cup mayonnaise or salad dressing
- 1 teaspoon Dijon mustard
- ¼ teaspoon sugar
- ¼ teaspoon salt
- ⅛ teaspoon pepper

1. Cook pasta to desired doneness as directed on package. Drain; rinse with cold water to cool.

2. In large bowl, combine cooked pasta and all remaining salad ingredients; toss gently.

3. In small bowl, combine all dressing ingredients; blend well. Add to salad; toss gently to coat. Serve immediately, or cover and refrigerate until serving time.

Nutrition Information Per Serving: Calories 440 • Total Fat 28g • Saturated Fat 4g • Cholesterol 35mg • Sodium 530mg • Total Carbohydrate 28g • Dietary Fiber 1g • Sugars 3g • Protein 19g. **Dietary Exchanges:** 2 Starch • 2 Very Lean Meat • 5 Fat OR 2 Carbohydrate • 2 Very Lean Meat • 5 Fat.

oven-fried fish

PREP TIME: 20 MINUTES
READY TO SERVE: 40 MINUTES
SERVINGS: 4

- 3 tablespoons margarine or butter
- ¼ cup all-purpose flour
- ½ teaspoon onion salt
- 1 egg, slightly beaten
- 1 tablespoon water
- 1 tablespoon lemon juice
- ½ to ¾ cup crushed corn flakes, crackers or bread crumbs
- 1 lb. fish fillets (½ inch thick)

1. Heat oven to 350°F. Melt margarine in 13x9-inch (3-quart) glass baking dish in oven. In shallow pan, combine flour and onion salt.

2. In medium bowl, combine egg, water and lemon juice. Place corn flakes in another medium bowl. Coat fish fillets with flour mixture; dip in egg mixture. Coat with corn flakes. Place fish in baking dish; turn to coat with melted margarine.

3. Bake at 350°F for 15 to 20 minutes or until fish flakes easily with fork.

Nutrition Information Per Serving: Calories 280 • Total Fat 11g • Saturated Fat 2g • Cholesterol 100mg • Sodium 800mg • Total Carbohydrate 20g • Dietary Fiber 1g • Sugars 1g • Protein 24g. **Dietary Exchanges:** 1½ Starch • 3 Lean Meat OR 1½ Carbohydrate • 3 Lean Meat.

lemon-poached salmon

READY TO SERVE: 20 MINUTES
SERVINGS: 4

* super fast

- 3 cups water
- 2 tablespoons sliced green onions
- ½ lemon, sliced
- ⅛ teaspoon salt
  Dash pepper
- 4 (4-oz.) salmon steaks

1. In large skillet, combine all ingredients except salmon. Bring to a boil. Reduce heat to low; simmer 5 minutes to blend flavors.

2. Add salmon; cover and simmer 6 to 9 minutes or until salmon flakes easily with fork. With slotted spoon, remove salmon from liquid; place on serving platter. If desired, garnish with dill and additional lemon slices.

Nutrition Information Per Serving: Calories 200 • Total Fat 11g • Saturated Fat 2g • Cholesterol 85mg • Sodium 65mg • Total Carbohydrate 0g • Dietary Fiber 0g • Sugars 0g • Protein 26g. **Dietary Exchange:** 3½ Lean Meat.

pasta seafood salad

✳ super fast

- 8 oz. uncooked small shell pasta (3 cups)
- ½ cup frozen sweet peas
- 1 cup mayonnaise
- ¼ cup milk
- 2 tablespoons chopped fresh dill or 2 teaspoons dried dill weed
- 4 teaspoons lemon juice
- ½ teaspoon Worcestershire sauce
- 3 (8-oz.) pkg. imitation crabmeat (surimi), chopped (4 cups)
- 1 (8-oz.) can sliced water chestnuts, drained
- 1 red bell pepper, chopped
- ½ cup sliced green onions

1. Cook pasta to desired doneness as directed on package, adding peas during last 2 minutes of cooking time. Drain; rinse with cold water to cool.

2. Meanwhile, in large bowl, combine mayonnaise, milk, dill, lemon juice and Worcestershire sauce; mix well.

3. Add cooked macaroni and peas and all remaining ingredients to mayonnaise mixture; mix well. Serve immediately, or cover and refrigerate until serving time.

Nutrition Information Per Serving: Calories 570 • Total Fat 32g • Saturated Fat 5g • Cholesterol 45mg • Sodium 1190mg • Total Carbohydrate 50g • Dietary Fiber 3g • Sugars 13g • Protein 20g. **Dietary Exchanges:** 3 Starch • 1 Vegetable • 1½ Very Lean Meat • 6 Fat OR 3 Carbohydrate • 1 Vegetable • 1½ Very Lean Meat • 6 Fat.

maryland deviled crab

- 3 tablespoons margarine or butter
- 2 tablespoons chopped onion
- 2 tablespoons chopped green bell pepper
- 2 tablespoons all-purpose flour
- ¾ cup milk
- 8 oz. cooked crabmeat, drained, flaked (2 cups)
- 1 tablespoon chopped fresh parsley
- ½ teaspoon dry mustard
- 2 teaspoons lemon juice
- ½ teaspoon Worcestershire sauce
- ½ teaspoon hot pepper sauce
- 1 egg, slightly beaten
- ½ cup soft bread crumbs
- 2 tablespoons margarine or butter, melted

1. Heat oven to 400°F. Lightly grease 1-quart casserole or 4 individual baking dishes or shells. Melt 3 tablespoons margarine in medium saucepan over medium heat. Add onion and bell pepper; cook and stir until tender. Stir in flour. Gradually add milk. Cook until mixture boils and thickens, stirring constantly.

2. Add all remaining ingredients except bread crumbs and 2 tablespoons margarine; mix well. Spoon into greased casserole. In small bowl, combine bread crumbs and 2 tablespoons margarine. Sprinkle evenly over crab mixture.

3. Bake at 400°F for 15 to 20 minutes or until thoroughly heated.

Nutrition Information Per Serving: Calories 260 • Total Fat 18g • Saturated Fat 4g • Cholesterol 85mg • Sodium 860mg • Total Carbohydrate 9g • Dietary Fiber 0g • Sugars 3g • Protein 15g. **Dietary Exchanges:** ½ Starch • 2 Very Lean Meat • 3½ Fat OR ½ Carbohydrate • 2 Very Lean Meat • 3½ Fat.

HOW TO EAT HARD-SHELL CRAB

To remove meat from a cooked hardshell crab, first twist off the legs and claws close to the body. Carefully break each claw and leg using a nutcracker; remove the meat with a cocktail fork or nut pick.

Holding the crab in both hands, insert your thumb under the shell by the apron hinge. Pull the body away from the shell.

With a spoon, remove the meat and roe from the shell. Discard the stomach bag located between the eyes. Discard the shell.

grilled salmon with herbed tartar sauce

READY TO SERVE: 20 MINUTES
SERVINGS: 4

✳ super fast

sauce

- ½ cup mayonnaise
- 2 tablespoons chopped fresh herbs (basil, dill weed, chives and/or parsley)
- ¼ teaspoon Worcestershire sauce

salmon

- 2 tablespoons olive or vegetable oil
- 1 tablespoon lemon juice
- 4 (6-oz.) salmon fillets
- ⅛ teaspoon salt
- ⅛ teaspoon pepper

1. Heat grill. In blender container or food processor bowl with metal blade, combine all sauce ingredients; blend at high speed until well mixed, stopping often to scrape down sides. Place in serving bowl; refrigerate.

2. In small bowl, combine oil and lemon juice; mix well.

3. When ready to grill, brush salmon fillets with lemon mixture; sprinkle with salt and pepper. Carefully oil grill rack. Place salmon on gas grill over medium heat or on charcoal grill 4 to 6 inches from medium coals. Cook 8 to 12 minutes or until fish flakes easily with fork, turning once. Serve with sauce.

Nutrition Information Per Serving: Calories 520 • Total Fat 40g • Saturated Fat 6g • Cholesterol 140mg • Sodium 330mg • Total Carbohydrate 1g • Dietary Fiber 0g • Sugars 1g • Protein 40g. **Dietary Exchanges:** 5½ Lean Meat • 6 Fat.

catfish cakes

READY TO SERVE: 25 MINUTES
SERVINGS: 5

✳ super fast

- 1 lb. catfish fillets
- ¾ cup cornmeal
- 1 teaspoon baking powder
- ¼ cup chopped green onions
- ¼ cup finely chopped red or green bell pepper
- 1 teaspoon dried Creole seasoning
- ¼ cup buttermilk
- 1 egg
- 2 to 3 tablespoons oil

1. Poach catfish following directions in Poached Fish, page 214.

2. Place catfish in large bowl; break into small pieces with fork. Add cornmeal, baking powder, onions, bell pepper and Creole seasoning; mix well. In small bowl, combine buttermilk and egg; mix well. Add to catfish mixture; mix well.

3. Heat 1 tablespoon of the oil on griddle or in large skillet over medium-high heat. Drop catfish mixture by rounded tablespoonfuls onto hot griddle; flatten to form patty. Cook 2 to 4 minutes or until lightly browned, turning once during cooking. Add remaining 1 to 2 tablespoons oil as needed during cooking.

Nutrition Information Per Serving: Calories 300 • Total Fat 13g • Saturated Fat 2g • Cholesterol 85mg • Sodium 360mg • Total Carbohydrate 25g • Dietary Fiber 2g • Sugars 2g • Protein 20g. **Dietary Exchanges:** 1½ Starch • 2 Medium-Fat Meat • ½ Fat OR 1½ Carbohydrate • 2 Medium-Fat Meat • ½ Fat.

deviled crab and cheese rolls

PREP TIME: 10 MINUTES
READY TO SERVE: 50 MINUTES
SERVINGS: 6

MICHAEL W. WEAVER ✳ SAN FRANCISCO, CALIFORNIA
BAKE-OFF® CONTEST 42, 2006

½ cup whipped cream cheese (from 8-oz. container)

1 tablespoon fresh lemon juice

1 to 2 teaspoons red pepper sauce

¼ cup finely shredded mild Cheddar cheese (1 oz.)

2 tablespoons finely chopped green onions (2 medium)

1 teaspoon paprika

½ cup garlic-herb dry bread crumbs

3 (6-oz.) cans white crabmeat, well drained

1 (11-oz.) can refrigerated original breadsticks

1 egg, slightly beaten

1. Heat oven to 350°F. Spray cookie sheet with cooking spray or line with a silicone baking mat. In medium bowl, mix cream cheese, lemon juice and red pepper sauce until smooth. Stir in Cheddar cheese, onions and paprika. Reserve 2 tablespoons bread crumbs for topping; stir remaining bread crumbs into cream cheese mixture. Gently stir in crabmeat. Shape crabmeat mixture into 6 balls, using about ⅓ cup mixture for each; flatten slightly.

2. Unroll dough; separate into 6 (2-breadstick) portions. Seal seam halfway up length of each portion; place 1 ball on sealed side of each. Holding dough and ball in one hand, stretch dough strips over balls, crisscrossing and tucking ends under opposite side; place on cookie sheet.

3. Lightly brush tops and sides of dough with beaten egg; sprinkle with reserved 2 tablespoons bread crumbs.

4. Bake 20 to 30 minutes or until golden brown. Cool 10 minutes. Serve warm.

Nutrition Information Per Serving: Calories 330 • Total Fat 11g • Saturated Fat 5g • Trans Fat 0.5g • Cholesterol 120mg • Sodium 890mg • Total Carbohydrate 33g • Dietary Fiber 0g • Sugars 4g • Protein 24g. **Dietary Exchanges:** 2 Starch • 2½ Lean Meat • ½ Fat.

orange roughy with dill butter

PREP TIME: 20 MINUTES
READY TO SERVE: 40 MINUTES
SERVINGS: 4

3 tablespoons butter

4 (4 to 6-oz.) orange roughy fillets

1/2 teaspoon dried dill weed

Dash salt

Dash pepper

1 1/2 teaspoons butter

2 tablespoons unseasoned dry bread crumbs

1. Heat oven to 350°F. Melt 3 tablespoons butter in 12x8-inch (2-quart) baking dish in the oven.

2. Place orange roughy in dish; turn it to coat with butter. Sprinkle the fillets with dill, salt and pepper.

3. Bake at 350°F for 15 to 20 minutes or until fish flakes easily with fork.

4. Meanwhile, melt 1 1/2 teaspoons butter in small skillet or saucepan over medium heat. Add bread crumbs; cook until crumbs are light golden brown, stirring constantly. Sprinkle over fish during last 3 minutes of baking time.

Nutrition Information Per Serving: Calories 190 • Total Fat 11g • Saturated Fat 6g • Cholesterol 55mg • Sodium 250mg • Total Carbohydrate 2g • Dietary Fiber 0g • Sugars 0g • Protein 21g. **Dietary Exchanges:** 3 Very Lean Meat • 2 Fat.

salmon-broccoli salad in shells

READY TO SERVE: 35 MINUTES
SERVINGS: 4

* meal-in-one

1 (9-oz.) pkg. frozen cut broccoli in a pouch

12 uncooked jumbo pasta shells

1 (6-oz.) can salmon, drained, flaked

1 cup cherry tomatoes, quartered

1/4 cup sliced green onions

1/4 cup purchased ranch salad dressing

1/4 cup light mayonnaise

1 tablespoon chopped fresh parsley

4 lettuce leaves

1. Cook broccoli pouch as directed on package. Drain; cool.

2. Cook pasta shells to desired doneness as directed on package. Drain; return to saucepan. Cover with cold water to cool.

3. In medium bowl, combine cooked broccoli, salmon, tomatoes and green onions. Add salad dressing, mayonnaise and parsley; stir gently to coat.

4. Line 4 individual plates with lettuce. Drain water from cooked pasta shells. Spoon about 1/4 cup salmon mixture into each shell. Arrange stuffed shells over lettuce.

Nutrition Information Per Serving: Calories 340 • Total Fat 18g • Saturated Fat 3g • Cholesterol 25mg • Sodium 570mg • Total Carbohydrate 31g • Dietary Fiber 3g • Sugars 4g • Protein 14g. **Dietary Exchanges:** 2 Starch • 1 Lean Meat • 3 Fat OR 2 Carbohydrate • 1 Lean Meat • 3 Fat.

speedy sides & sauces

corn off the cob ✳ p. 233

lemon-buttered asparagus ✳ p. 239

spicy nuggets and vegetables ✳ p. 245

green beans with cashew butter ✳ p. 251

swiss vegetable casserole * p. 237

penne provençal

READY TO SERVE: 30 MINUTES
SERVINGS: 6

8 oz. uncooked penne
(2 cups)

3 cups diced peeled eggplant

2 (14.5-oz.) cans diced
tomatoes, undrained

1 (15-oz.) can navy beans,
drained, rinsed

3 garlic cloves, minced

2 teaspoons sugar

2 tablespoons chopped fresh
Italian parsley

1. Cook penne to desired doneness as directed on package. Drain; cover to keep warm.

2. Meanwhile, in Dutch oven or large saucepan, combine eggplant, tomatoes, beans, garlic and sugar; mix well. Bring to a boil over medium-high heat. Reduce heat to low; simmer 10 to 15 minutes or until eggplant is tender. If desired, add coarse ground black pepper to taste.

3. Add penne to eggplant mixture; toss gently to mix. Sprinkle with parsley.

Nutrition Information Per Serving: Calories 270 • Total Fat 1g • Saturated Fat 0g • Cholesterol 0mg • Sodium 370mg • Total Carbohydrate 53g • Dietary Fiber 7g • Sugars 9g • Protein 12g. **Dietary Exchanges:** 3 Starch • 1 Vegetable OR 3 Carbohydrate • 1 Vegetable.

A PENNE FOR YOUR PASTA

Penne pasta is a tube-shaped, Italian delight. In fact, it is one of the best-known Italian pastas of all time. Penne means "pen" in Italian, and the pasta is angled at each end to resemble the quill of a pen. With its hollow center and many ridges, penne is perfect for holding lots of marinara or Alfredo sauce! Enjoy it in this recipe and all of your favorite pasta dishes.

eggs foo yong

READY TO SERVE: 30 MINUTES
SERVINGS: 5

eggs

- 6 eggs
- ½ cup finely chopped onion
- 2 tablespoons chopped green bell pepper
- ½ teaspoon salt
  Dash pepper
- 1 (16-oz.) can bean sprouts, drained, rinsed
- 2 tablespoons oil

sauce

- 1 tablespoon cornstarch
- 2 teaspoons sugar
- 1 vegetable or chicken-flavor instant bouillon
  Dash ginger
- 1 cup water
- 2 tablespoons soy sauce

1. Heat oven to 300°F. In large bowl, beat eggs well. Add onion, bell pepper, salt, pepper and bean sprouts; mix well.

2. Heat oil in large skillet over medium heat. Drop egg mixture by tablespoonfuls into skillet. Cook until golden brown on both sides. Drain on paper towels. If necessary, add more oil to skillet. Place egg patties on ovenproof dish; keep warm in 300°F oven while preparing sauce.

3. In small saucepan, combine all sauce ingredients; blend well. Cook until mixture boils and thickens, stirring constantly. Serve egg patties with sauce.

Nutrition Information Per Serving: Calories 170 • Total Fat 12g • Saturated Fat 3g • Cholesterol 255mg • Sodium 1030mg • Total Carbohydrate 7g • Dietary Fiber 1g • Sugars 4g • Protein 9g. **Dietary Exchanges:** ½ Starch • 1 Medium-Fat Meat • 1 Fat OR ½ Carbohydrate • 1 Medium-Fat Meat • 1 Fat.

pea pod medley

READY TO SERVE: 10 MINUTES
SERVINGS: 4

✳ super fast

- 1 cup frozen sweet peas
- 1 cup frozen sugar snap peas
- 1 tablespoon margarine or butter
- 1 garlic clove, minced

1. In 1½-quart microwave-safe casserole, combine all ingredients; cover.

2. Microwave on high for 5 to 6 minutes or until vegetables are thoroughly heated, stirring twice during cooking.

Nutrition Information Per Serving: Calories 60 • Total Fat 3g • Saturated Fat 1g • Cholesterol 0mg • Sodium 70mg • Total Carbohydrate 6g • Dietary Fiber 2g • Sugars 2g • Protein 2g. **Dietary Exchanges:** 1 Vegetable • ½ Fat.

low-fat french fries

PREP TIME: 10 MINUTES
READY TO SERVE: 35 MINUTES
SERVINGS: 6

- 3 large baking potatoes, unpeeled, cut into ⅜-inch-thick strips
- 1 tablespoon oil
  Seasoned salt

1. Heat oven to 425°F. Spray large cookie sheet with cooking spray.

2. Place potatoes and oil in plastic bag; shake until well coated. Arrange in single layer on sprayed cookie sheet.

3. Bake at 425°F for 15 minutes. Carefully turn potatoes; sprinkle lightly with seasoned salt. Bake an additional 5 minutes or until tender. If desired, broil 1 to 2 minutes for additional browning.

Nutrition Information Per Serving: Calories 100 • Total Fat 2g • Saturated Fat 0g • Cholesterol 0mg • Sodium 70mg • Total Carbohydrate 18g • Dietary Fiber 2g • Sugars 1g • Protein 2g. **Dietary Exchanges:** 1 Starch • ½ Fat OR 1 Carbohydrate • ½ Fat.

linguine with roasted vegetables

READY TO SERVE: 35 MINUTES
SERVINGS: 6

6 oz. uncooked linguine

4 tomatoes, coarsely chopped

1 eggplant, unpeeled, cubed

1 red bell pepper, cut into 1-inch pieces

1 zucchini, sliced

4 garlic cloves, minced

3 tablespoons olive or vegetable oil

1 teaspoon dried basil leaves

1/2 teaspoon salt

1/8 teaspoon pepper

2 oz. shredded fresh Parmesan cheese (1/2 cup)

1. Cook linguine to desired doneness as directed on package. Drain; cover to keep warm.

2. Meanwhile, heat oven to 450°F. Spray 15x10x1-inch baking pan with cooking spray. In large bowl, combine tomatoes, eggplant, bell pepper, zucchini and garlic. Toss with 2 tablespoons of the oil, basil, salt and pepper. Place vegetables on sprayed pan.

3. Bake at 450°F for 12 to 15 minutes or until vegetables are tender and lightly browned.

4. Place cooked linguine in serving bowl. Add remaining 1 tablespoon oil and roasted vegetables; toss gently to mix. Sprinkle with cheese.

Nutrition Information Per Serving: Calories 240 • Total Fat 10g • Saturated Fat 3g • Cholesterol 5mg • Sodium 340mg • Total Carbohydrate 29g • Dietary Fiber 3g • Sugars 5g • Protein 9g. **Dietary Exchanges:** 1 1/2 Starch • 1 Vegetable • 1/2 Lean Meat • 1 1/2 Fat OR 1 1/2 Carbohydrate • 1 Vegetable • 1/2 Lean Meat • 1 1/2 Fat.

ravioli with salsa-black bean sauce

READY TO SERVE: 15 MINUTES
SERVINGS: 3

* super fast

1 (9-oz.) pkg. refrigerated cheese-filled ravioli

1 (14.5-oz.) can salsa-style tomatoes, undrained

1 (15-oz.) can black beans, drained

2 teaspoons chili powder

1/2 teaspoon cumin

2 tablespoons chopped fresh cilantro

1. In large saucepan, cook ravioli to desired doneness as directed on package. Drain in colander; cover to keep warm.

2. In same saucepan, combine tomatoes, beans, chili powder and cumin; mix well. Cook over medium heat for 5 minutes or until thoroughly heated, stirring occasionally.

3. Carefully stir in cooked ravioli. Spoon onto serving platter; sprinkle with cilantro.

Nutrition Information Per Serving: Calories 450 • Total Fat 11g • Saturated Fat 5g • Cholesterol 75mg • Sodium 930mg • Total Carbohydrate 64g • Dietary Fiber 10g • Sugars 6g • Protein 23g. **Dietary Exchanges:** 4 Starch • 1 Vegetable • 1 Very Lean Meat • 1 1/2 Fat OR 4 Carbohydrate • 1 Vegetable • 1 Very Lean Meat • 1 1/2 Fat.

zesty seafood cocktail sauce

READY TO SERVE: 20 MINUTES
SERVINGS: 6

* super fast

1/2 cup chili sauce

2 tablespoons lemon juice

1 teaspoon prepared horseradish

1/2 teaspoon celery seed

1/2 teaspoon Worcestershire sauce

1. In small bowl, combine all ingredients; mix well.

2. Cover; refrigerate 15 minutes or until chilled.

Nutrition Information Per Serving: Calories 10 • Total Fat 0g • Saturated Fat 0g • Cholesterol 0mg • Sodium 160mg • Total Carbohydrate 3g • Dietary Fiber 0g • Sugars 2g • Protein 0g. **Dietary Exchange:** Free.

linguine with roasted vegetables

sunny cauliflower-broccoli toss

READY TO SERVE: 25 MINUTES
SERVINGS: 8

✳ super fast

dressing

- ½ cup mayonnaise or salad dressing
- 2 tablespoons sugar
- 1 tablespoon cider vinegar

salad

- 3 slices bacon
- 2 cups fresh cauliflower florets
- 2 cups cut-up fresh broccoli (including tender part of stalks)
- ½ cup raisins
- ¼ cup sliced green onions
- ¼ cup shelled sunflower seeds

1. In small bowl, combine all dressing ingredients; blend with wire whisk until smooth. Set aside.

2. Cook bacon until crisp. Drain on paper towels; crumble.

3. In large bowl, combine bacon and all remaining salad ingredients; toss gently. Pour dressing over salad; toss to coat. If desired, sprinkle with additional sunflower seeds.

Nutrition Information Per Serving: Calories 200 • Total Fat 15g • Saturated Fat 2g • Cholesterol 10mg • Sodium 160mg • Total Carbohydrate 14g • Dietary Fiber 2g • Sugars 11g • Protein 3g. **Dietary Exchanges:** ½ Starch • ½ Fruit • ½ Vegetable • 3 Fat OR 1 Carbohydrate • ½ Vegetable • 3 Fat.

mexican rice and veggie skillet

READY TO SERVE: 30 MINUTES
SERVINGS: 4

- 1 (15.5 or 15-oz.) can kidney beans, drained, rinsed
- 1 (14.5-oz.) can stewed tomatoes, undrained
- 1 (10-oz.) can mild enchilada sauce
- 1 cup water
- 2 cups frozen mixed vegetables
- 1½ cups uncooked instant brown rice

1. In large skillet, combine all ingredients except rice; mix well. Bring to a boil. Stir in rice. Reduce heat to low; cover and simmer 18 to 20 minutes or until liquid is absorbed and rice is tender, stirring occasionally.

2. Remove skillet from heat. Fluff mixture with fork. If desired, add salt and pepper to taste.

Nutrition Information Per Serving: Calories 300 • Total Fat 3g • Saturated Fat 0g • Cholesterol 0mg • Sodium 640mg • Total Carbohydrate 58g • Dietary Fiber 8g • Sugars 5g • Protein 11g. **Dietary Exchanges:** 2½ Starch • 1 Fruit • 1 Vegetable • ½ Fat OR 3½ Carbohydrate • 1 Vegetable • ½ Fat.

brussels sprouts with bacon and pecans

READY TO SERVE: 25 MINUTES
SERVINGS: 6

* super fast

1½ lb. fresh Brussels sprouts

4 slices bacon

1 teaspoon all-purpose flour

1 tablespoon brown sugar

1 tablespoon water

1 tablespoon cider vinegar

1 teaspoon Dijon mustard

¼ cup chopped pecans

1. Wash and trim Brussels sprouts. With tip of knife, cut an "X" in base of each. Place in large saucepan; add just enough water to cover. Bring to a boil over high heat. Reduce heat; simmer 8 to 10 minutes or until tender.

2. Meanwhile, in medium skillet, cook bacon until crisp. Drain, reserving 2 tablespoons bacon drippings in skillet; cool. Add flour to cooled drippings; cook and stir over medium-low heat until bubbly. Remove from heat.

3. In small bowl, combine brown sugar, water, vinegar and mustard; mix well. Gradually stir into bacon drippings mixture.

4. Drain Brussels sprouts; place in serving bowl. Add hot bacon dressing mixture; toss gently. Crumble bacon over Brussels sprouts. Sprinkle with pecans.

Nutrition Information Per Serving: Calories 120 • Total Fat 8g • Saturated Fat 2g • Cholesterol 4mg • Sodium 40mg • Total Carbohydrate 10g • Dietary Fiber 3g • Sugars 4g • Protein 3g. **Dietary Exchanges:** ½ Starch • 1 Vegetable • 1½ Fat OR ½ Carbohydrate • 1 Vegetable • 1½ Fat.

fettuccine with garlic-herb butter

READY TO SERVE: 25 MINUTES
SERVINGS: 4

* super fast

6 oz. uncooked fettuccine

1 teaspoon butter

1 large garlic clove, minced

2 to 3 tablespoons chopped
fresh herbs (such as
1 tablespoon parsley,
1 tablespoon basil,
1 teaspoon marjoram and
1 teaspoon thyme)

1 tablespoon butter, softened

⅛ teaspoon salt

Dash pepper

1. In large saucepan, cook fettuccine to desired doneness as directed on package. Drain; return to saucepan.

2. Meanwhile, in small saucepan, melt 1 teaspoon butter over medium heat. Add garlic; cook 30 to 60 seconds or until garlic begins to turn golden brown.

3. In small bowl, combine herbs, 1 tablespoon butter, salt, pepper and cooked garlic; mix well. Add to fettuccine; toss to coat.

Nutrition Information Per Serving: Calories 200 • Total Fat 6g • Saturated Fat 3g • Cholesterol 50mg • Sodium 180mg • Total Carbohydrate 31g • Dietary Fiber 1g • Sugars 1g • Protein 6g. **Dietary Exchanges:** 2 Starch • 1 Fat OR 2 Carbohydrate • 1 Fat.

cauliflower parmesan

READY TO SERVE: 25 MINUTES
SERVINGS: 6

* super fast

4 cups fresh cauliflower florets (1 medium head)

1 tablespoon olive oil

2 tablespoons all-purpose flour

½ cup skim milk

⅓ cup water

½ teaspoon chicken-flavor instant bouillon

¼ cup grated Parmesan cheese

¼ cup fresh bread crumbs

¼ teaspoon paprika

1. In medium saucepan, combine cauliflower and ¼ cup water. Bring to a boil. Reduce heat; cover and simmer 5 to 6 minutes or until cauliflower is crisp-tender. Drain; spoon cauliflower into ungreased 1-quart ovenproof casserole. Set aside.

2. In same saucepan, heat oil over medium heat until hot. With wire whisk, stir in flour; cook and stir 1 minute. Add milk, ⅓ cup water and bouillon; blend well. Cook 3 minutes or until sauce boils and thickens, stirring constantly. Stir in cheese; cook and stir until cheese is melted. Pour sauce over cauliflower. Sprinkle with bread crumbs and paprika.

3. Broil 4 to 6 inches from heat for 2 minutes or until bread crumbs are golden brown.

Nutrition Information Per Serving: Calories 80 • Total Fat 4g • Saturated Fat 1g • Cholesterol 4mg • Sodium 125mg • Total Carbohydrate 8g • Dietary Fiber 2g • Sugars 3g • Protein 4g. **Dietary Exchanges:** 1 Vegetable • 1 Fat.

peas and mushrooms

READY TO SERVE: 10 MINUTES
SERVINGS: 5

* super fast

2 tablespoons margarine or butter

¼ cup chopped celery

2 tablespoons finely chopped onion

1 (2.5-oz.) jar sliced mushrooms, drained

2 cups frozen sweet peas, thawed

1 (2-oz.) jar diced pimientos, drained

1. Melt margarine in medium saucepan over medium heat. Stir in celery and onion; cook 3 to 4 minutes or until crisp-tender.

2. Stir in all remaining ingredients; cook 3 to 5 minutes or until thoroughly heated.

Nutrition Information Per Serving: Calories 100 • Total Fat 5g • Saturated Fat 1g • Cholesterol 0mg • Sodium 180mg • Total Carbohydrate 10g • Dietary Fiber 3g • Sugars 2g • Protein 3g. **Dietary Exchanges:** 2 Vegetable • 1 Fat.

zucchini with tomatoes and basil

READY TO SERVE: 15 MINUTES
SERVINGS: 5

* super fast

4 (½-lb.) zucchini, cut into ½-inch-thick slices

1 cup coarsely chopped tomatoes

2 tablespoons chopped fresh basil

¼ teaspoon salt

⅛ teaspoon pepper

2 teaspoons lemon juice

2 tablespoons shredded fresh Parmesan cheese, if desired

1. In medium saucepan, combine zucchini and ¼ cup water. Cook over medium heat for 3 to 4 minutes or until crisp-tender. Drain well.

2. Add tomatoes, basil, salt, pepper and lemon juice; mix well. Cook and stir about 1 minute or until thoroughly heated. Sprinkle with cheese.

Nutrition Information Per Serving: Calories 30 • Total Fat 1g • Saturated Fat 0g • Cholesterol 0mg • Sodium 150mg • Total Carbohydrate 3g • Dietary Fiber 1g • Sugars 2g • Protein 2g. **Dietary Exchange:** 1 Vegetable.

broccoli with sharp cheddar sauce

READY TO SERVE: 20 MINUTES
SERVINGS: 12

* super fast

2 lb. fresh broccoli florets
  (about 15 cups)

2¾ cups skim milk

⅓ cup all-purpose flour

5 oz. shredded reduced-fat
  sharp Cheddar cheese
  (1¼ cups)

¾ teaspoon salt

⅛ teaspoon ground red
  pepper (cayenne)

1 teaspoon Dijon mustard

1 tablespoon grated
  Parmesan cheese

1. Place about 4 cups water in Dutch oven; bring to a boil. Add broccoli; return to a boil. Reduce heat to medium; cover tightly and cook 5 to 7 minutes or until broccoli is crisp-tender, stirring once.

2. Meanwhile, place 2 cups of the milk in large saucepan; place over medium heat. In small bowl, combine remaining ¾ cup milk and flour; blend with wire whisk until smooth. Add to milk in skillet; cook 8 to 10 minutes or until thickened, stirring constantly.

3. Remove saucepan from heat. Add Cheddar cheese, salt, ground red pepper and mustard; stir until thoroughly blended.

4. Drain broccoli; place in shallow ovenproof casserole. Spoon sauce over broccoli; sprinkle with Parmesan cheese.

Nutrition Information Per Serving: Calories 100 • Total Fat 3g • Saturated Fat 2g • Cholesterol 10mg • Sodium 300mg • Total Carbohydrate 10g • Dietary Fiber 2g • Sugars 4g • Protein 8g. **Dietary Exchanges:** ½ Starch • 1 Vegetable • ½ Medium-Fat Meat OR ½ Carbohydrate • 1 Vegetable • ½ Medium-Fat Meat.

bow ties and broccoli alfredo

bow ties and broccoli alfredo

PREP TIME: 25 MINUTES
READY TO SERVE: 55 MINUTES
SERVINGS: 4

6 oz. uncooked bow tie pasta
(3 cups)

2 cups frozen broccoli florets

½ cup sliced purchased
roasted red bell peppers
(from 7.25-oz. jar)

½ teaspoon dried basil leaves

⅛ teaspoon pepper

1 (10-oz.) container
refrigerated Alfredo sauce

2 tablespoons shredded fresh
Parmesan cheese

1. Heat oven to 350°F. Grease 2-quart casserole. Cook pasta to desired doneness as directed on package, adding broccoli during last 2 to 3 minutes of cooking time. Drain.

2. In greased casserole, combine all ingredients except cheese; mix well. Cover.

3. Bake at 350°F for 20 minutes. Uncover casserole; sprinkle with cheese. Bake, uncovered, an additional 5 to 10 minutes or until cheese is light golden brown.

Nutrition Information Per Serving: Calories 420 • Total Fat 24g • Saturated Fat 13g • Cholesterol 50mg • Sodium 370mg • Total Carbohydrate 39g • Dietary Fiber 2g • Sugars 4g • Protein 12g. Dietary Exchanges: 2½ Starch • 1 Vegetable • ½ High-Fat Meat • 3½ Fat OR 2½ Carbohydrate • 1 Vegetable • ½ High-Fat Meat • 3½ Fat.

dill baby carrots

READY TO SERVE: 15 MINUTES
SERVINGS: 7

* super fast

1 lb. fresh baby carrots

1 tablespoon margarine or
butter

1 teaspoon chopped fresh dill
or ¼ teaspoon dried dill
weed

1 teaspoon fresh lemon juice

¼ teaspoon salt

⅛ teaspoon pepper

1. In medium saucepan, bring ¾ cup water to a boil. Add carrots; cover and cook over medium heat for 10 to 12 minutes or until tender.

2. Drain carrots; return to saucepan. Add all remaining ingredients; stir until margarine is melted.

Nutrition Information Per Serving: Calories 50 • Total Fat 2g • Saturated Fat 0g • Cholesterol 0mg • Sodium 120mg • Total Carbohydrate 7g • Dietary Fiber 2g • Sugars 4g • Protein 1g. Dietary Exchanges: 1 Vegetable • ½ Fat.

sweet-sour red cabbage

READY TO SERVE: 35 MINUTES
SERVINGS: 6

6 cups shredded red cabbage

2 tart green apples, chopped

¼ cup firmly packed brown
sugar

1 teaspoon salt

½ teaspoon caraway seed

⅛ teaspoon pepper

½ cup water

¼ to ⅓ cup vinegar

1. In large saucepan, combine all ingredients; mix gently.

2. Cover; simmer 20 to 25 minutes or until cabbage is tender, stirring occasionally.

Nutrition Information Per Serving: Calories 90 • Total Fat 0g • Saturated Fat 0g • Cholesterol 0mg • Sodium 370mg • Total Carbohydrate 21g • Dietary Fiber 3g • Sugars 18g • Protein 1g. Dietary Exchanges: 1 Fruit • 1 Vegetable OR 1 Carbohydrate • 1 Vegetable.

easy cheesy savory polenta

PREP TIME: 45 MINUTES
READY TO SERVE: 1 HOUR
SERVINGS: 6

3 cups water

1 cup yellow cornmeal

2 teaspoons chicken-flavor instant bouillon

½ teaspoon garlic powder

½ teaspoon dried basil leaves

¼ teaspoon hot pepper sauce

1 tablespoon margarine or butter, melted

2 oz. shredded provolone cheese (½ cup)

1. Spray 9-inch pie pan with cooking spray. In large saucepan, combine 1 cup of the water and cornmeal; mix until smooth. Stir in remaining 2 cups water, bouillon, garlic powder, basil and hot pepper sauce.

2. Bring to a boil over medium-high heat. Reduce heat to low; cook 10 to 15 minutes or until very thick, stirring frequently. Pour polenta into sprayed pie pan. Let stand 15 minutes.

3. Cut polenta into wedges; place on broiler pan. Drizzle wedges lightly with half of margarine. Broil 4 to 6 inches from heat for 5 to 7 minutes or until bubbly.

4. Turn wedges. Drizzle with remaining margarine; sprinkle with cheese. Broil an additional 3 to 5 minutes or until cheese is bubbly and golden brown.

Nutrition Information Per Serving: Calories 130 • Total Fat 5g • Saturated Fat 2g • Cholesterol 5mg • Sodium 440mg • Total Carbohydrate 16g • Dietary Fiber 2g • Sugars 1g • Protein 4g. **Dietary Exchanges:** 1 Starch • 1 Fat OR 1 Carbohydrate • 1 Fat.

potatoes curry

READY TO SERVE: 40 MINUTES
SERVINGS: 4

4 cups coarsely chopped cauliflower

¾ lb. small red potatoes (about 8), cut into ¾-inch pieces (2 to 2½ cups)

1 cup frozen sweet peas, thawed

2 medium tomatoes, chopped

1 (15-oz.) can garbanzo beans, drained, rinsed

3 teaspoons curry powder

¼ teaspoon salt

2 teaspoons olive oil

½ cup water

1. Heat grill. In large bowl, combine cauliflower, potatoes, peas, tomatoes and garbanzo beans. Add curry powder and salt; mix well. Add oil; toss to coat.

2. Cut four 12-inch squares of heavy-duty foil or double thicknesses of regular foil. Divide vegetable mixture evenly onto foil squares. Sprinkle each with 2 tablespoons water. Wrap each packet securely using double-fold seals, allowing room for heat expansion.

3. When ready to grill, place packets on gas grill over medium heat or on charcoal grill 4 to 6 inches from medium coals. Cook 15 to 20 minutes or until potatoes are tender.

Nutrition Information Per Serving: Calories 290 • Total Fat 5g • Saturated Fat 1g • Cholesterol 0mg • Sodium 380mg • Total Carbohydrate 50g • Dietary Fiber 12g • Sugars 6g • Protein 11g. **Dietary Exchanges:** 3 Starch • 1 Vegetable • ½ Fat OR 3 Carbohydrate • 1 Vegetable • ½ Fat.

corn off the cob

READY TO SERVE: 20 MINUTES
SERVINGS: 3

* super fast

6 ears corn, husked, cleaned

2 tablespoons margarine or butter

2 tablespoons chopped green onions

½ teaspoon salt

⅛ teaspoon pepper

¼ cup whipping cream or milk

1. With sharp knife, cut kernels of corn from cob.

2. Melt margarine in medium skillet over low heat. Add corn and all remaining ingredients except whipping cream; cook 4 to 6 minutes or until corn is crisp-tender.

3. Stir in whipping cream; cook about 2 minutes or until cream coats corn.

Nutrition Information Per Serving: Calories 370 • Total Fat 17g • Saturated Fat 6g • Cholesterol 25mg • Sodium 480mg • Total Carbohydrate 47g • Dietary Fiber 5g • Sugars 5g • Protein 7g. **Dietary Exchanges:** 3 Starch • 3 Fat OR 3 Carbohydrate • 3 Fat.

quick mushroom risotto

READY TO SERVE: 20 MINUTES
SERVINGS: 8

* super fast

2 tablespoons butter

½ cup chopped onion

1 (4.5-oz.) jar sliced mushrooms, drained

2 cups uncooked instant white rice

1 teaspoon garlic powder

¼ teaspoon pepper

2 (14½-oz.) cans ready-to-serve chicken broth

⅓ cup whipping cream or half-and-half

⅓ cup grated Parmesan cheese

1 tablespoon grated Parmesan cheese, if desired

1. In large skillet, melt butter over medium-high heat. Add onion and mushrooms; cook and stir 3 minutes. Add rice, garlic powder and pepper; cook 2 minutes.

2. Stir in 1 can of the broth; cook 4 minutes, stirring constantly. Gradually stir in remaining can of broth; cook 7 minutes or until liquid is almost absorbed, stirring frequently.

3. Stir in whipping cream. Remove from heat. Stir in ⅓ cup cheese. Spoon into serving dish; sprinkle with 1 tablespoon cheese.

Nutrition Information Per Serving: Calories 200 • Total Fat 9g • Saturated Fat 5g • Cholesterol 25mg • Sodium 500mg • Total Carbohydrate 23g • Dietary Fiber 1g • Sugars 1g • Protein 7g. **Dietary Exchanges:** 1½ Starch • 2 Fat OR 1½ Carbohydrate • 2 Fat.

carrots and broccoli with orange browned butter

READY TO SERVE: 15 MINUTES
SERVINGS: 8

✳ super fast

1 (16-oz.) pkg. fresh baby
   carrots
1 (14-oz.) pkg. frozen broccoli
   florets
⅓ cup butter
1 teaspoon grated orange
   peel
½ teaspoon grated gingerroot
2 tablespoons orange juice

1. Place carrots in large saucepan; cover with water. Bring to a boil. Reduce heat; cover and simmer 3 minutes. Add the broccoli; cook 2 to 3 minutes or until the vegetables are crisp-tender.

2. Meanwhile, in small saucepan, cook butter over medium-high heat until golden brown; immediately remove from heat. Add orange peel, gingerroot and orange juice; mix well.

3. Drain vegetables. Pour butter sauce over vegetables; toss lightly to coat.

Nutrition Information Per Serving: Calories 120 • Total Fat 8g • Saturated Fat 5g • Cholesterol 20mg • Sodium 110mg • Total Carbohydrate 9g • Dietary Fiber 8g • Sugars 5g • Protein 2g. **Dietary Exchanges:** Fruit • 1 Vegetable • 1 Fat OR Carbohydrate • 1 Vegetable • 1 Fat.

seasoned oven potatoes

PREP TIME: 10 MINUTES
READY TO SERVE: 1 HOUR 10 MINUTES
SERVINGS: 4

½ teaspoon dried parsley
   flakes
½ teaspoon onion powder
½ teaspoon salt
2 tablespoons oil
3 to 4 medium baking
   potatoes, cut into 1 to
   1½-inch cubes (3 cups)

1. Heat oven to 350°F. In ungreased 12x8-inch (2-quart) baking dish, combine parsley flakes, onion powder, salt and oil; blend well. Add potatoes; toss to coat well.

2. Bake at 350°F for 50 to 60 minutes or until tender, stirring once during baking. Drain potatoes on paper towels.

Nutrition Information Per Serving: Calories 200 • Total Fat 7g • Saturated Fat 1g • Cholesterol 0mg • Sodium 280mg • Total Carbohydrate 31g • Dietary Fiber 3g • Sugars 1g • Protein 3g. **Dietary Exchanges:** 2 Starch • 1 Fat OR 2 Carbohydrate • 1 Fat.

steamed nutmeg spinach

READY TO SERVE: 15 MINUTES
SERVINGS: 3

* super fast

1 tablespoon olive or vegetable oil

1 (10-oz.) pkg. fresh prewashed spinach (about 12 cups)

2 tablespoons apple juice

¼ teaspoon nutmeg

1. Heat oil in large skillet or Dutch oven over medium-high heat until hot. Add half of spinach; cook and stir 1 to 2 minutes or until spinach starts to wilt.

2. Add remaining spinach; cook and stir until wilted. Reduce heat; cover and simmer 5 to 7 minutes or until tender.

3. With slotted spoon, place spinach in serving bowl. Add the apple juice and nutmeg; stir gently.

Nutrition Information Per Serving: Calories 80 • Total Fat 5g • Saturated Fat 1g • Cholesterol 0mg • Sodium 75mg • Total Carbohydrate 5g • Dietary Fiber 3g • Sugars 1g • Protein 3g. **Dietary Exchanges:** 1 Vegetable • 1 Fat.

rice and barley medley

READY TO SERVE: 30 MINUTES
SERVINGS: 7

2 teaspoons olive oil

½ cup sliced fresh mushrooms

¼ cup chopped onion

1 garlic clove, minced

1 (14½-oz.) can ready-to-serve vegetable broth

½ cup uncooked quick-cooking barley

½ cup uncooked instant brown rice

½ cup chopped fresh broccoli

¼ cup shredded carrot

1. Heat oil in medium skillet over high heat until hot. Add mushrooms, onion and garlic; cook until tender.

2. Add broth; bring to a boil. Stir in barley and rice. Reduce heat; cover and simmer 10 to 12 minutes or until most of liquid is absorbed, adding broccoli and carrot during last 5 minutes of cooking time.

3. Remove skillet from heat; let stand 5 minutes. Fluff mixture with fork before serving.

Nutrition Information Per Serving: Calories 90 • Total Fat 2g • Saturated Fat 0g • Cholesterol 0mg • Sodium 270mg • Total Carbohydrate 15g • Dietary Fiber 2g • Sugars 1g • Protein 1g. **Dietary Exchanges:** 1 Starch OR 1 Carbohydrate.

harvard beets

READY TO SERVE: 20 MINUTES
SERVINGS: 4

* super fast

1 (15-oz.) can sliced or baby whole beets

Water

¼ cup sugar

1 tablespoon cornstarch

¾ teaspoon salt

Dash pepper

3 tablespoons vinegar

1. Drain beets, reserving liquid. Measure liquid; add water to make ¾ cup. Set beets aside.

2. In medium saucepan, combine sugar, cornstarch, salt and pepper; mix well. Gradually stir beet liquid and vinegar into sugar mixture; blend until smooth. Cook until mixture boils and thickens, stirring constantly.

3. Add beets; cook until thoroughly heated.

Nutrition Information Per Serving: Calories 90 • Total Fat 0g • Saturated Fat 0g • Cholesterol 0mg • Sodium 670mg • Total Carbohydrate 22g • Dietary Fiber 1g • Sugars 18g • Protein 1g. **Dietary Exchanges:** 1 Fruit • 1 Vegetable OR 1 Carbohydrate • 1 Vegetable.

swiss vegetable casserole

PREP TIME: 20 MINUTES
READY TO SERVE: 50 MINUTES
SERVINGS: 8

1 (1-lb.) pkg. frozen broccoli florets, carrots and cauliflower

2 tablespoons margarine or butter

6 green onions, cut into ¹/₂-inch pieces (¹/₂ cup)

2 tablespoons all-purpose flour

¼ teaspoon salt

¹/₈ teaspoon pepper

1¹/₂ cups milk

4 oz. shredded Swiss cheese (1 cup)

¼ cup crushed round buttery crackers

1. Heat oven to 350°F. Grease 1 to 1¹/₂-quart casserole. Cook frozen vegetables as directed on package. Drain.

2. Meanwhile, melt margarine in medium saucepan over medium heat. Add onions; cook and stir 2 to 3 minutes or until tender.

3. Stir in flour, salt and pepper; mix well. Gradually add milk, stirring constantly. Cook and stir until mixture is bubbly and thickened. Remove from heat.

4. Add ¾ cup of the cheese; stir until melted. Stir in cooked vegetables. Spoon mixture into greased casserole. Sprinkle with crushed crackers and remaining ¼ cup cheese.

5. Bake at 350°F for 25 to 30 minutes or until topping is golden brown and casserole is bubbly.

Nutrition Information Per Serving: Calories 130 • Total Fat 6g • Saturated Fat 2g • Cholesterol 10mg • Sodium 190mg • Total Carbohydrate 10g • Dietary Fiber 2g • Sugars 4g • Protein 8g. Dietary Exchanges: ½ Starch • 1 Vegetable • ½ High-Fat Meat • ½ Fat OR ½ Carbohydrate • 1 Vegetable • ½ High-Fat Meat • ½ Fat.

buttered parmesan noodles

READY TO SERVE: 25 MINUTES
SERVINGS: 5

* super fast

5 oz. uncooked wide egg noodles (2¹/₂ cups)

2 to 3 tablespoons butter

¼ cup grated Parmesan cheese

1¹/₂ teaspoons chopped fresh parsley or 1 teaspoon dried parsley flakes

1. Cook noodles to desired doneness as directed on package. Drain; cover to keep warm.

2. In same saucepan, melt butter over low heat. Gently stir in noodles. Add cheese and parsley; toss to coat.

Nutrition Information Per Serving: Calories 190 • Total Fat 10g • Saturated Fat 2g • Cholesterol 30mg • Sodium 180mg • Total Carbohydrate 20g • Dietary Fiber 1g • Sugars 1g • Protein 6g. Dietary Exchanges: 1 Starch • ½ Lean Meat • 1½ Fat OR 1 Carbohydrate • ½ Lean Meat • 1½ Fat.

quick brown rice pilaf

READY TO SERVE: 15 MINUTES
SERVINGS: 5

* super fast

1¼ cups chicken broth

1 tablespoon margarine or butter

1 to 1¹/₂ cups uncooked instant brown rice

¹/₂ cup shredded carrot

¹/₃ cup sliced green onions

¹/₂ teaspoon dried rosemary or marjoram leaves

1. In medium saucepan, combine broth and margarine. Bring to a boil. Stir in all remaining ingredients. Reduce heat to low; cover and simmer 5 minutes.

2. Remove saucepan from heat; stir. Cover; let stand 5 minutes. Fluff mixture with fork before serving.

Nutrition Information Per Serving: Calories 140 • Total Fat 4g • Saturated Fat 1g • Cholesterol 0mg • Sodium 230mg • Total Carbohydrate 22g • Dietary Fiber 2g • Sugars 1g • Protein 4g. Dietary Exchanges: 1½ Starch • ½ Fat OR 1½ Carbohydrate • ½ Fat.

swiss vegetable casserole

roasted peppers with garlic

READY TO SERVE: 25 MINUTES
SERVINGS: 4

dressing

- 2 garlic cloves, minced
- 2 tablespoons red wine vinegar
- 2 tablespoons olive oil
- ¼ teaspoon salt
- ¼ teaspoon freshly ground black pepper

salad

- 1 roasted red bell pepper, cut into strips
- 1 roasted green bell pepper, cut into strips
- 1 roasted yellow bell pepper, cut into strips
- ⅓ cup halved ripe olives

  Leaf lettuce
- 2 tablespoons chopped fresh basil

1. In jar with tight-fitting lid, combine all dressing ingredients; shake well. Set aside.

2. In medium bowl, combine pepper strips and olives. Pour dressing over pepper mixture; let stand 10 minutes.

3. Line serving platter with lettuce. Decoratively arrange peppers and olives over lettuce. Sprinkle with basil. Serve warm or at room temperature.

Nutrition Information Per Serving: Calories 100 • Total Fat 8g • Saturated Fat 1g • Cholesterol 0mg • Sodium 280mg • Total Carbohydrate 6g • Dietary Fiber 1g • Sugars 1g • Protein 1g. **Dietary Exchanges:** 1 Vegetable • 1½ Fat.

lemon-buttered asparagus

READY TO SERVE: 20 MINUTES
SERVINGS: 4

* super fast

1. Snap off tough ends of asparagus. In large skillet, combine asparagus spears and ½ cup water. Bring to a boil over medium heat. Cook 5 to 10 minutes or until crisp-tender. Drain.

2. Meanwhile, melt butter in small saucepan. Stir in lemon juice and lemon peel.

3. Place asparagus on serving platter; pour butter mixture over spears.

Nutrition Information Per Serving: Calories 110 • Total Fat 9g • Saturated Fat 5g • Cholesterol 25mg • Sodium 90mg • Total Carbohydrate 5g • Dietary Fiber 2g • Sugars 2g • Protein 2g. **Dietary Exchanges:** 1 Vegetable • 2 Fat.

1 lb. fresh asparagus spears

3 tablespoons butter

1 tablespoon lemon juice

½ teaspoon grated lemon peel

new potato, pasta and vegetable stir-fry

READY TO SERVE: 30 MINUTES
SERVINGS: 4

8 oz. uncooked bow tie pasta (3 cups)

2 tablespoons olive or vegetable oil

1 medium onion, cut into 8 wedges

4 new red potatoes, unpeeled, sliced

8 oz. fresh asparagus spears, trimmed, cut into 2-inch pieces

1 medium red or yellow bell pepper, cut into strips

2 tablespoons chopped fresh oregano

½ teaspoon salt

⅛ teaspoon pepper

4 oz. shredded Swiss cheese (1 cup)

1. Cook pasta to desired doneness as directed on package. Drain.

2. Meanwhile, heat oil in large skillet over medium-high heat until hot. Add onion; cook and stir 2 minutes. Add potatoes; cover and cook 5 to 6 minutes or until partially cooked, stirring occasionally.

3. Stir in asparagus, bell pepper, oregano, salt and pepper. Reduce heat to medium-low; cover and cook 5 to 8 minutes or until vegetables are tender, stirring occasionally.

4. Stir in cooked pasta; cook until thoroughly heated. Remove from heat. Sprinkle with cheese. Cover; let stand until cheese is melted.

Nutrition Information Per Serving: Calories 510 • Total Fat 16g • Saturated Fat 6g • Cholesterol 25mg • Sodium 350mg • Total Carbohydrate 72g • Dietary Fiber 6g • Sugars 7g • Protein 19g. **Dietary Exchanges:** 4½ Starch • 1 Vegetable • ½ High-Fat Meat • 2 Fat OR 4½ Carbohydrate • 1 Vegetable • ½ High-Fat Meat • 2 Fat.

BUYING FRESH

Fresh vegetables are usually least expensive and of best quality during their peak growing season. Unlike fruits, most vegetables do not continue to ripen after harvesting.

Look for produce that is crisp, nicely colored, firm and unblemished. Avoid vegetables that show signs of wilting, bruising, spoilage or dryness.

Most vegetables lose nutrients and flavor in prolonged storage. It's a good idea to buy a few days' supply of vegetables at a time. Good "keepers" with longer storage time include potatoes, onions, winter squash, carrots and cabbage.

tartar sauce

READY TO SERVE: 20 MINUTES
YIELD: 1-1/2 CUPS

✳ super fast

1 cup mayonnaise or salad dressing

¼ cup finely chopped dill pickle or pickle relish

2 tablespoons finely chopped fresh parsley

1 tablespoon lemon juice

1 tablespoon chopped pimientos

½ teaspoon finely chopped onion

¼ teaspoon Worcestershire sauce

1. In small bowl, combine all ingredients; mix well.

2. Cover; refrigerate 15 minutes or until chilled.

Nutrition Information Per Serving: Calories: 60 • Total Fat 7g • Saturated Fat 1g • Cholesterol 5mg • Sodium 75mg • Total Carbohydrate 0g • Dietary Fiber 0g • Sugars 0g • Protein 0g. Dietary Exchange: 1½ Fat.

new potatoes with chive butter

PREP TIME: 15 MINUTES
READY TO SERVE: 40 MINUTES
SERVINGS: 6

1 to 1½ lb. small new potatoes

1 tablespoon butter, melted

1 tablespoon chopped fresh chives

¼ to ½ teaspoon salt

Dash pepper

1. Scrub or peel potatoes. In medium saucepan, cook potatoes in small amount of boiling water for 15 to 25 minutes or until fork-tender. Drain well. Return potatoes to saucepan or place in serving bowl.

2. Add butter, chives, salt and pepper; toss gently to coat.

Nutrition Information Per Serving: Calories 150 • Total Fat 2g • Saturated Fat 1g • Cholesterol 5mg • Sodium 210mg • Total Carbohydrate 29g • Dietary Fiber 3g • Sugars 1g • Protein 3g. Dietary Exchanges: 1½ Starch • ½ Fat OR 1½ Carbohydrate • ½ Fat.

savory couscous

READY TO SERVE: 20 MINUTES
SERVINGS: 4

* super fast

1 tablespoon margarine or butter

¼ cup chopped red onion

2 cups water

1 teaspoon dried parsley flakes

½ teaspoon seasoned salt

¼ teaspoon dried sage leaves

¼ teaspoon dried thyme leaves

1⅓ cups uncooked couscous

1. Melt margarine in medium saucepan over medium-high heat. Add onion; cook 1 minute or until tender, stirring occasionally.

2. Add water, parsley, seasoned salt, sage and thyme. Increase heat to high; bring to a boil. Stir in couscous. Remove from heat; cover and let stand 5 minutes. Fluff lightly with fork before serving.

Nutrition Information Per Serving: Calories 260 • Total Fat 3g • Saturated Fat 1g • Cholesterol 0mg • Sodium 230mg • Total Carbohydrate 49g • Dietary Fiber 4g • Sugars 2g • Protein 8g. **Dietary Exchanges:** 3 Starch • ½ Fat OR 3 Carbohydrate • ½ Fat.

cabbage stir-fry

READY TO SERVE: 15 MINUTES
SERVINGS: 4

* super fast

2 tablespoons oil

1 teaspoon sesame oil

1 garlic clove, minced

1 teaspoon grated gingerroot

1 cup shredded cabbage

1 cup shredded Chinese (napa) cabbage

1 cup shredded bok choy

½ cup chopped green onions

1 tablespoon soy sauce

2 teaspoons sesame seed, toasted if desired

1. In large skillet or wok, heat oils over high heat until hot. Add garlic and gingerroot; cook a few seconds.

2. Add cabbage, Chinese cabbage, bok choy, onions and soy sauce; mix well. Cook 2 to 3 minutes or until cabbage is crisp-tender, stirring constantly. Place in serving bowl. Sprinkle with sesame seed.

Nutrition Information Per Serving: Calories 110 • Total Fat 9g • Saturated Fat 1g • Cholesterol 0mg • Sodium 290mg • Total Carbohydrate 4g • Dietary Fiber 1g • Sugars 2g • Protein 2g. **Dietary Exchanges:** 1 Vegetable • 2 Fat.

TOASTING SESAME SEED

To toast sesame seed, spread in small nonstick skillet; stir over medium-high heat for 1 to 2 minutes or until light golden brown.

asparagus stir-fry

asparagus stir-fry

2 cups uncooked instant rice

2 cups water

1 teaspoon olive oil

3 carrots, sliced (about 1 cup)

1 small onion, cut into 8 wedges

1 lb. fresh asparagus, cut into 1-inch pieces

1 (8-oz.) pkg. fresh whole mushrooms, quartered

⅓ cup water

1 teaspoon grated lemon peel

¼ teaspoon dried thyme leaves

¼ teaspoon pepper

1. Cook rice in water as directed on package.

2. Meanwhile, heat oil in 12-inch skillet over medium-high heat until hot. Add carrots and onion; cook and stir 2 minutes. Add asparagus and mushrooms; cook and stir 4 minutes or just until asparagus is crisp-tender.

3. Stir in water, lemon peel, thyme and pepper. Cover; cook over medium heat for 2 to 3 minutes or until vegetables are crisp-tender. Serve over rice.

Nutrition Information Per Serving: Calories 250 • Total Fat 2g • Saturated Fat 0g • Cholesterol 0mg • Sodium 30mg • Total Carbohydrate 49g • Dietary Fiber 6g • Sugars 7g • Protein 8g. **Dietary Exchanges:** 2½ Starch • 2 Vegetable OR 2½ Carbohydrate • 2 Vegetable.

spicy corn and zucchini with ramen noodles

noodles

1 (3-oz.) pkg. any flavor ramen noodle soup mix

sauce

1 teaspoon sugar

1 teaspoon cornstarch

¼ to ½ teaspoon crushed red pepper flakes

¼ cup water

2 tablespoons soy sauce

stir-fry

1 tablespoon oil

2 medium zucchini, cut into ¼-inch-thick slices (2 cups)

1 medium onion, cut into thin wedges

1 garlic clove, minced

1 (14-oz.) can baby corn nuggets, drained, rinsed

1. In medium saucepan, bring 2 cups water to a boil. Add noodles from soup mix; boil 2 to 3 minutes or until noodles are tender. Drain; cover to keep warm. (Discard seasoning packet or reserve for another use.)

2. Meanwhile, in small bowl, combine all sauce ingredients; mix well. Set aside.

3. Heat oil in large skillet over medium-high heat until hot. Add zucchini, onion and garlic; cook and stir 2 minutes. Reduce heat to medium-low; stir in corn and sauce mixture. Cook 2 to 4 minutes or until vegetables are crisp-tender and mixture is bubbly and thickened, stirring frequently. Stir in cooked noodles.

Nutrition Information Per Serving: Calories 180 • Total Fat 8g • Saturated Fat 2g • Cholesterol 0mg • Sodium 710mg • Total Carbohydrate 21g • Dietary Fiber 4g • Sugars 6g • Protein 5g. **Dietary Exchanges:** 1½ Starch • 1½ Fat OR 1½ Carbohydrate • 1½ Fat.

summer squash sauté

READY TO SERVE: 20 MINUTES
SERVINGS: 6

* super fast

1 tablespoon olive or vegetable oil

2 small zucchini, sliced

2 small yellow summer squash, sliced

2 large garlic cloves, minced

1 small onion, thinly sliced

1½ cups sliced fresh mushrooms (4 oz.)

1 tablespoon chopped fresh dill

1 tablespoon chopped fresh chives

¼ teaspoon salt

Dash coarse ground black pepper

1. Heat oil in large skillet over medium-high heat until hot. Add zucchini, summer squash, garlic and onion; cook 2 to 3 minutes, stirring frequently.

2. Add mushrooms, dill, chives, salt and pepper; mix gently. Cook 3 to 4 minutes or until vegetables are crisp-tender, stirring occasionally.

Nutrition Information Per Serving: Calories 60 • Total Fat 3g • Saturated Fat 0g • Cholesterol 0mg • Sodium 95mg • Total Carbohydrate 7g • Dietary Fiber 3g • Sugars 3g • Protein 2g. **Dietary Exchanges:** 1 Vegetable • ½ Fat.

garden beans with hot bacon dressing

READY TO SERVE: 25 MINUTES
SERVINGS: 8

* super fast

4 slices bacon, cut into ½-inch pieces

1 beef bouillon cube or 1 teaspoon beef-flavor instant bouillon

⅓ cup boiling water

1 tablespoon sugar

⅛ teaspoon pepper

4 cups fresh yellow wax or green beans, cut into 2-inch pieces

½ cup chopped onion

2 tablespoons red wine vinegar

¼ cup sliced almonds

1. In large skillet, cook bacon until crisp, stirring occasionally. With slotted spoon, remove bacon from skillet; drain on paper towels. Set aside.

2. Dissolve bouillon in water. Add bouillon, sugar and pepper to bacon drippings; mix well. Add wax beans and onion; mix well. Cover; cook 4 to 6 minutes or until crisp-tender.

3. Remove skillet from heat. Stir in vinegar. Spoon into serving dish. Sprinkle with bacon and almonds.

Nutrition Information Per Serving: Calories 70 • Total Fat 3g • Saturated Fat 1g • Cholesterol 3mg • Sodium 160mg • Total Carbohydrate 7g • Dietary Fiber 2g • Sugars 3g. **Dietary Exchanges:** 1½ Vegetable • ½ Fat.

chunky marinara sauce

PREP TIME: 20 MINUTES
READY TO SERVE: 40 MINUTES
YIELD: 2/3 CUP

2 teaspoons olive or vegetable oil

¼ cup chopped green bell pepper

¼ cup chopped onion

1 garlic clove, minced

1 (14.5-oz.) can diced tomatoes, undrained

1 (8-oz.) can tomato sauce

1 teaspoon sugar

½ teaspoon dried oregano leaves

¼ teaspoon salt

1. Heat oil in medium saucepan over medium-high heat until hot. Add bell pepper, onion and garlic; cook 2 to 4 minutes or until vegetables are crisp-tender, stirring frequently.

2. Add all remaining ingredients; mix well. Bring to a boil. Reduce heat to low; simmer 15 to 20 minutes or until flavors are blended, stirring frequently. Serve over hot cooked pasta.

Nutrition Information Per Serving: Calories 80 • Total Fat 3g • Saturated Fat 0g • Cholesterol 0mg • Sodium 630mg • Total Carbohydrate 11g • Dietary Fiber 2g • Sugars 6g • Protein 2g. **Dietary Exchanges:** 2 Vegetable • ½ Fat.

spicy nuggets and vegetables

READY TO SERVE: 25 MINUTES
SERVINGS: 4

* super fast

4½ oz. uncooked pasta nuggets (1½ cups)

2 cups frozen broccoli florets, carrots and cauliflower

4 oz. mild Mexican pasteurized process cheese spread with jalapeño peppers, cubed (½ cup)

1 tablespoon milk

1. In large saucepan, cook pasta nuggets as directed on package, adding vegetables during last 3 to 5 minutes of cooking time. Cook until pasta nuggets and vegetables are tender. Drain well; return to saucepan.

2. Add cheese and milk; cook over medium heat, stirring constantly, until cheese is melted and pasta and vegetables are coated.

Nutrition Information Per Serving: Calories 220 • Total Fat 7g • Saturated Fat 4g • Cholesterol 15mg • Sodium 400mg • Total Carbohydrate 29g • Dietary Fiber 2g • Sugars 5g • Protein 10g. **Dietary Exchanges:** 1½ Starch • 1 Vegetable • ½ High-Fat Meat • ½ Fat OR 1½ Carbohydrate • 1 Vegetable • ½ High-Fat Meat • ½ Fat.

maple-cinnamon sweet potatoes

READY TO SERVE: 20 MINUTES
SERVINGS: 8

✳ **super fast**

4 small dark-orange sweet potatoes, peeled, cut into ³⁄4-inch cubes (about 4 cups)

¼ cup real maple syrup or maple-flavored syrup

½ teaspoon cinnamon

2 tablespoons finely chopped walnuts

1. In large saucepan, bring 4 cups water to a boil. Add sweet potatoes; return to a boil. Cook over medium heat for 8 to 12 minutes or until tender. Drain well. Return sweet potatoes to saucepan or place in serving bowl.

2. Meanwhile, in small bowl, combine syrup and cinnamon; mix well. Add to sweet potatoes; toss gently to coat. Just before serving, sprinkle with walnuts.

Nutrition Information Per Serving: Calories 110 • Total Fat 1g • Saturated Fat 0g • Cholesterol 0mg • Sodium 10mg • Total Carbohydrate 23g • Dietary Fiber 2g • Sugars 10g • Protein 1g. **Dietary Exchanges:** 1 Starch • ½ Fruit OR 1½ Carbohydrate.

cashew-rice pilaf

PREP TIME: 10 MINUTES
READY TO SERVE: 40 MINUTES
SERVINGS: 3

2 tablespoons margarine or butter

2 to 3 tablespoons finely chopped onion

½ cup uncooked regular long-grain white rice

1 cup chicken broth

¼ teaspoon salt

¼ cup cashews, coarsely chopped

2 tablespoons chopped fresh parsley

1. Melt margarine in medium saucepan. Add onion; cook until tender. Add rice; stir until coated with margarine.

2. Add broth and salt. Cover; simmer 25 to 30 minutes or until rice is tender and liquid is absorbed. Stir in cashews and parsley.

Nutrition Information Per Serving: Calories 280 • Total Fat 15g • Saturated Fat 3g • Cholesterol 0mg • Sodium 620mg • Total Carbohydrate 31g • Dietary Fiber 1g • Sugars 2g • Protein 6g. **Dietary Exchanges:** 2 Starch • 3 Fat OR 2 Carbohydrate • 3 Fat.

southern succotash

READY TO SERVE: 15 MINUTES
SERVINGS: 4

✳ **super fast**

1 tablespoon butter

½ cup chopped red bell pepper

1 cup frozen whole kernel corn

1 (9-oz.) pkg. frozen baby lima beans in a pouch

¼ teaspoon salt

¼ teaspoon dried marjoram leaves, if desired

⅛ teaspoon pepper

1. Melt butter in medium skillet over medium heat. Add bell pepper; cook and stir 1 minute.

2. Add all remaining ingredients; mix well. Cook 3 to 5 minutes or until vegetables are crisp-tender, stirring occasionally.

Nutrition Information Per Serving: Calories 160 • Total Fat 4g • Saturated Fat 2g • Cholesterol 10mg • Sodium 200mg • Total Carbohydrate 25g • Dietary Fiber 5g • Sugars 3g • Protein 6g. **Dietary Exchanges:** 1½ Starch • ½ Fat OR 1½ Carbohydrate • ½ Fat.

parmesan mushrooms and onions

READY TO SERVE: 15 MINUTES
SERVINGS: 3

* super fast

2 tablespoons margarine or butter

2 cups small fresh mushrooms (6 oz.)

⅓ cup sliced sweet onion

½ teaspoon dried marjoram leaves

¼ teaspoon salt

¼ teaspoon pepper

1 tablespoon dry white wine

1 to 2 tablespoons grated fresh Parmesan cheese

1. Melt margarine in small skillet over medium-high heat.

2. Add all remaining ingredients except Parmesan cheese; cook 5 to 10 minutes or until mushrooms are tender, stirring occasionally. Remove from heat. Sprinkle with cheese.

Nutrition Information Per Serving: Calories 120 • Total Fat 9g • Saturated Fat 2g • Cholesterol 3mg • Sodium 350mg • Total Carbohydrate 5g • Dietary Fiber 1g • Sugars 1g • Protein 3g. **Dietary Exchanges:** 1 Vegetable • 2 Fat.

apricot-glazed carrots

READY TO SERVE: 15 MINUTES
SERVINGS: 8

✳ **super fast**

5 cups julienne-cut (2x⅛x⅛-inch) carrots

¼ teaspoon salt

¼ cup apricot preserves

1. In medium saucepan, combine carrots and ¾ cup water; bring to a boil. Reduce heat to low; cover and simmer until carrots are tender. Drain.

2. Add salt and apricot preserves; stir to coat. Cook over low heat for 1 to 2 minutes or until thoroughly heated.

Nutrition Information Per Serving: Calories 60 • Total Fat 0g • Saturated Fat 0g • Cholesterol 0mg • Sodium 100mg • Total Carbohydrate 14g • Dietary Fiber 2g • Sugars 10g • Protein 1g. Dietary Exchanges: ½ Fruit • 1 Vegetable OR ½ Carbohydrate • 1 Vegetable.

quick fried rice

READY TO SERVE: 20 MINUTES
SERVINGS: 4

✳ **super fast**

1½ cups uncooked instant white rice

1½ cups water

1 teaspoon oil

2 eggs, beaten

4 teaspoons dark sesame oil

½ cup frozen early June peas

⅓ cup sliced green onions

1 cup fresh bean sprouts

¼ cup soy sauce

1. Cook rice in water as directed on package.

2. Meanwhile, heat 1 teaspoon oil in large skillet over medium-high heat until hot. Add beaten eggs; tilt pan to form thin layer of egg. Lift edges of egg with small spatula to let uncooked egg flow to bottom of skillet. Cover; cook 1 minute or until set. Slide egg from skillet onto cutting board. Set aside.

3. In same skillet, heat 4 teaspoons sesame oil over medium-high heat until hot. Add peas and onions; cook and stir 1 to 2 minutes or until vegetables are crisp-tender.

4. Add cooked rice, sprouts and soy sauce; cook and stir until rice is thoroughly heated.

5. Roll up egg; cut into small strips. Cut strips into 2-inch lengths; fold into rice mixture. Heat thoroughly. If desired, serve with additional soy sauce.

Nutrition Information Per Serving: Calories 250 • Total Fat 8g • Saturated Fat 2g • Cholesterol 105mg • Sodium 1090mg • Total Carbohydrate 36g • Dietary Fiber 2g • Sugars 3g • Protein 9g. Dietary Exchanges: 2 Starch • 1 Vegetable • 1½ Fat OR 2 Carbohydrate • 1 Vegetable • 1½ Fat.

fresh herb scones

PREP TIME: 20 MINUTES
READY TO SERVE: 40 MINUTES
SERVINGS: 8 SCONES

2 cups all-purpose flour

¼ cup chopped fresh parsley

1 tablespoon sugar

1 tablespoon chopped fresh thyme or 1 teaspoon dried thyme leaves

3 teaspoons baking powder

1 teaspoon chopped fresh rosemary or ¼ teaspoon dried rosemary leaves, crushed

½ teaspoon salt

⅓ cup margarine or butter

½ cup milk

1 egg, slightly beaten

1. Heat oven to 400°F. Lightly grease cookie sheet. In large bowl, combine flour, parsley, sugar, thyme, baking powder, rosemary and salt; mix well. With pastry blender or fork, cut in margarine until mixture resembles coarse crumbs. Stir in milk and egg just until moistened.

2. On floured surface, gently knead dough 10 times. Place on greased cookie sheet; roll or pat dough into 6-inch round. Cut into 8 wedges; separate slightly.

3. Bake at 400°F for 15 to 20 minutes or until golden brown. Serve warm.

Nutrition Information Per Serving: Calories 210 • Total Fat 9g • Saturated Fat 2g • Cholesterol 30mg • Sodium 420mg • Dietary Fiber 1g. **Dietary Exchanges:** 1½ Starch • ½ Fruit • 1½ Fat OR 2 Carbohydrate • 1½ Fat.

three-bean salad

PREP TIME: 15 MINUTES
READY TO SERVE: 4 HOURS 15 MINUTES
SERVINGS: 12

* plan ahead

salad

1 (15.5 or 15-oz.) can kidney beans, drained

1 (14.5-oz.) can cut yellow wax beans, drained

1 (14.5-oz.) can cut green beans, drained

1 medium red onion, sliced, separated into rings

1 green bell pepper, cut into strips

dressing

¾ cup vinegar

½ cup sugar

½ cup oil

1 tablespoon chopped fresh parsley

1 teaspoon celery seed

¼ teaspoon pepper

1. In large bowl, combine all salad ingredients.

2. In jar with tight-fitting lid, combine all dressing ingredients; shake well. Pour dressing over salad; toss to coat. Cover; refrigerate at least 4 hours or overnight to blend flavors.

Nutrition Information Per Serving: Calories 160 • Total Fat 9g • Saturated Fat 1g • Cholesterol 0mg • Sodium 150mg • Total Carbohydrate 17g • Dietary Fiber 2g • Sugars 10g • Protein 2g. **Dietary Exchanges:** 1 Starch • 2 Fat OR 1 Carbohydrate • 2 Fat.

OIL AND VINEGAR SALAD DRESSING

The classic dressing ratio is three parts oil to one part vinegar with seasoning to taste, but you can always adjust the proportions to suit your taste. Add more vinegar if you like a tangier dressing or if you want to reduce the fat content.

Oil and vinegar have a natural tendency to separate. Mix them in a blender or shake them well in a tightly closed jar to blend them together.

To mix oil and vinegar by hand, begin whisking the vinegar and pour in the oil a drop or two at a time, then pour in a slow steady stream, all the while whisking vigorously.

If a dressing separates after it has stood for a while, simply rewhisk (or shake) the mixture before tossing it with the salad.

---

chinese chicken salad with rice vinegar dressing

READY TO SERVE: 30 MINUTES
SERVINGS: 4

dressing

- 3 tablespoons sugar
- 1 teaspoon ginger
- 1/8 teaspoon crushed red pepper flakes
- 1/2 cup rice vinegar
- 4 teaspoons soy sauce

salad

- 3 boneless skinless chicken breast halves
- 1/2 small head Chinese (napa) cabbage, shredded (4 cups)
- 1 medium carrot, shredded
- 2 tablespoons sliced green onions
- 1/4 cup chow mein noodles, if desired

1. In small bowl, combine all dressing ingredients; blend well. Place chicken breast halves in medium skillet. Drizzle 3 tablespoons dressing over chicken. Let stand at room temperature for 10 minutes.

2. Add 3 tablespoons water. Bring to a boil. Reduce heat; cover and simmer 10 minutes or until chicken is no longer pink. Drain; cool slightly. Shred or chop chicken.

3. In large bowl, combine chicken, cabbage, carrot and onions. Add remaining dressing; toss to coat. Top with chow mein noodles.

Nutrition Information Per Serving: Calories 180 • Total Fat 3g • Saturated Fat 1g • Cholesterol 55 mg • Sodium 460 mg • Total Carbohydrate 17g • Dietary Fiber 2g • Sugars 11g • Protein 22g. Dietary Exchanges: 1/2 Fruit • 2 Vegetable • 2 1/2 Very Lean Meat OR 1/2 Carbohydrate • 2 Vegetable • 2 1/2 Very Lean Meat.

stuffed sweet potatoes

READY TO SERVE: 45 MINUTES
SERVINGS: 6

- 6 dark-orange sweet potatoes (about 8 oz. each)
- 2/3 cup buttermilk
- 2 tablespoons sliced green onions
- 1/4 teaspoon salt
- 1/8 teaspoon pepper
- 3 tablespoons shredded reduced-fat sharp Cheddar cheese

1. Scrub potatoes; pierce several times with tip of knife. Place in microwave on microwave-safe paper towel; cover with another paper towel. Microwave on high for 15 to 20 minutes or until potatoes are tender, rearranging once.

2. Spray 13x9-inch (3-quart) baking dish with cooking spray. Cut thin slice from top of each cooked potato. Scoop out each potato, leaving 1/4-inch-thick shell. Place potato pulp in large bowl; mash with electric mixer on medium-low speed or potato masher.

3. Add buttermilk, onions, salt and pepper; mix well. Fill potato shells with mixture; place in sprayed baking dish. Sprinkle cheese over tops of potatoes.

4. Broil 4 to 6 inches from heat for about 1 minute or until cheese is melted.

Nutrition Information Per Serving: Calories 270 • Total Fat 2g • Saturated Fat 1g • Cholesterol 3mg • Sodium 180mg • Total Carbohydrate 57g • Dietary Fiber 7g • Sugars 14g • Protein 6g. Dietary Exchanges: 3 1/2 Starch OR 3 1/2 Carbohydrate.

green beans with cashew butter

READY TO SERVE: 10 MINUTES
SERVINGS: 6

* super fast

3½ cups frozen cut green beans

⅓ cup butter

⅓ cup coarsely chopped cashews

1. Cook green beans as directed on package. Drain; spoon into serving bowl.

2. Meanwhile, melt butter in small saucepan. Add the cashews; cook and stir over low heat for 2 minutes or until cashews are very light brown. Pour cashew butter over the hot green beans.

Nutrition Information Per Serving: Calories 180 • Total Fat 15g • Saturated Fat 7g • Cholesterol 30mg • Sodium 170mg • Total Carbohydrate 9g • Dietary Fiber 2g • Sugars 2g • Protein 3g. **Dietary Exchanges:** 1½ Vegetable • 3 Fat.

swift snacks & sweets

grands!® strawberry shortcakes * p. 257

pizza melts * p. 289

aloha peach pies * p. 271

lemon-ginger thumbprints * p. 290

coconut-pineapple tart ✳ p. 276

easy pesto pinwheels

READY TO SERVE: 30 MINUTES
SERVINGS: 16 APPETIZERS

1 (8-oz.) can refrigerated
crescent dinner rolls

⅓ cup purchased pesto

¼ cup chopped roasted red
bell peppers (from 7.25-oz.
jar)

1. Heat oven to 350°F. Unroll dough into 2 long rectangles. Firmly press perforations to seal. Spread rectangles with pesto to within ¼ inch of edges. Sprinkle with roasted peppers.

2. Starting at shortest side, roll up each rectangle; pinch edges to seal. Cut each roll into 8 slices. Place, cut side down, on ungreased cookie sheet.

3. Bake at 350°F for 13 to 17 minutes or until golden brown. Immediately remove from cookie sheet. Serve warm.

Nutrition Information Per Serving: Calories 60 • Total Fat 4g • Saturated Fat 1g • Cholesterol 0 mg • Sodium 125mg • Total Carbohydrate 6g • Dietary Fiber 0g • Sugars 1g • Protein 1g. **Dietary Exchanges:** ½ Starch • ½ Fat OR ½ Carbohydrate • ½ Fat.

grands!® little pies

PREP TIME: 20 MINUTES
READY TO SERVE: 55 MINUTES
SERVINGS: 16

S. LEA MEAD ✳ SAN MATEO, CALIFORNIA
BAKE-OFF® CONTEST 40, 2002

¾ cup all-purpose flour

½ cup packed brown sugar

1 teaspoon ground cinnamon

½ cup butter or margarine

½ cup chopped nuts, if desired

1 (16.3-oz.) can large refrigerated original or buttermilk flaky biscuits

1 (21-oz.) can apple, blueberry or cherry pie filling

1 to 1½ cups whipping cream

Cinnamon-sugar

1. Heat oven to 350°F. In medium bowl, mix flour, brown sugar and cinnamon. With pastry blender or fork, cut in butter until mixture resembles coarse crumbs. Stir in nuts.

2. Separate dough into 8 biscuits. Split each biscuit in half to make 16 rounds. With floured fingers, flatten each to form 4-inch round. Press each biscuit round in ungreased 2¾x1¼-inch muffin cup.

3. Spoon 2 tablespoons pie filling into each biscuit-lined cup. Sprinkle each with about 2 tablespoons flour mixture. (Cups will be full.)

4. Bake 15 to 22 minutes or until golden brown. Cool 5 minutes. Remove from muffin cups; place on wire rack. Cool 10 minutes.

5. In small bowl, beat whipping cream with electric mixer on high speed until stiff peaks form. Top each serving with whipped cream; sprinkle with cinnamon-sugar. Store pies in refrigerator.

Nutrition Information Per Serving: Calories 280 • Total Fat 14g • Saturated Fat 8g • Trans Fat 2g • Cholesterol 30mg • Sodium 340mg • Total Carbohydrate 34g • Dietary Fiber 0g • Sugars 18g • Protein 3g. **Dietary Exchanges:** 1 Starch • 1½ Other Carbohydrate • 2½ Fat.

choco-toffee bars

PREP TIME: 20 MINUTES
READY TO SERVE: 3 HOURS
SERVINGS: 36 BARS

✳ plan ahead

crust

1 (18-oz.) pkg. Pillsbury® Refrigerated Chocolate Chip Cookies

filling

1 cup toffee bits

¼ cup firmly packed brown sugar

1 teaspoon vanilla

1 (3-oz.) pkg. cream cheese, softened

1 egg

⅔ cup butterscotch chips, melted

topping

½ cup miniature semisweet chocolate chips

1. Heat oven to 350°F. Cut cookie dough into ½-inch slices. Arrange slices in bottom of ungreased 13x9-inch pan. With floured fingers, press dough evenly in pan to form crust. Sprinkle with ½ cup of the toffee bits. Bake at 350°F for 16 to 18 minutes or until golden brown.

2. Meanwhile, in small bowl, combine brown sugar, vanilla, cream cheese and egg; beat at medium speed until blended. Add melted butterscotch chips; blend well.

3. Remove partially baked crust from oven. With spatula, gently press edges of crust down to make surface flat. Spoon and spread filling over crust. Sprinkle with remaining ½ cup toffee bits and chocolate chips.

4. Return to oven; bake an additional 20 to 25 minutes or until edges are deep golden brown and center is set. Cool 10 minutes. Run knife around sides of pan to loosen. Cool 2 hours or until completely cooled. Cut into bars. Store in refrigerator.

Nutrition Information Per Serving: Calories 140 • Total Fat 7g • Saturated Fat 4g • Cholesterol 15mg • Sodium 90mg • Total Carbohydrate 17g • Dietary Fiber 0g • Sugars 14g • Protein 1g. **Dietary Exchanges:** ½ Starch • ½ Fruit • 1½ Fat OR 1 Carbohydrate • 1½ Fat.

zebra brownie doughnuts

PREP TIME: 20 MINUTES
READY TO SERVE: 40 MINUTES
SERVINGS: 12

ROSEMARY LEICHT ✳ BETHEL, OHIO
BAKE-OFF® CONTEST 40, 2002

doughnuts
- 1 (15.8-oz.) box double chocolate brownie mix with chocolate syrup
- ½ cup buttermilk
- ¼ cup light or extra-light olive oil
- 1 egg

glaze
- 1½ cups powdered sugar
- 1 teaspoon vanilla
- 3 to 4 tablespoons milk

1. Heat oven to 400°F. Grease 12 miniature fluted tube cake cups (six 1-cup fluted cups per pan) with shortening.

2. Reserve chocolate syrup packet from brownie mix. In large bowl, beat brownie mix, buttermilk, oil and egg with electric mixer on medium speed 1 minute 30 seconds to 2 minutes or until smooth. Spoon 2 heaping measuring tablespoonfuls of batter into each cup.

3. Bake 10 to 15 minutes or until toothpick inserted in center comes out clean. Cool 5 minutes. Run knife around edge of each doughnut to loosen. Remove from cups; place on wire rack.

4. In small bowl, blend all glaze ingredients until smooth, adding enough milk for desired glazing consistency. Brush or spoon glaze over fluted side of each doughnut. Cut off small corner from chocolate syrup packet; drizzle syrup over doughnuts.

Nutrition Information Per Serving: Calories 270 • Total Fat 9g • Saturated Fat 2.5g • Trans Fat 0.5g • Cholesterol 20mg • Sodium 110mg • Total Carbohydrate 45g • Dietary Fiber 1g • Sugars 37g • Protein 2g. **Dietary Exchanges:** 1 Starch • 2 Other Carbohydrate • 1½ Fat.

roasted chicken nachos

READY TO SERVE: 25 MINUTES
SERVINGS: 8

✳ **super fast**

- 8 oz. tortilla chips
- ¾ cup chunky style salsa
- 1 (15-oz.) can black beans, drained, rinsed
- 3 frozen charbroiled mesquite chicken breast patties, thawed, chopped
- 1 tomato, chopped
- 8 oz. finely shredded Mexican natural cheese blend (2 cups)

1. Heat oven to 400°F. Line 15x10x1-inch baking pan with foil. Spread half of tortilla chips evenly in foil-lined pan.

2. In medium bowl, combine salsa and beans; mix well. Spoon half of bean mixture over chips. Top with half each of chicken, tomato and cheese. Repeat layers.

3. Bake at 400°F for 12 to 14 minutes or until cheese is melted. Serve immediately.

Nutrition Information Per Serving: Calories 360 • Total Fat 19g • Saturated Fat 8g • Cholesterol 40mg • Sodium 780mg • Total Carbohydrate 29g • Dietary Fiber 4g • Sugars 2g • Protein 18g. **Dietary Exchanges:** 2 Starch • 1½ Medium-Fat Meat • 2 Fat OR 2 Carbohydrate • 1½ Medium-Fat Meat • 2 Fat.

grands!® strawberry shortcakes

READY TO SERVE: 30 MINUTES
SERVINGS: 5

shortcakes

- 1 (10.2-oz.) can Pillsbury® Grands!® Refrigerated Buttermilk Biscuits (5 biscuits)
- 2 tablespoons margarine or butter, melted
- ¼ cup sugar

strawberry mixture

- 1½ pints fresh strawberries, sliced (3 cups)
- ⅓ cup sugar

sweetened whipped cream

- ½ cup whipping cream
- 2 tablespoons sugar
- ¼ teaspoon vanilla, if desired

1. Heat oven to 375°F. Separate dough into 5 biscuits. Dip tops and sides of each biscuit in margarine; dip in ¼ cup sugar. Place on ungreased cookie sheet. Bake at 375°F for 13 to 17 minutes or until golden brown. Cool 5 minutes.

2. Meanwhile, in medium bowl, combine sliced strawberries and ⅓ cup sugar; mix well. Set aside.

3. In another small bowl, beat whipping cream and 2 tablespoons sugar until soft peaks form. Beat in vanilla.

4. To serve, split biscuits; place on individual dessert plates. Top with sweetened whipped cream and strawberry mixture.

Nutrition Information Per Serving: Calories 460 • Total Fat 22g • Saturated Fat 9g • Cholesterol 35mg • Sodium 660mg • Total Carbohydrate 60g • Dietary Fiber 3g • Sugars 39g • Protein 5g. **Dietary Exchanges:** 2 Starch • 2 Fruit • 4 Fat OR 4 Carbohydrate • 4 Fat.

crab-filled crescent snacks

crab-filled crescent snacks

PREP TIME: 25 MINUTES
READY TO SERVE: 45 MINUTES
SERVINGS: 32 SNACKS

1 (6-oz.) can crabmeat, rinsed, well drained

1 (3-oz.) pkg. cream cheese, softened

2 tablespoons sliced green onions

¼ teaspoon garlic salt

2 (8-oz.) cans Pillsbury® Refrigerated Crescent Dinner Rolls

1 egg yolk

1 tablespoon water

1 teaspoon sesame seed

1. Heat oven to 375°F. Spray large cookie sheet with cooking spray. In small bowl, combine crabmeat, cream cheese, green onions and garlic salt; mix well.

2. Separate both cans of dough into 16 triangles. Cut each triangle in half lengthwise to make 32 triangles.

3. Place 1 teaspoon crab mixture on center of each triangle about 1 inch from short side. Fold short ends of each triangle over filling; pinch sides to seal. Roll up. Place on sprayed cookie sheet.

4. In small bowl, combine egg yolk and water; mix well. Brush egg mixture over snacks. Sprinkle with sesame seed. Discard any remaining egg mixture.

5. Bake at 375°F for 15 to 20 minutes or until golden brown. Serve warm.

Nutrition Information Per Serving: Calories 65 • Total Fat 3g • Saturated Fat 1g • Cholesterol 15mg • Sodium 200mg • Total Carbohydrate 7g • Dietary Fiber 0g • Sugars 2g • Protein 2g. **Dietary Exchanges:** ½ Starch • ½ Fat OR ½ Carbohydrate • ½ Fat.

sweet apple dumplings

PREP TIME: 20 MINUTES
READY TO SERVE: 55 MINUTES
SERVINGS: 8

filling

4 cups coarsely chopped apples

½ cup sugar

½ teaspoon cinnamon

¼ teaspoon nutmeg

dumplings

1 (16.3-oz.) can Pillsbury® Grands!® Refrigerated Flaky Biscuits

syrup

1½ cups water

2 tablespoons all-purpose flour

¾ cup firmly packed brown sugar

½ cup corn syrup

2 tablespoons margarine or butter

¼ teaspoon cinnamon

⅛ teaspoon nutmeg

1. Heat oven to 375°F. In medium bowl, combine all filling ingredients.

2. Separate dough into 8 biscuits. Press or roll each biscuit to form 6-inch round. Place ½ cup of filling on center of each biscuit; stretch dough around mixture, completely covering fruit. Pinch to seal. Place seam side down in ungreased 13x9-inch (3-quart) glass baking dish.

3. In medium saucepan, combine water and flour; blend thoroughly. Stir in all remaining syrup ingredients. Bring to a boil, stirring occasionally. Pour syrup evenly over dumplings, completely coating each.

4. Bake at 375°F for 25 to 35 minutes or until deep golden brown. To serve, spoon warm dumplings and syrup into individual dessert dishes.

Nutrition Information Per Serving: Calories 460 • Total Fat 12g • Saturated Fat 3g • Cholesterol 0mg • Sodium 620mg • Total Carbohydrate 84g • Dietary Fiber 3g • Sugars 51g • Protein 4g. **Dietary Exchanges:** 1½ Starch • 4 Fruit • 2½ Fat OR 5½ Carbohydrate • 2½ Fat.

NEWS ON NUTMEG

A pinch of nutmeg adds a down-home, spiced touch to the Sweet Apple Dumplings above. For the freshest flavor, consider purchasing whole rather than ground nutmeg. Whole nutmeg is grated on a special small-hole nutmeg grater, available at specialty cooking shops. Garnish the finished apple dumplings with just a tiny sprinkle of the freshly grated spice.

fabulous fudge pie

PREP TIME: 20 MINUTES
READY TO SERVE: 50 MINUTES
SERVINGS: 10

1 Pillsbury® Pet-Ritz™ frozen deep-dish pie crust (from 12-oz. pkg.)

½ cup butter or margarine, softened

¾ cup packed brown sugar

3 eggs

1 (12-oz.) pkg. semisweet chocolate chips, melted

2 teaspoons instant coffee (dry)

1 teaspoon vanilla

½ cup all-purpose flour

1 cup coarsely chopped walnuts

Whipped cream or ice cream, if desired

1. Heat oven to 375°F. Partially bake pie crust 5 to 7 minutes.

2. Meanwhile, in large bowl, beat butter and brown sugar on medium speed until light and fluffy. Beat in eggs, one at a time, beating well after each addition. Add melted chocolate, dry coffee and vanilla; mix well. Stir in flour and walnuts.

3. Pour mixture into partially baked crust. Bake 25 to 30 minutes or until set. Serve warm with whipped cream or ice cream, if desired.

Nutrition Information Per Serving: Calories 510 • Total Fat 32g • Saturated Fat 13g • Cholesterol 90mg • Sodium 150mg • Total Carbohydrate 51g • Dietary Fiber 3g • Sugars 35g • Protein 7g. **Dietary Exchanges:** 2 Starch • 1½ Other Carbohydrate • 6 Fat.

individual cheesy apple crisps

PREP TIME: 30 MINUTES
READY TO SERVE: 55 MINUTES
SERVINGS: 6

3 slices Cheddar cheese (0.75 oz. each)

4 cups sliced peeled apples (4 medium)

½ cup granulated sugar

½ teaspoon ground cinnamon

1 tablespoon lemon juice

½ cup all-purpose flour

½ cup old-fashioned oats

¼ cup packed brown sugar

¼ cup butter or margarine

1. Heat oven to 375°F. Using seasonal cookie cutters, cut 2 shapes from each cheese slice. Cover; refrigerate. Chop remaining cheese scraps; set aside.

2. In large bowl, toss apples, granulated sugar, cinnamon and lemon juice to coat apple slices. In medium bowl, mix flour, oats and brown sugar. Using pastry blender or fork, cut in butter until mixture is consistency of coarse crumbs. Spoon apple mixture into each of 6 ungreased 6-ounce custard cups. Top with chopped cheese; sprinkle with crumb mixture. Place cups in 15x10x1-inch pan.

3. Bake 18 to 25 minutes or until apples are tender and topping is golden brown. Top each with cheese cutout; bake 1 to 2 minutes longer or until cheese begins to melt.

Nutrition Information Per Serving: Calories 320 • Total Fat 12g • Saturated Fat 7g • Trans Fat 0.5g • Cholesterol 30mg • Sodium 125mg • Total Carbohydrate 48g • Dietary Fiber 2g • Sugars 33g • Protein 5g. **Dietary Exchanges:** 1 Starch • ½ Fruit • 1½ Other Carbohydrate • 2½ Fat.

APPLE OPTIONS

Granny Smith apples work well in crisps. They keep their firm, crunchy texture and do not turn mushy as they bake. Granny Smith apples also have a tart taste, which complements the sweet, sugary topping of the crisp.

curried chicken turnovers

PREP TIME: 15 MINUTES
READY TO SERVE: 40 MINUTES
SERVINGS: 14 APPETIZERS

⅓ cup raisins

⅓ cup sour cream

¼ cup mango chutney

1¼ teaspoons curry powder

1 (5-oz.) can chunk chicken in water, drained

1 (15-oz.) pkg. Pillsbury® Refrigerated Pie Crusts, softened as directed on package

1. Heat oven to 400°F. In medium bowl, combine all ingredients except pie crusts; mix well.

2. Remove pie crusts from pouches. Unfold crusts; press out fold lines. With 3½-inch round cutter, cut 14 rounds from crusts.

3. Place about 1 tablespoon chicken mixture in center of each dough round. Brush edge of each round with water. Fold in half over filling; press edges with fork to seal. Place on ungreased cookie sheet.

4. Bake at 400°F for 18 to 23 minutes or until light golden brown. Serve warm.

Nutrition Information Per Serving: Calories 105 • Total Fat 5g • Saturated Fat 3g • Cholesterol 15mg • Sodium 90mg • Total Carbohydrate 12g • Dietary Fiber 0g • Sugars 0g • Protein 3g. **Dietary Exchanges:** 1 Starch • ½ Fat OR 1 Carbohydrate • ½ Fat.

fudgy triple-chocolate pudding cake

PREP TIME: 15 MINUTES
READY TO SERVE: 1 HOUR 30 MINUTES
SERVINGS: 9

JANICE KOLLAR ✳ WOODBRIDGE, NEW JERSEY
BAKE-OFF® CONTEST 39, 2000

1 (15.8-oz.) box double chocolate brownie mix with chocolate syrup

½ teaspoon baking powder

½ cup milk

¼ cup butter or margarine, melted

1 teaspoon vanilla

1½ cups water

1½ teaspoons instant espresso coffee granules

1 cup chocolate fudge creamy ready-to-spread frosting (from 1-lb. container)

Whipped cream or vanilla ice cream

1. Heat oven to 350°F. Spray 9- or 8-inch square pan with cooking spray. In large bowl, mix brownie mix and baking powder. Stir in milk, butter, vanilla and chocolate syrup from packet in brownie mix. Spread batter in pan.

2. In 2-quart saucepan, heat water to boiling. Add espresso granules; stir to dissolve. Add frosting; cook over low heat, stirring frequently, until melted and smooth. Slowly pour over batter in pan. Do not stir.

3. Bake 40 to 45 minutes or until edges are bubbly and cake begins to pull away from sides of pan (top may appear shiny in spots). Cool 30 minutes before serving. Serve warm or cold with whipped cream or ice cream. Store cake in refrigerator.

Nutrition Information Per Serving: Calories 410 • Total Fat 18g • Saturated Fat 11g • Trans Fat 1g • Cholesterol 15mg • Sodium 200mg • Total Carbohydrate 59g • Dietary Fiber 2g • Sugars 46g • Protein 3g. **Dietary Exchanges:** 1 Starch • 3 Other Carbohydrate • 3½ Fat.

SWEET FINALE

For a final burst of color and flavor, accent a decadent chocolate dessert with whipped cream or ice cream, then top it all off with chocolate shavings. Simply use a hand grater to shave a cool, firm block of bittersweet or semisweet chocolate. As you grate, remove the chocolate shavings from the hand grater frequently to prevent it from becoming clogged.

chocolate chip cookies

READY TO SERVE: 40 MINUTES
SERVINGS: 3 DOZEN COOKIES

¾ cup firmly packed brown sugar

½ cup sugar

½ cup margarine or butter, softened

½ cup shortening

1½ teaspoons vanilla

1 egg

1¾ cups all-purpose flour

1 teaspoon baking soda

½ teaspoon salt

1 (6-oz.) pkg. semisweet chocolate chips (1 cup)

½ cup chopped nuts or shelled sunflower seeds, if desired

1. Heat oven to 375°F. In large bowl, combine brown sugar, sugar, margarine and shortening; beat until light and fluffy. Add vanilla and egg; blend well.

2. Add flour, baking soda and salt; mix well. Stir in chocolate chips and nuts. Drop dough by rounded teaspoonfuls 2 inches apart onto ungreased cookie sheets.

3. Bake at 375°F for 8 to 10 minutes or until light golden brown. Cool 1 minute; remove from cookie sheets.

Nutrition Information Per Serving: Calories 140 • Total Fat 8g • Saturated Fat 2g • Cholesterol 5mg • Sodium 100mg • Total Carbohydrate 15g • Dietary Fiber 1g • Sugars 10g • Protein 1g. **Dietary Exchanges:** ½ Starch • ½ Fruit • 1½ Fat OR 1 Carbohydrate • 1½ Fat.

blueberry crumble

PREP TIME: 10 MINUTES
READY TO SERVE: 40 MINUTES
SERVINGS: 6

fruit mixture

4 cups fresh or frozen blueberries

¼ cup raisins

2 tablespoons cornstarch

1 teaspoon grated lemon peel

1 tablespoon lemon juice

⅓ cup apricot preserves

topping

½ cup all-purpose flour

½ cup firmly packed brown sugar

1 teaspoon cinnamon

¼ cup margarine or butter, softened

Whipped topping or vanilla ice cream, if desired

1. Heat oven to 400°F. Grease 10x6-inch (1½-quart) or 8-inch square (2-quart) baking dish. In large bowl, combine blueberries, raisins, cornstarch, lemon peel and lemon juice; mix well. Spoon mixture evenly into greased baking dish. Dot with apricot preserves.

2. In medium bowl, combine flour, brown sugar and cinnamon; mix well. With pastry blender or fork, cut in margarine until mixture is crumbly. Sprinkle topping evenly over fruit mixture.

3. Bake at 400°F for 20 to 30 minutes or until topping is golden brown. Serve warm or at room temperature. If desired, top with whipped topping or ice cream.

Nutrition Information Per Serving: Calories 320 • Total Fat 8g • Saturated Fat 1g • Cholesterol 0mg • Sodium 110mg • Total Carbohydrate 59g • Dietary Fiber 4g • Sugars 38g • Protein 2g. **Dietary Exchanges:** 1 Starch • 3 Fruit • 1½ Fat OR 4 Carbohydrate • 1½ Fat.

raspberry-sauced fresh pear dumplings

READY TO SERVE: 45 MINUTES
SERVINGS: 8

dumplings

2 firm ripe pears, peeled, cored and coarsely chopped

¼ cup golden raisins

¼ cup firmly packed brown sugar

1 Pillsbury® Refrigerated Pie Crust (from 15-oz. pkg.), softened as directed on package

1 tablespoon milk

1 tablespoon sugar

sauce

1 (10-oz.) pkg. frozen raspberries in syrup, thawed

3 tablespoons sugar

1 teaspoon cornstarch

1. Heat oven to 425°F. In medium bowl, combine pears, golden raisins and brown sugar; mix well.

2. Remove pie crusts from pouches. Unfold crusts; cut each into quarters. Place about ⅓ cup pear mixture on each crust quarter. Brush crust edges lightly with water. Bring sides of each crust up to top of pears; press edges to seal, making 3 seams.

3. With pancake turner, carefully place each dumpling seam side up in ungreased 15x10x1-inch baking pan. Brush with milk. Sprinkle with 1 tablespoon sugar.

4. Bake at 425°F for 15 to 20 minutes or until deep golden brown. Cool on wire rack for 10 minutes.

5. Meanwhile, place raspberries in food processor bowl with metal blade or blender container; process until smooth. If desired, place strainer over small saucepan; pour raspberries into strainer. Press berries with back of spoon through strainer to remove seeds; discard seeds. Add 3 tablespoons sugar and cornstarch to raspberries in saucepan; cook over medium heat until mixture comes to a boil, stirring constantly. Place in freezer for 5 to 10 minutes to cool quickly.

6. To serve, spoon raspberry sauce evenly onto individual dessert plates. Top each with dumpling.

Nutrition Information Per Serving: Calories 370 • Total Fat 14g • Saturated Fat 6g • Cholesterol 15mg • Sodium 210mg • Total Carbohydrate 59g • Dietary Fiber 3g • Sugars 30g • Protein 2g. **Dietary Exchanges:** ½ Starch • 3½ Fruit • 2½ Fat OR 4 Carbohydrate • 2½ Fat.

scandinavian almond bars

PREP TIME: 10 MINUTES
READY TO SERVE: 1 HOUR 5 MINUTES
SERVINGS: 48 BARS

1 (16.5-oz.) roll refrigerated sugar cookies

½ teaspoon ground cinnamon

1 teaspoon almond extract

1 egg white

1 tablespoon water

1 cup sliced almonds

¼ cup sugar

1. Heat oven to 350°F. Grease 15x10x1-inch pan with shortening. In large bowl, break up cookie dough. Add cinnamon and almond extract; mix well. With floured fingers, press dough mixture evenly in bottom of pan.

2. In small bowl, beat egg white and water until frothy. Brush over dough. Sprinkle evenly with almonds and sugar.

3. Bake 17 to 22 minutes or until edges are golden brown. Cool completely, about 30 minutes. For diamond-shaped bars, cut 5 straight parallel lines about 1½ inches apart down length of pan; cut diagonal lines about 1½ inches apart across straight lines.

Nutrition Information Per Serving: Calories 60 • Total Fat 3g • Saturated Fat 0.5g • Trans Fat 0g • Cholesterol 5mg • Sodium 25mg • Total Carbohydrate 7g • Dietary Fiber 0g • Sugars 4g • Protein 0g. **Dietary Exchanges:** ½ Other Carbohydrate • ½ Fat.

raspberry-sauced fresh pear dumplings

easy lemon cheesecake

PREP TIME: 10 MINUTES
READY TO SERVE: 4 HOURS 10 MINUTES
SERVINGS: 16

AMELIA VILLERS ✳ LEE'S SUMMIT, MISSOURI
BAKE-OFF® CONTEST 36, 1994

crust

1 (18.25-oz.) box lemon or yellow cake mix with pudding

½ cup butter or margarine, softened

filling

2 (8-oz.) pkg. cream cheese, softened

3 eggs

1 (8-oz.) container lemon yogurt

1 (1-lb.) container lemon creamy ready-to-spread frosting

1. Heat oven to 325°F. Lightly grease bottom only of a 9- or 10-inch springform pan with shortening. In large bowl, beat cake mix and butter with electric mixer on low speed until crumbly. Reserve 1 cup crumb mixture for topping. With floured fingers, press remaining crumb mixture in bottom and 1½ inches up side of pan.

2. In same bowl, beat all filling ingredients on medium speed until smooth. Pour into crust-lined pan. Sprinkle reserved crumb mixture evenly over filling.

3. Bake 1 hour to 1 hour 30 minutes or just until center is set and edge is golden brown. Cool on wire rack 30 minutes.

4. Run knife around side of pan to loosen; remove side of pan. Refrigerate at least 2 hours before serving. Store cheesecake in refrigerator.

Nutrition Information Per Serving: Calories 440 • Total Fat 24g • Saturated Fat 15g • Trans Fat 1g • Cholesterol 90mg • Sodium 370mg • Total Carbohydrate 50g • Dietary Fiber 0g • Sugars 43g • Protein 5g. **Dietary Exchanges:** 3½ Other Carbohydrate • ½ High-Fat Meat • 4 Fat.

gingerbread with lemon sauce

PREP TIME: 20 MINUTES
READY TO SERVE: 50 MINUTES
SERVINGS: 9

gingerbread

- 1 cup all-purpose flour
- 1/3 cup wheat germ
- 1/4 cup firmly packed brown sugar
- 1/2 teaspoon baking powder
- 1/2 teaspoon baking soda
- 3/4 teaspoon ginger
- 3/4 teaspoon cinnamon
- 1/2 teaspoon allspice
- 1/2 cup unsweetened apple juice
- 1/3 cup molasses
- 1/4 cup oil
- 1 egg

sauce

- 1/4 cup sugar
- 2 teaspoons cornstarch
- 1/2 cup hot water
- 1 tablespoon lemon juice
- 1 teaspoon grated lemon peel

1. Heat oven to 350°F. Grease bottom only of an 8-inch square pan. In large bowl, combine flour, wheat germ, brown sugar, baking powder, baking soda, ginger, cinnamon and allspice; mix well. Add all remaining gingerbread ingredients; blend well. Pour into greased pan.

2. Bake at 350°F for 30 to 40 minutes or until toothpick inserted in the center comes out clean.

3. Meanwhile, in medium saucepan, combine sugar and cornstarch. Gradually stir in hot water. Cook over medium heat until mixture comes to a boil and is slightly thickened and clear, stirring constantly. Stir in lemon juice and lemon peel. Serve warm sauce over warm gingerbread.

Nutrition Information Per Serving: Calories 220 • Total Fat 7g • Saturated Fat 1g • Cholesterol 25mg • Sodium 115mg • Total Carbohydrate 35g • Dietary Fiber 1g • Sugars 20g • Protein 3g. **Dietary Exchanges:** 1 Starch • 1 1/2 Fruit • 1 Fat OR 2 1/2 Carbohydrate • 1 Fat.

RECIPE FOR SUCCESS

Unless you're an expert baker, stick precisely to the recipe when preparing a cake. For instance, it really does matter whether you preheat the oven to the right temperature or use the specified size of cake pan. It is equally important to measure the ingredients accurately and add them in the correct order. Also, follow the recipe's instructions for cooling the cake.

milk chocolate-butterscotch café cookies

PREP TIME: 20 MINUTES
READY TO SERVE: 40 MINUTES
SERVINGS: 9 COOKIES

- 1 (18-oz.) pkg. Pillsbury® Refrigerated Sugar Cookies
- 1/3 cup firmly packed brown sugar
- 1 teaspoon vanilla
- 3/4 cup old-fashioned rolled oats
- 1/2 cup butterscotch chips
- 2 (1.55-oz.) milk chocolate candy bars, unwrapped, finely chopped

1. Heat oven to 350°F. Spray 1 large or 2 small cookie sheets with cooking spray. Break up cookie dough into large bowl. Add brown sugar and vanilla; mix well. Add oats, chips and chocolate; mix well. (Dough will be stiff.)

2. Drop dough by rounded 1/4 cupfuls 2 inches apart onto sprayed cookie sheet. Flatten to 1/2-inch thickness.

3. Bake at 350°F for 13 to 18 minutes or until cookies are slightly puffed and edges are golden brown. Cool 1 minute; remove from cookie sheet.

Nutrition Information Per Serving: Calories 400 • Total Fat 16g • Saturated Fat 7g • Cholesterol 15mg • Sodium 220mg • Total Carbohydrate 59g • Dietary Fiber 2g • Sugars 38g • Protein 4g. **Dietary Exchanges:** 1 1/2 Starch • 2 1/2 Fruit • 3 Fat OR 4 Carbohydrate • 3 Fat.

caramel apple cobbler

PREP TIME: 25 MINUTES
READY TO SERVE: 50 MINUTES
SERVINGS: 10

MARGARET BLAKELY ✳ NEW PHILADELPHIA, OHIO
BAKE-OFF® CONTEST 27, 1976

3 cups chunky applesauce
(from 48-oz. jar)

1 (12-oz.) jar caramel topping
(1 cup)

¾ cup coconut

¼ cup sugar

1 (12-oz.) can refrigerated
original or buttermilk flaky
biscuits

3 tablespoons butter or
margarine, melted

Vanilla ice cream or
whipped cream, if desired

1. Heat oven to 400°F. In ungreased 13x9-inch (3-quart) glass baking dish, mix applesauce and caramel topping.

2. Bake 10 to 15 minutes or until hot and bubbly around edges. Meanwhile, in small bowl, mix coconut and sugar.

3. Remove baking dish from oven. Separate dough into 10 biscuits. Cut each in half crosswise. Dip each biscuit half in melted butter; roll in coconut mixture to coat. Arrange biscuit halves, cut side down, over hot applesauce mixture. Sprinkle any remaining coconut mixture over biscuits.

4. Bake 20 to 25 minutes longer or until biscuits are golden brown. Serve warm with ice cream or whipped cream, if desired.

Nutrition Information Per Serving: Calories 330 • Total Fat 10g • Saturated Fat 5g • Trans Fat 1.5g • Cholesterol 10mg • Sodium 520mg • Total Carbohydrate 59g • Dietary Fiber 1g • Sugars 39g • Protein 3g. Dietary Exchanges: 1 Starch • 3 Other Carbohydrate • 1½ Fat.

chocolate chip cookie bars

READY TO SERVE: 40 MINUTES
SERVINGS: 36 BARS

¾ cup firmly packed brown
sugar

½ cup sugar

½ cup margarine or butter,
softened

½ cup shortening

1½ teaspoons vanilla

1 egg

1¾ cups all-purpose flour

1 teaspoon baking soda

½ teaspoon salt

1 (6-oz.) pkg. semisweet
chocolate chips (1 cup)

½ cup chopped nuts or shelled
sunflower seeds, if desired

1. Heat oven to 375°F. In large bowl, combine brown sugar, sugar, margarine and shortening; beat until light and fluffy. Add vanilla and egg; blend well.

2. Add flour, baking soda and salt; mix well. Stir in chocolate chips and nuts. Spread dough in ungreased 13x9-inch pan.

3. Bake at 375°F for 15 to 25 minutes or until light golden brown. Cool completely. Cut into bars.

Nutrition Information Per Serving: Calories 140 • Total Fat 8g • Saturated Fat 2g • Cholesterol 5mg • Sodium 100mg • Total Carbohydrate 15g • Dietary Fiber 1g • Sugars 10g • Protein 1g. Dietary Exchanges: ½ Starch • ½ Fruit • 1½ Fat OR 1 Carbohydrate • 1½ Fat.

CHIPS CHOICES

Baking chips come in all kinds of deliciously different flavors these days. For a fun flavor alternative, substitute 1 cup white chocolate, caramel or peanut butter chips for the chocolate chips called for in the recipe above.

cherry cheesecake dessert

PREP TIME: 15 MINUTES
READY TO SERVE: 1 HOUR 15 MINUTES
SERVINGS: 12

filling
1 (8-oz.) pkg. cream cheese, softened
¼ cup sugar
1 tablespoon all-purpose flour
½ teaspoon vanilla
1 egg
crust
1 (18-oz.) pkg. Pillsbury® Refrigerated Sugar Cookies
topping
2 (21-oz.) cans cherry pie filling
½ teaspoon almond extract

1. Heat oven to 375°F. In small bowl, combine all of the filling ingredients; beat until well blended.

2. Remove cookie dough from wrapper. With floured fingers, press dough evenly in bottom of ungreased 13x9-inch pan to form crust. Spoon and spread filling over crust.

3. Bake at 375°F for 17 to 20 minutes or until edges begin to brown. Cool 40 minutes or until completely cooled.

4. Meanwhile, in medium bowl, combine topping ingredients; mix well. Spread over top. Cut into squares. Store in refrigerator.

Nutrition Information Per Serving: Calories 380 • Total Fat 14g • Saturated Fat 6g • Cholesterol 45mg • Sodium 240mg • Total Carbohydrate 60g • Dietary Fiber 1g • Sugars 42g • Protein 4g. **Dietary Exchanges:** 1 Starch • 3 Fruit • 2½ Fat OR 4 Carbohydrate • 2½ Fat.

blackberry-cherry cobbler

PREP TIME: 20 MINUTES
READY TO SERVE: 50 MINUTES
SERVINGS: 10

filling
2 cups frozen blackberries
1 (21-oz.) can cherry fruit pie filling
¼ teaspoon cinnamon
topping
1 (12-oz.) can Pillsbury® Golden Layers™ Refrigerated Flaky Biscuits
¼ cup sugar
½ teaspoon cinnamon
2 tablespoons margarine or butter, melted
¼ cup sliced almonds
1 cup half-and-half, if desired

1. Heat oven to 350°F. In medium saucepan, combine all filling ingredients. Cook over medium heat until mixture is bubbly and hot, stirring occasionally. Pour into ungreased 12x8-inch (2-quart) glass baking dish.

2. Separate dough into 10 biscuits. In small bowl, combine sugar and ½ teaspoon cinnamon. Dip each biscuit in margarine; dip in sugar mixture. Arrange biscuits over hot fruit mixture around edge of baking dish. Sprinkle with almonds and any remaining sugar mixture.

3. Bake at 350°F for 20 to 30 minutes or until biscuits are golden brown. Serve warm with half-and-half.

Nutrition Information Per Serving: Calories 305 • Total Fat 10g • Saturated Fat 0g • Cholesterol 9mg • Sodium 340mg • Total Carbohydrate 50g • Dietary Fiber 0g • Sugars 0g • Protein 4g. **Dietary Exchanges:** 1 Starch • 2 Fruit • 2 Fat OR 3 Carbohydrate • 2 Fat.

aloha peach pies

aloha peach pies

PREP TIME: 10 MINUTES
READY TO SERVE: 45 MINUTES
SERVINGS: 2

CANDACE McMENAMIN ✻ LEXINGTON, SOUTH CAROLINA
BAKE-OFF® CONTEST 42, 2006

2 refrigerated buttermilk biscuits (twin-pack from 21-oz. pkg.)

1 cup organic frozen sliced peaches (from 10-oz. bag), thawed as directed on bag

2 big refrigerated white chunk macadamia nut cookies (from 18-oz. pkg.)

2 tablespoons cinnamon-flavored chips

2 tablespoons flaked coconut

1 pint vanilla ice cream, if desired (2 cups)

1. Heat oven to 350°F (325°F for dark cookie sheet). Spray cookie sheet with cooking spray. Place biscuits 3 inches apart on cookie sheet. Press each into 5-inch round with ¼-inch-high rim around outer edge.

2. For each pie, spoon half of peaches onto biscuit. Crumble 1 cookie dough round evenly over peaches. Top with 1 tablespoon chips and 1 tablespoon coconut.

3. Bake 22 to 28 minutes or until edges are deep golden brown. Cool 5 minutes. Serve warm with ice cream.

Nutrition Information Per Serving: Calories 540 • Total Fat 27g • Saturated Fat 10g • Trans Fat 6g • Cholesterol 10mg • Sodium 670mg • Total Carbohydrate 68g • Dietary Fiber 2g • Sugars 37g • Protein 8g. **Dietary Exchanges:** 2 Starch • 1 Fruit • 1½ Other Carbohydrate • 5 Fat.

luscious lemon bars

PREP TIME: 15 MINUTES
READY TO SERVE: 1 HOUR 35 MINUTES
SERVINGS: 36 BARS

✻ plan ahead

crust
1 (18-oz.) pkg. Pillsbury® Refrigerated Sugar Cookies

filling
4 eggs, slightly beaten

1½ cups sugar

¼ cup all-purpose flour

1 teaspoon baking powder

¼ cup lemon juice

garnish
1 to 2 tablespoons powdered sugar

1. Heat oven to 350°F. Cut cookie dough into slices as directed on package. Arrange slices in bottom of ungreased 13x9-inch pan. With lightly floured fingers, press dough evenly in pan to form crust.

2. Bake at 350°F for 15 to 20 minutes or until light golden brown.

3. Meanwhile, in large bowl, combine eggs, sugar, flour and baking powder; blend well. Stir in lemon juice.

4. Remove partially baked crust from oven. Pour egg mixture over warm crust.

5. Return to oven; bake an additional 20 to 30 minutes or until top is light golden brown. Cool 30 minutes or until completely cooled. Sprinkle with powdered sugar. Cut into bars.

Nutrition Information Per Serving: Calories 100 • Total Fat 3g • Saturated Fat 1g • Cholesterol 25mg • Sodium 70mg • Total Carbohydrate 18g • Dietary Fiber 0g • Sugars 13g • Protein 1g. **Dietary Exchanges:** 1 Starch • ½ Fat OR 1 Carbohydrate • ½ Fat.

simple fruit crisp

PREP TIME: 10 MINUTES
READY TO SERVE: 40 MINUTES
SERVINGS: 8

fruit

1 (21-oz.) can fruit pie filling (apple, apricot, cherry, blueberry, peach or raspberry)

topping

¾ cup all-purpose flour

⅓ cup firmly packed brown sugar

½ teaspoon cinnamon, if desired

½ teaspoon nutmeg, if desired

¼ cup margarine or butter, softened

1. Heat oven to 375°F. Spread the pie filling in ungreased 8-inch square (2-quart) baking dish.

2. In medium bowl, combine all topping ingredients; mix until crumbly. Sprinkle over pie filling.

3. Bake at 375°F for 25 to 30 minutes or until bubbly and golden brown. If desired, serve warm with frozen yogurt or whipped topping.

Nutrition Information Per Serving: Calories 220 • Total Fat 6g • Saturated Fat 1g • Cholesterol 0mg • Sodium 75mg • Total Carbohydrate 40g • Dietary Fiber 1g • Sugars 28g • Protein 2g. **Dietary Exchanges:** 1 Starch • 1½ Fruit • 1 Fat OR 2½ Carbohydrate • 1 Fat.

rocky road cookie pizza

PREP TIME: 10 MINUTES
READY TO SERVE: 1 HOUR 10 MINUTES
SERVINGS: 12

crust

1 (18-oz.) pkg. Pillsbury® Refrigerated Sugar Cookies

topping

½ cup salted peanuts

1 cup miniature marshmallows

1 (6-oz.) pkg. semisweet chocolate chips (1 cup)

⅓ cup caramel ice cream topping

1. Heat oven to 350°F. Grease 12-inch pizza pan or spray with cooking spray. With floured fingers, press dough evenly in bottom of greased pan.

2. Bake at 350°F for 15 to 20 minutes or until light golden brown.

3. Remove partially baked crust from oven. Sprinkle peanuts, marshmallows and chocolate chips evenly over crust. Drizzle with caramel topping.

4. Return to oven; bake an additional 8 to 10 minutes or until topping is melted. Cool 30 minutes or until completely cooled. Cut into wedges or squares.

Nutrition Information Per Serving: Calories 325 • Total Fat 13g • Saturated Fat 4g • Cholesterol 0mg • Sodium 210mg • Total Carbohydrate 48g • Dietary Fiber 2g • Sugars 32g • Protein 4g. **Dietary Exchanges:** 1 Starch • 2 Fruit • 3 Fat OR 3 Carbohydrate • 3 Fat.

COOKIE PIZZA CREATIVITY

The cookie pizza recipe above offers room for variation. For example, you could branch out from the rocky road flavor and try different toppings, such as coconut, chocolate candy baking bits, pecans, walnuts or toffee bits.

black-bottom peanut butter pie

PREP TIME: 25 MINUTES
READY TO SERVE: 3 HOURS 25 MINUTES
SERVINGS: 8

CLAUDIA SHEPARDSON ✳ SOUTH YARMOUTH, MASSACHUSETTS
BAKE-OFF® CONTEST 42, 2006

crust

- 1 refrigerated pie crust (from 15-oz. box), softened as directed on box

fudge layer and drizzle

- 1¼ cups dark or semisweet chocolate chips (7½ oz.)
- ½ cup whipping cream
- 2 tablespoons butter

filling

- 1¼ cups milk
- 1 (6-oz.) container French vanilla low-fat yogurt
- 1 (4-serving size) box white chocolate instant pudding and pie filling mix
- 3 tablespoons butter
- 1 (10-oz.) bag peanut butter chips (1⅔ cups)

topping

- 4 peanut butter crunchy granola bars (2 pouches from 8.9-oz. box), crushed (¾ cup)

1. Heat oven to 450°F. Make pie crust as directed on box for One-Crust Baked Shell using 9-inch glass pie plate. Cool on wire rack 20 minutes.

2. Meanwhile, in 1-quart heavy saucepan, mix all fudge layer ingredients. Cook over low heat, stirring constantly, until chips are melted. Remove from heat; stir until smooth. Reserve ¼ cup fudge mixture in small microwavable bowl for drizzle; set remaining mixture aside to cool.

3. In large bowl, beat milk, yogurt and pudding mix with electric mixer on high speed about 3 minutes or until smooth and thickened. Set aside.

4. In another small microwavable bowl, microwave 3 tablespoons butter and the peanut butter chips on high 45 seconds. Stir; if necessary, continue to microwave in 10-second increments, stirring after each, until chips are melted and mixture is smooth. On low speed, gradually beat peanut butter mixture into pudding mixture until combined; beat on high speed until filling is smooth and fluffy, scraping side of bowl occasionally.

5. Spread cooled fudge layer mixture evenly in bottom of cooled baked shell. Carefully spoon and spread filling over fudge layer. Sprinkle crushed granola bars evenly over top. Refrigerate until set, 3 to 4 hours.

6. To serve, microwave reserved fudge mixture on high 15 to 20 seconds or until drizzling consistency. Drizzle over top of pie. Cut into wedges to serve. Store in refrigerator.

Nutrition Information Per Serving: Calories 690 • Total Fat 40g • Saturated Fat 18g • Trans Fat 0.5g • Cholesterol 45mg • Sodium 520mg • Total Carbohydrate 72g • Dietary Fiber 3g • Sugars 48g • Protein 10g. **Dietary Exchanges:** 2 Starch • 3 Other Carbohydrate • ½ High-Fat Meat • 7 Fat.

mexican chocolate-filled cornmeal cookies

READY TO SERVE: 55 MINUTES
SERVINGS: 20 COOKIES

cookies

- 1 (18-oz.) pkg. Pillsbury® Refrigerated Sugar Cookies
- ¼ cup yellow cornmeal
- 20 dark chocolate candy miniatures (from 11-oz. pkg.), unwrapped

glaze

- ⅓ cup cinnamon chips
- 1 teaspoon shortening
  Dash ground red pepper (cayenne), if desired

1. Heat oven to 375°F. Spray cookie sheets with cooking spray. Break up cookie dough into large bowl. Add cornmeal; mix well. Shape rounded tablespoon of dough around each candy, covering completely. Place 2 inches apart on sprayed cookie sheets.

2. Bake at 375°F for 9 to 12 minutes or until edges are light golden brown. Cool 1 minute. Remove from cookie sheets; place on wire rack. Cool 10 minutes or until completely cooled.

3. In small microwave-safe bowl, combine chips and shortening. Microwave on high for 30 to 45 seconds, stirring every 15 seconds until smooth. Stir in ground red pepper. Drizzle glaze over cookies.

Nutrition Information Per Serving: Calories 180 • Total Fat 8g • Saturated Fat 3g • Cholesterol 5mg • Sodium 100mg • Total Carbohydrate 24g • Dietary Fiber 1g • Sugars 14g • Protein 2g. **Dietary Exchanges:** ½ Starch • 1 Fruit • 1½ Fat OR 1½ Carbohydrate • 1½ Fat.

cherry-nut-crescent crisp

PREP TIME: 15 MINUTES
READY TO SERVE: 55 MINUTES
SERVINGS: 12

BETTY CHROMZACK ✳ NORTHLAKE, ILLINOIS
BAKE-OFF® CONTEST 23, 1972

1 cup all-purpose flour

¾ cup chopped pecans

½ cup granulated sugar

½ cup packed brown sugar

1 teaspoon ground cinnamon

½ cup butter or margarine, softened

2 (8-oz.) cans refrigerated crescent dinner rolls

1 (21-oz.) can cherry pie filling

Powdered sugar, if desired

1. Heat oven to 375°F. In medium bowl, mix flour, pecans, granulated sugar, brown sugar, cinnamon and butter until crumbly. Sprinkle ⅓ of crumb mixture evenly in bottom of ungreased 13x9-inch pan.

2. Separate both cans of dough into 4 long rectangles. Place 3 rectangles over crumb mixture in pan; bring dough 1 inch up sides of pan to form crust. Sprinkle half of remaining crumb mixture over dough.

3. Spoon pie filling into crust. Sprinkle with remaining crumb mixture. Cut remaining dough rectangle into strips; place diagonally over pie filling to form a crisscross pattern.

4. Bake 30 to 40 minutes or until golden brown. Sprinkle with powdered sugar; serve warm.

Nutrition Information Per Serving: Calories 420 • Total Fat 21g • Saturated Fat 8g • Trans Fat 2.5g • Cholesterol 20mg • Sodium 350mg • Total Carbohydrate 53g • Dietary Fiber 2g • Sugars 31g • Protein 5g. Dietary Exchanges: 1½ Starch • 2 Other Carbohydrate • 4 Fat.

pineapple upside-down cake

PREP TIME: 20 MINUTES
READY TO SERVE: 1 HOUR
SERVINGS: 6

½ cup firmly packed brown sugar

¼ cup margarine or butter, melted

6 canned pineapple slices, drained

6 maraschino cherries

2 eggs, separated

½ cup sugar

¾ cup all-purpose flour

½ teaspoon baking powder

¼ teaspoon salt

¼ cup pineapple juice

Whipped cream

1. Heat oven to 350°F. In small bowl, combine brown sugar and margarine; blend well. Spread in bottom of ungreased 9-inch round cake pan. Arrange pineapple slices and maraschino cherries over brown sugar mixture. Set aside.

2. In small bowl, beat egg yolks until thick and lemon colored. Gradually add sugar; beat well. Add flour, baking powder, salt and pineapple juice; mix well.

3. In another small bowl, beat egg whites until stiff peaks form. Fold into batter. Pour batter evenly over pineapple slices and cherries.

4. Bake at 350°F for 30 to 35 minutes or until toothpick inserted in center comes out clean. Cool upright in pan 2 minutes. Invert cake onto serving plate. Serve warm with whipped cream.

Nutrition Information Per Serving: Calories 370 • Total Fat 15g • Saturated Fat 5g • Cholesterol 90mg • Sodium 250mg • Total Carbohydrate 55g • Dietary Fiber 1g • Sugars 43g • Protein 4g. Dietary Exchanges: 1 Starch • 2½ Fruit • 3 Fat OR 3½ Carbohydrate • 3 Fat.

GARNISHING CAKE PLATES

For a little weeknight flair, drizzle individual cake plates with raspberry ice cream topping or chocolate syrup before adding each slice of cake. You can also use vanilla pudding that you've thinned with milk or chocolate chips you've melted in the microwave. Make swirls, zigzags, polka dots or other designs, then set a slice of cake on the decorated plate.

coconut-pineapple tart

PREP TIME: 15 MINUTES
READY TO SERVE: 1 HOUR 5 MINUTES
SERVINGS: 12

MARY ANN LEE ✽ MARCO ISLAND, FLORIDA
BAKE-OFF® CONTEST 38, 1998

1 refrigerated pie crust (from 15-oz. box), softened as directed on box

½ cup pineapple preserves

½ cup sliced almonds, toasted

2 egg whites

¼ cup sugar

1 cup shredded coconut

½ teaspoon vanilla

1. Heat oven to 400°F. Remove pie crust from pouch; unroll on ungreased cookie sheet. Fold in crust edge 1 inch to form border; flute. Spread preserves evenly over crust; sprinkle with almonds.

2. In small bowl, beat egg whites with electric mixer on high speed until slightly thickened. Gradually add sugar, beating until soft peaks form. Fold in coconut and vanilla. Spread over almonds.

3. Bake 15 to 20 minutes or until crust is light golden brown and top is lightly toasted. Cool 30 minutes. Serve warm or cool.

Nutrition Information Per Serving: Calories 200 • Total Fat 10g • Saturated Fat 4.5g • Trans Fat 0g • Cholesterol 0mg • Sodium 105mg • Total Carbohydrate 27g • Dietary Fiber 1g • Sugars 14g • Protein 2g. Dietary Exchanges: ½ Starch • 1 Other Carbohydrate • 2 Fat.

double chocolate chip cookies

READY TO SERVE: 30 MINUTES
SERVINGS: 24 COOKIES

½ cup firmly packed brown sugar

¼ cup margarine or butter, softened

½ teaspoon vanilla

1 egg white

1 cup all-purpose flour

3 tablespoons unsweetened cocoa

½ teaspoon baking soda

⅛ teaspoon salt

½ cup semisweet chocolate chips

1. Heat oven to 375°F. In large bowl, combine brown sugar and margarine; beat until light and fluffy. Add vanilla and egg white; blend well.

2. Add flour, cocoa, baking soda and salt; mix well. Stir in chocolate chips. Drop dough by teaspoonfuls 2 inches apart onto ungreased cookie sheets.

3. Bake at 375°F for 8 to 9 minutes or until set. Do not overbake. Cool 1 minute; remove from cookie sheets.

Nutrition Information Per Serving: Calories 70 • Total Fat 3g • Saturated Fat 1g • Cholesterol 0mg • Sodium 65mg • Total Carbohydrate 11g • Dietary Fiber 1g • Sugars 7g • Protein 1g. Dietary Exchanges: ½ Starch • ½ Fruit • ½ Fat OR 1 Carbohydrate • ½ Fat.

TIPS FOR DROP COOKIES

Use a teaspoon or tablespoon to scoop up some dough, then transfer it onto the baking sheet with a second spoon or a narrow rubber scraper. Keep the dough uniformly sized so cookies will bake evenly.

coconut-pineapple tart

streusel fruit custard

PREP TIME: 15 MINUTES
READY TO SERVE: 1 HOUR 10 MINUTES
SERVINGS: 6

MARTIE A. KIAN ✳ EDINBORO, PENNSYLVANIA
BAKE-OFF® CONTEST 24, 1973

fruit mixture

1 (15.25-oz.) can sliced pears, drained

1 (15.25-oz.) can sliced peaches, drained

2 eggs

¼ cup all-purpose flour

¼ cup sugar

1 cup sour cream

1 teaspoon vanilla

topping

¾ cup all-purpose flour

½ cup packed brown sugar

½ teaspoon ground nutmeg

¼ cup butter or margarine, softened

Vanilla ice cream or whipped cream

1. Heat oven to 325°F. In ungreased 8-inch square or 11x7-inch (2-quart) glass baking dish, arrange pears and peaches. In medium bowl, beat eggs with wire whisk until blended. Beat in remaining fruit mixture ingredients until smooth. Pour over fruit.

2. In same bowl, mix all topping ingredients until crumbly. Sprinkle over fruit mixture.

3. Bake 30 to 40 minutes or until topping is golden brown and center is set. Cool at least 15 minutes. Serve warm with ice cream. Store custard in refrigerator.

Nutrition Information Per Serving: Calories 390 • Total Fat 17g • Saturated Fat 10g • Trans Fat 0.5g • Cholesterol 115mg • Sodium 100mg • Total Carbohydrate 54g • Dietary Fiber 3g • Sugars 36g • Protein 6g. **Dietary Exchanges:** 2 Starch • 1½ Other Carbohydrate • 3 Fat.

individual hot fudge sundae cakes

PREP TIME: 10 MINUTES
READY TO SERVE: 35 MINUTES
SERVINGS: 6

1 cup all-purpose flour

½ cup sugar

2 tablespoons unsweetened cocoa

1½ teaspoons baking powder

⅔ cup skim milk

2 tablespoons margarine or butter, melted

1 teaspoon vanilla

¾ cup firmly packed brown sugar

¼ cup unsweetened cocoa

1½ cups hot water

1. Heat oven to 350°F. In small bowl, combine flour, sugar, 2 tablespoons cocoa and baking powder; mix well. Add milk, margarine and vanilla; blend well. Spoon evenly into 6 ungreased 10-oz. custard cups. Place cups in 15x10x1-inch baking pan.

2. In small bowl, combine brown sugar and ¼ cup cocoa; mix well. Spoon 2 to 3 tablespoons mixture evenly over batter in each cup. Pour ¼ cup hot water evenly over sugar mixture in each cup.

3. Bake at 350°F for 20 to 25 minutes or until center is set and firm to the touch. Serve warm. If desired, sprinkle with powdered sugar, or serve with nonfat frozen yogurt or light whipped topping.

Nutrition Information Per Serving: Calories 320 • Total Fat 5g • Saturated Fat 1g • Cholesterol 0mg • Sodium 150mg • Total Carbohydrate 64g • Dietary Fiber 2g • Sugars 45g • Protein 4g. **Dietary Exchanges:** 1½ Starch • 2½ Fruit • 1 Fat OR 4 Carbohydrate • 1 Fat.

SWEET ACCENTS

To decorate the top of each dessert with powdered sugar, cut a stencil of a favorite holiday shape from paper, or use a paper doily. Place the stencil on the dessert; dust with powdered sugar. Remove the stencil.

---

homemade chewy granola bars

PREP TIME: 15 MINUTES
READY TO SERVE: 1 HOUR 30 MINUTES
SERVINGS: 24 BARS

* plan ahead

1 cup firmly packed brown sugar

⅔ cup peanut butter

½ cup light corn syrup

½ cup margarine or butter, melted

2 teaspoons vanilla

3 cups quick-cooking rolled oats

½ cup coconut

½ cup shelled sunflower seeds

½ cup raisins

⅓ cup wheat germ

2 tablespoons sesame seed

1 (6-oz.) pkg. semisweet chocolate chips or carob chips, if desired (1 cup)

1. Heat oven to 350°F. Grease 13x9-inch pan. In large bowl, combine brown sugar, peanut butter, corn syrup, margarine and vanilla; blend well. Add all remaining ingredients; mix well. Press evenly in greased pan.

2. Bake at 350°F for 15 to 20 minutes or until light golden brown. Cool 1 hour or until completely cooled. Cut into bars.

Nutrition Information Per Serving: Calories 270 • Total Fat 13g • Saturated Fat 3g • Cholesterol 0mg • Sodium 95mg • Total Carbohydrate 32g • Dietary Fiber 3g • Sugars 19g • Protein 5g. **Dietary Exchanges:** 1½ Starch • ½ Fruit • 2½ Fat OR 2 Carbohydrate • 2½ Fat.

giant oatmeal-candy cookies

READY TO SERVE: 1 HOUR
SERVINGS: 12 COOKIES

1 (18-oz.) pkg. Pillsbury® Refrigerated Sugar Cookies

1 cup miniature candy-coated chocolate baking bits

½ cup quick-cooking rolled oats

½ cup raisins

2 teaspoons quick-cooking rolled oats

1. Heat oven to 325°F. Break up cookie dough into large bowl. Add baking bits, ½ cups oats and raisins; mix well.

2. Shape cookie dough into 12 (2-inch) balls. Place 3 inches apart on ungreased large cookie sheets. Flatten each ball to form 3-inch round. Sprinkle with 2 teaspoons oats.

3. Bake at 325°F for 14 to 19 minutes or until set and dry in center. Cool 2 minutes; remove from cookie sheets.

Nutrition Information Per Serving: Calories 300 • Total Fat 12g • Saturated Fat 5g • Cholesterol 15mg • Sodium 160mg • Total Carbohydrate 45g • Dietary Fiber 2g • Sugars 29g • Protein 3g. **Dietary Exchanges:** 1 Starch • 2 Fruit • 2½ Fat OR 3 Carbohydrate • 2½ Fat.

CHOCK-FULL OF GOODNESS

These large, colorful treats are great for folks who like cookies packed with plenty of good "stuff." If you would like, you can always replace some or all of the raisins or baking bits with other chopped dried fruit or chocolate, peanut butter or butterscotch baking chips. Toss in a handful of your favorite chopped nuts if you wish. Or, add some toffee bits or white chocolate chunks.

scotchie s´mores

READY TO SERVE: 10 MINUTES
SERVINGS: 4

* super fast

8 graham cracker squares

Prepared butterscotch ice cream topping

2 (1.55-oz.) milk chocolate candy bars, halved

4 large marshmallows

4 long-handled forks

1. On each of 4 graham cracker squares, place candy bar half. Drizzle with the ice cream topping.

2. Spear each marshmallow on long-handled fork; toast over campfire coals or over grill with low heat.

3. Place 1 toasted marshmallow over the ice cream topping. Top each with cracker; press together and hold for a few seconds to melt chocolate.

sweet pizza pie

PREP TIME: 25 MINUTES
READY TO SERVE: 45 MINUTES
SERVINGS: 12

1 (15-oz.) box Pillsbury refrigerated pie crusts, softened as directed on box

1 (14-oz.) can sweetened condensed milk (not evaporated)

1½ cups semisweet chocolate chips

½ cup cream cheese frosting (from 16-oz. can)

1 medium banana, sliced

1 cup sliced fresh strawberries

1. Heat oven to 450°F. Remove pie crusts from pouches; unroll crusts on work surface. Place 1 crust on ungreased cookie sheet or 12-inch pizza pan. Place second crust on first crust. Press edges together with fork.

2. Bake crust 10 to 14 minutes or until golden brown. Cool 25 minutes or until completely cooled.

3. Meanwhile, heat sweetened condensed milk in medium saucepan over low heat until warm. Add chocolate chips; cook until chips are melted, stirring constantly. Remove from heat. Cover; let stand until crust is cool.

4. To assemble pie, place cooled baked crust on serving platter. Spread cream cheese frosting evenly over baked crust. Arrange banana and strawberry slices over frosting. Drizzle with ½ cup of the chocolate mixture. (Save remaining chocolate mixture to use as a topping for ice cream or cake.) To serve, cut into wedges. Store in refrigerator.

Nutrition Information Per Serving: Calories 270 • Total Fat 13g • Saturated Fat 6g • Cholesterol 10mg • Sodium 170mg • Total Carbohydrate 36g • Dietary Fiber 1g • Sugars 18g • Protein 2g.
Dietary Exchanges: 1 Starch • 1½ Fruit • 2½ Other Carbohydrate • 2½ Fat.

maple baked apples

maple baked apples

PREP TIME: 20 MINUTES
READY TO SERVE: 1 HOUR 10 MINUTES
SERVINGS: 6

6 large baking apples
2 tablespoons lemon juice
½ cup raisins
½ teaspoon cinnamon
1 cup real maple or maple-flavored syrup
¼ cup water

1. Heat oven to 350°F. Core apples and remove a 1-inch strip of peel around top to prevent splitting. Brush tops and insides with lemon juice. Place apples in ungreased 8-inch square (2-quart) baking dish.

2. In small bowl, combine raisins and cinnamon; fill center of each apple with mixture. Pour maple syrup over apples. Add ¼ cup water to baking dish.

3. Bake at 350°F for 45 to 50 minutes or until apples are tender, occasionally spooning syrup mixture over apples.

Nutrition Information Per Serving: Calories 320 • Total Fat 1g • Saturated Fat 0g • Cholesterol 0mg • Sodium 5mg • Total Carbohydrate 78g • Dietary Fiber 6g • Sugars 70g • Protein 1g. Dietary Exchanges: 5½ Fruit OR 5½ Carbohydrate.

peach and crescent dessert

PREP TIME: 10 MINUTES
READY TO SERVE: 35 MINUTES
SERVINGS: 12

DOLORES LAMMERS ✳ MORRIS, MINNESOTA
BAKE-OFF® CONTEST 27, 1976

1 (8-oz.) can refrigerated crescent dinner rolls
2 tablespoons butter or margarine, softened
½ cup coconut, if desired
1 cup sour cream
1 egg
1 (28-oz.) can sliced peaches, well drained (2 cups)
½ cup packed brown sugar
Vanilla ice cream or whipped cream, if desired

1. Heat oven to 350°F. Separate dough into 2 long rectangles; place in ungreased 13x9-inch pan. Press dough to cover bottom of pan, firmly pressing perforations to seal. Spread with butter; sprinkle with coconut.

2. Bake 5 to 7 minutes or until crust is very lightly browned. Meanwhile, in small bowl, beat sour cream and egg until well blended.

3. Arrange peach slices over partially baked crust. Pour sour cream mixture over peaches; sprinkle with brown sugar. Bake 22 to 25 minutes longer or until crust is golden brown. Cut into squares. Serve warm with ice cream. Store dessert in refrigerator.

Nutrition Information Per Serving: Calories 190 • Total Fat 10g • Saturated Fat 5g • Trans Fat 1g • Cholesterol 35mg • Sodium 180mg • Total Carbohydrate 21g • Dietary Fiber 1g • Sugars 14g • Protein 3g. Dietary Exchanges: 1 Starch • ½ Other Carbohydrate • 2 Fat.

HELP FOR HARD BROWN SUGAR

If your brown sugar has become hard, soften it by placing a slice of bread or an apple wedge with the sugar in a covered container for a few days. If you're in a hurry, microwave the sugar on high for 20-30 seconds. Repeat if necessary, but watch carefully because the sugar may begin to melt during heating. Always store brown sugar in an airtight container.

cranberry-pear cobbler

PREP TIME: 10 MINUTES
READY TO SERVE: 50 MINUTES
SERVINGS: 10

MARSHA MICHAEL ✳ BLOOMINGTON, MINNESOTA
BAKE-OFF® CONTEST 38, 1998

fruit mixture

2 (15-oz.) cans pear halves or slices, drained, liquid reserved

½ cup sweetened dried cranberries

½ cup applesauce

¼ teaspoon ground cinnamon

topping

½ cup sugar

½ teaspoon ground cinnamon

1 (12-oz.) can refrigerated buttermilk biscuits

2½ teaspoons butter or margarine

Vanilla ice cream or whipped cream

1. Heat oven to 450°F. Cut pears into 1-inch chunks. In ungreased 11x7- or 8-inch square (2-quart) glass baking dish, arrange pear chunks. Sprinkle with cranberries. In small bowl, mix applesauce and ¼ teaspoon cinnamon. Spoon over fruit.

2. Bake 8 to 10 minutes or until hot and bubbly. Remove from oven. Reduce oven temperature to 400°F.

3. In small bowl, mix sugar and ½ teaspoon cinnamon. Separate dough into 10 biscuits. Dip each biscuit into reserved pear liquid; coat all sides with sugar-cinnamon mixture. Arrange biscuits over hot fruit in 2 rows of 5 biscuits each. Top each biscuit with about ¼ teaspoon butter.

4. Bake 15 to 20 minutes or until biscuits are golden brown. Cool 10 minutes before serving. Serve warm with ice cream.

Nutrition Information Per Serving: Calories 230 • Total Fat 5g • Saturated Fat 1.5g • Trans Fat 1.5g • Cholesterol 0mg • Sodium 370mg • Total Carbohydrate 43g • Dietary Fiber 2g • Sugars 27g • Protein 2g. **Dietary Exchanges:** 1 Starch • 1 Fruit • 1 Other Carbohydrate • ½ Fat.

peanut butter cookies

READY TO SERVE: 45 MINUTES
SERVINGS: 4 DOZEN COOKIES

½ cup sugar

½ cup firmly packed brown sugar

½ cup margarine or butter, softened

½ cup peanut butter

1 teaspoon vanilla

1 egg

1¼ cups all-purpose flour

1 teaspoon baking soda

½ teaspoon salt

4 teaspoons sugar

1. Heat oven to 375°F. In large bowl, combine ½ cup sugar, brown sugar and margarine; beat until light and fluffy. Add peanut butter, vanilla and egg; blend well.

2. Add flour, baking soda and salt; mix well. Shape dough into 1-inch balls. Place 2 inches apart on ungreased cookie sheets. With fork dipped in 4 teaspoons sugar, flatten balls in crisscross pattern.

3. Bake at 375°F for 6 to 9 minutes or until set and golden brown. Immediately remove from cookie sheets.

Nutrition Information Per Serving: Calories 60 • Total Fat 3g • Saturated Fat 1g • Cholesterol 4mg • Sodium 85mg • Total Carbohydrate 8g • Dietary Fiber 0g • Sugars 5g • Protein 1g. **Dietary Exchanges:** ½ Starch • ½ Fat OR ½ Carbohydrate • ½ Fat.

cinnamon-apple crostata

PREP TIME: 20 MINUTES
READY TO SERVE: 50 MINUTES
SERVINGS: 8

crust

1 refrigerated pie crust (from 15-oz. box), softened as directed on box

filling

½ cup sugar

4 teaspoons cornstarch

2 teaspoons cinnamon

4 cups thinly sliced, peeled apples (4 medium)

1 teaspoon sugar

2 tablespoons chopped pecans or walnuts

1. Heat oven to 450°F. Remove pie crust from pouch. Unfold pie crust; place on ungreased cookie sheet. Press out fold lines.

2. In medium bowl, combine ½ cup sugar, cornstarch and cinnamon; mix well. Add apples; toss gently. Spoon apple mixture onto center of crust, spreading to within 2 inches of edges. Fold edges of crust over filling, ruffling decoratively. Brush crust edge with water. Sprinkle with 1 teaspoon sugar.

3. Bake at 450°F for 15 minutes or until crust is golden brown. Sprinkle pecans over apple mixture. Bake an additional 5 to 15 minutes or until apples are tender.

Nutrition Information Per Serving: Calories 210 • Total Fat 7g • Saturated Fat 3g • Cholesterol 5mg • Sodium 110mg • Total Carbohydrate 36g • Dietary Fiber 1g • Sugars 20g • Protein 1g. **Dietary Exchanges:** ½ Starch • 2 Fruit • 1 Fat OR 2½ Carbohydrate • 1 Fat.

chocolate chip-coconut cheesecake bars

PREP TIME: 10 MINUTES
READY TO SERVE: 2 HOURS 20 MINUTES
SERVINGS: 16 BARS

* plan ahead

1 (8-oz.) pkg. cream cheese, softened

½ cup sugar

1 egg

½ cup coconut

1 (18-oz.) pkg. Pillsbury® Refrigerated Chocolate Chip Cookies

1. Heat oven to 350°F. In small bowl, combine cream cheese, sugar and egg; beat until smooth. Stir in coconut.

2. Press half of dough in bottom of ungreased 8- or 9-inch square pan. Spread cream cheese mixture over dough. Crumble and sprinkle remaining half of cookie dough over cream cheese mixture.

3. Bake at 350°F for 35 to 40 minutes or until golden brown and firm to the touch. Cool 30 minutes. Refrigerate at least 1 hour or until chilled. Cut into bars. Store in refrigerator.

Nutrition Information Per Serving: Calories 240 • Total Fat 13g • Saturated Fat 6g • Cholesterol 35mg • Sodium 150mg • Total Carbohydrate 27g • Dietary Fiber 1g • Sugars 19g • Protein 3g. **Dietary Exchanges:** 1 Starch • 1 Fruit • 2½ Fat OR 2 Carbohydrate • 2½ Fat.

flaky reuben slices

flaky reuben slices

READY TO SERVE: 25 MINUTES
SERVINGS: 24

* super fast

rolls

1 (8-oz.) can Pillsbury® Refrigerated Crescent Dinner Rolls

¼ lb. thinly sliced corned beef

2 oz. finely shredded Swiss cheese (½ cup)

⅓ cup well-drained sauerkraut

dipping sauce

½ cup purchased Thousand Island salad dressing

1 tablespoon milk

1. Heat oven to 375°F. Unroll dough into 2 long rectangles. Press each to form 12-inch-long rectangle; press perforations to seal.

2. Layer half of corned beef on each dough rectangle, cutting to fit if necessary. Top each with cheese and sauerkraut. Starting at long side, roll up each tightly; seal long edges. Place seam side down on ungreased cookie sheet; tuck edges under.

3. Bake at 375°F for 12 to 14 minutes or until golden brown.

4. Meanwhile, in small bowl, combine dipping sauce ingredients; mix well.

5. To serve, cut warm rolls into 1-inch slices; place on serving platter. Serve with dipping sauce.

Nutrition Information Per Serving: Calories 70 • Total Fat 5g • Saturated Fat 1g • Cholesterol 10mg • Sodium 170mg • Total Carbohydrate 5g • Dietary Fiber 0g • Sugars 1g • Protein 2g. **Dietary Exchanges:** ½ Starch • 1 Fat OR ½ Carbohydrate • 1 Fat.

coconut macaroons

READY TO SERVE: 30 MINUTES
SERVINGS: 12 COOKIES

2 egg whites

⅓ cup sugar

2 tablespoons all-purpose flour

Dash salt

¼ teaspoon almond extract

2 cups coconut

1. Heat oven to 325°F. Grease and lightly flour cookie sheet. In medium bowl, beat egg whites until frothy. Add sugar, flour, salt and almond extract; mix well. Stir in coconut. Drop dough by tablespoonfuls 2 inches apart onto greased and floured cookie sheet.

2. Bake at 325°F for 13 to 17 minutes or until set and light golden brown. Immediately remove from cookie sheet.

Nutrition Information Per Serving: Calories 90 • Total Fat 4g • Saturated Fat 4g • Cholesterol 0mg • Sodium 50mg • Total Carbohydrate 1g • Dietary Fiber 1g • Sugars 10g • Protein 1g. **Dietary Exchanges:** ½ Starch • ½ Fruit • ½ Fat OR 1 Carbohydrate • ½ Fat.

rainy days s´mores

READY TO SERVE: 10 MINUTES
SERVINGS: 4

* super fast

8 graham cracker squares

2 milk chocolate candy bars (1.55-oz. each), each halved

4 tablespoons marshmallow creme

1. On each of 4 graham cracker squares, place candy bar half.

2. Top each candy bar half with 1 tablespoon marshmallow creme.

3. Top each with a cracker; press together and hold for a few seconds.

grands!® meatball pops

READY TO SERVE: 30 MINUTES
SERVINGS: 10 APPETIZERS

1 (10.2-oz.) can Pillsbury®
Grands!® Refrigerated
Southern Style or Buttermilk
Biscuits (5 biscuits)

1⅓ oz. shredded Monterey Jack
or Cheddar cheese (⅓ cup)

10 refrigerated or frozen
cooked beef meatballs,
thawed

¼ cup margarine or butter,
melted

⅔ cup finely crushed seasoned
croutons

10 large appetizer picks or
lollipop sticks, if desired

1. Heat oven to 375°F. Line cookie sheet with parchment paper or spray with cooking spray. Separate dough into 5 biscuits. With serrated knife, cut each biscuit in half horizontally to make 10 rounds. Press out each biscuit half to form 3-inch round.

2. Sprinkle each biscuit round with cheese to within ½ inch of edge. Top each with meatball. Bring up sides of dough over meatball; pinch edges to seal. Brush rounded tops and sides of dough with margarine; coat with croutons. Place seam side down on paper-lined cookie sheet.

3. Bake at 375°F for 10 to 15 minutes or until golden brown.

4. To serve, place appetizer pick in each warm biscuit-wrapped meatball to form meatball pop.

Nutrition Information Per Serving: Calories 275 • Total Fat 16g • Saturated Fat 5g • Cholesterol 35mg • Sodium 690mg • Total Carbohydrate 22g • Dietary Fiber 1g • Sugars 5g • Protein 9g. **Dietary Exchanges:** 1½ Starch • ½ High-Fat Meat • 2 Fat OR 1½ Carbohydrate • ½ High-Fat Meat • 2 Fat.

pizza melts

PREP TIME: 15 MINUTES
READY TO SERVE: 40 MINUTES
SERVINGS: 32 APPETIZERS

2 (8-oz.) cans Pillsbury® refrigerated crescent dinner rolls

¼ cup pizza sauce or 3 tablespoons tomato paste with basil, garlic and oregano

1 (3.5-oz.) pkg. sliced pepperoni

2 cups shredded mozzarella cheese (8 oz.)

1 egg, beaten

2 tablespoons grated Parmesan cheese

1 teaspoon dried oregano leaves

1 cup pizza sauce, if desired

1. Heat oven to 375°F. Grease cookie sheet. On cookie sheet, unroll 1 can of dough into 1 large rectangle. With floured rolling pin or fingers, roll or press dough into 12x9-inch rectangle, firmly pressing perforations to seal.

2. Spread ¼ cup pizza sauce over dough to within ¼ inch of edges. Top with pepperoni and mozzarella cheese.

3. On 14-inch length of parchment paper, unroll remaining can of dough. Press to make 12x9-inch rectangle, firmly pressing perforations to seal. While holding paper with dough, turn dough upside down to cover cheese. Remove paper. Brush with beaten egg. Sprinkle with Parmesan cheese and oregano.

4. Bake 12 to 15 minutes or until golden brown. Let stand on cooling rack 5 to 10 minutes. Move to cutting board. Using pizza cutter, cut into 16 squares. Cut each square in half diagonally. Serve with 1 cup pizza sauce.

Nutrition Information Per Serving: Calories 90 • Total Fat 6g • Sodium 220mg • Total Carbohydrate 6g • Dietary Fiber 0g • Sugars 1g. **Dietary Exchanges:** ½ Starch • ½ High-Fat Meat.

lemon-ginger thumbprints

READY TO SERVE: 45 MINUTES
SERVINGS: 3 DOZEN COOKIES

1 (16.5-oz.) roll refrigerated gingerbread cookies

3 tablespoons graham cracker crumbs

½ cup lemon curd or lemon pie filling

1. Heat oven to 350°F. Cut cookie dough into 3 equal pieces. Work with 1 piece of dough at a time; refrigerate remaining dough until ready to use.

2. In shallow dish, place graham cracker crumbs. Shape each piece of dough into twelve 1-inch balls; roll in crumbs to coat. Place balls 1 inch apart on ungreased large cookie sheet.

3. Bake 8 to 11 minutes or until cookies are almost set. Cool 2 minutes on cookie sheet. With thumb or handle of wooden spoon, make slight indentation in center of each cookie. Remove cookies from cookie sheet. Cool completely, about 15 minutes.

4. In small resealable food-storage plastic bag, place lemon curd; partially seal bag. Cut small hole in bottom corner of bag. Squeeze bag to pipe small dollop of lemon curd into indentation in each cookie. Store in refrigerator.

Nutrition Information Per Serving: Calories 80 • Total Fat 3.5g • Saturated Fat 0.5g • Trans Fat 1g • Cholesterol 10mg • Sodium 50mg • Total Carbohydrate 11g • Dietary Fiber 0g • Sugars 7g • Protein 0g. **Dietary Exchanges:** ½ Other Carbohydrate • 1 Fat.

SHEDDING LIGHT ON LEMON CURD

Lemon curd is a rich, thick spread made of a cooked mixture of butter, sugar, egg yolks and lemon juice. Plan to make the cookie recipe above? Look for lemon curd alongside the jams and jellies in your grocery store.

stuffed crust pizza snacks

PREP TIME: 25 MINUTES
READY TO SERVE: 50 MINUTES
YIELD: 48 SNACKS

2 (10-oz.) cans Pillsbury® Refrigerated Pizza Crust

8 oz. mozzarella cheese, cut into 48 cubes

48 slices pepperoni (3 oz.)

¼ cup olive or vegetable oil

1½ teaspoons dried Italian seasoning

2 tablespoons grated Parmesan cheese

1. Heat oven to 400°F. Spray two 9-inch pie pans or one 13x9-inch pan with cooking spray. Remove dough from both cans; unroll. Starting at center, press out each dough rectangle to form 12x8-inch rectangle. Cut each rectangle into 24 squares.

2. Top each square with cheese cube and pepperoni slice. Wrap dough around filling to completely cover; firmly press edges to seal. Place seam side down with sides touching in sprayed pie pans.

3. In small bowl, combine oil and Italian seasoning; mix well. Drizzle over filled dough in pans. Sprinkle with Parmesan cheese.

4. Bake at 400°F for 16 to 22 minutes or until golden brown. Serve warm.

Nutrition Information Per Serving: Calories 65 • Total Fat 3g • Saturated Fat 1g • Cholesterol 5mg • Sodium 150mg • Total Carbohydrate 6g • Dietary Fiber 0g • Sugars 1g • Protein 3g. **Dietary Exchanges:** ½ Starch • ½ Fat OR ½ Carbohydrate • ½ Fat.

lemon-ginger thumbprints

General Recipe Index